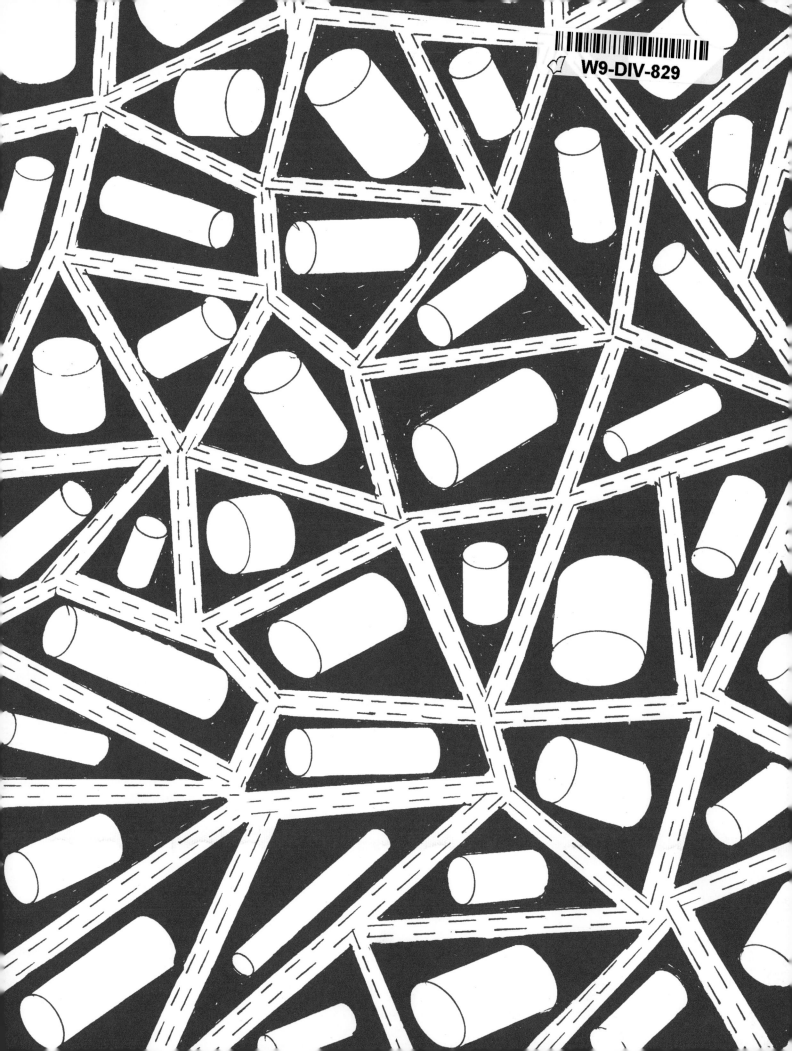

This
story was first
published as a three part
series by the author
himself.

ARSÈNE SCHRAUWEN

FOR Gary From Olivier

HELLO.
I AM O. SCHRAUWEN, GRAPHIC NOVELIST.

THIS BOOK IS ABOUT MY GRANDFATHER, ARSÈNE.

MY GRANDFATHER GAVE ME MY NOSE, MY EYES AND A CLEFT CHIN.

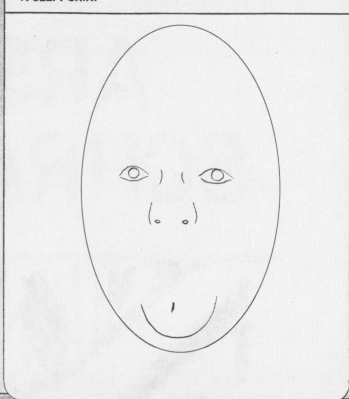

NOW, IN THE YEAR 2014, NOT MUCH REMAINS OF GRANDPA.

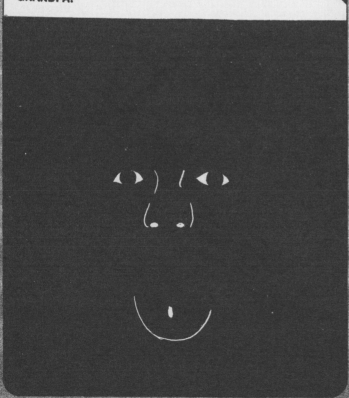

IN 1947, THOUGH, HE WAS STILL VERY MUCH ALIVE.

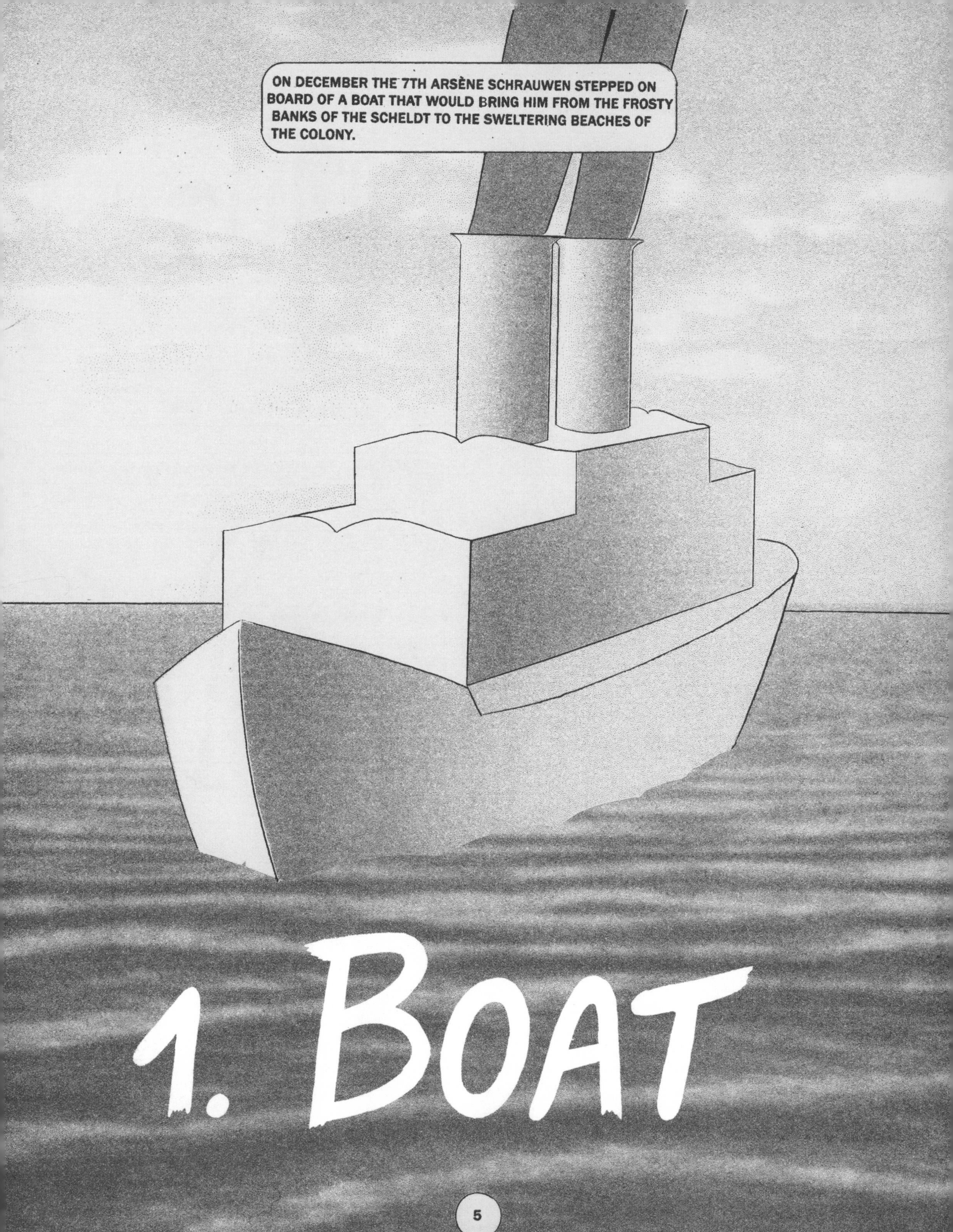
ON DECEMBER THE 7TH ARSÈNE SCHRAUWEN STEPPED ON BOARD OF A BOAT THAT WOULD BRING HIM FROM THE FROSTY BANKS OF THE SCHELDT TO THE SWELTERING BEACHES OF THE COLONY.
1. BOAT

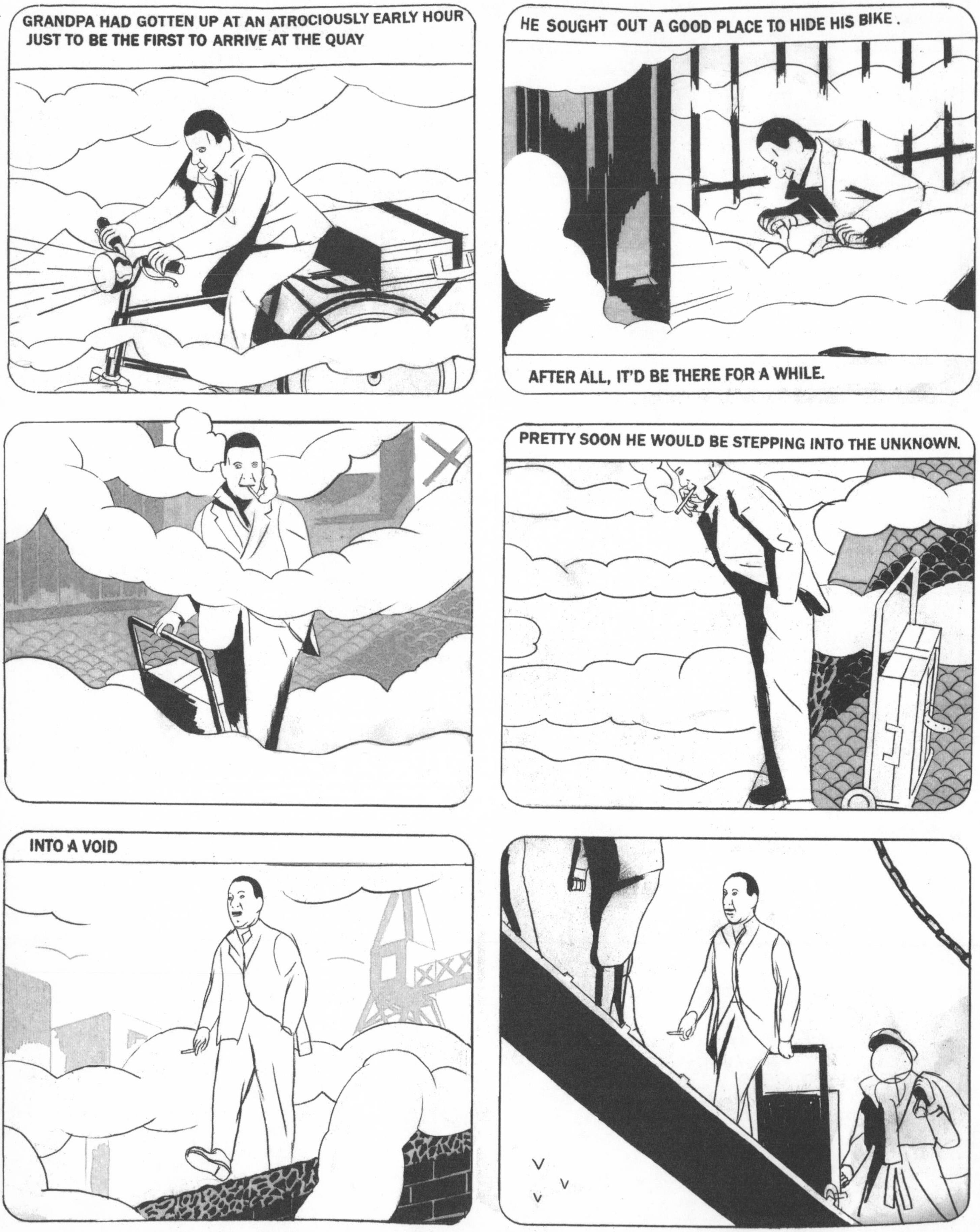
GRANDPA HAD GOTTEN UP AT AN ATROCIOUSLY EARLY HOUR JUST TO BE THE FIRST TO ARRIVE AT THE QUAY
HE SOUGHT OUT A GOOD PLACE TO HIDE HIS BIKE.
AFTER ALL, IT'D BE THERE FOR A WHILE.
PRETTY SOON HE WOULD BE STEPPING INTO THE UNKNOWN.
INTO A VOID

ARSÈNE HAD BEEN TOLD THAT THE BOAT WOULD LIKELY BE SWARMING WITH PICKPOCKETS AND BULLSHIT ARTISTS.

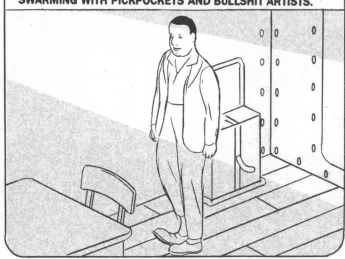

HE OUGHT TO BE WARY OF THEIR SMOOTH TALK AND DEVIOUS WAYS.

SO GRANDPA STAYED IN HIS CABIN MOST OF THE TIME ,

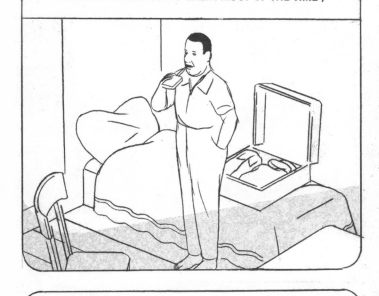

SMOKING

...UNTIL, AS THE BOAT CRAWLED TOWARDS THE TROPICS,

THE TEMPERATURE INSIDE BECAME INTOLERABLE.

BUT THIS DIDN'T MAKE HIM VENTURE ONTO THE DECK;
HIS NEIGHBOR DID...
A CORPULENT WOMAN HAD KNOCKED ON HIS DOOR, WALING, BEGGING HIM FOR HIS HELP.
AS HE RELUCTANTLY STEPPED INTO HER CABIN
SOMETHING WHIZZED BY, THEN BOUNCED OFF THE WALL.
WHIZ
BOUNCE
A FLYING FISH
(FREEZE FRAME)
THE WOMAN WANTED HIM TO KILL IT, BUT HE COULDN'T.
INSTEAD HE MANAGED TO CORNER IT
... AND CRADLE IT IN HIS HANDS.

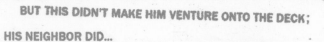

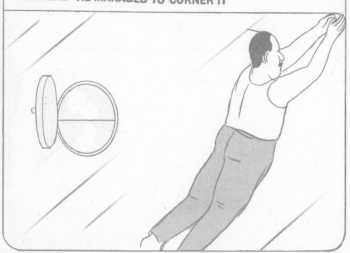

IT WAS HIS FIRST TIME ON THE DECK AND HE IMMEDIATELY DREW ATTENTION.

AS HE RELEASED THE CHIMERICAL WONDER, SOME PEOPLE CLAPPED.

WHIZ

WATCHING IT SLASH INTO THE WATER HE IMAGINED A CONTRAPTION THAT'D ENABLE HIM TO KEEP IT AS A PET.

AN OLD MAN WITH A CANE WALKED UP TO HIM

"BRAVO"

"THERE'S ANOTHER BIRD ABOUT TO FLY AWAY."

ARSÈNE CONSIDERED THIS RIDDLE FOR A SPLIT SECOND, THEN PULLED UP HIS UNDONE ZIPPER HASTILY.

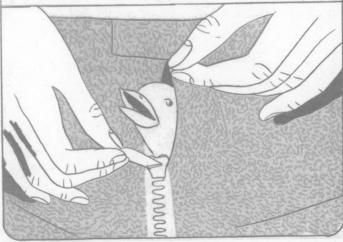

THE OLD MAN SQUEEZED GRANDFATHER'S CHEEK WITH LUST, AS IF IT WERE A TIT.

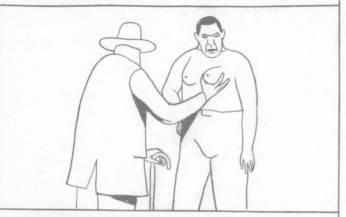

"HAHA. YOU'RE NOT ONLY VENTUROUS, YOU'RE ALSO QUICK-WITTED!"

"LET'S HAVE A DRINK, BOY!"

HIS NAME WAS LIPPENS, HE HAD DROOPY EYES AND, FUNNILY, RATHER BIG LIPS.

THE WAY HIS LIPS CARRESSED THE RIM OF THE GLASS WAS ALMOST OBSCENE.

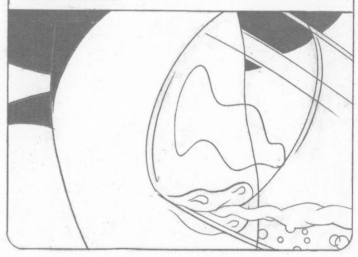

THE LIPS MOVED CEASELESSLY.   LIKE A TRUMPETER, HE SEEMED TO HAVE MASTERED CIRCULAR BREATHING. HE PRODUCED   A CONTINUOUS STREAM OF WORDS...

ARE YOU AN ENTREPRENEUR BOY? I MYSE

MOST OF IT PASSED THROUGH GRANDPA'S EAR, UNPROCESSED.

IT BECAME MORE INTERESTING HOWEVER, WHEN LIPPENS' STREAM OF WORDS MEANDERED TO THE TOPIC OF THE COLONY.

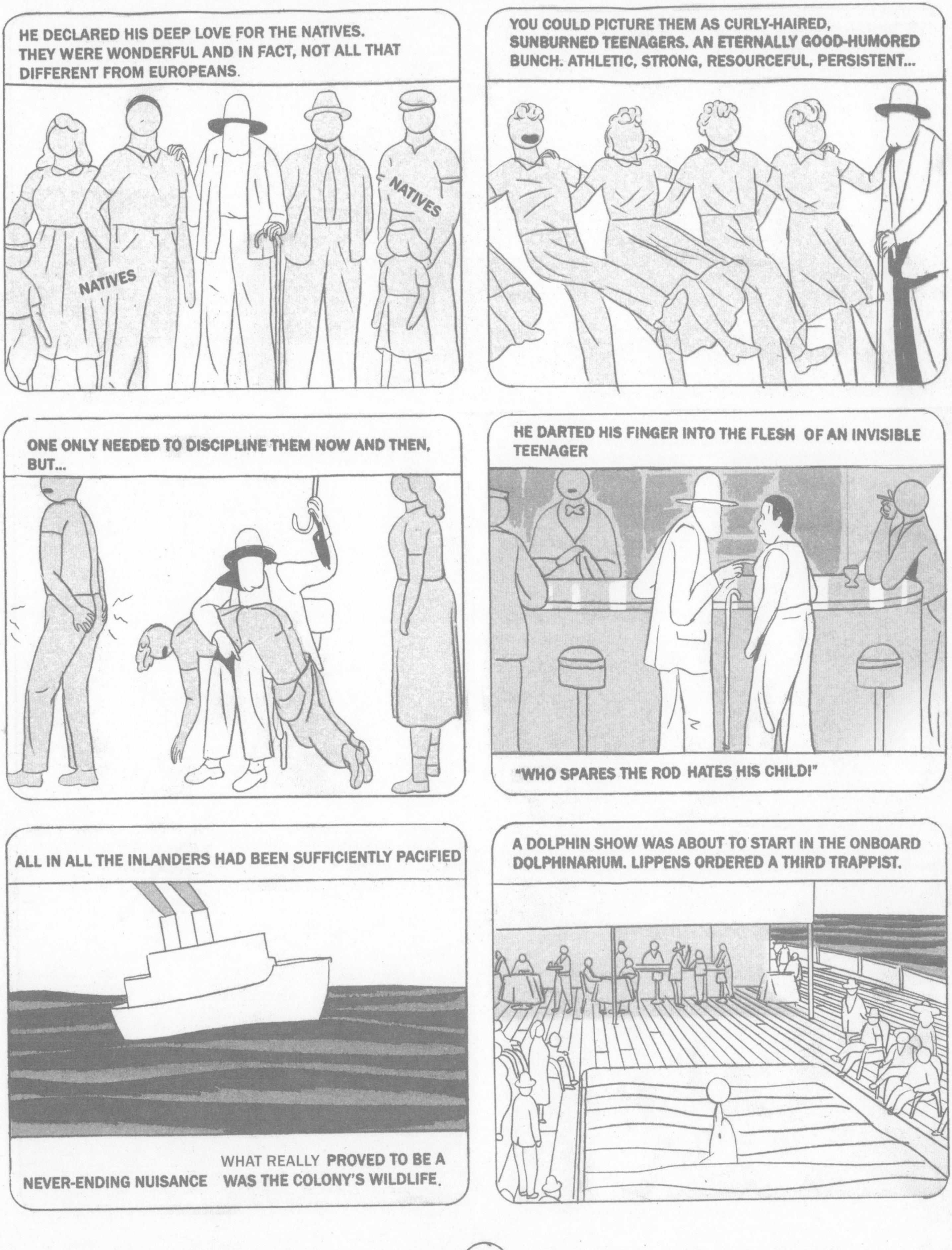
HE DECLARED HIS DEEP LOVE FOR THE NATIVES. THEY WERE WONDERFUL AND IN FACT, NOT ALL THAT DIFFERENT FROM EUROPEANS.
NATIVES
NATIVES
YOU COULD PICTURE THEM AS CURLY-HAIRED, SUNBURNED TEENAGERS. AN ETERNALLY GOOD-HUMORED BUNCH. ATHLETIC, STRONG, RESOURCEFUL, PERSISTENT...
ONE ONLY NEEDED TO DISCIPLINE THEM NOW AND THEN, BUT...
HE DARTED HIS FINGER INTO THE FLESH OF AN INVISIBLE TEENAGER
"WHO SPARES THE ROD HATES HIS CHILD!"
ALL IN ALL THE INLANDERS HAD BEEN SUFFICIENTLY PACIFIED
NEVER-ENDING NUISANCE
WHAT REALLY PROVED TO BE A WAS THE COLONY'S WILDLIFE.
A DOLPHIN SHOW WAS ABOUT TO START IN THE ONBOARD DOLPHINARIUM. LIPPENS ORDERED A THIRD TRAPPIST.

ONE THING IN PARTICULAR THAT WARRANTED EXTREME CAUTION WAS THE ELEPHANT WORM.

THE ELEPHANT WORM WAS A TINY INVERTEBRATE, BUT WHEN IT ENTERED A HUMAN BODY IT COULD DO ENORMOUS DAMAGE.

THE VILE PARASITE DWELLED IN RIVERS, POOLS AND PUDDLES ALL ACROSS THE COLONY. YOU'D FIND IT IN THE TAP, IN DRINKING WATER, IN SOUP, IN THE RAIN ...IN SOMEONE'S TEARS!

IN FACT EVERY LIQUID WAS SUSPECT, UNLESS IT HAD COME FROM THE MAINLAND IN A SEALED CONTAINER.

IT WOULD ENTER YOUR BODY AND START LAYING EGGS. THE EGGS WOULD HATCH IN A MATTER OF MINUTES, AND NEW WORMS WOULD COME OUT, LAYING NEW EGGS, ETC

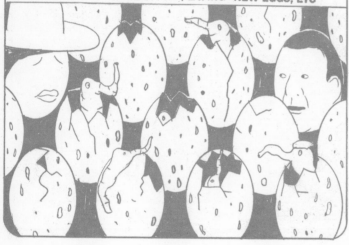

WHEREVER IT ENTERED, IT'LL MAKE YOUR MEMBERS SWELL IN THE MOST GROTESQUE FORMS.

SOON YOU'D BE NOTHING MORE THAN AN AMORPHOUS MASS OF FLESH.

LIPPENS HAD KNOWN OF A MAN WHO'D PISSED IN A DITCH. AN ELEPHANT-WORM CAME SWIMMING INTO THE STREAM OF URINE. LIKE A SALMON!

SOON IT HAD RESHAPED THIS MAN'S PENIS IN THE FORM OF A CAULIFLOWER!

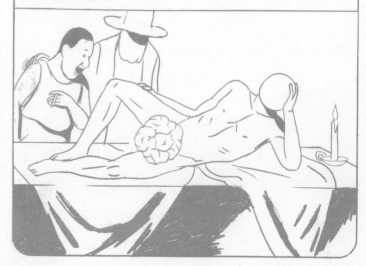

TO PREVENT THE WORM FROM CREEPING INTO ONE OF HIS LOWER ORIFICES, LIPPENS TIED UP THE EDGES OF HIS UNDERPANTS.

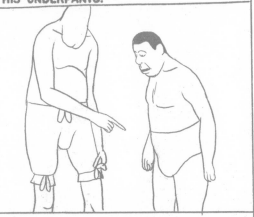

ARSÈNE HAD TO PROMISE TO DO LIKEWISE.

THEY TOASTED WITH THEIR FOURTH TRAPPIST AND LIPPENS SHUT UP FOR A MOMENT. THEN, QUIETLY, HE UTTERED.

"OH YES... THERE'S ALSO THE LEOPARD-MEN."

NOW LIPPENS' LIP HUNG DOWN LIKE PIECE OF MEAT ON A HOOK.

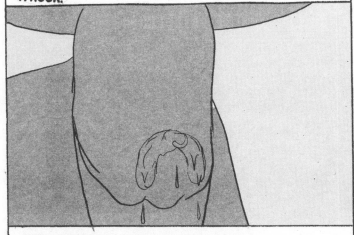

"JUST PRAY YOU DON'T RUN INTO THAT LOT..."

MENTIONING THE LEOPARD-MEN SEEMED TO SOBER HIM UP COMPLETELY.

SUDDENLY THERE WAS AN UNCOMFORTABLE SILENCE. LIPPENS GAVE GRANDPA A SERIOUS LOOK.

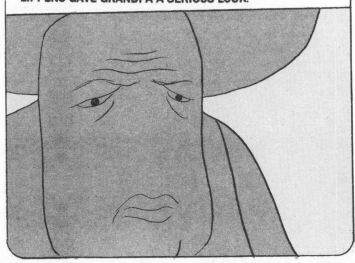

GRANDPA TOOK IT AS HIS CUE TO PAY FOR THE DRINKS. HE REACHED IN HIS POCKET, PULLED OUT HIS WALLET AND CLEARED THE GLASSES OFF THE TABLE.

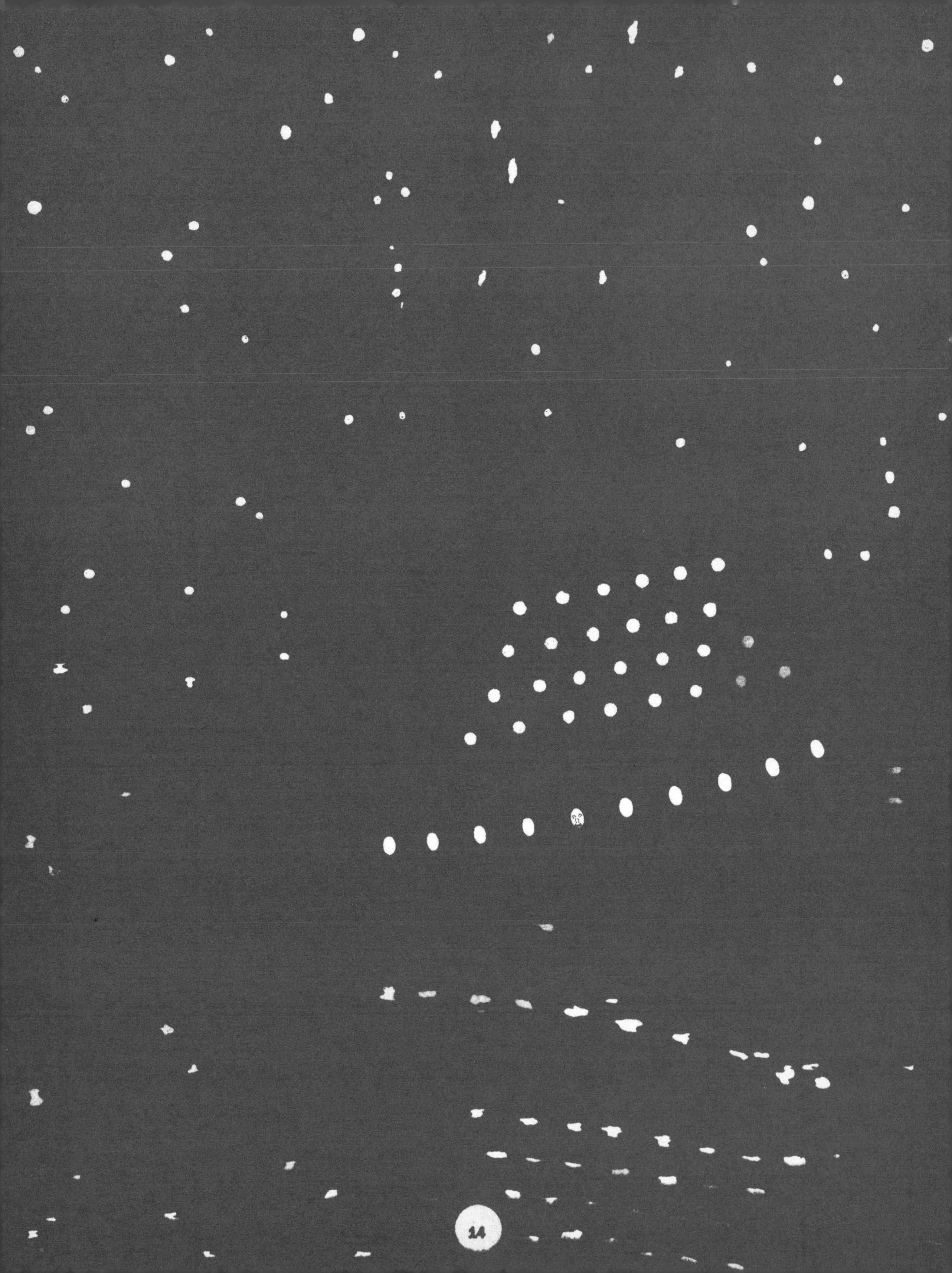

2. Colony

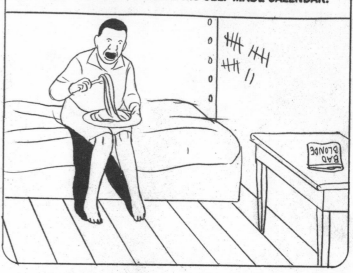

GRANDPA WOULD REMAIN IN HIS CABIN FOR THE REST OF THE TRIP.
HE'D KEEP TRACK OF TIME ON HIS SELF MADE CALENDAR.
BAD BLONDE
WHEN THE DAY OF ARRIVAL CAME HE PUT ON HIS NEW BLAZER, CEREMONIALLY....
... AND SPOONED HIS FEET INTO HIS PRETTY BEACHSIDE SHOES.
HE POSITIONED HIMSELF IN FRONT OF THE DOOR, AND PUT HIS HAND ON THE DOOR HANDLE.
IT WOULD TAKE THE BOAT ANOTHER TWO HOURS TO REACH THE FIRST PORT OF THE COLONY.
ALL THE WHILE HE STOOD THERE LIKE A SALT PILLAR, AS IF STUCK IN TIME .

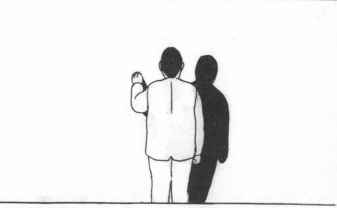

WHEN THE STEAMBOAT WHISTLE FINALLY BLEW, HE SIMPLY PUSHED DOWN THE HANDLE, LEFT HIS ROOM AND WENT ONTO THE DECK.

OUTSIDE, THE HEAT HIT HIM LIKE A PIANO DROPPED FROM A FIVE-STORY BUILDING.

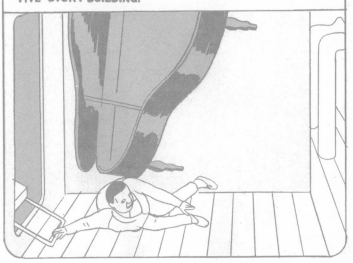

WITHIN SECONDS HE WAS DRENCHED IN SWEAT. IT LAY ON HIS BODY LIKE AN OILY FILM.

THE BOAT HALTED AT A SMALL MOORING PLACE ABOUT 50 KILOMETERS NORTH OF THE MAIN HAVEN. THE FACT THAT HE WAS THE ONLY ONE GETTING OUT DREW ATTENTION.

HE WALKED OFF THE GANGWAY AND ONTO A SMALL PLATFORM

. . . AND WAVED.

INSTEAD OF PAUSING FOR A MOMENT TO TAKE IN HIS NEW SURROUNDINGS, ARSÈNE TOOK OUT THE LETTER HE'D GOTTEN FROM HIS COUSIN ROGER DESMET.
IN IT DESMET HAD DRAWN PRECISE DIRECTIONS TO HIS HOUSE.
ARSÈNE IMMEDIATELY ACCEPTED THE PLAN AS HIS NEW REALITY.
Shrubbery
Coast
Sea
Pont
Pont
Sea
WITH HIS BACK FACING THE SEASIDE, ARSÈNE HAD TO TAKE FIVE STEPS OFF THE PLATFORM UNTIL HE STOOD UPON A GRAVEL ROAD.
Shrubbery
Peer
ON THE ROAD HE HAD TO TAKE A 90° RIGHT TURN AND PROCEED FORWARD UNTIL REACHING A ROAD ON HIS LEFT MARKED WITH A BALL-SHAPED TAXUS...
Shrubbery
vel road
Peer
GRANDPA FOLLOWED THE DIRECTIONS LIKE AN AUTOMATON,
Threes
Threes
Shrubbery
Shrubl
Bal
shape
taxus
AS IF INCAPABLE OF MAKING A MOVE THAT WASN'T IN ACCORDANCE TO DESMET'S PLAN.
Threes
Shru
Shrubbery
Ball-shaped taxus
Gravel road
Gravel

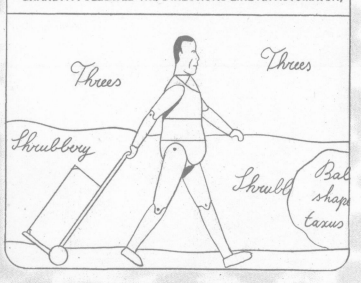

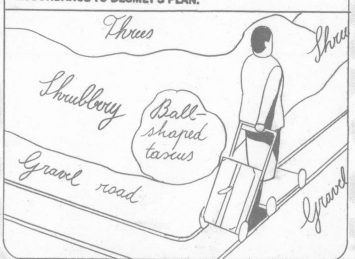

HE QUICKLY CAME UPON A SMALL GATE...
Wall
Bingo!
ugly plants chosen by my wife
P.S. key is hidden under yellow rock left.
BEHIND IT WAS A PRETTY GARDEN.
THERE WERE FUNNY MODERNISTIC STATUES SCATTERED ALL OVER.
A SMALL PATH LET INTO A LAWN IN THE MIDST OF WHICH LAY ANOTHER SCULPTURE.
A BEAM OF LIGHT FALLING THROUGH THE FOLIAGE FLATTERED ITS FORMS EXQUISITELY.
NOW THE STATUE MOVED AND REVEALED ITSELF AS A RATHER LARGE, WELL- BUILT WOMAN.

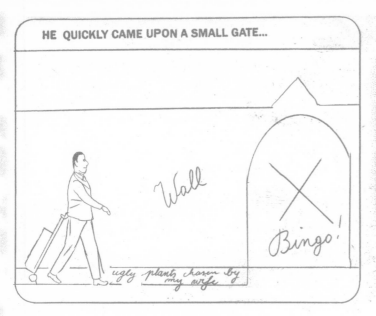

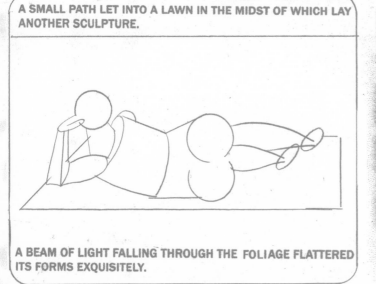

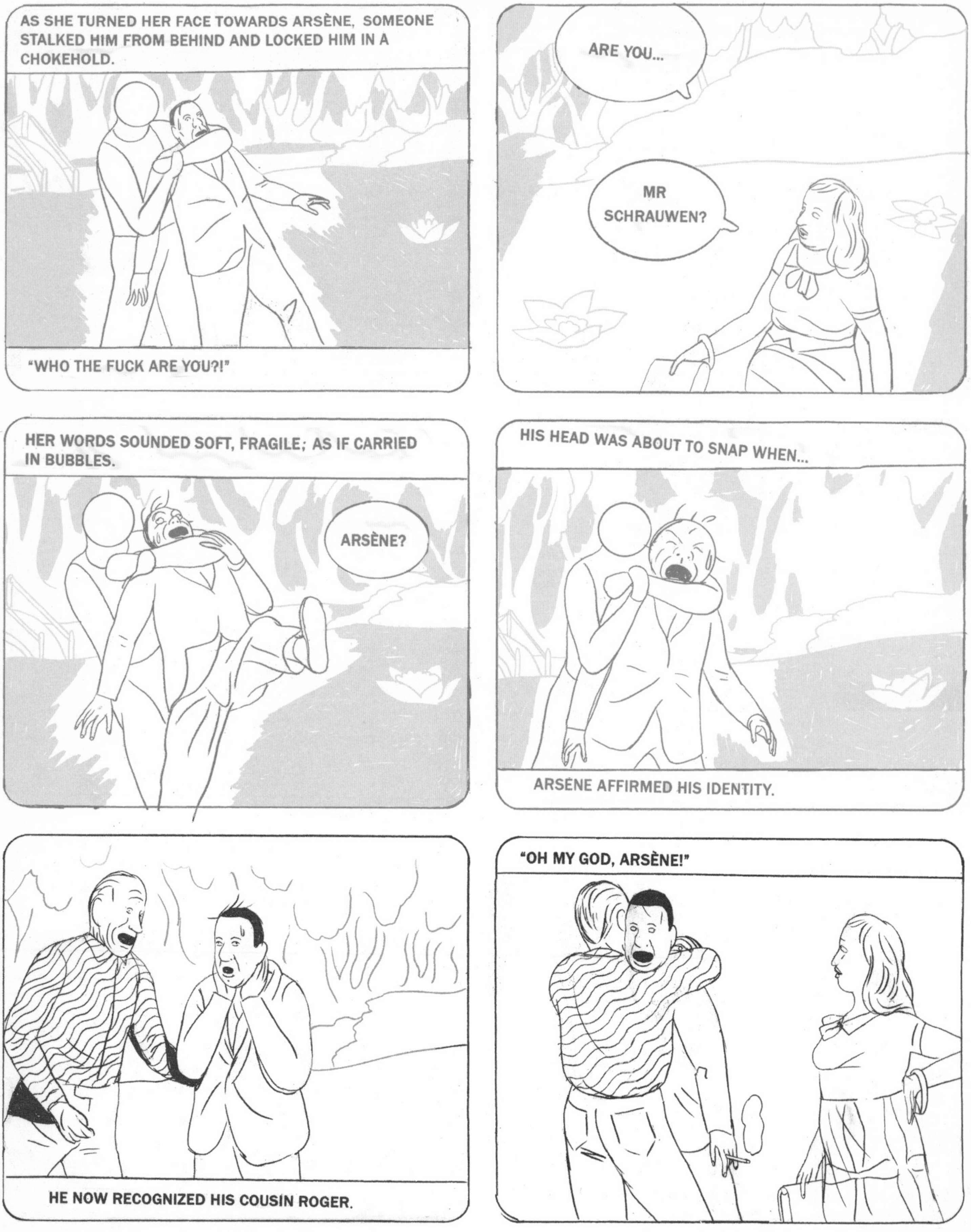

AS SHE TURNED HER FACE TOWARDS ARSÈNE, SOMEONE STALKED HIM FROM BEHIND AND LOCKED HIM IN A CHOKEHOLD.
"WHO THE FUCK ARE YOU?!"
ARE YOU...
MR SCHRAUWEN?
HER WORDS SOUNDED SOFT, FRAGILE; AS IF CARRIED IN BUBBLES.
ARSÈNE?
HIS HEAD WAS ABOUT TO SNAP WHEN...
ARSÈNE AFFIRMED HIS IDENTITY.
HE NOW RECOGNIZED HIS COUSIN ROGER.
"OH MY GOD, ARSÈNE!"

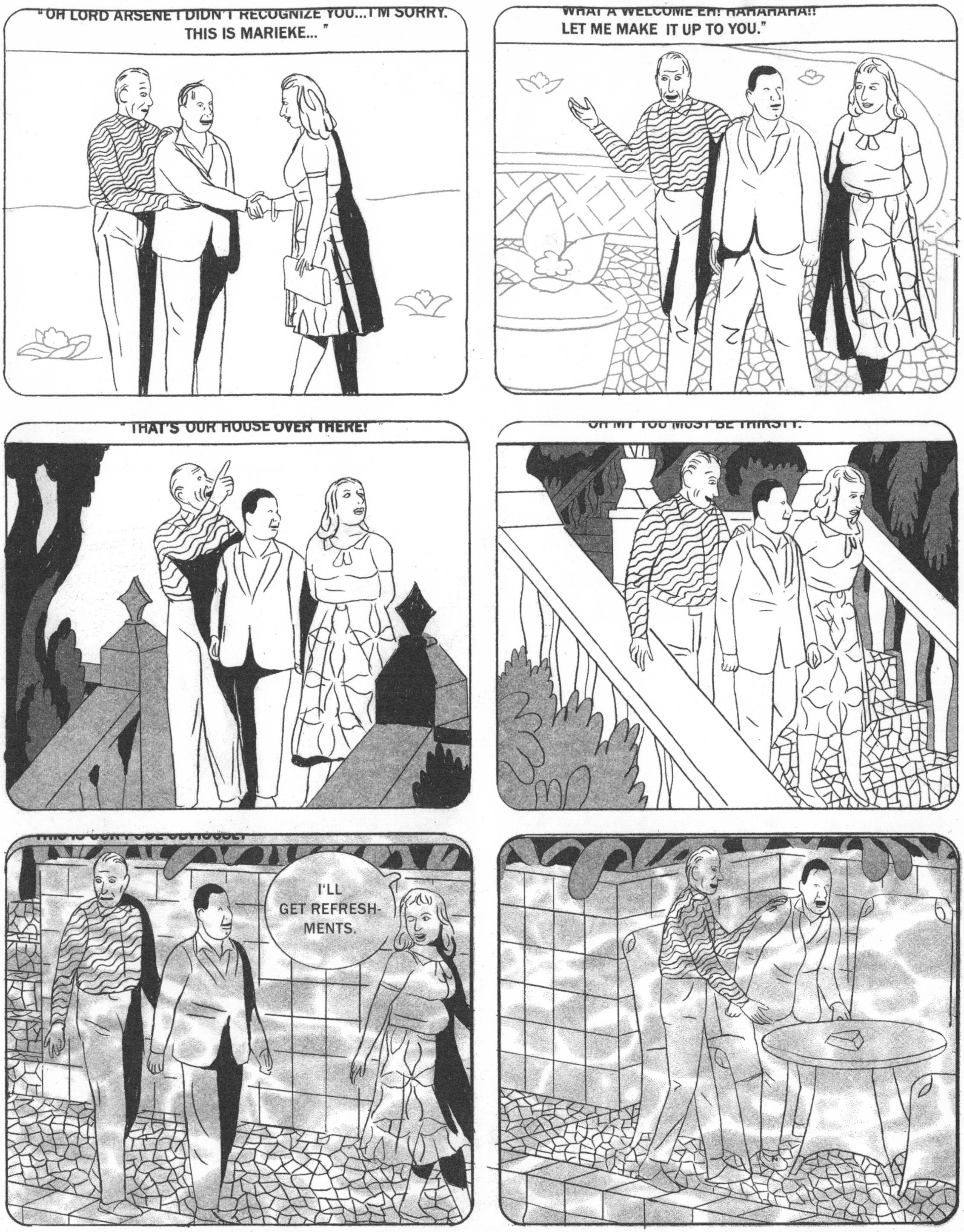
"OH LORD ARSENE I DIDN'T RECOGNIZE YOU...I'M SORRY. THIS IS MARIEKE..."
WHAT A WELCOME EH! HAHAHAHA!! LET ME MAKE IT UP TO YOU."
"THAT'S OUR HOUSE OVER THERE!"
OH MY YOU MUST BE THIRSTY.
I'LL GET REFRESH-MENTS.

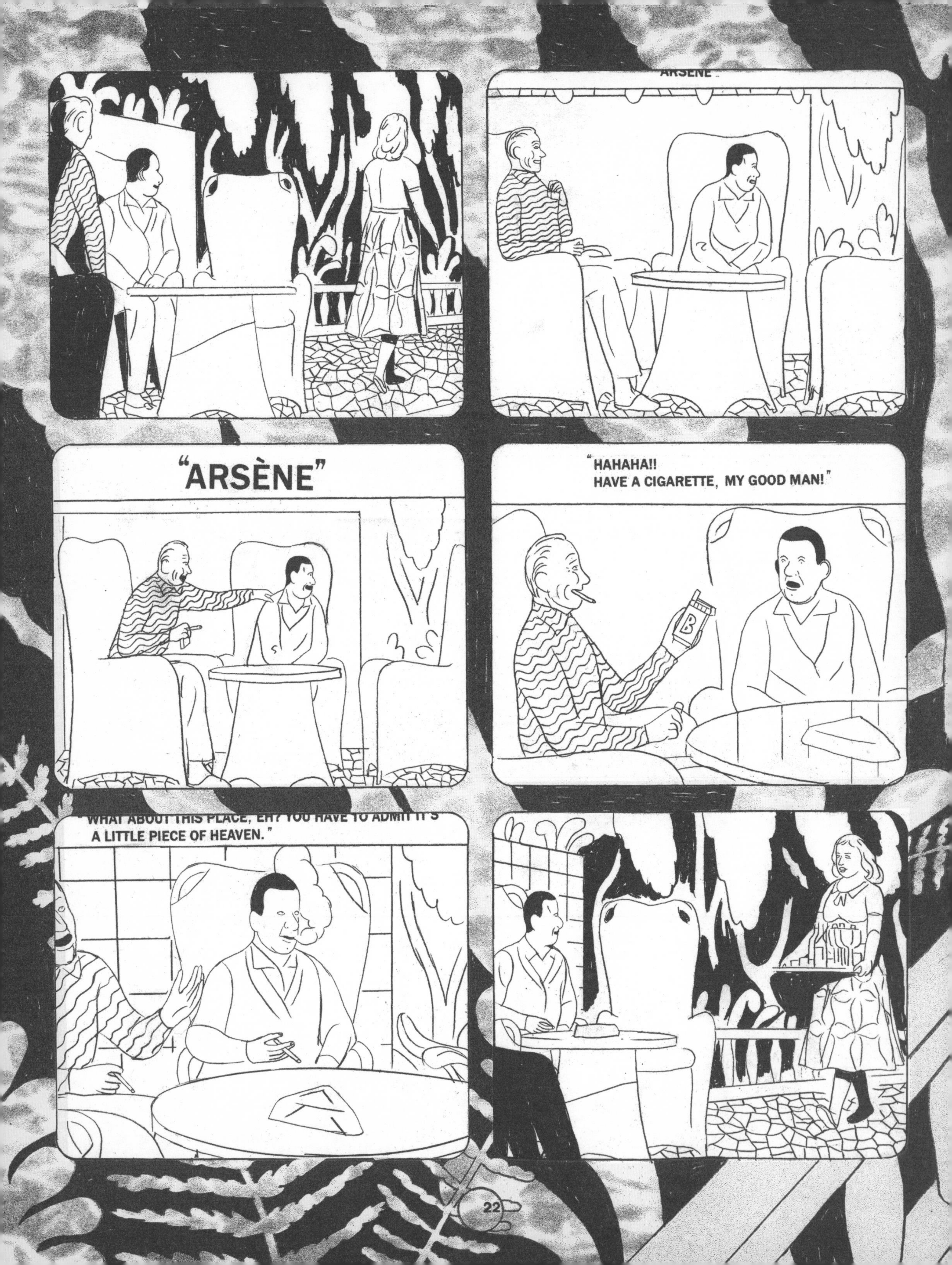
"ARSÈNE"
"HAHAHA!!
HAVE A CIGARETTE, MY GOOD MAN!"
"WHAT ABOUT THIS PLACE, EH? YOU HAVE TO ADMIT IT'S A LITTLE PIECE OF HEAVEN."

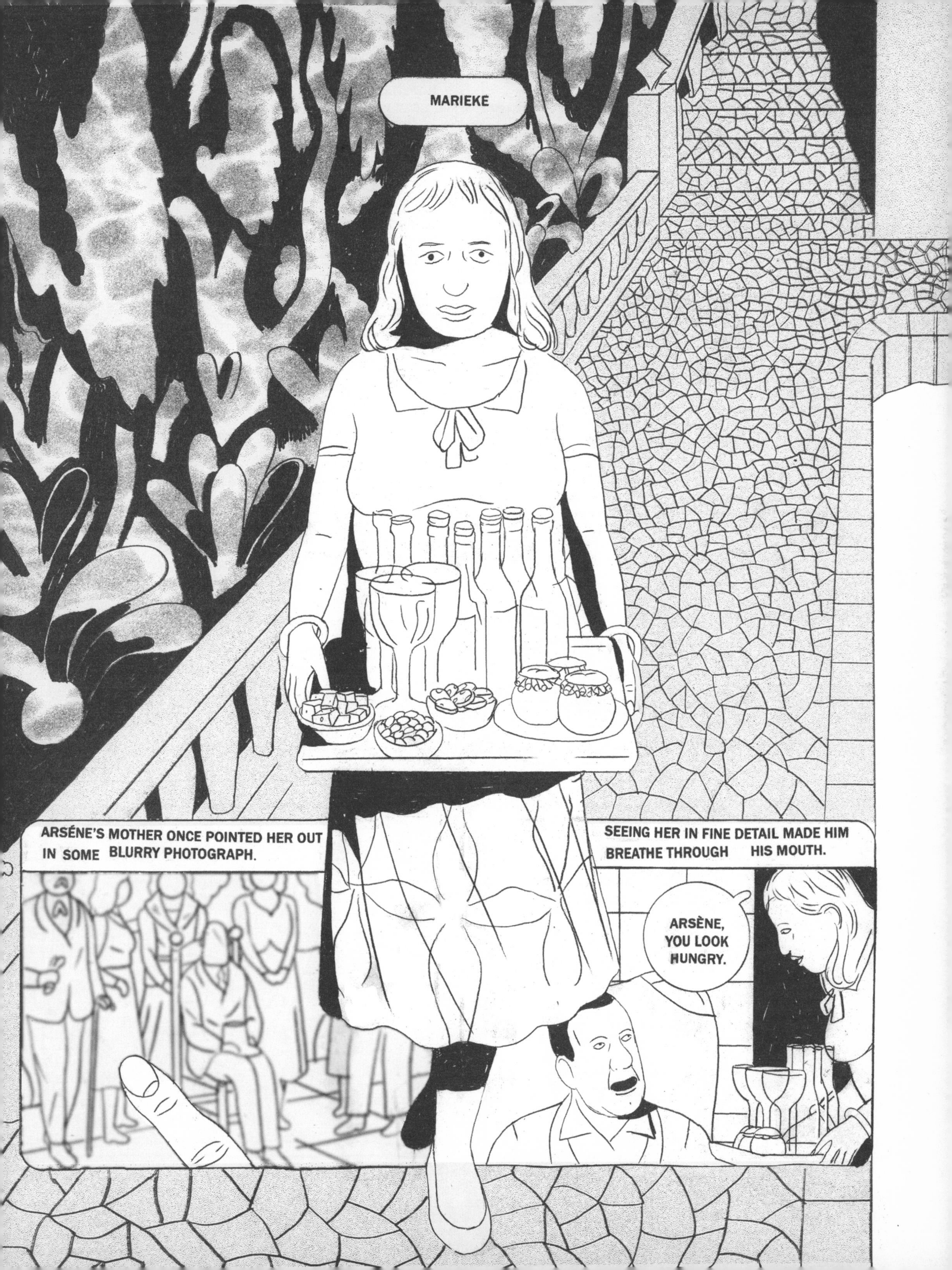
MARIEKE
ARSÉNE'S MOTHER ONCE POINTED HER OUT IN SOME BLURRY PHOTOGRAPH.
SEEING HER IN FINE DETAIL MADE HIM BREATHE THROUGH HIS MOUTH.
ARSÈNE, YOU LOOK HUNGRY.

HER REMARK MADE HIM AWARE OF HIS GAZE. HE BLUSHED AND AVERTED HIS EYES.

DESMET TOLD HIM WHERE TO LOOK.
"ARSÈNE, BEHOLD THESE TOMATE CREVETTES . AREN'T THEY MARVELOUS?"

"AND DO TRY THE TRAPPIST, IT'S OF SUPERIOR QUALITY."

NOW DESMET STARTED INQUIRING ABOUT HIS VOYAGE. HOW HIS FAMILY WAS DOING. HOW WORLD WAR II HAD BEEN.

ROGER PROVED TO BE A CHARMING CONVERSATIONALIST. IT SPURRED GRANDPA TO ANSWER IN SHORT, OCCASIONALLY WITTY ANSWERS.

HE MADE MARIEKE LAUGH ON SEVERAL OCCASIONS !

ALL THE WHILE ARSÈNE SCRUTINIZED THE TRAPPIST BOTTLE,
FOCUSING ON DIFFERENT SECTIONS OF ITS PECULIAR LABEL

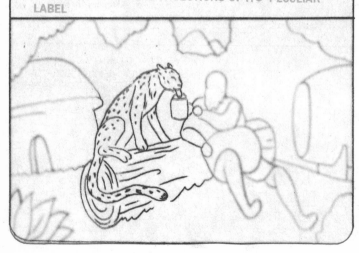

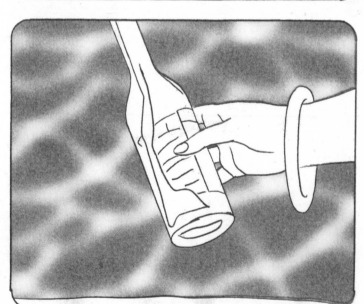

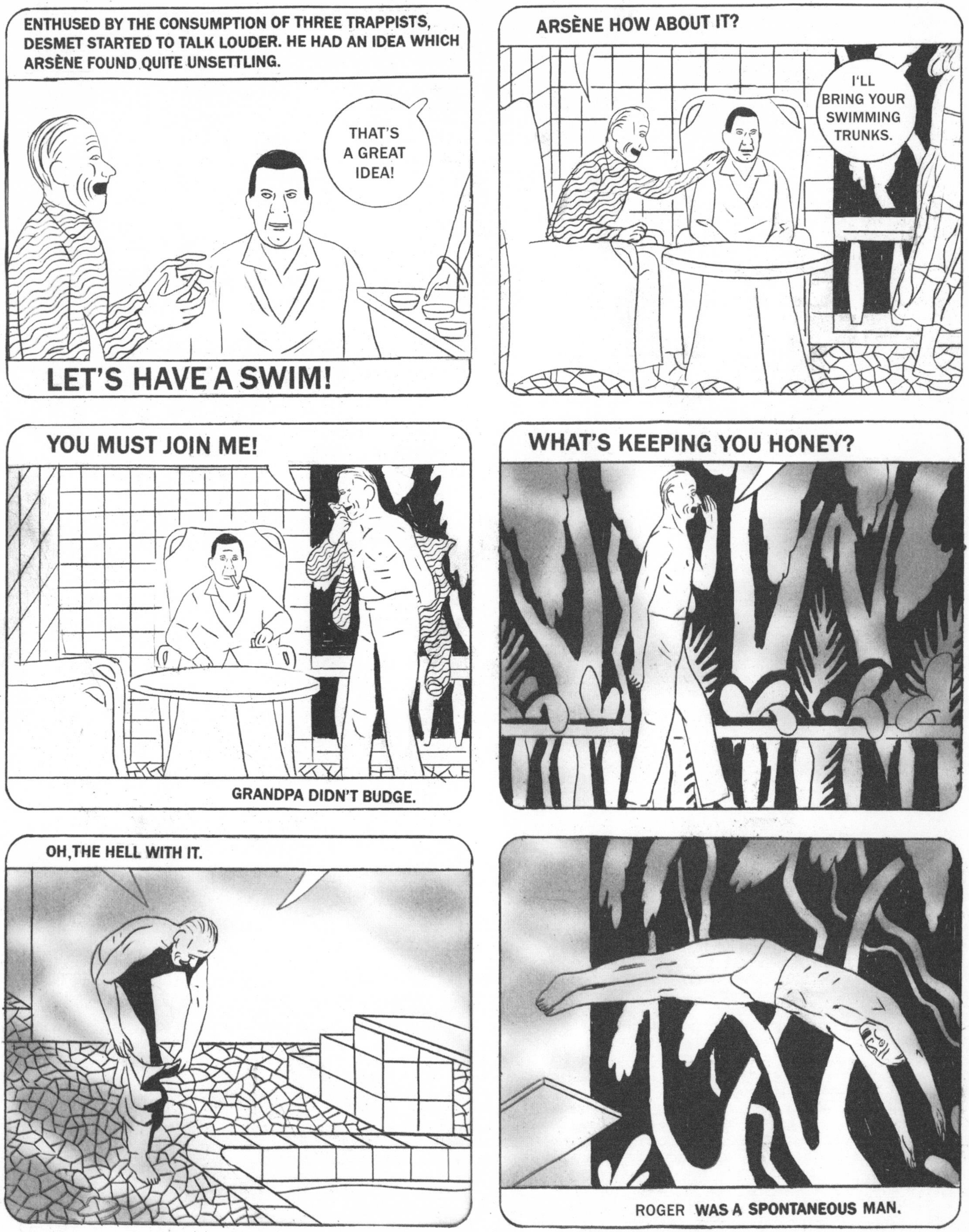
ENTHUSED BY THE CONSUMPTION OF THREE TRAPPISTS, DESMET STARTED TO TALK LOUDER. HE HAD AN IDEA WHICH ARSÈNE FOUND QUITE UNSETTLING.
THAT'S A GREAT IDEA!
LET'S HAVE A SWIM!
ARSÈNE HOW ABOUT IT?
I'LL BRING YOUR SWIMMING TRUNKS.
YOU MUST JOIN ME!
GRANDPA DIDN'T BUDGE.
WHAT'S KEEPING YOU HONEY?
OH, THE HELL WITH IT.
ROGER WAS A SPONTANEOUS MAN.

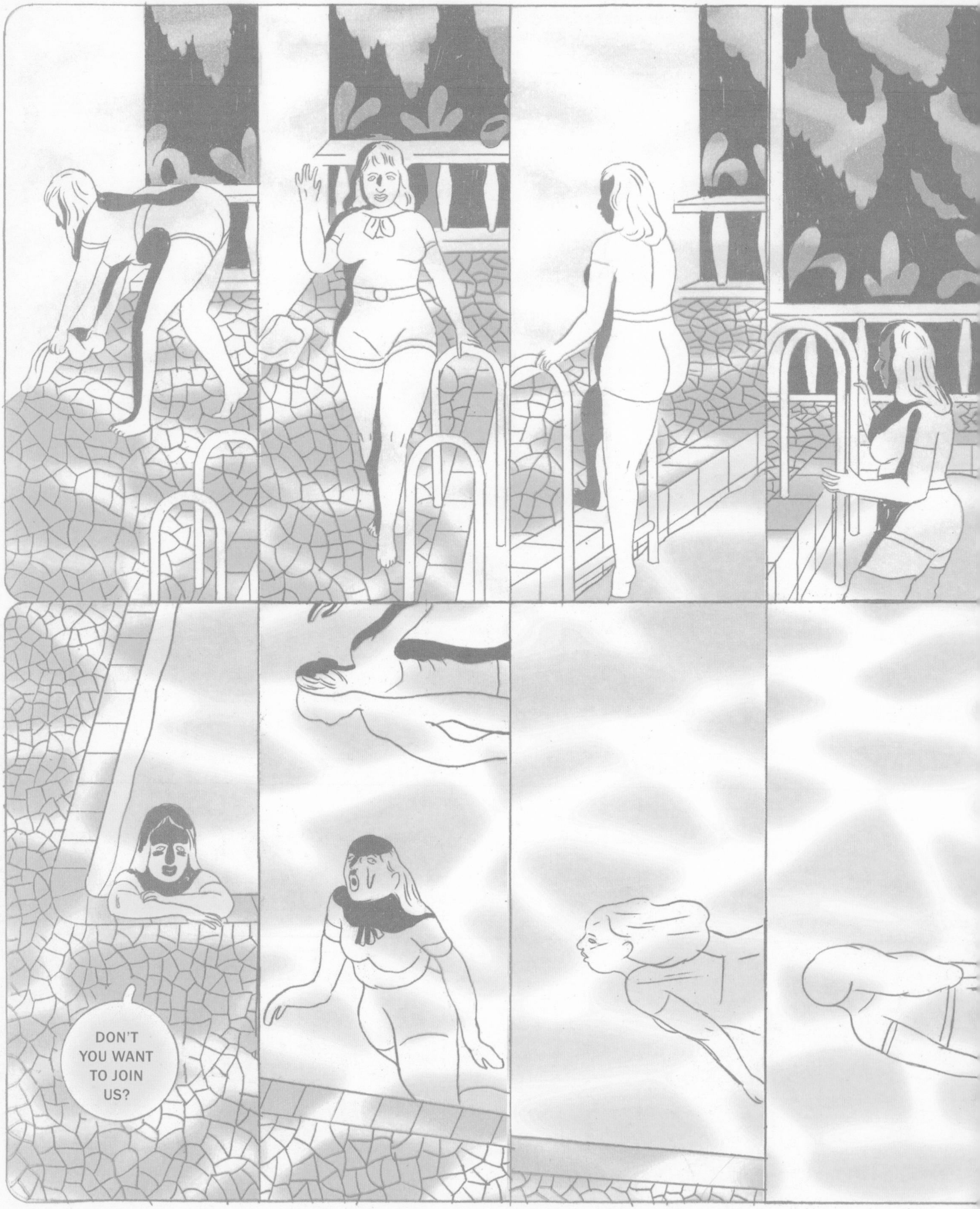
DON'T YOU WANT TO JOIN US?

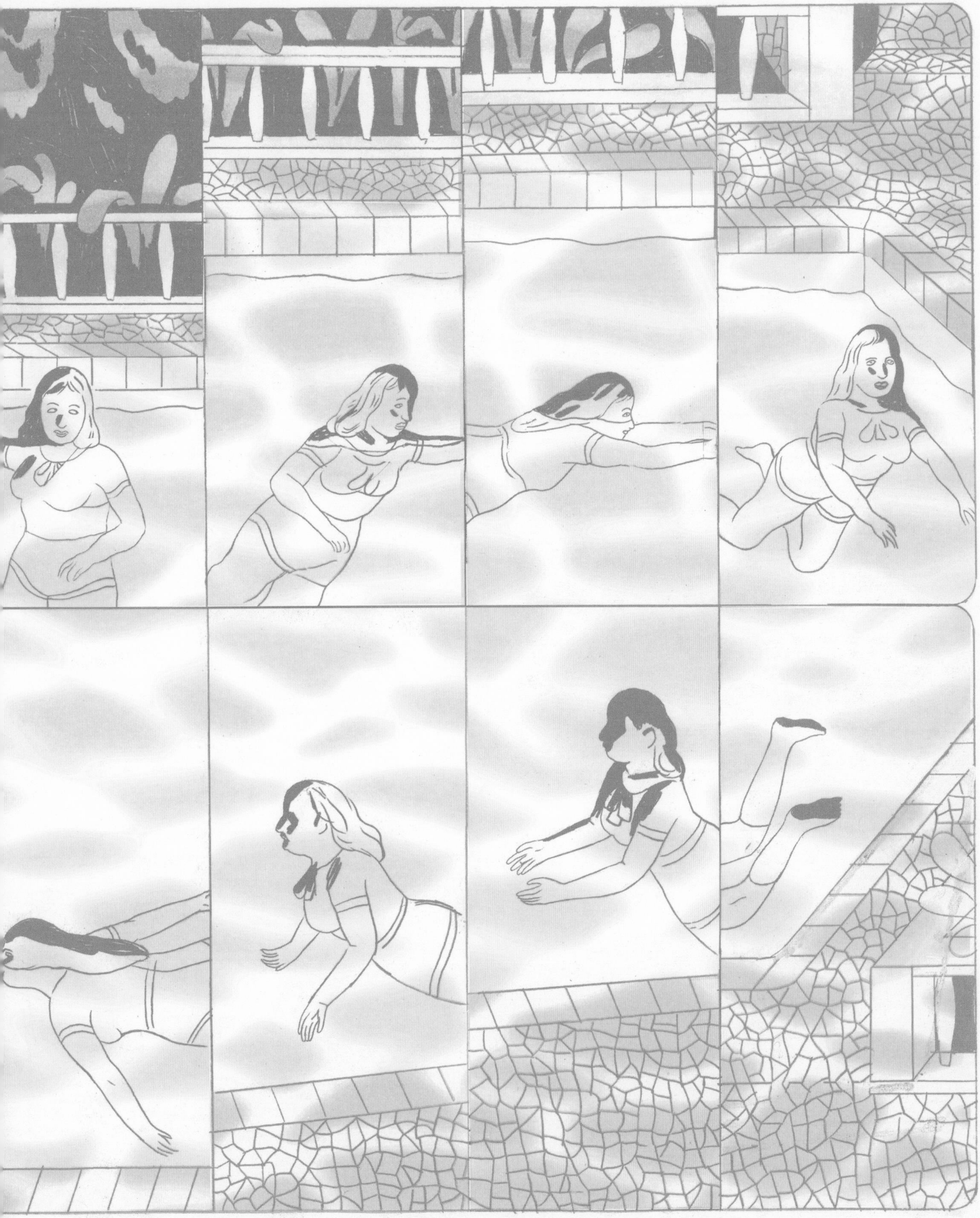

A RAY OF LIGHT HAD PENETRATED THE FOLIAGE AND SHONE UPON GRANDPA.

IF IT WERE AN X-RAY IT MIGHT'VE REVEALED HOW HIS BRIEFS WERE TAPED TO HIS THIGHS AND BELLY.

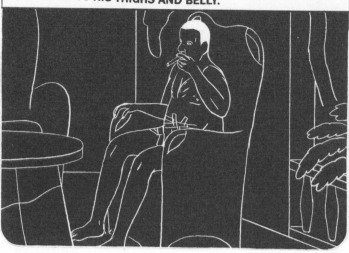

IT MIGHT'VE EXPOSED HOW HE'D DEVELOPED AN ERECTION THAT WOULD FLATTER A RANDY DONKEY.

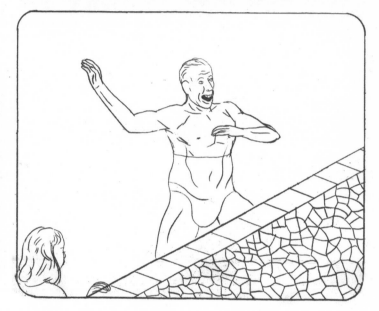

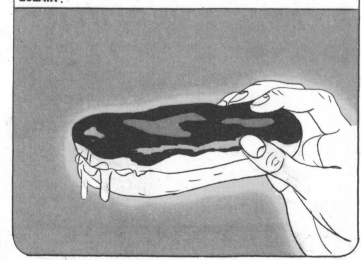

DINNER WAS ROUNDED OFF WITH A COFFEE-COGNAC AND AN ÉCLAIR.

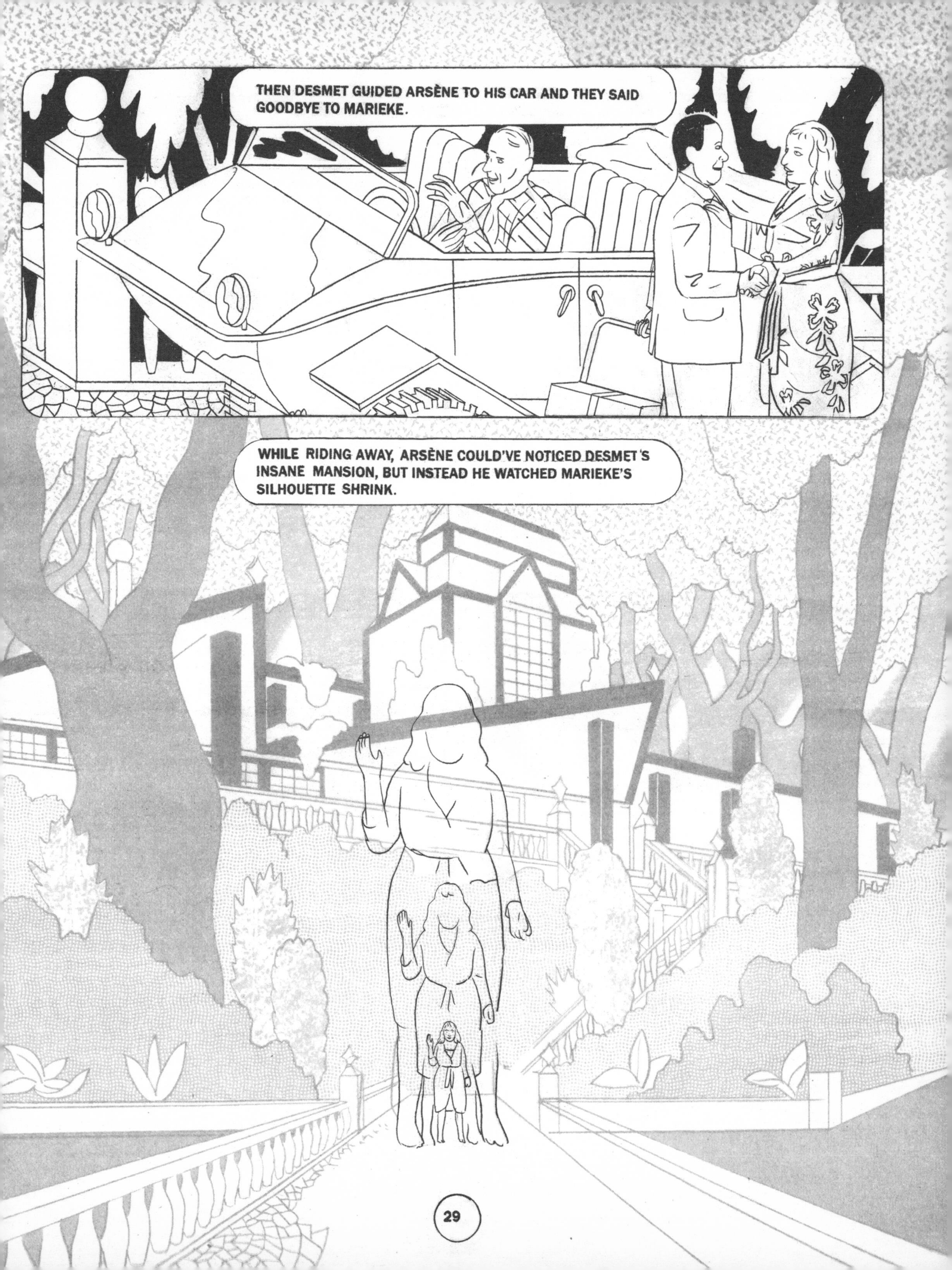
THEN DESMET GUIDED ARSÈNE TO HIS CAR AND THEY SAID GOODBYE TO MARIEKE.
WHILE RIDING AWAY, ARSÈNE COULD'VE NOTICED DESMET'S INSANE MANSION, BUT INSTEAD HE WATCHED MARIEKE'S SILHOUETTE SHRINK.

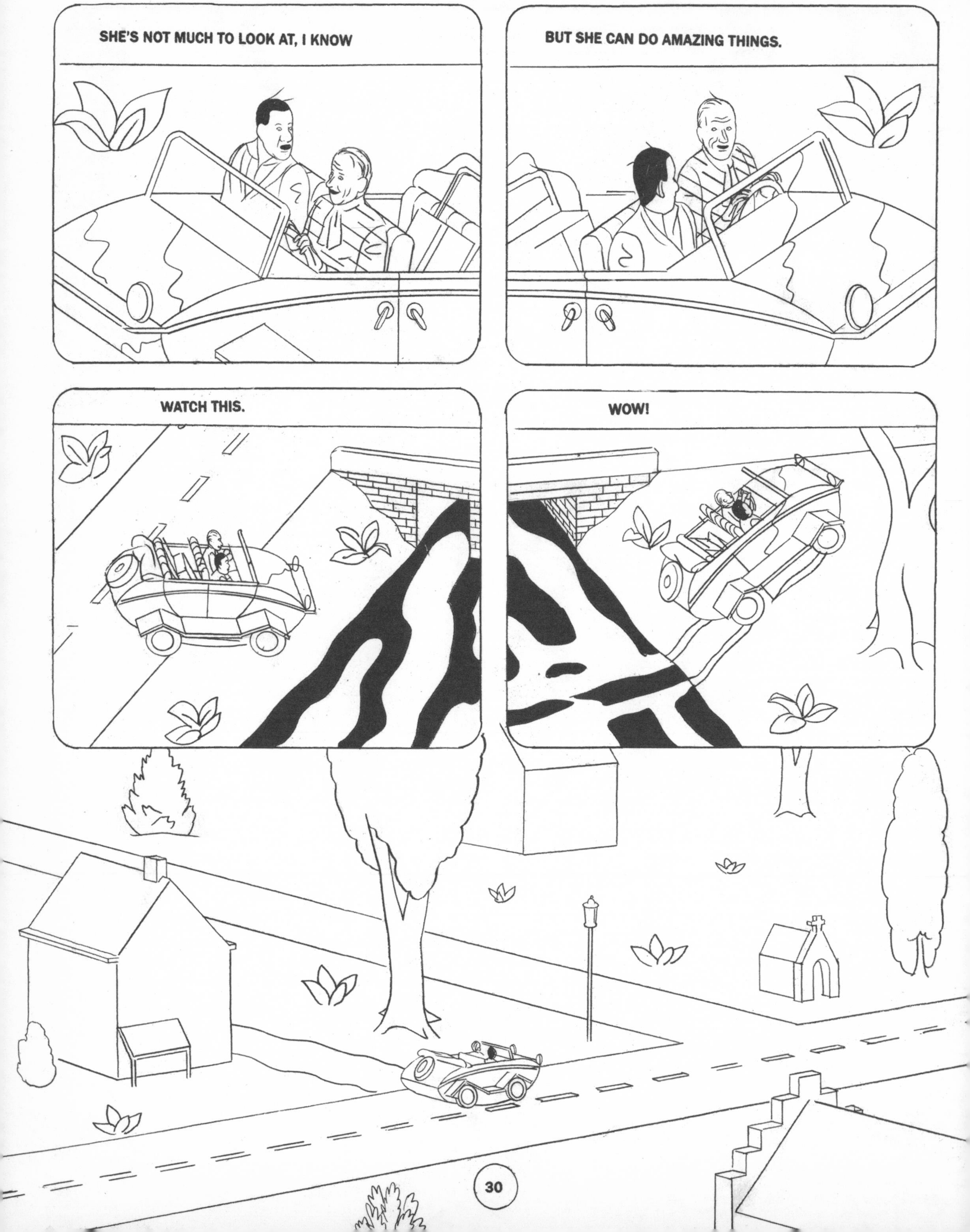
SHE'S NOT MUCH TO LOOK AT, I KNOW
BUT SHE CAN DO AMAZING THINGS.
WATCH THIS.
WOW!

SOON THEY ROLLED INTO A SMALLISH TOWN. DESMET POINTED OUT THE TOWN HALL, THE MAYOR'S OFFICE. THE

POLICE OFFICE, THE LIBRARY, THE FLOWER STORE, ETC.

THERE WERE PEOPLE ALL OVER, GOING ABOUT THEIR BUSINESS, SOME LOUNGING IN SHADE OF THE VERANDAS THAT SEEMED TO BE ATTACHED TO EVERY HOUSE.

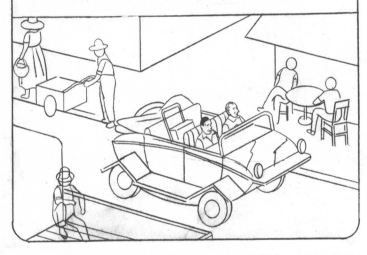

IT DIDN'T LOOK MUCH DIFFERENT THAN ANY SMALL FLEMISH TOWN ON A HOT SUMMER DAY.

WHEN ARSÈNE POINTED THIS OUT TO DESMET, HE EXCLAIMED: "THAT'S EXACTLY WHAT'S WRONG WITH THIS PLACE!"

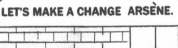

THEY PULLED UP AT A LARGE WAREHOUSE.

LET'S MAKE A CHANGE ARSÈNE.

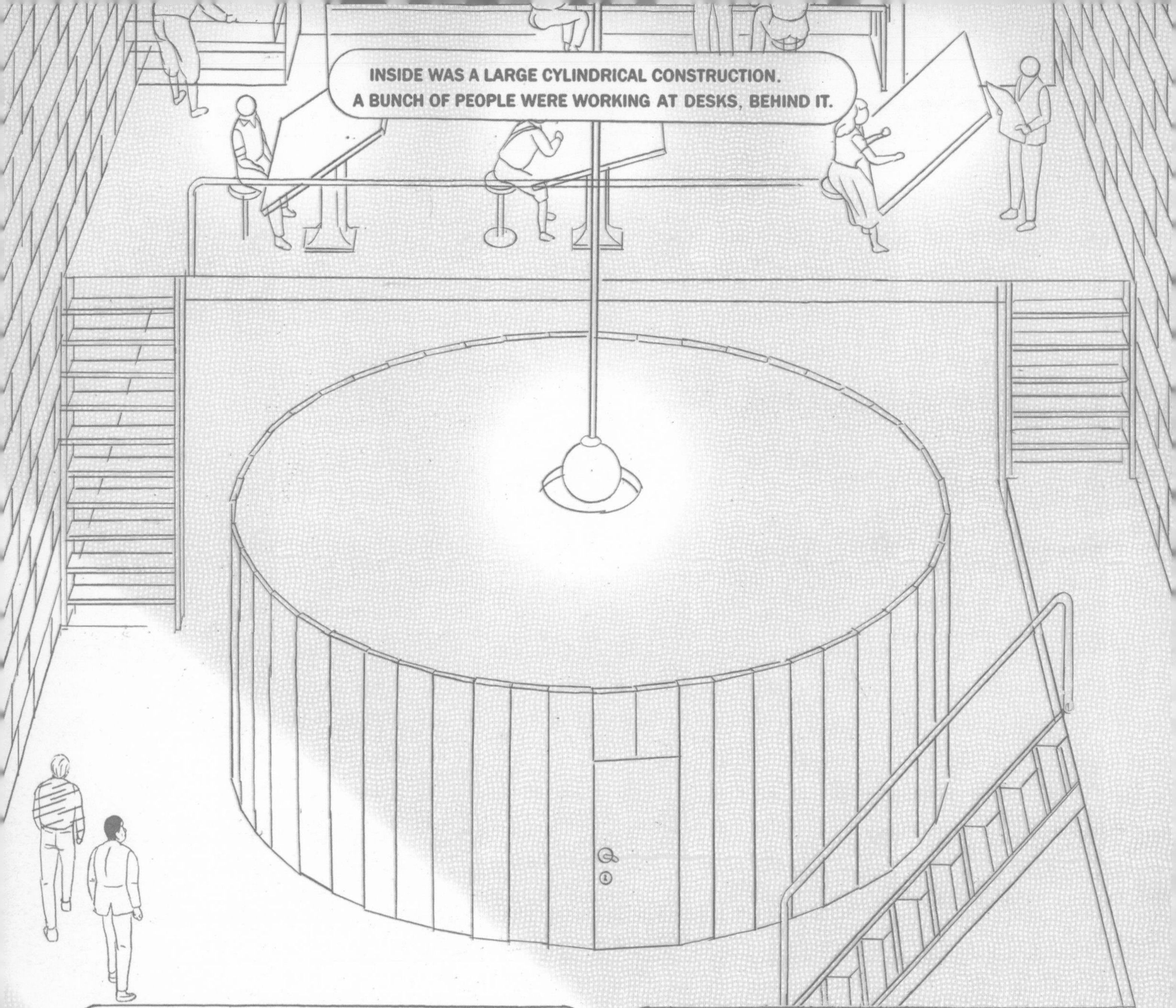
INSIDE WAS A LARGE CYLINDRICAL CONSTRUCTION.
A BUNCH OF PEOPLE WERE WORKING AT DESKS, BEHIND IT.

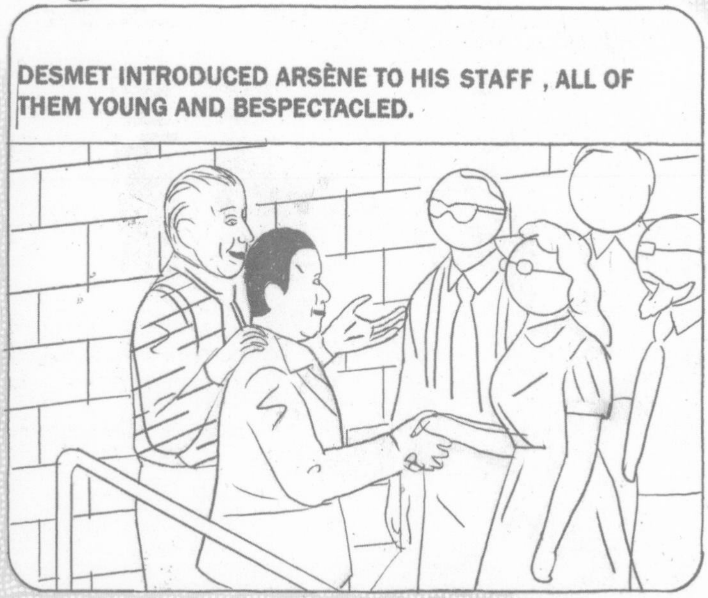
DESMET INTRODUCED ARSÈNE TO HIS STAFF , ALL OF THEM YOUNG AND BESPECTACLED.

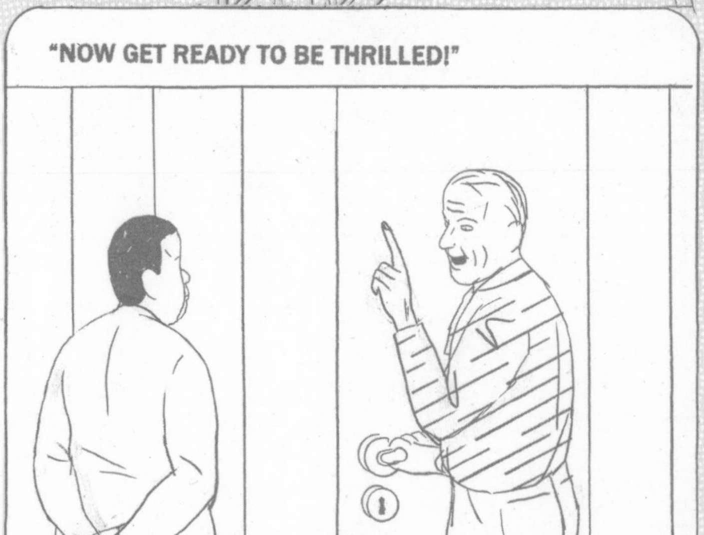
"NOW GET READY TO BE THRILLED!"

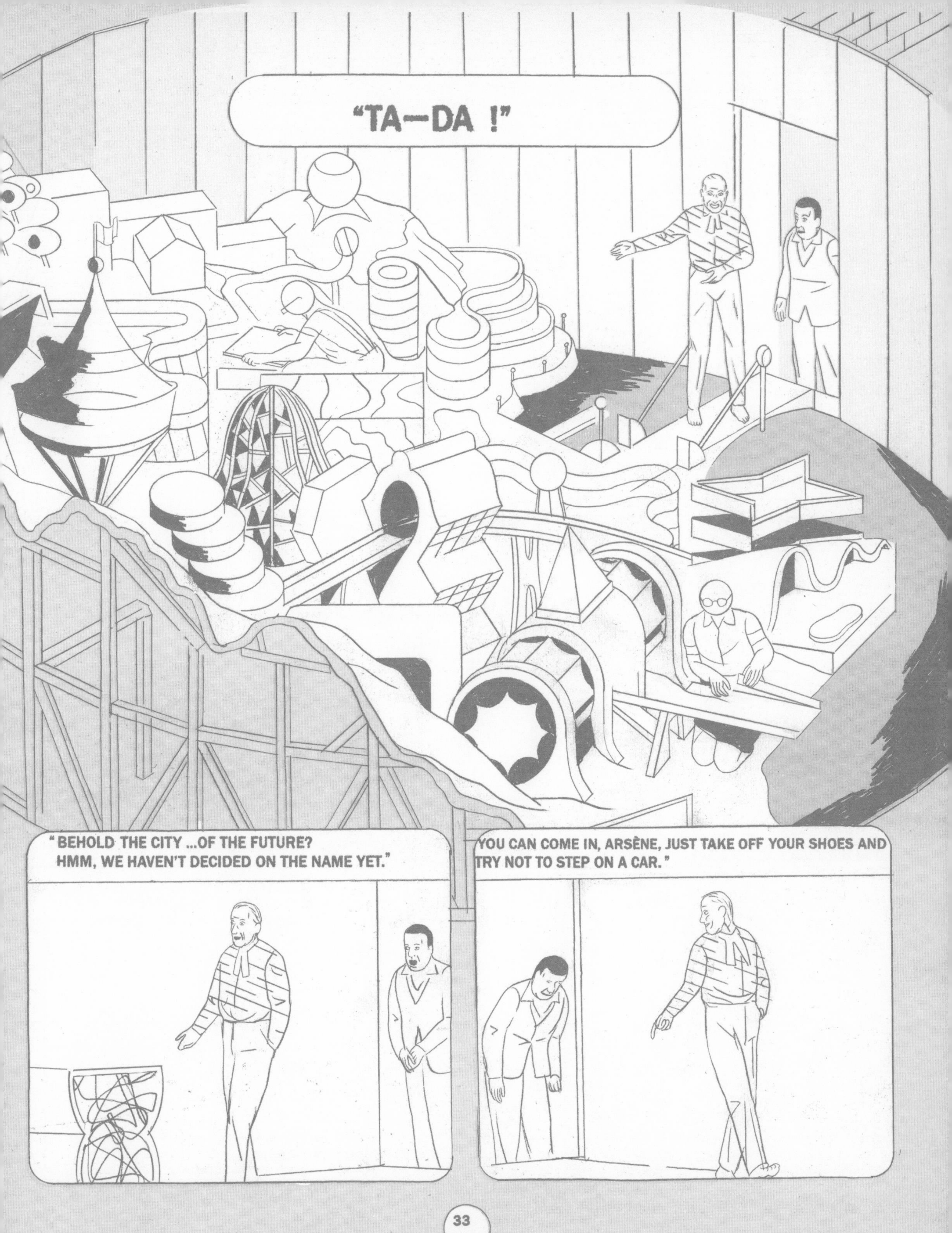
"TA—DA !"
" BEHOLD THE CITY ...OF THE FUTURE? HMM, WE HAVEN'T DECIDED ON THE NAME YET."
YOU CAN COME IN, ARSÈNE, JUST TAKE OFF YOUR SHOES AND TRY NOT TO STEP ON A CAR. "

THE WHOLE CYLINDER WAS FILLED WITH WHAT LOOKED LIKE TINY, HANDSOMELY CRAFTED SCULPTURES.

THE SCENE WAS DENSE WITH DETAIL, ALMOST TOO MUCH TO TAKE IN.

THE WAY THE INFRASTRUCTURE WAS COMPOSED, THE TISSUE OF INTERWOVEN STREETS AND CANALS THAT CONNECTED PARKS AND PLAZAS SEEMED ORGANIC.

THE WHOLE THING LAID IN A CARDBOARD VALLEY LIKE A MAN RESTING IN A PILE OF HAY.

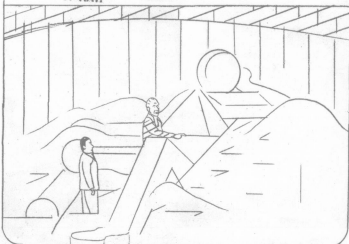

ARSENE TRIED TO GUESS WHAT PURPOSE THE BUILDINGS MIGHT HAVE.

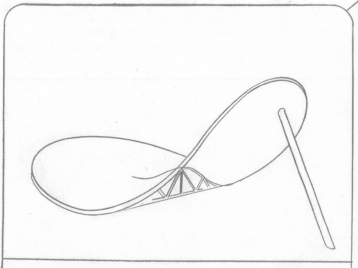

PRETTY SOON HE WAS AT A LOSS...

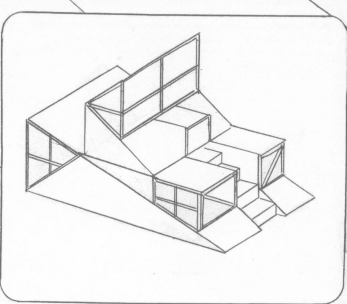

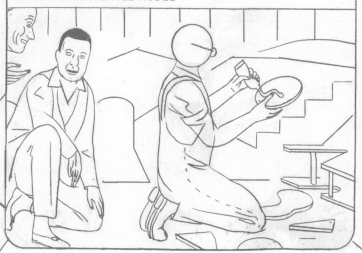

DESMET INVITED HIM TO GRAB SOME TOOLS AND MAKE HIS OWN LITTLE MODEL

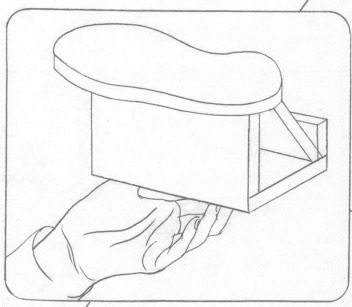

"GO AHEAD, STICK YOUR HEAD IN IT!"

GRANDAD'S FAMILIARITY WITH MODERN ARCHITECTURE WAS MINIMAL.

HE EXPERIENCED EVERYTHING IN THE WIDE-EYED, OPEN-MOUTHED MANNER OF A CHILD

AS A SPECTACLE OF LIGHT AND COLOR, FORMS AND SHAPES.

ACCORDING TO DESMET, ALL HUMAN ARTIFACTS COULD BE BROKEN DOWN INTO A SET OF UNIVERSAL FORMS. THESE COULD BE INTERCHANGED AND RECOMBINED, ACROSS CULTURES, IN EXCITING NEW CONFIGURATIONS.

SO EVERY DESIGN IN THIS CITY WAS FORMULATED USING A VOCABULARY OF THESE ELEMENTARY FORMS. THE STUFF THAT BINDS ALL PEOPLE.

DESMET EXPLAINED HOW THIS CITY WOULD DIFFER FROM JUST ABOUT ANY CITY IN THE WORLD. HOW IT WOULD ACCOMMODATE THE AWESOME VARIETY OF PEOPLES THAT WOULD COME TO INHABIT IT.

IT WOULD SEEK COMMUNITY WHILE RESPECTING THE PERSONAL AND CULTURAL INTEGRITY OF THE INDIVIDUAL.

THERE WOULDN'T BE ANY SEGREGATION HERE. ALL PEOPLES, WEATHER NATIVE OR EUROPEAN, MAN OR WOMAN...

SLIGHTLY DISTRACTED, ARSÉNE'S EYES WANDERED OFF TO A SMALL, ODD-LOOKING PIECE OF 'BRICOLAGE' IN THE MIDDLE OF THE MAQUETTE.

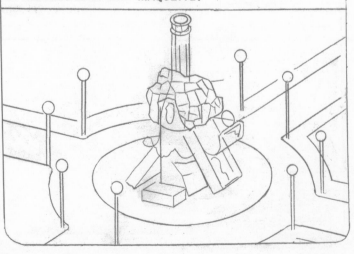

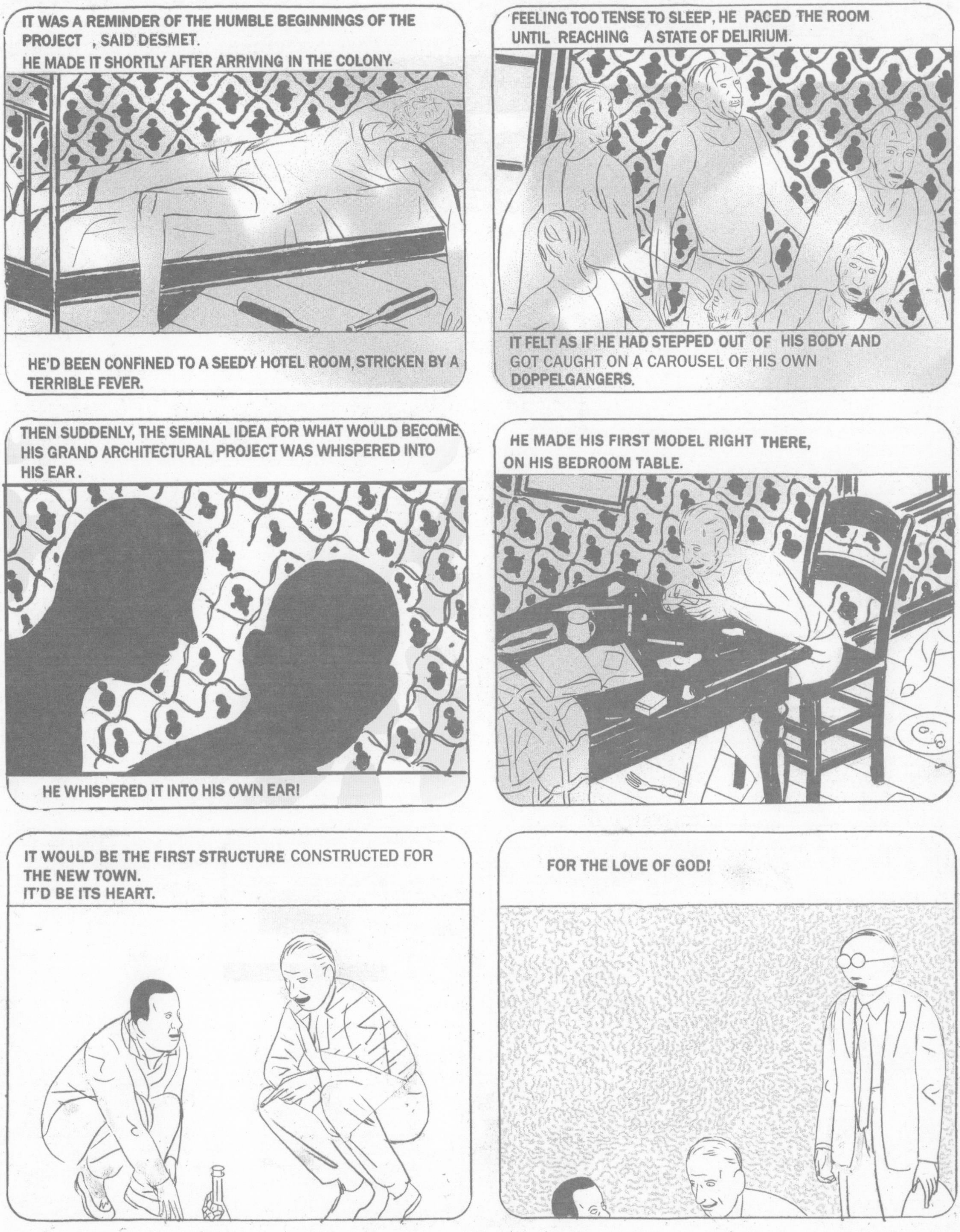
IT WAS A REMINDER OF THE HUMBLE BEGINNINGS OF THE PROJECT , SAID DESMET.
HE MADE IT SHORTLY AFTER ARRIVING IN THE COLONY.
HE'D BEEN CONFINED TO A SEEDY HOTEL ROOM, STRICKEN BY A TERRIBLE FEVER.
FEELING TOO TENSE TO SLEEP, HE PACED THE ROOM UNTIL REACHING A STATE OF DELIRIUM.
IT FELT AS IF HE HAD STEPPED OUT OF HIS BODY AND GOT CAUGHT ON A CAROUSEL OF HIS OWN DOPPELGANGERS.
THEN SUDDENLY, THE SEMINAL IDEA FOR WHAT WOULD BECOME HIS GRAND ARCHITECTURAL PROJECT WAS WHISPERED INTO HIS EAR.
HE WHISPERED IT INTO HIS OWN EAR!
HE MADE HIS FIRST MODEL RIGHT THERE, ON HIS BEDROOM TABLE.
IT WOULD BE THE FIRST STRUCTURE CONSTRUCTED FOR THE NEW TOWN.
IT'D BE ITS HEART.
FOR THE LOVE OF GOD!

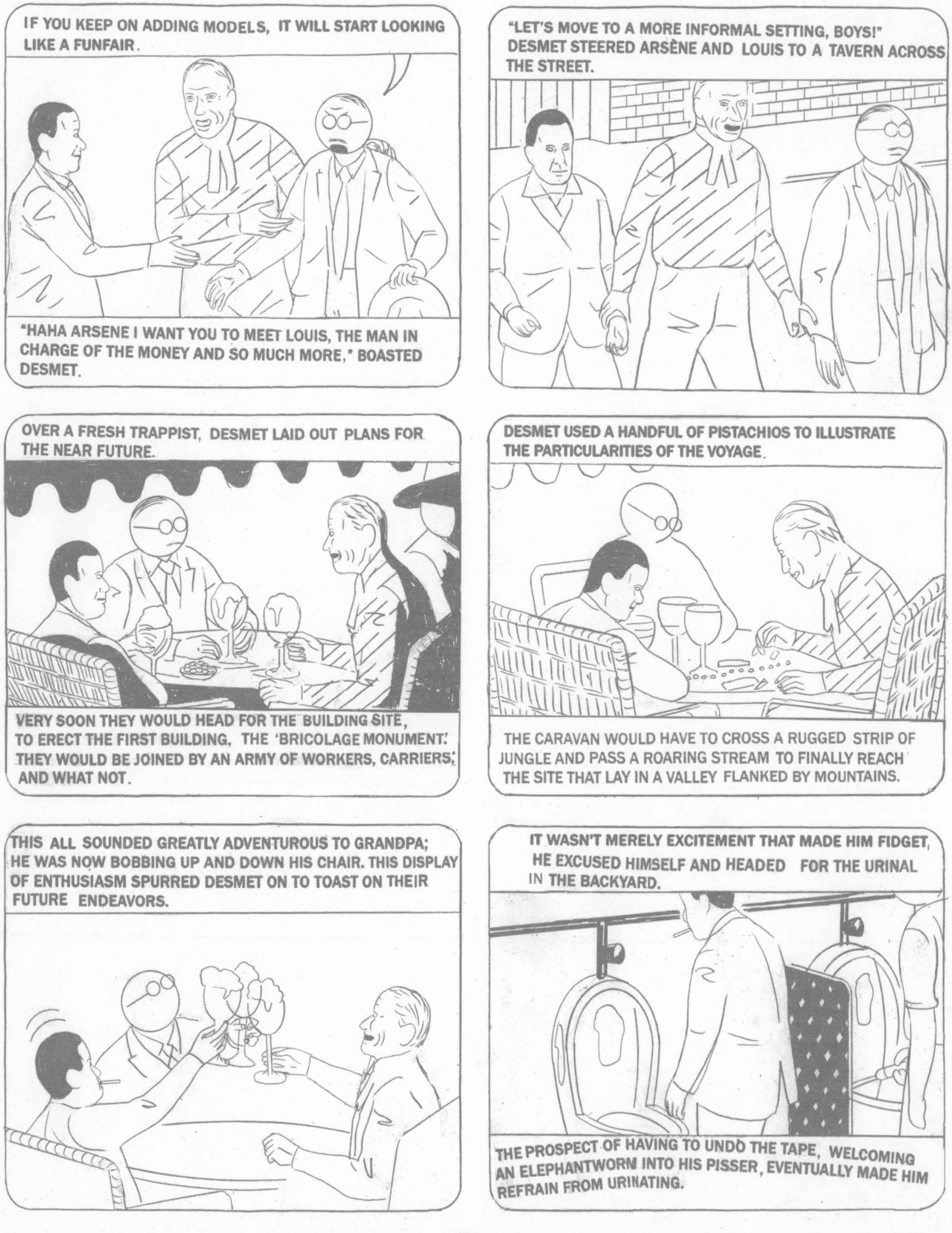
IF YOU KEEP ON ADDING MODELS, IT WILL START LOOKING LIKE A FUNFAIR.
"HAHA ARSENE I WANT YOU TO MEET LOUIS, THE MAN IN CHARGE OF THE MONEY AND SO MUCH MORE," BOASTED DESMET.
"LET'S MOVE TO A MORE INFORMAL SETTING, BOYS!" DESMET STEERED ARSÈNE AND LOUIS TO A TAVERN ACROSS THE STREET.
OVER A FRESH TRAPPIST, DESMET LAID OUT PLANS FOR THE NEAR FUTURE.
VERY SOON THEY WOULD HEAD FOR THE BUILDING SITE, TO ERECT THE FIRST BUILDING, THE 'BRICOLAGE MONUMENT.' THEY WOULD BE JOINED BY AN ARMY OF WORKERS, CARRIERS, AND WHAT NOT.
DESMET USED A HANDFUL OF PISTACHIOS TO ILLUSTRATE THE PARTICULARITIES OF THE VOYAGE.
THE CARAVAN WOULD HAVE TO CROSS A RUGGED STRIP OF JUNGLE AND PASS A ROARING STREAM TO FINALLY REACH THE SITE THAT LAY IN A VALLEY FLANKED BY MOUNTAINS.
THIS ALL SOUNDED GREATLY ADVENTUROUS TO GRANDPA; HE WAS NOW BOBBING UP AND DOWN HIS CHAIR. THIS DISPLAY OF ENTHUSIASM SPURRED DESMET ON TO TOAST ON THEIR FUTURE ENDEAVORS.
IT WASN'T MERELY EXCITEMENT THAT MADE HIM FIDGET, HE EXCUSED HIMSELF AND HEADED FOR THE URINAL IN THE BACKYARD.
THE PROSPECT OF HAVING TO UNDO THE TAPE, WELCOMING AN ELEPHANTWORM INTO HIS PISSER, EVENTUALLY MADE HIM REFRAIN FROM URINATING.

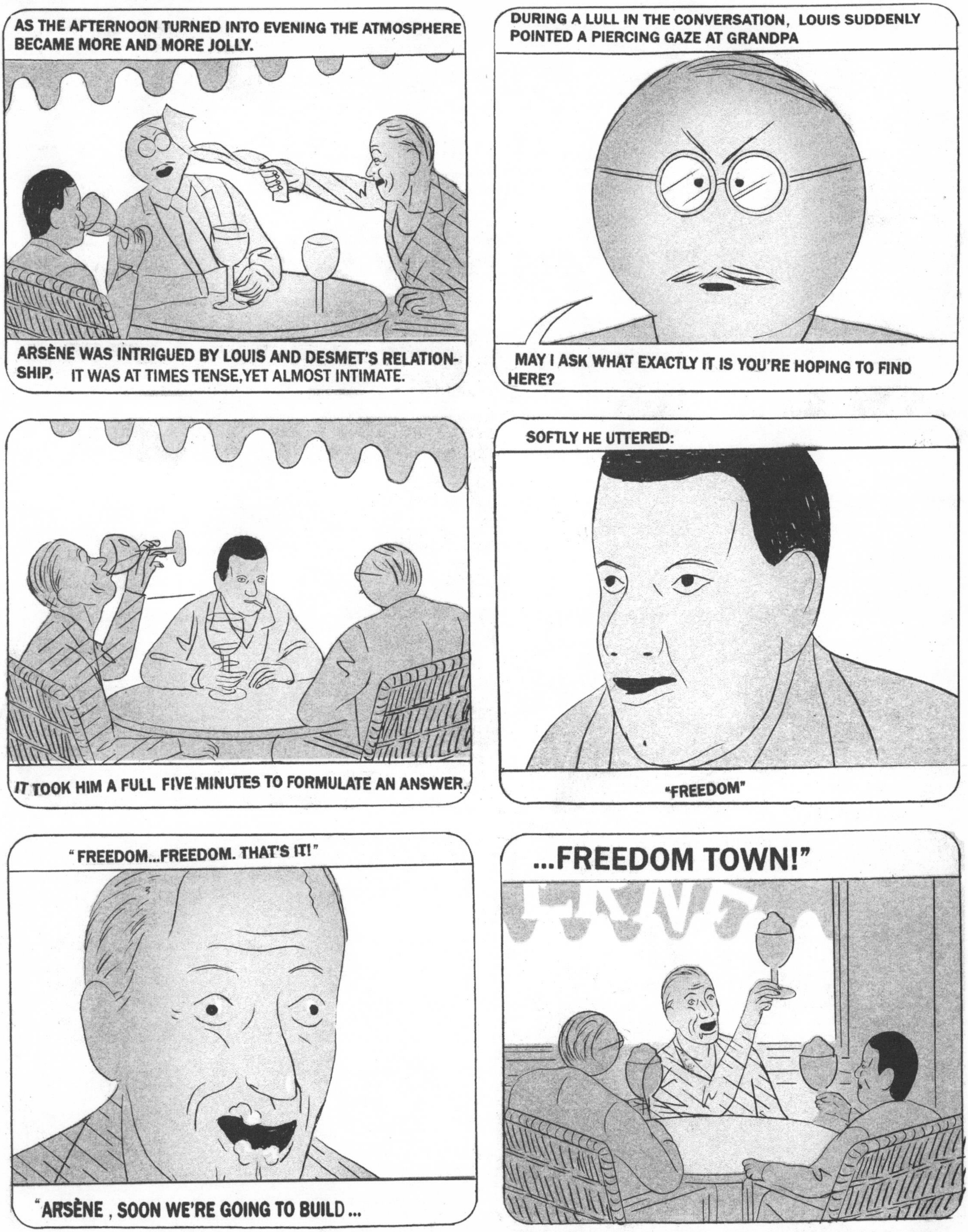
AS THE AFTERNOON TURNED INTO EVENING THE ATMOSPHERE BECAME MORE AND MORE JOLLY.
ARSÈNE WAS INTRIGUED BY LOUIS AND DESMET'S RELATION-SHIP. IT WAS AT TIMES TENSE, YET ALMOST INTIMATE.
DURING A LULL IN THE CONVERSATION, LOUIS SUDDENLY POINTED A PIERCING GAZE AT GRANDPA
MAY I ASK WHAT EXACTLY IT IS YOU'RE HOPING TO FIND HERE?
IT TOOK HIM A FULL FIVE MINUTES TO FORMULATE AN ANSWER.
SOFTLY HE UTTERED:
"FREEDOM"
" FREEDOM...FREEDOM. THAT'S IT!"
"ARSÈNE , SOON WE'RE GOING TO BUILD ...
...FREEDOM TOWN!"

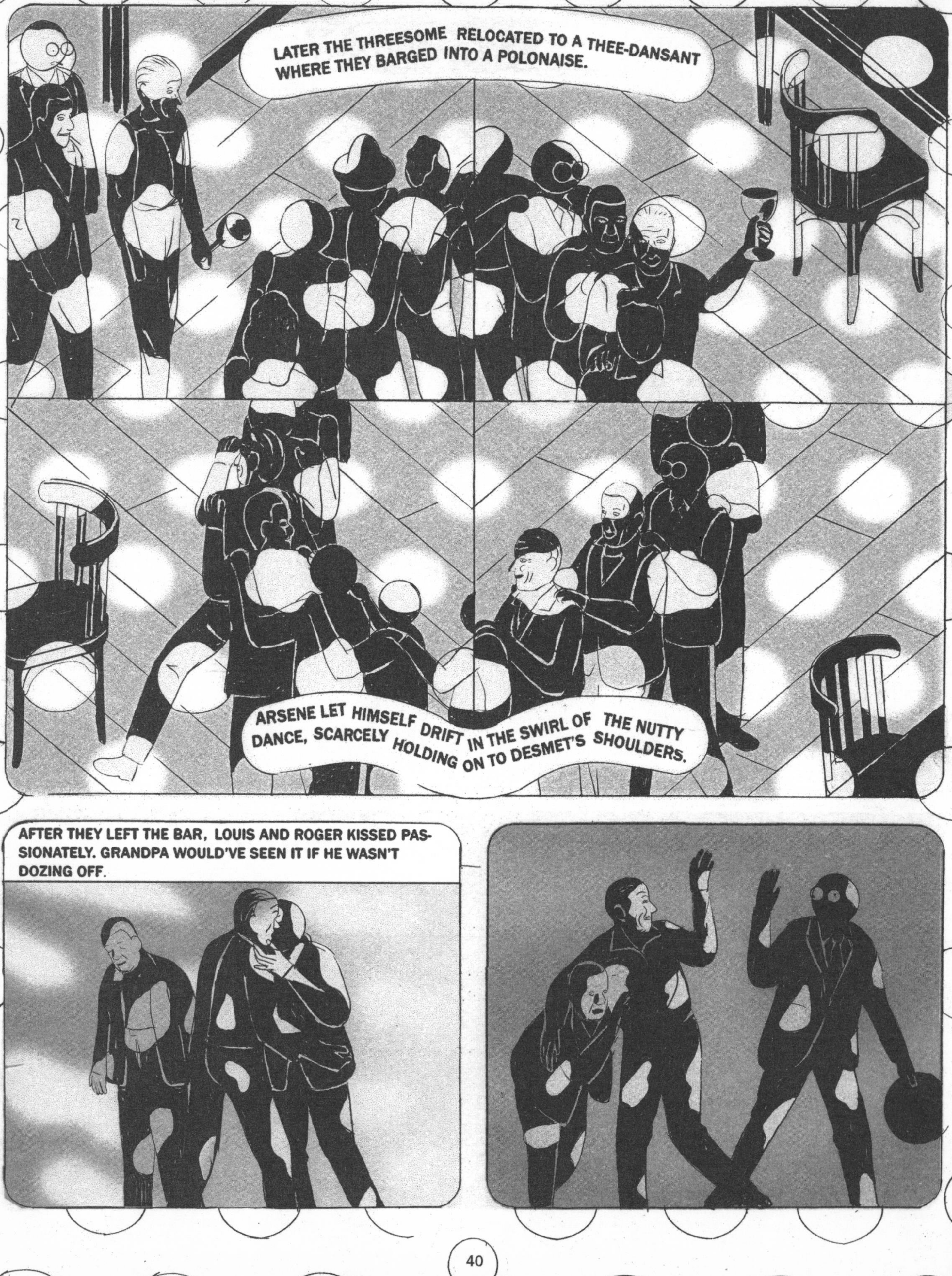
LATER THE THREESOME RELOCATED TO A THEE-DANSANT WHERE THEY BARGED INTO A POLONAISE.
ARSENE LET HIMSELF DRIFT IN THE SWIRL OF THE NUTTY DANCE, SCARCELY HOLDING ON TO DESMET'S SHOULDERS.
AFTER THEY LEFT THE BAR, LOUIS AND ROGER KISSED PASSIONATELY. GRANDPA WOULD'VE SEEN IT IF HE WASN'T DOZING OFF.

AS IF TIME HAD MADE A LEAP, GRANDPA SUDDENLY FOUND HIMSELF IN THE CAR. HE WAS EXHAUSTED.

THERE WAS NO LIGHT TO BE SEEN OUTSIDE THEY SEEMED TO CLEAVE THROUGH A SEA OF BLACKNESS.

MEANWHILE, DESMET WAS EXTREEMLY CHEERFUL AND TALKATIVE.

HE EXPRESSED HOW HAPPY HE WAS WITH ARSÈNE'S ARRIVAL AND HOW HE SAW HIM AS AN IDEAL SOUNDING BOARD.

A PALETTE ON WHICH TO SQUIRT PAINT AND MIX COLORS.

A BUILDING BLOCK.

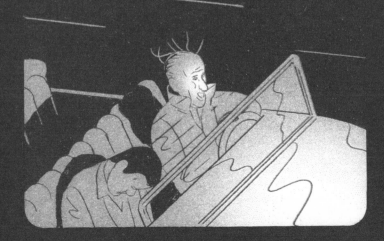

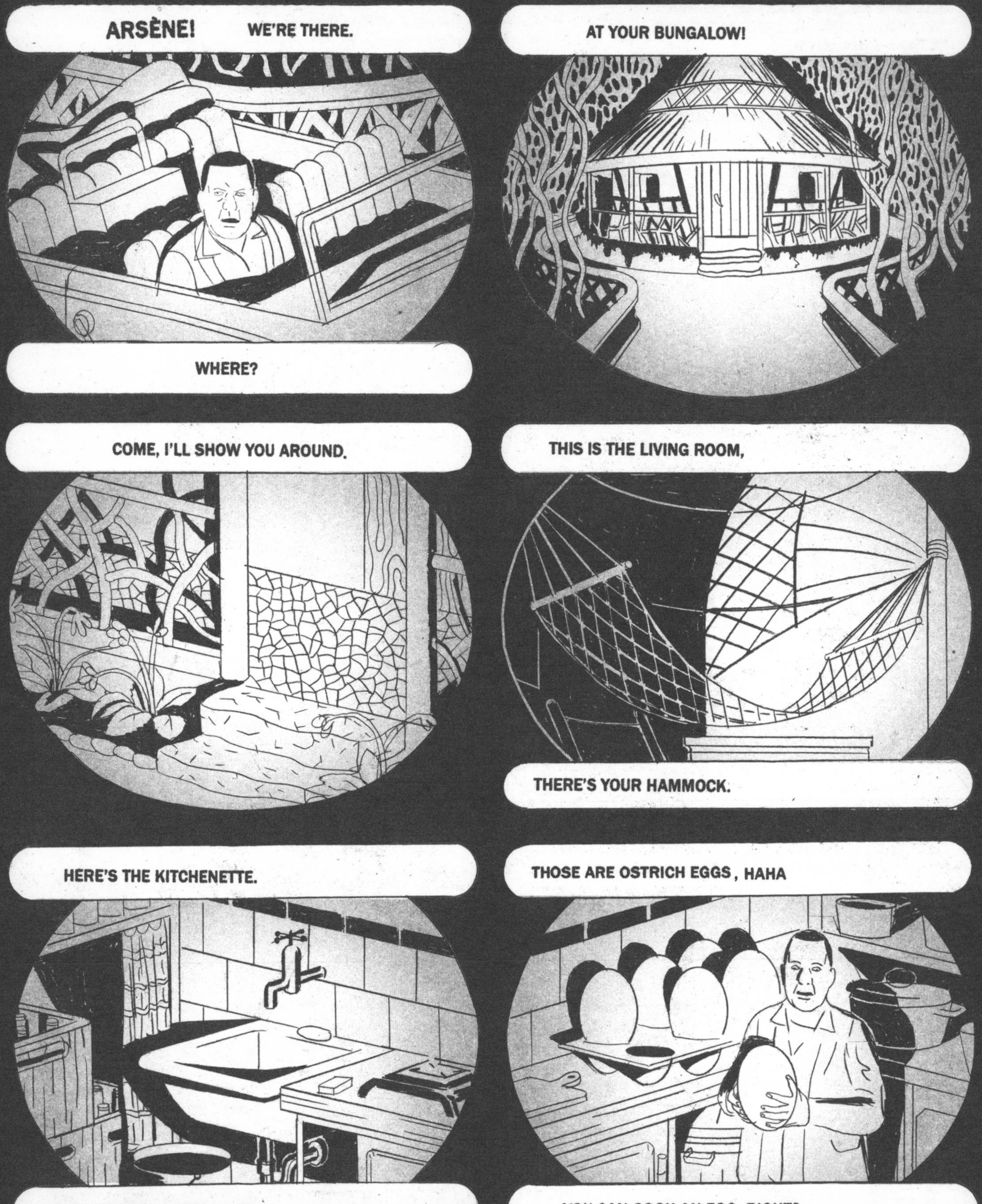
ARSÈNE! WE'RE THERE.
WHERE?
AT YOUR BUNGALOW!
COME, I'LL SHOW YOU AROUND.
THIS IS THE LIVING ROOM,
THERE'S YOUR HAMMOCK.
HERE'S THE KITCHENETTE.
THERE'S WATER, TRAPPIST...
THOSE ARE OSTRICH EGGS , HAHA
...YOU CAN COOK AN EGG, RIGHT?

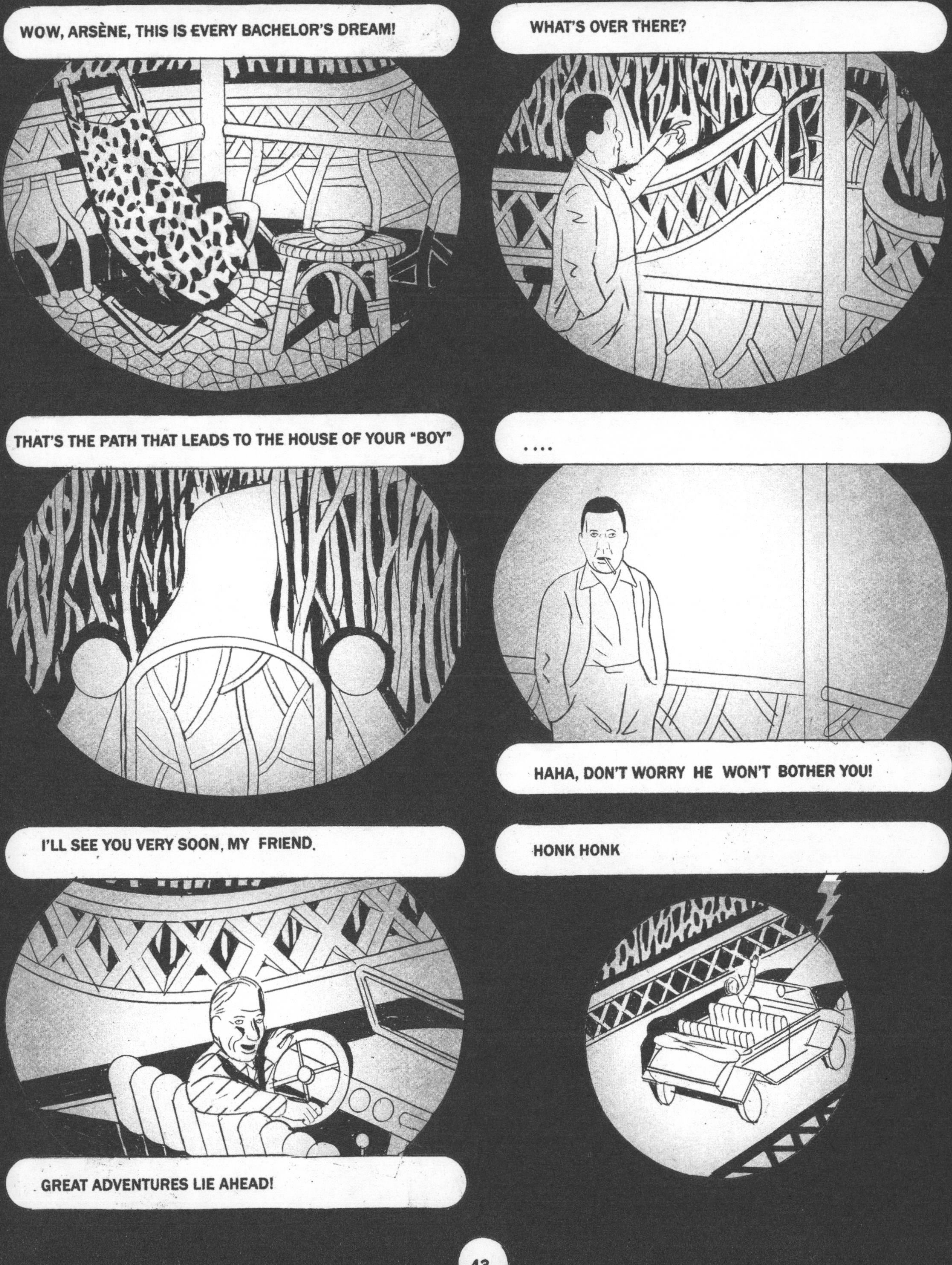
WOW, ARSÈNE, THIS IS EVERY BACHELOR'S DREAM!
WHAT'S OVER THERE?
THAT'S THE PATH THAT LEADS TO THE HOUSE OF YOUR "BOY"
....
HAHA, DON'T WORRY HE WON'T BOTHER YOU!
I'LL SEE YOU VERY SOON, MY FRIEND.
GREAT ADVENTURES LIE AHEAD!
HONK HONK

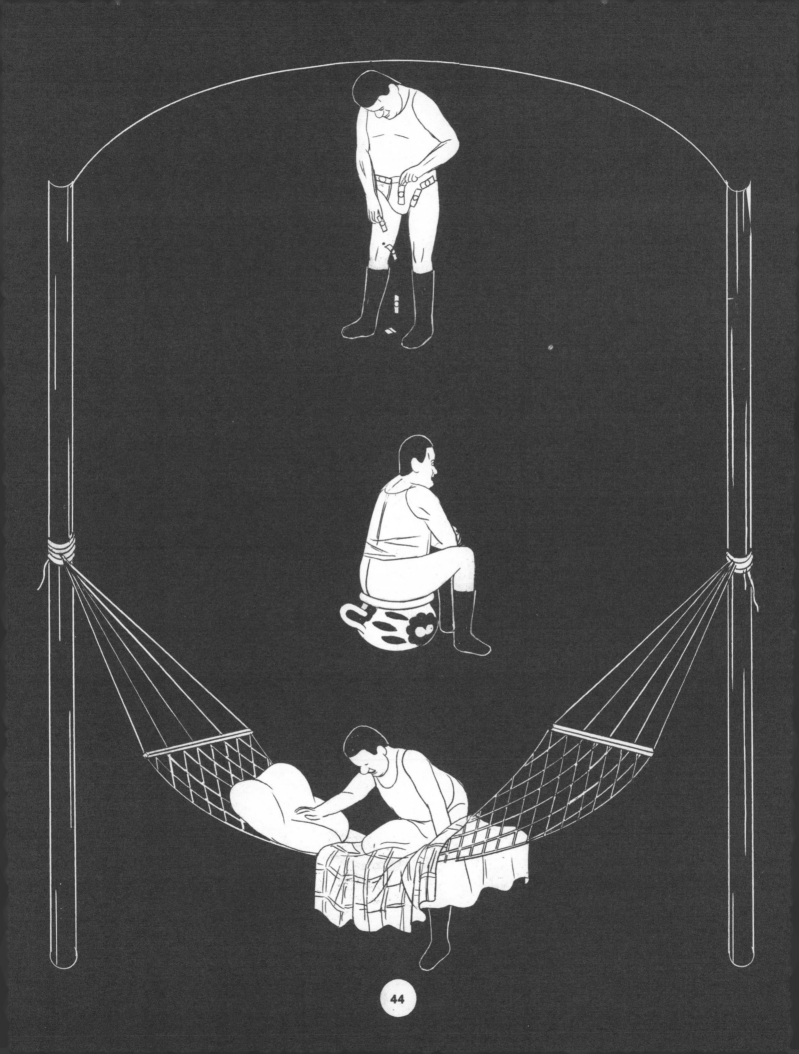

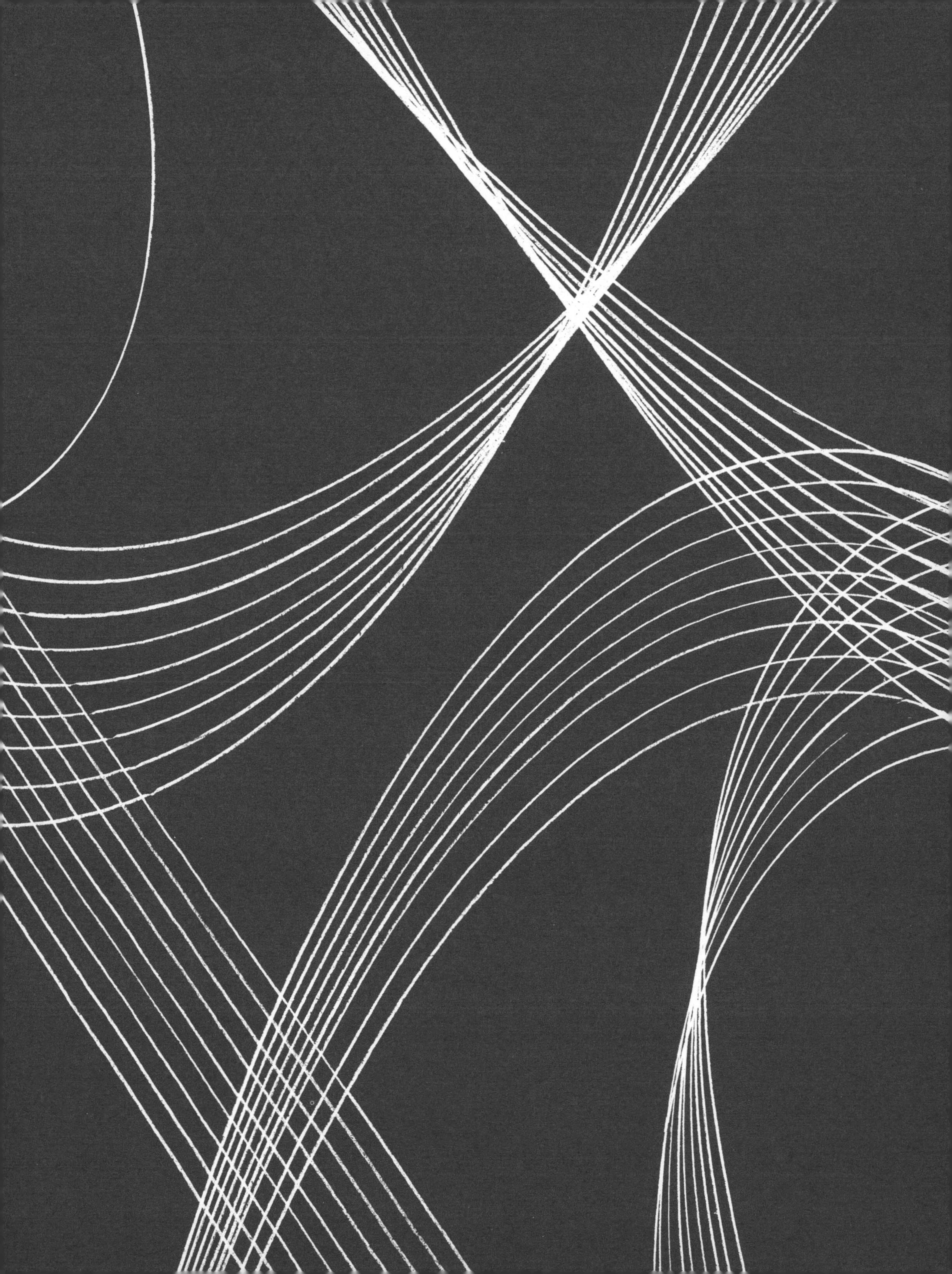

3. Bungalow

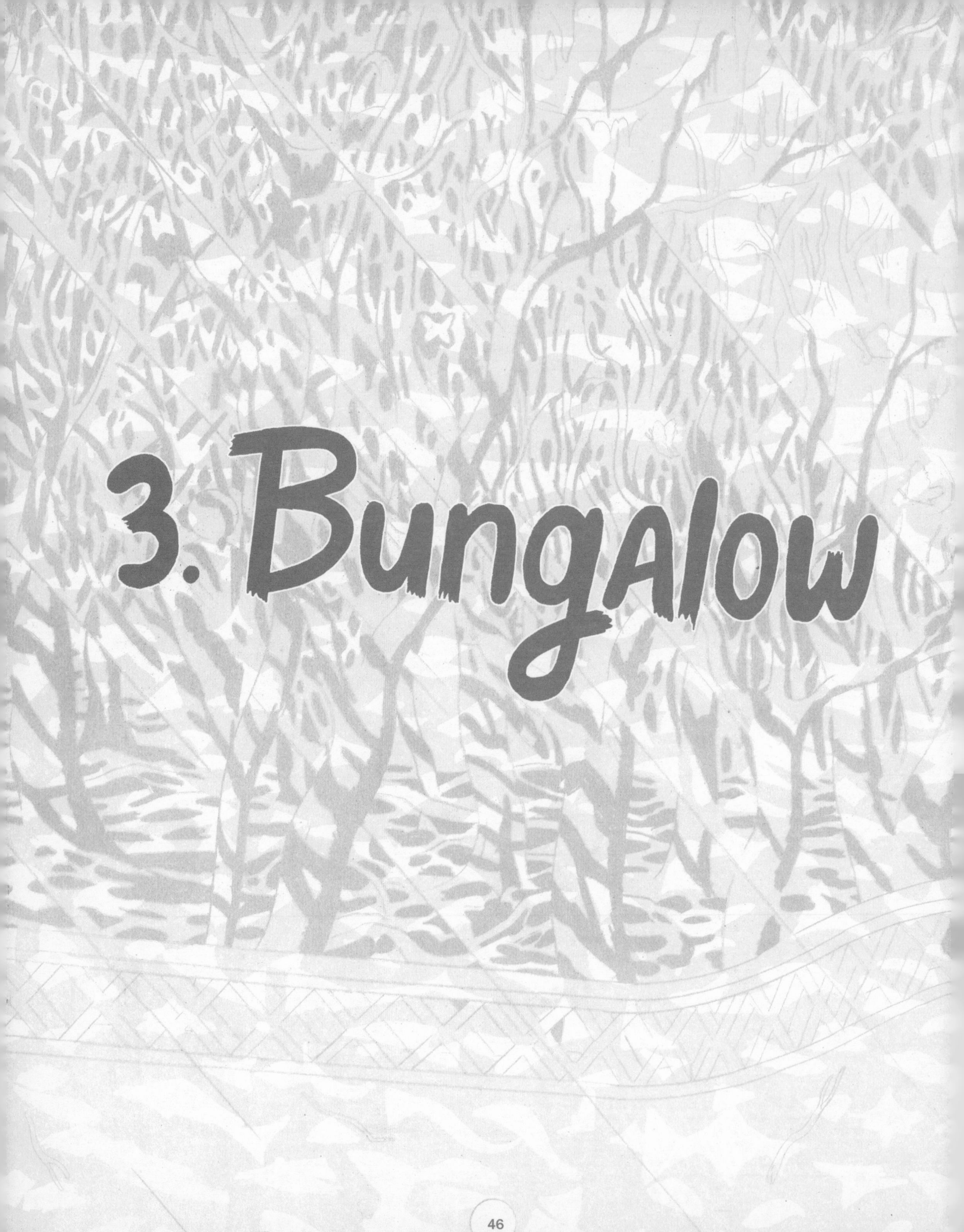

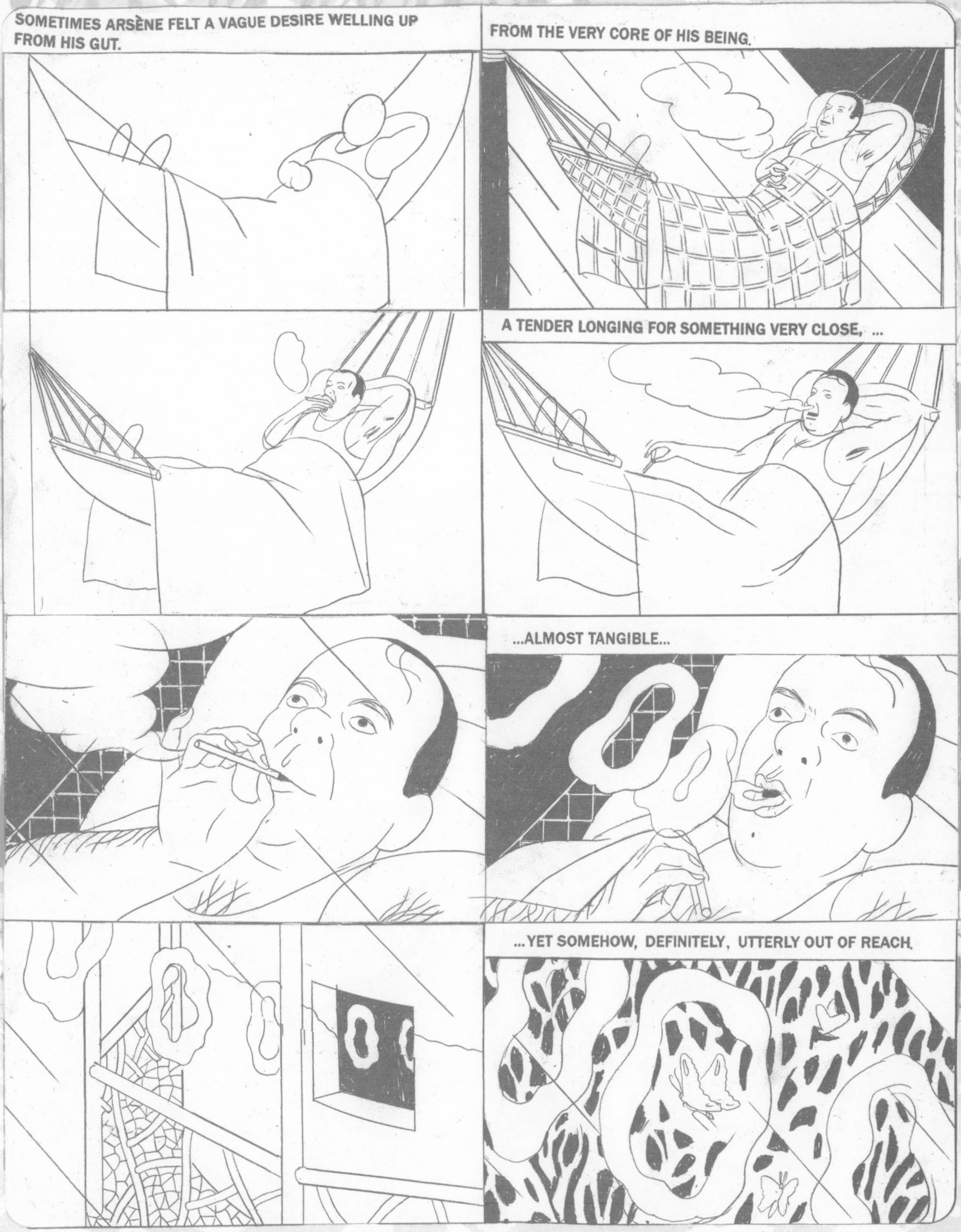

SOMETIMES ARSÈNE FELT A VAGUE DESIRE WELLING UP FROM HIS GUT.
FROM THE VERY CORE OF HIS BEING.
A TENDER LONGING FOR SOMETHING VERY CLOSE, ...
...ALMOST TANGIBLE...
...YET SOMEHOW, DEFINITELY, UTTERLY OUT OF REACH.

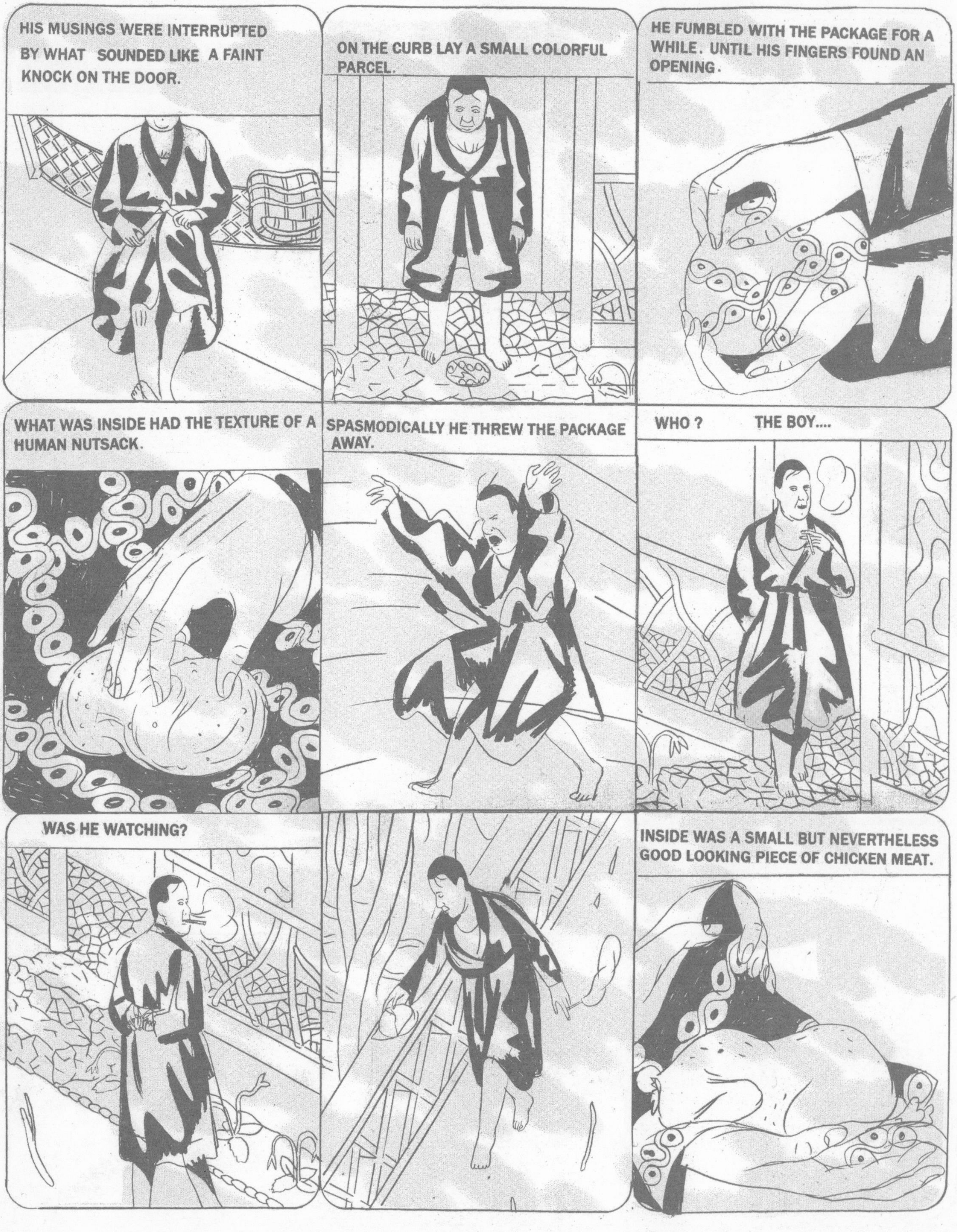
HIS MUSINGS WERE INTERRUPTED BY WHAT SOUNDED LIKE A FAINT KNOCK ON THE DOOR.
ON THE CURB LAY A SMALL COLORFUL PARCEL.
HE FUMBLED WITH THE PACKAGE FOR A WHILE. UNTIL HIS FINGERS FOUND AN OPENING.
WHAT WAS INSIDE HAD THE TEXTURE OF A HUMAN NUTSACK.
SPASMODICALLY HE THREW THE PACKAGE AWAY.
WHO ?
THE BOY....
WAS HE WATCHING?
INSIDE WAS A SMALL BUT NEVERTHELESS GOOD LOOKING PIECE OF CHICKEN MEAT.

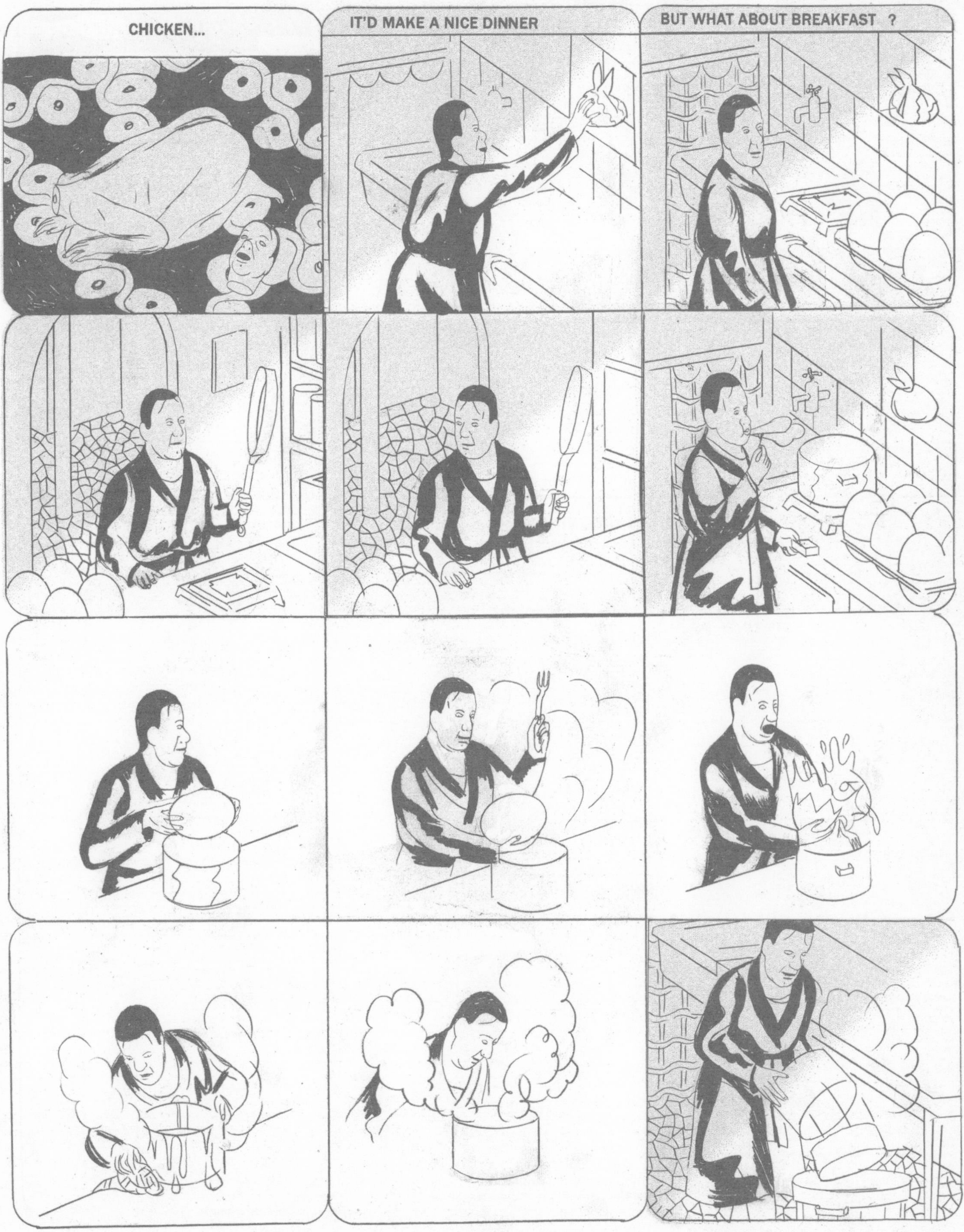
CHICKEN...
IT'D MAKE A NICE DINNER
BUT WHAT ABOUT BREAKFAST ?

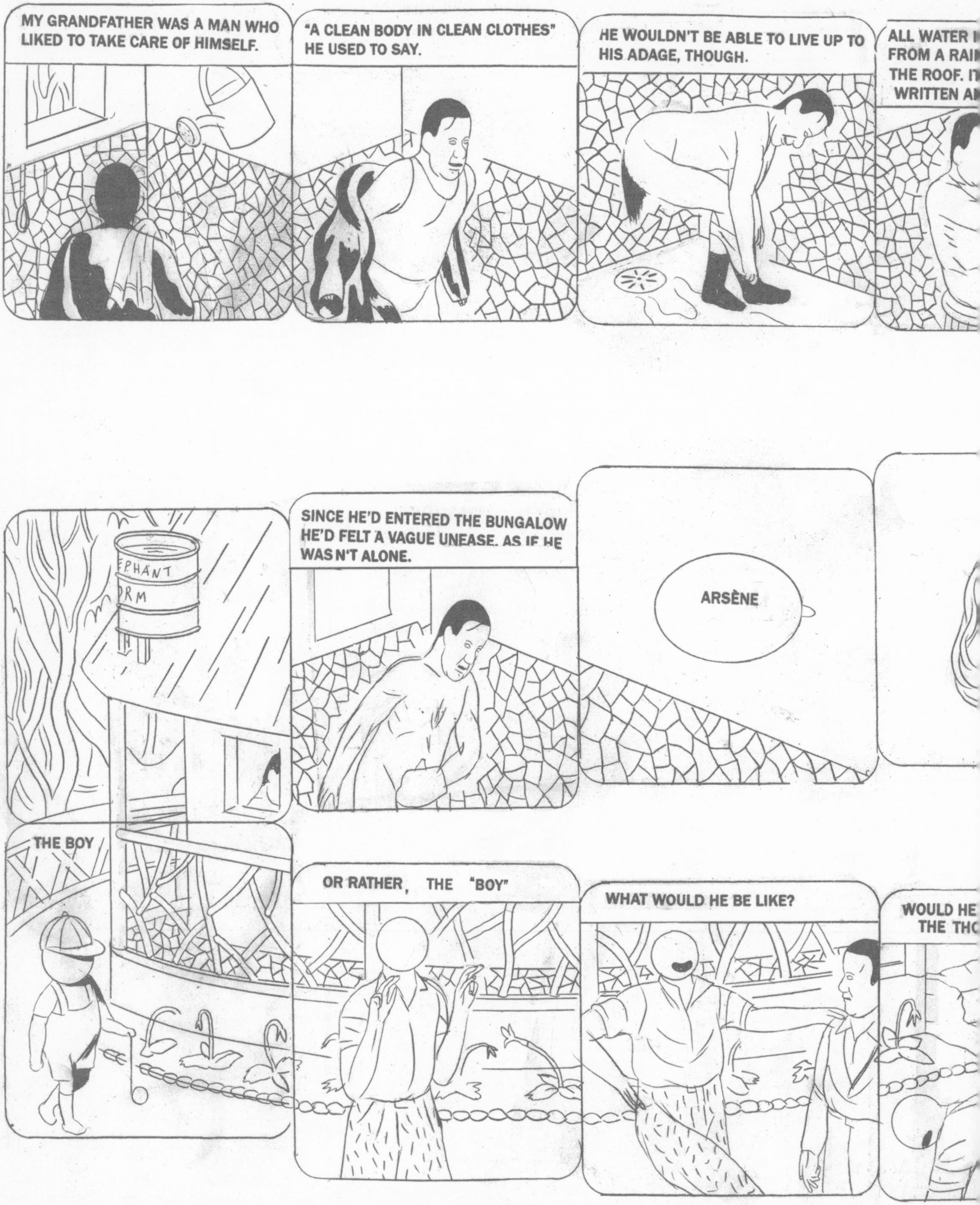
MY GRANDFATHER WAS A MAN WHO LIKED TO TAKE CARE OF HIMSELF.
"A CLEAN BODY IN CLEAN CLOTHES" HE USED TO SAY.
HE WOULDN'T BE ABLE TO LIVE UP TO HIS ADAGE, THOUGH.
ALL WATER
FROM A
THE ROOF.
WRITTEN
SINCE HE'D ENTERED THE BUNGALOW HE'D FELT A VAGUE UNEASE. AS IF HE WASN'T ALONE.
ARSÈNE
THE BOY
OR RATHER, THE "BOY"
WHAT WOULD HE BE LIKE?
WOULD HE
THE

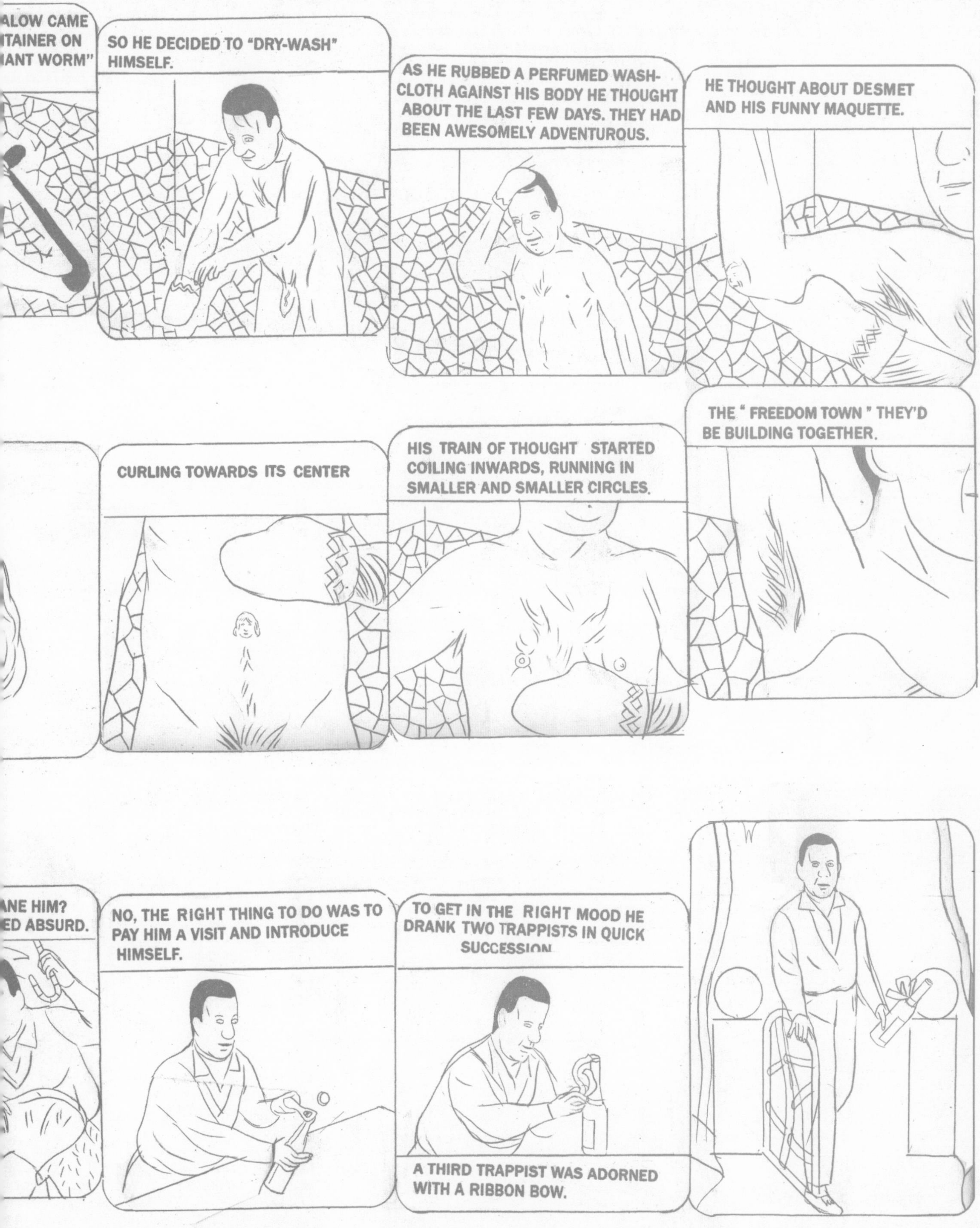
ALOW CAME
TAINER ON
IANT WORM"
SO HE DECIDED TO "DRY-WASH" HIMSELF.
AS HE RUBBED A PERFUMED WASH-CLOTH AGAINST HIS BODY HE THOUGHT ABOUT THE LAST FEW DAYS. THEY HAD BEEN AWESOMELY ADVENTUROUS.
HE THOUGHT ABOUT DESMET AND HIS FUNNY MAQUETTE.
CURLING TOWARDS ITS CENTER
HIS TRAIN OF THOUGHT STARTED COILING INWARDS, RUNNING IN SMALLER AND SMALLER CIRCLES.
THE " FREEDOM TOWN " THEY'D BE BUILDING TOGETHER.
ANE HIM?
ED ABSURD.
NO, THE RIGHT THING TO DO WAS TO PAY HIM A VISIT AND INTRODUCE HIMSELF.
TO GET IN THE RIGHT MOOD HE DRANK TWO TRAPPISTS IN QUICK SUCCESSION
A THIRD TRAPPIST WAS ADORNED WITH A RIBBON BOW.

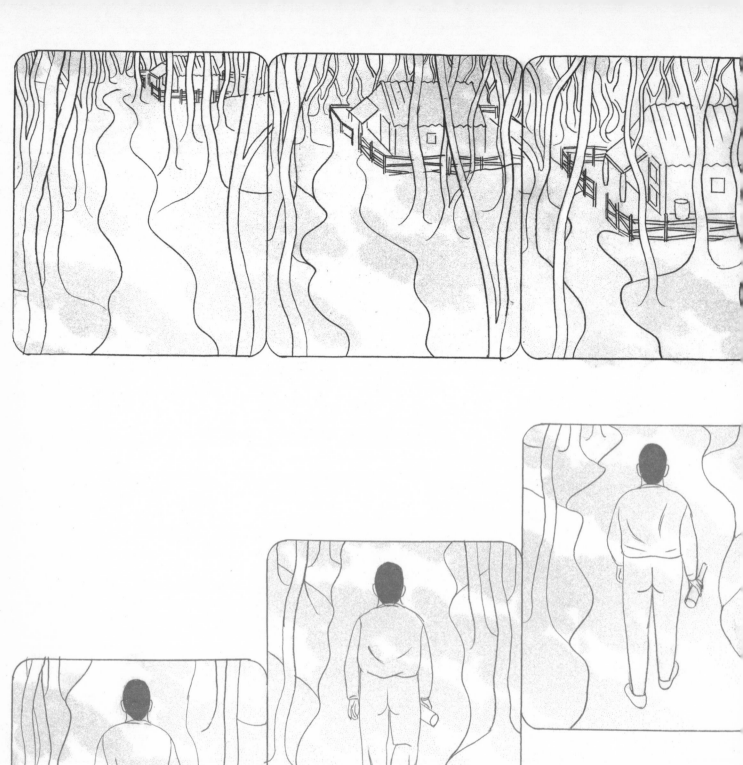
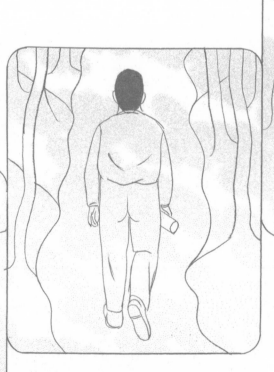

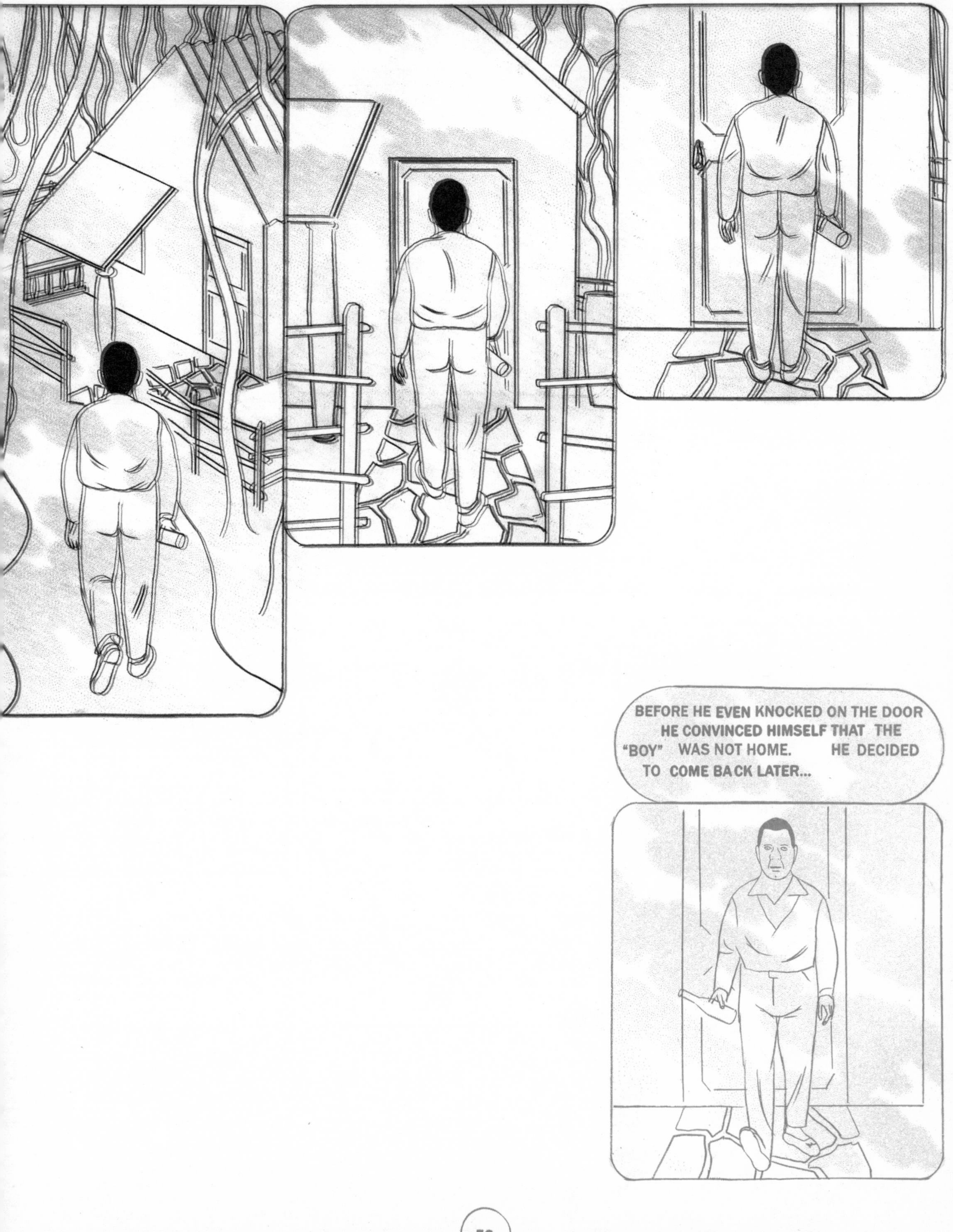
BEFORE HE EVEN KNOCKED ON THE DOOR HE CONVINCED HIMSELF THAT THE "BOY" WAS NOT HOME. HE DECIDED TO COME BACK LATER...

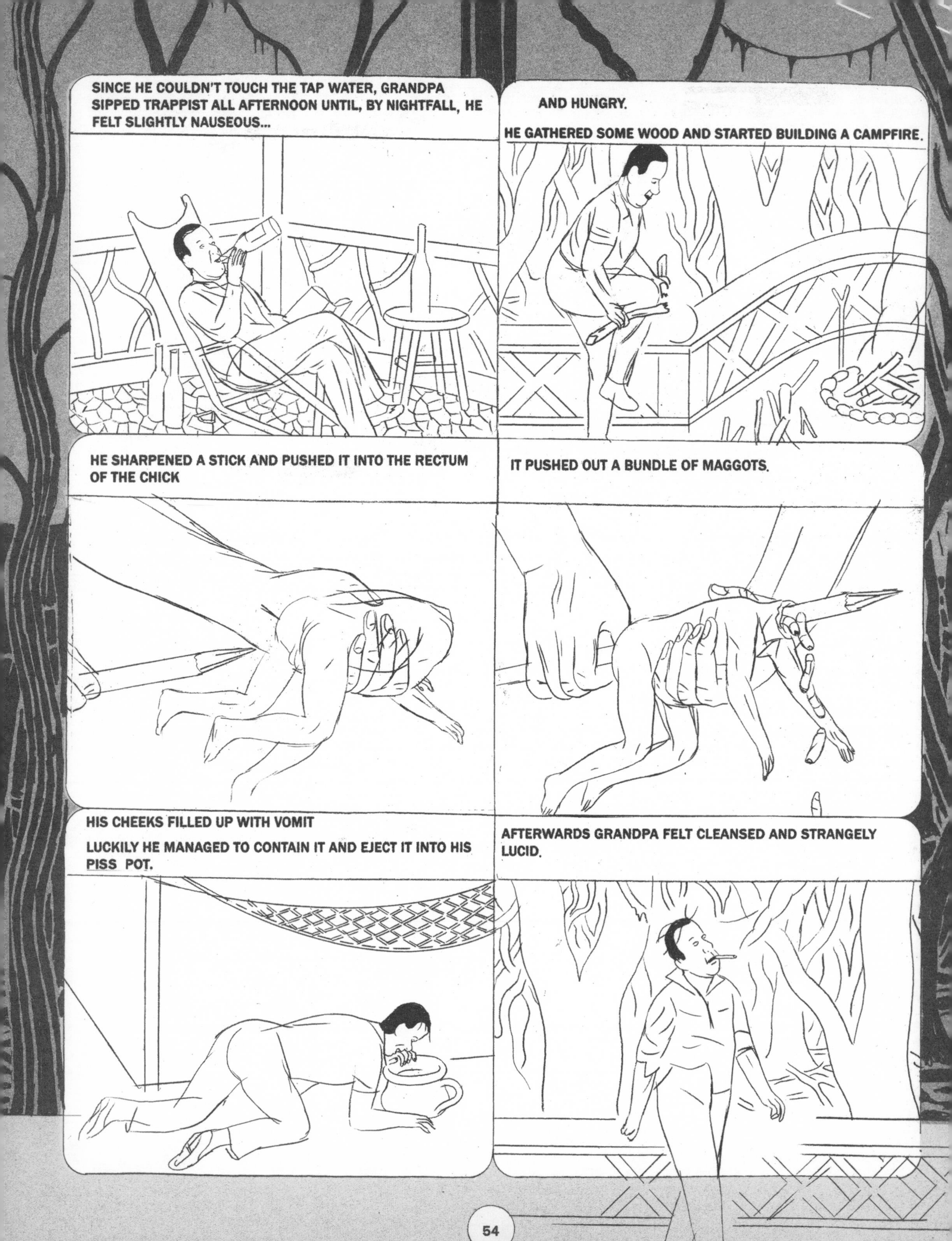

SINCE HE COULDN'T TOUCH THE TAP WATER, GRANDPA SIPPED TRAPPIST ALL AFTERNOON UNTIL, BY NIGHTFALL, HE FELT SLIGHTLY NAUSEOUS...
AND HUNGRY.
HE GATHERED SOME WOOD AND STARTED BUILDING A CAMPFIRE.
HE SHARPENED A STICK AND PUSHED IT INTO THE RECTUM OF THE CHICK
IT PUSHED OUT A BUNDLE OF MAGGOTS.
HIS CHEEKS FILLED UP WITH VOMIT
LUCKILY HE MANAGED TO CONTAIN IT AND EJECT IT INTO HIS PISS POT.
AFTERWARDS GRANDPA FELT CLEANSED AND STRANGELY LUCID.

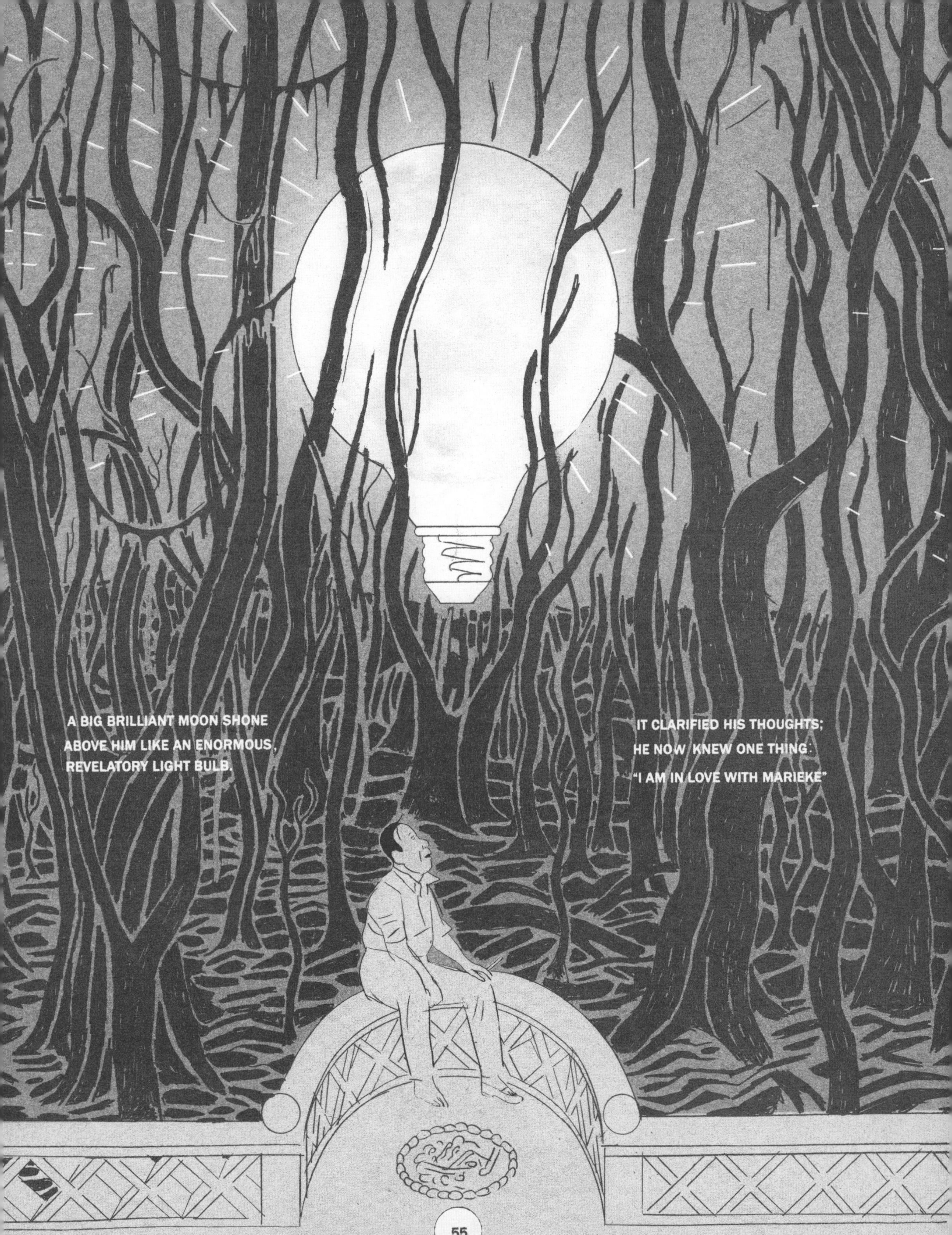
A BIG BRILLIANT MOON SHONE ABOVE HIM LIKE AN ENORMOUS, REVELATORY LIGHT BULB.
IT CLARIFIED HIS THOUGHTS; HE NOW KNEW ONE THING: "I AM IN LOVE WITH MARIEKE"

PLEASE
WAIT A WEEK
BEFORE READING
FURTHER

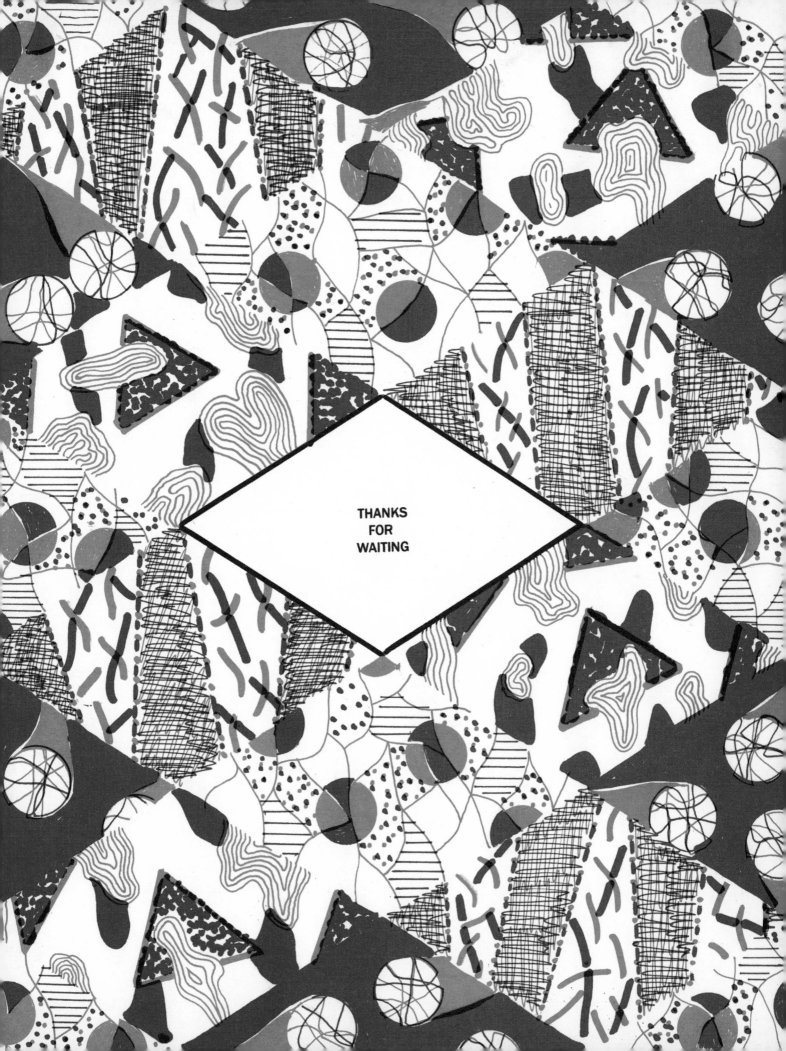

THANKS
FOR
WAITING

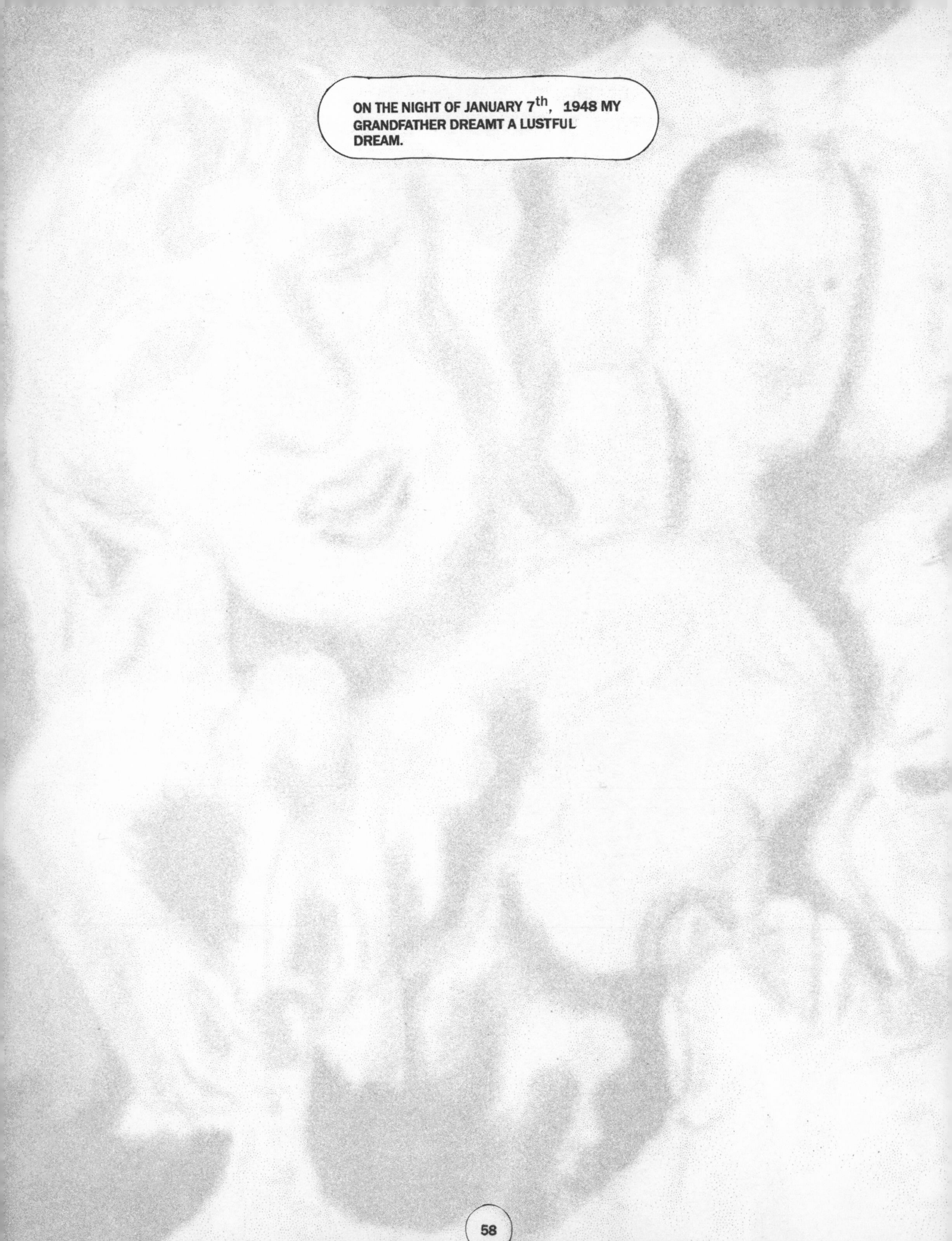
ON THE NIGHT OF JANUARY 7th, 1948 MY GRANDFATHER DREAMT A LUSTFUL DREAM.

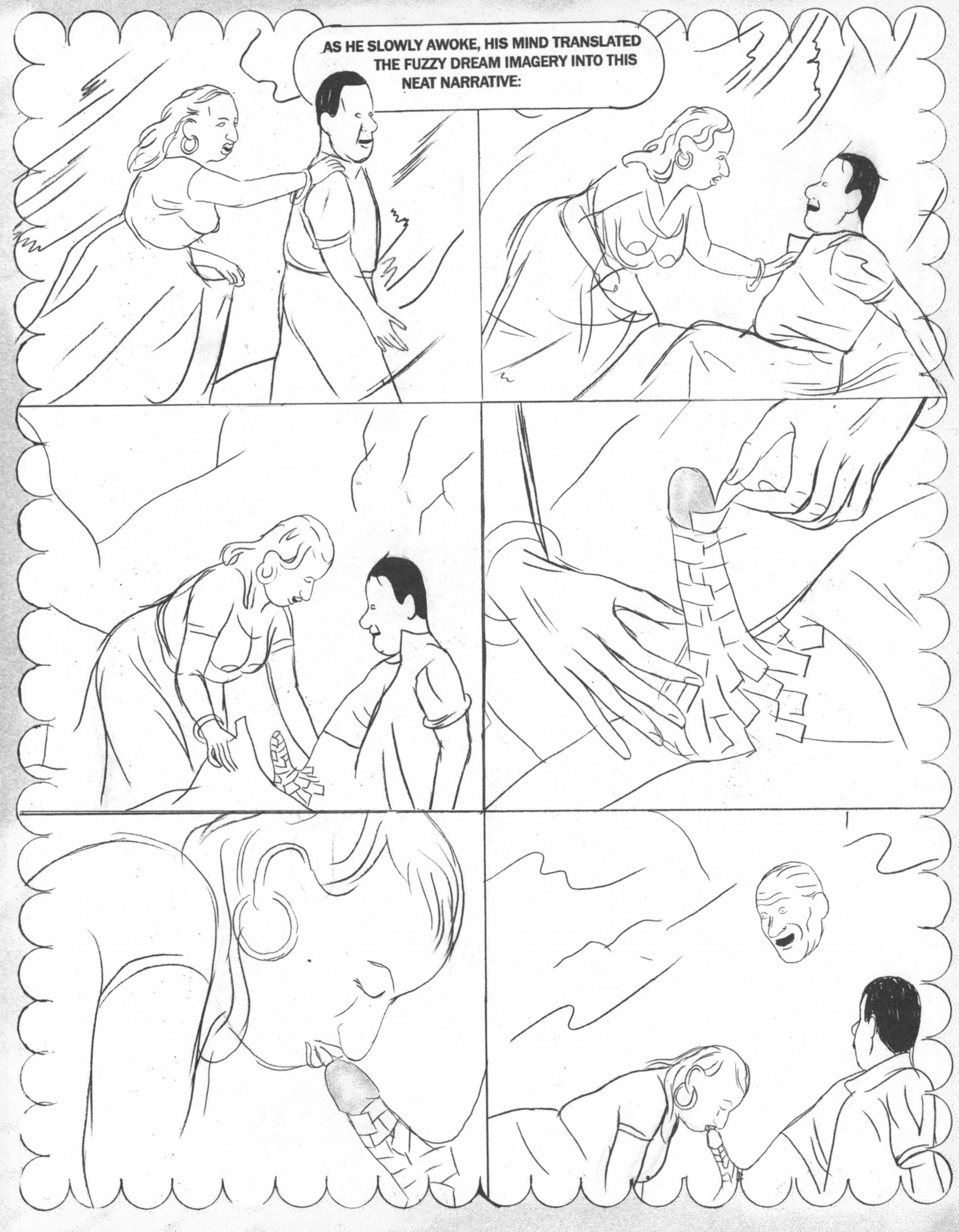
AS HE SLOWLY AWOKE, HIS MIND TRANSLATED THE FUZZY DREAM IMAGERY INTO THIS NEAT NARRATIVE:

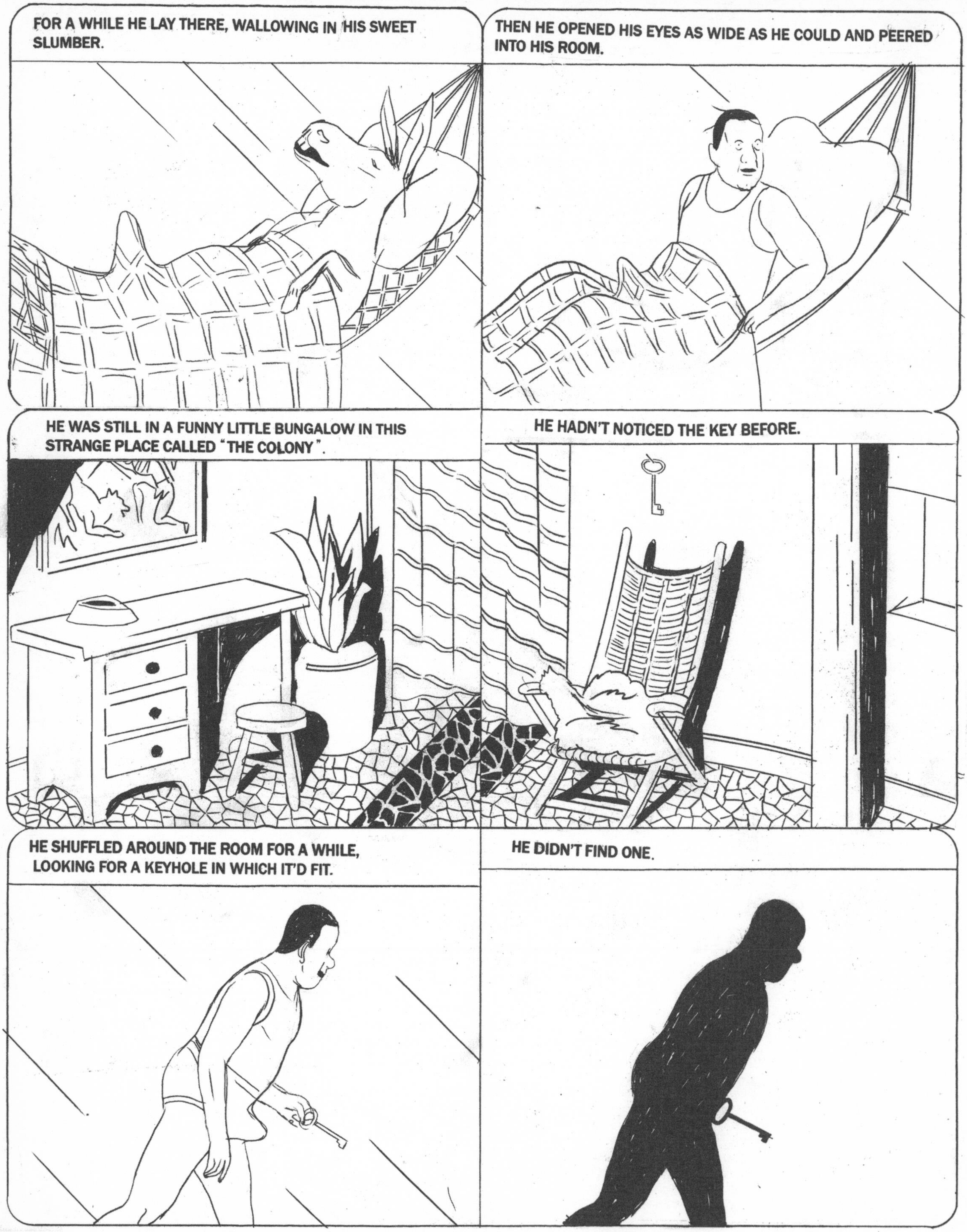
FOR A WHILE HE LAY THERE, WALLOWING IN HIS SWEET SLUMBER.
THEN HE OPENED HIS EYES AS WIDE AS HE COULD AND PEERED INTO HIS ROOM.
HE WAS STILL IN A FUNNY LITTLE BUNGALOW IN THIS STRANGE PLACE CALLED "THE COLONY".
HE HADN'T NOTICED THE KEY BEFORE.
HE SHUFFLED AROUND THE ROOM FOR A WHILE, LOOKING FOR A KEYHOLE IN WHICH IT'D FIT.
HE DIDN'T FIND ONE.

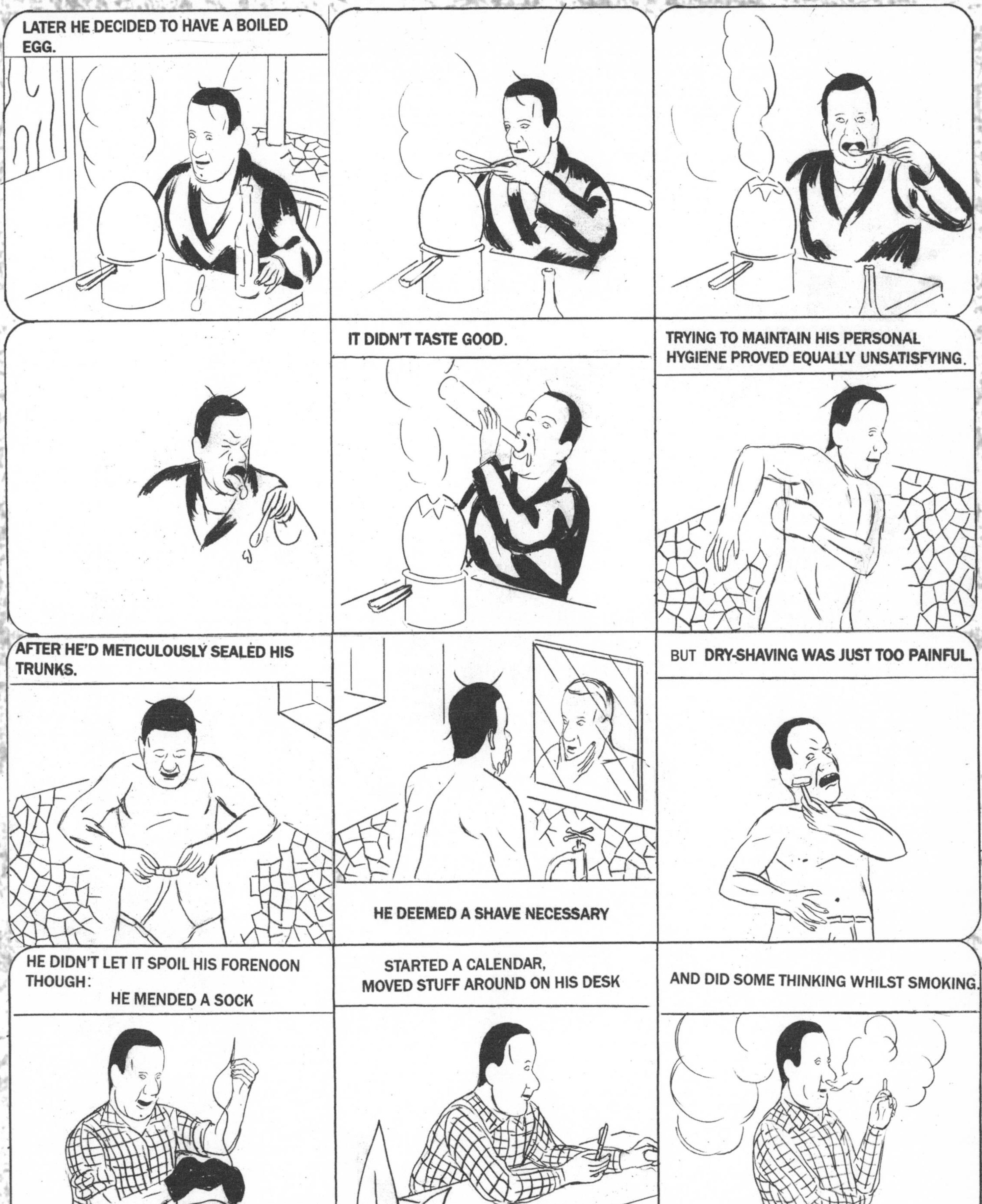
LATER HE DECIDED TO HAVE A BOILED EGG.
IT DIDN'T TASTE GOOD.
TRYING TO MAINTAIN HIS PERSONAL HYGIENE PROVED EQUALLY UNSATISFYING.
AFTER HE'D METICULOUSLY SEALED HIS TRUNKS.
HE DEEMED A SHAVE NECESSARY
BUT DRY-SHAVING WAS JUST TOO PAINFUL.
HE DIDN'T LET IT SPOIL HIS FORENOON THOUGH:
HE MENDED A SOCK
STARTED A CALENDAR,
MOVED STUFF AROUND ON HIS DESK
AND DID SOME THINKING WHILST SMOKING.

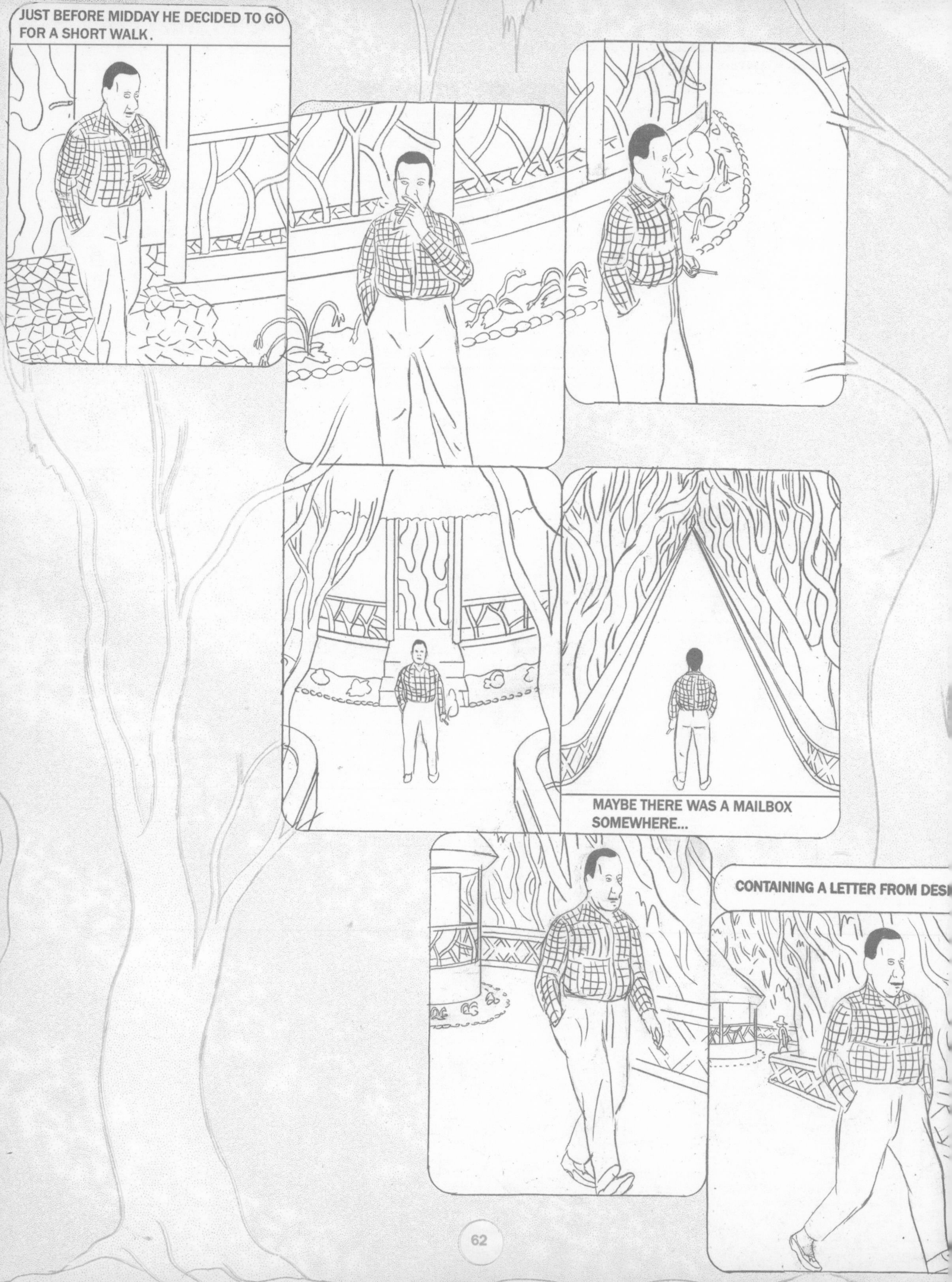
JUST BEFORE MIDDAY HE DECIDED TO GO FOR A SHORT WALK.
MAYBE THERE WAS A MAILBOX SOMEWHERE...
CONTAINING A LETTER FROM DES

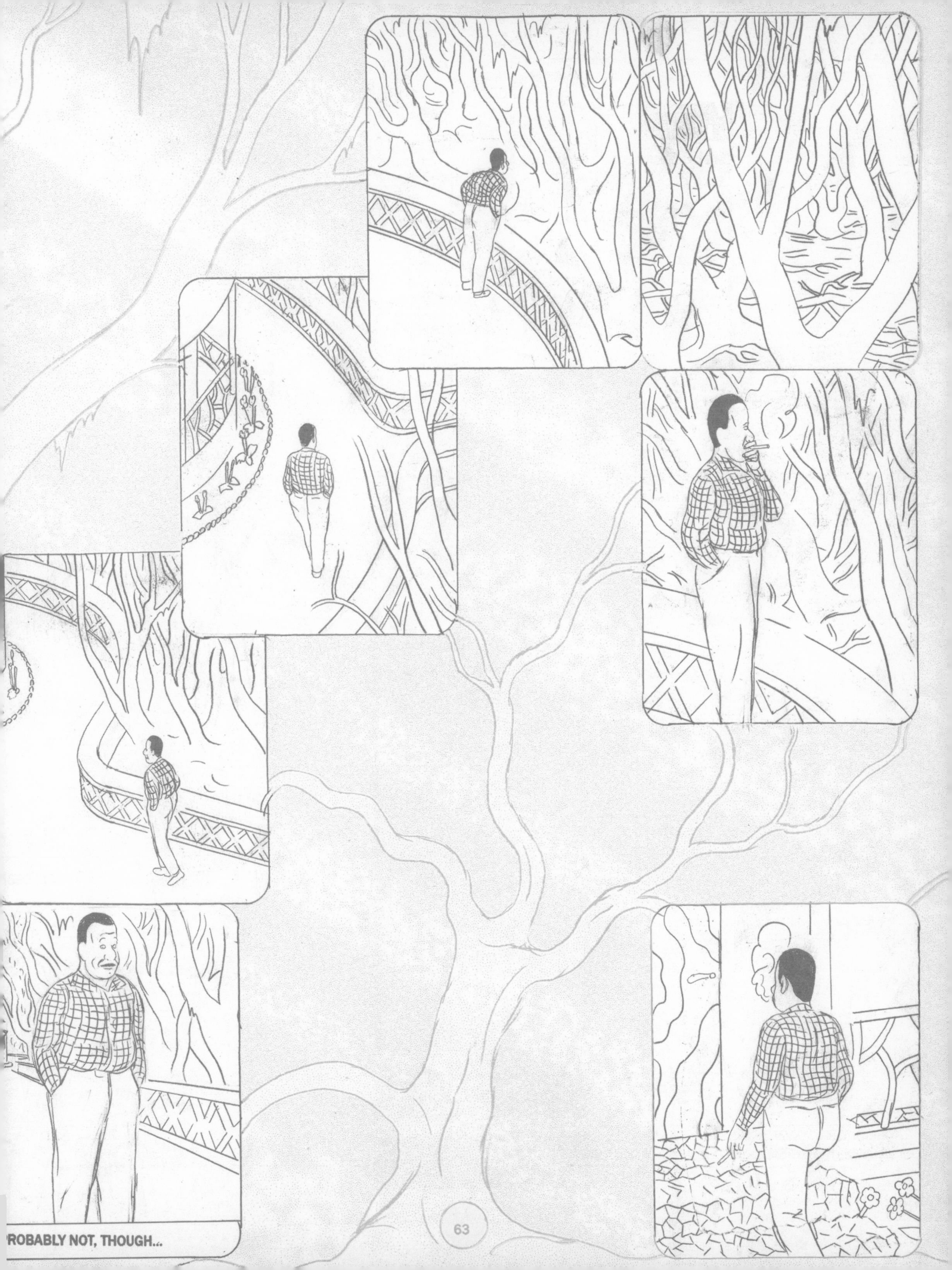
PROBABLY NOT, THOUGH...

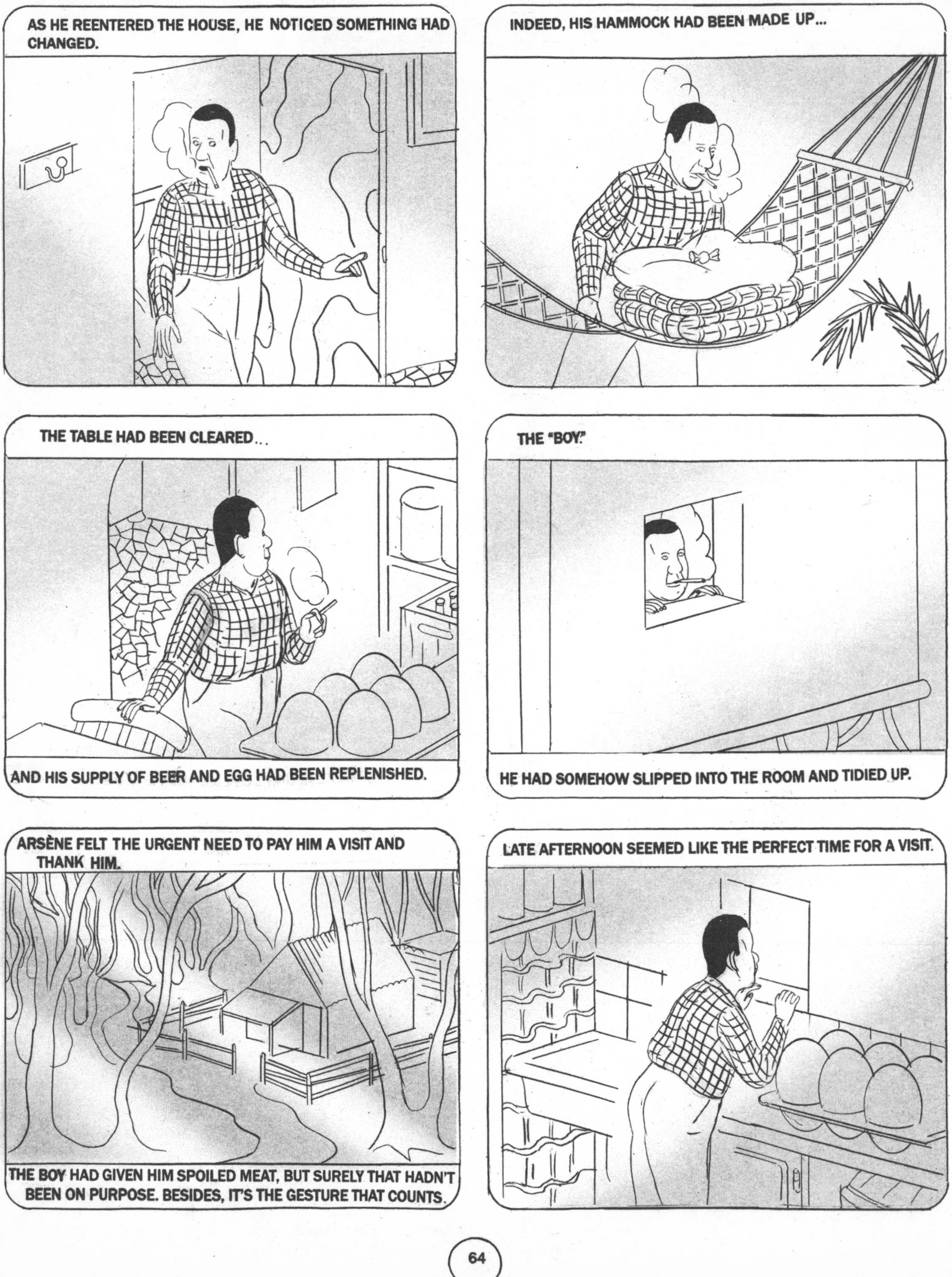
AS HE REENTERED THE HOUSE, HE NOTICED SOMETHING HAD CHANGED.
INDEED, HIS HAMMOCK HAD BEEN MADE UP...
THE TABLE HAD BEEN CLEARED...
AND HIS SUPPLY OF BEER AND EGG HAD BEEN REPLENISHED.
THE "BOY."
HE HAD SOMEHOW SLIPPED INTO THE ROOM AND TIDIED UP.
ARSÈNE FELT THE URGENT NEED TO PAY HIM A VISIT AND THANK HIM.
THE BOY HAD GIVEN HIM SPOILED MEAT, BUT SURELY THAT HADN'T BEEN ON PURPOSE. BESIDES, IT'S THE GESTURE THAT COUNTS.
LATE AFTERNOON SEEMED LIKE THE PERFECT TIME FOR A VISIT.

IN THE MEANTIME HE WOULD

...JUST...

IN THE MEANTIME HE WOULD ...

... ERR

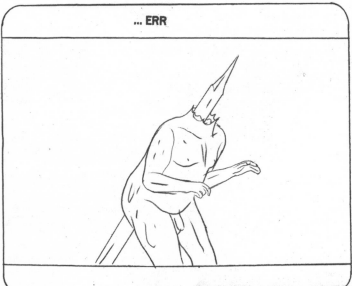

HE WOULD SIT DOWN AND AWAIT DESMET, WHO WOULD COME "VERY SOON."

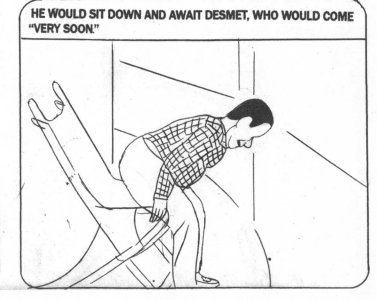

AND HE MIGHT AS WELL ENJOY HIS FREE TIME.

WHILST DRINKING ANOTHER TRAPPIST HE RESUMED READING HIS PULP OMNIBUS, "BAD BLONDE."

IT TOLD THE STORY OF SOME POOR FOOL WHO, UNDER THE SPELL OF A SEDUCTIVE BLONDE, WAS LURED INTO AN INTRIGUE THE SCOPE OF WHICH   HE COULD BARELY GRASP.

THE BLONDE USED HIM TO GET RID OF BOTH HER WEALTHY, EVIL FATHER AND HER LUNATIC HUSBAND.

AT FIRST ARSÈNE HAD FOUND IT HARD TO RELATE TO THE STORY, BUT EVENTUALLY IT STARTED TO GROW ON HIM.

ARSÈNE HAD FOUND THE MOMENT WHEN THE MAIN CHARACTER REALIZES HE'D BEEN DUPED BY HIS BELOVED BLONDE TO BE GENUINELY HEARTBREAKING.

THE STORY ENDED WITH THE BEHEADING OF THE POOR SUCKER. GRANDPA COULD ALMOST FEEL THE BLOW OF THE AXE COMING DOWN ON HIS NECK.

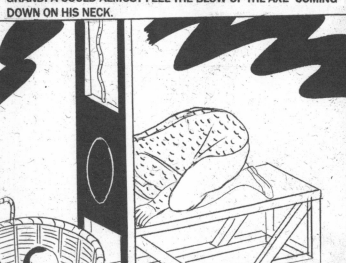

HE TURNED TO THE LAST PAGE OF THE BOOK HOPING FOR SOME MIRACULOUS RESURRECTION OF ITS PITIFUL PROTAGONIST.

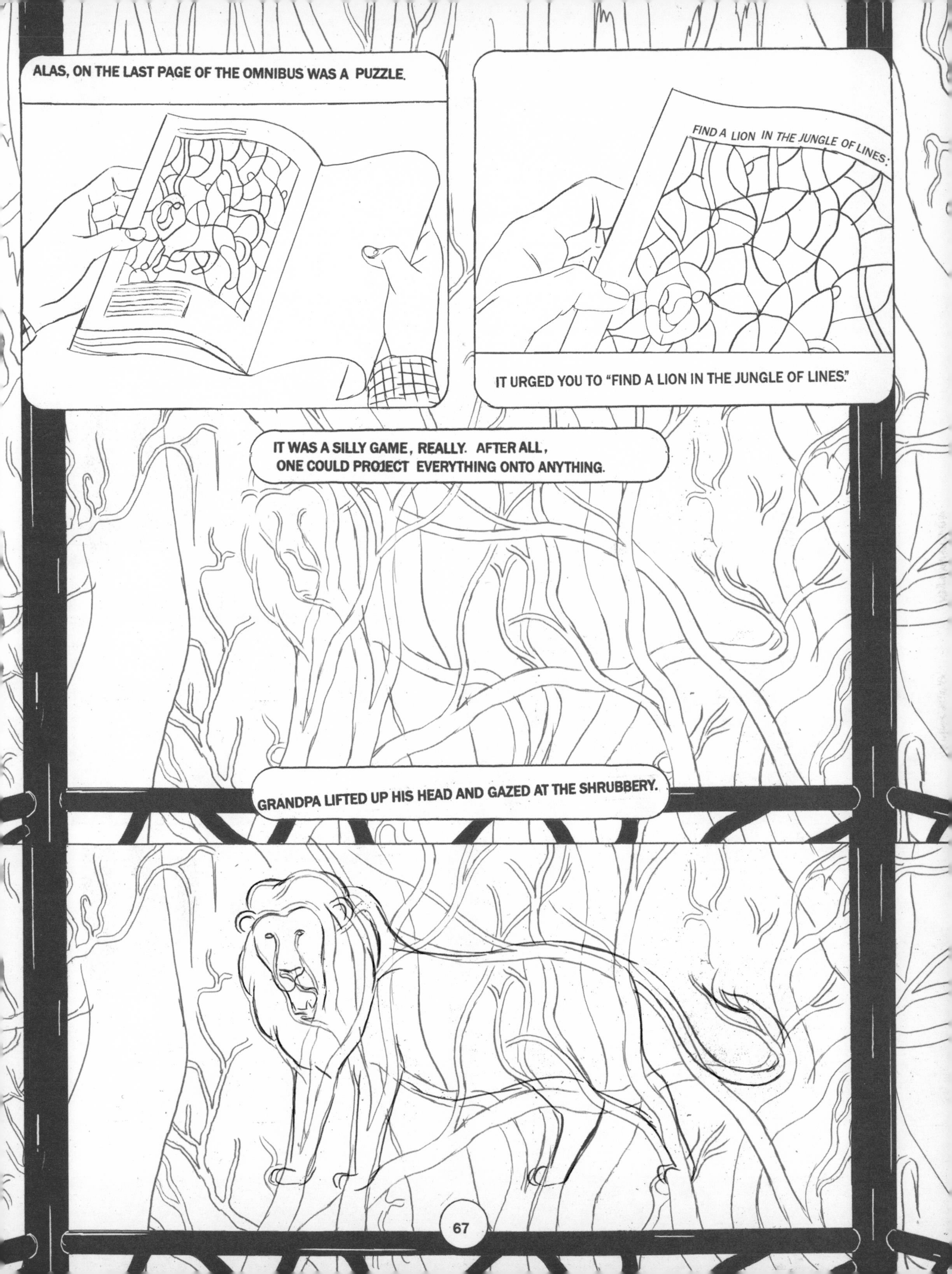
ALAS, ON THE LAST PAGE OF THE OMNIBUS WAS A PUZZLE.
FIND A LION IN THE JUNGLE OF LINES:
IT URGED YOU TO "FIND A LION IN THE JUNGLE OF LINES."
IT WAS A SILLY GAME, REALLY. AFTER ALL, ONE COULD PROJECT EVERYTHING ONTO ANYTHING.
GRANDPA LIFTED UP HIS HEAD AND GAZED AT THE SHRUBBERY.

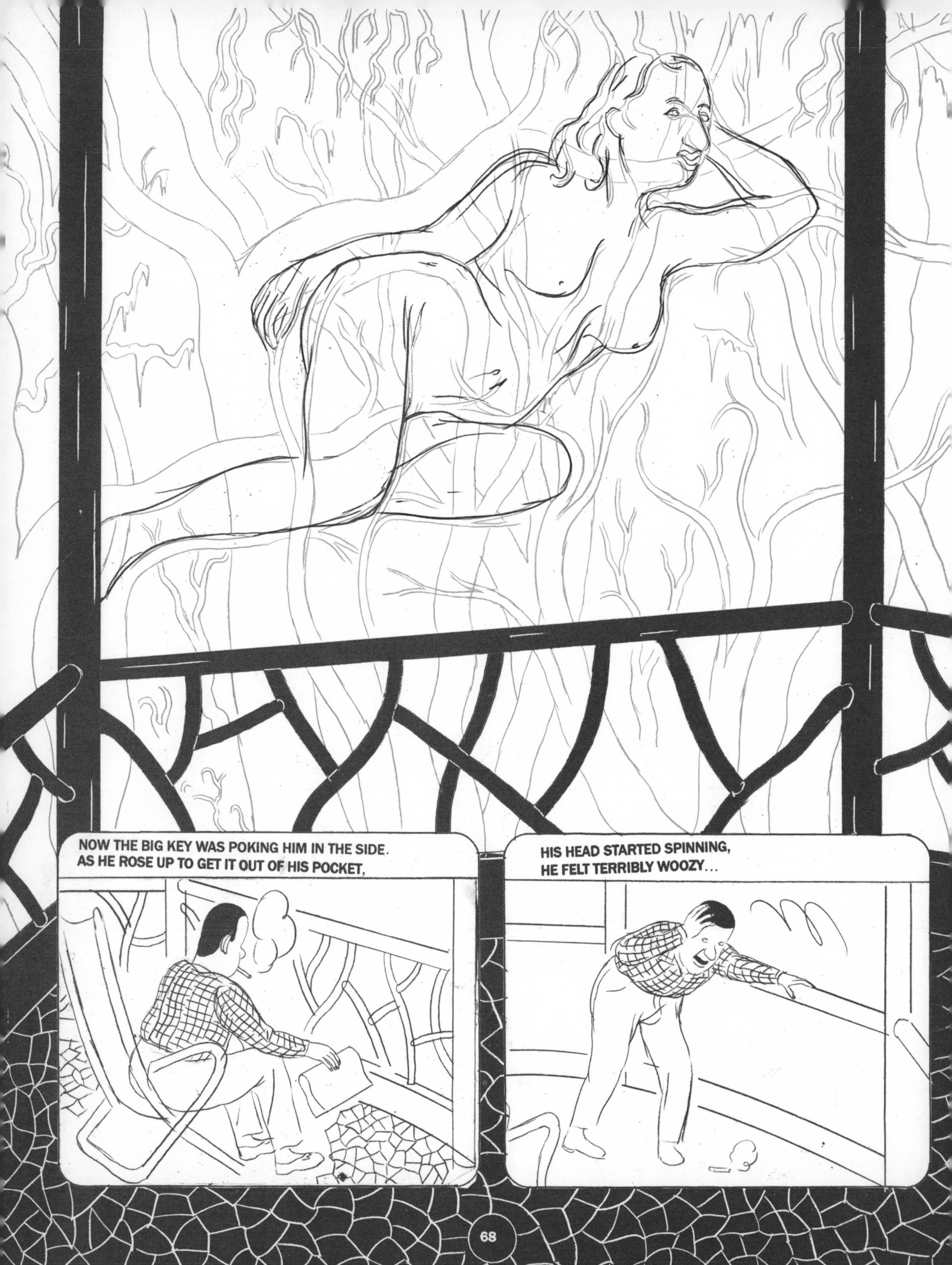
NOW THE BIG KEY WAS POKING HIM IN THE SIDE.
AS HE ROSE UP TO GET IT OUT OF HIS POCKET,
HIS HEAD STARTED SPINNING,
HE FELT TERRIBLY WOOZY...

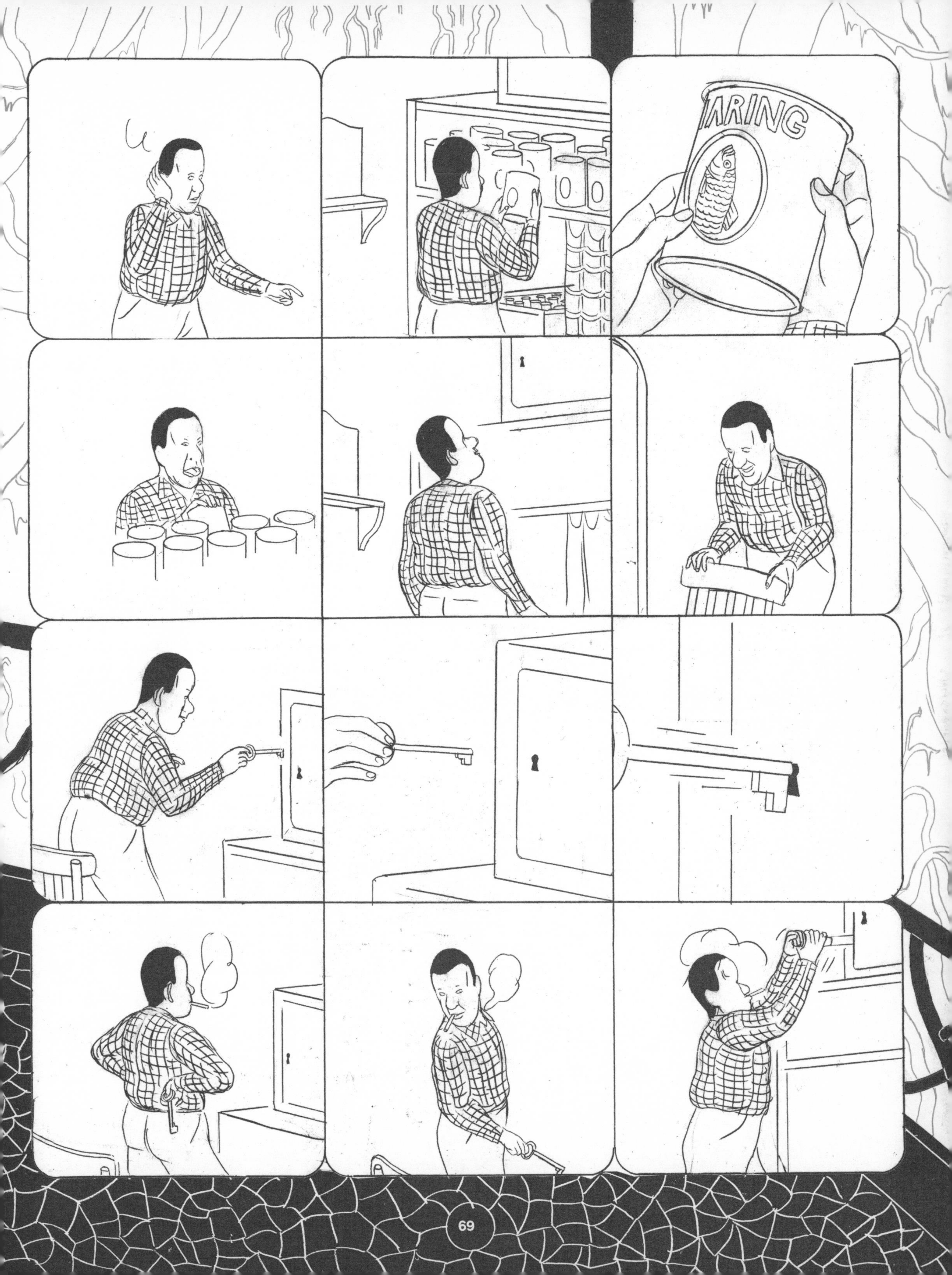
u
ARING

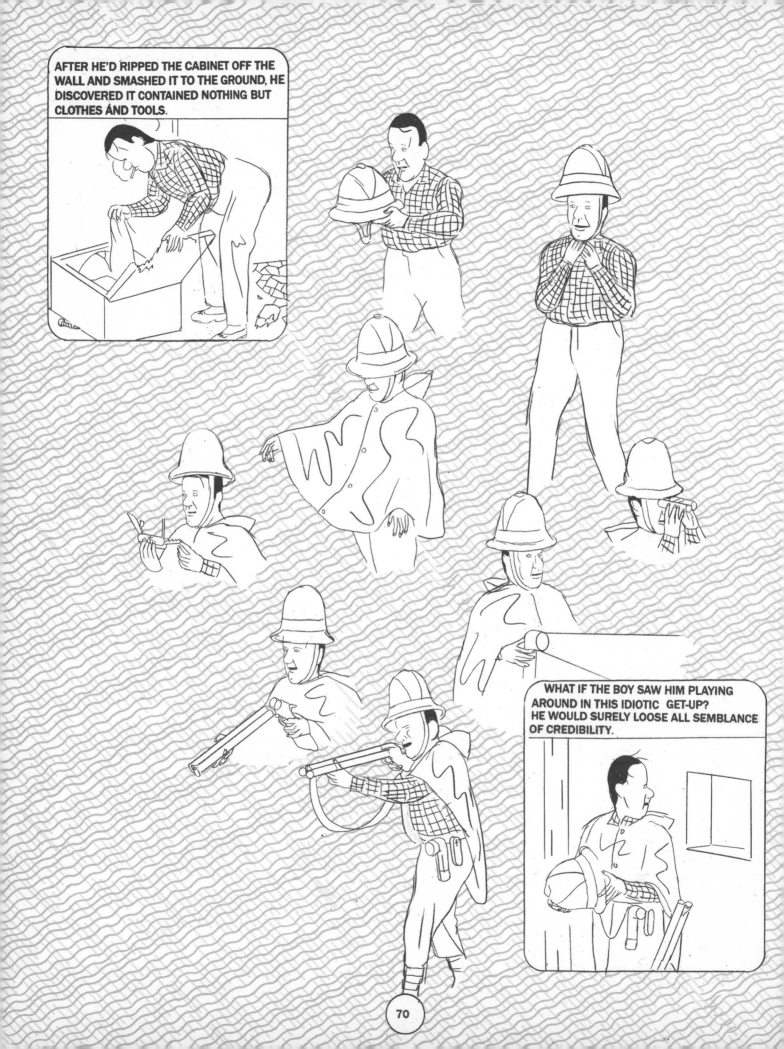

AFTER HE'D RIPPED THE CABINET OFF THE WALL AND SMASHED IT TO THE GROUND, HE DISCOVERED IT CONTAINED NOTHING BUT CLOTHES AND TOOLS.

WHAT IF THE BOY SAW HIM PLAYING AROUND IN THIS IDIOTIC GET-UP? HE WOULD SURELY LOOSE ALL SEMBLANCE OF CREDIBILITY.

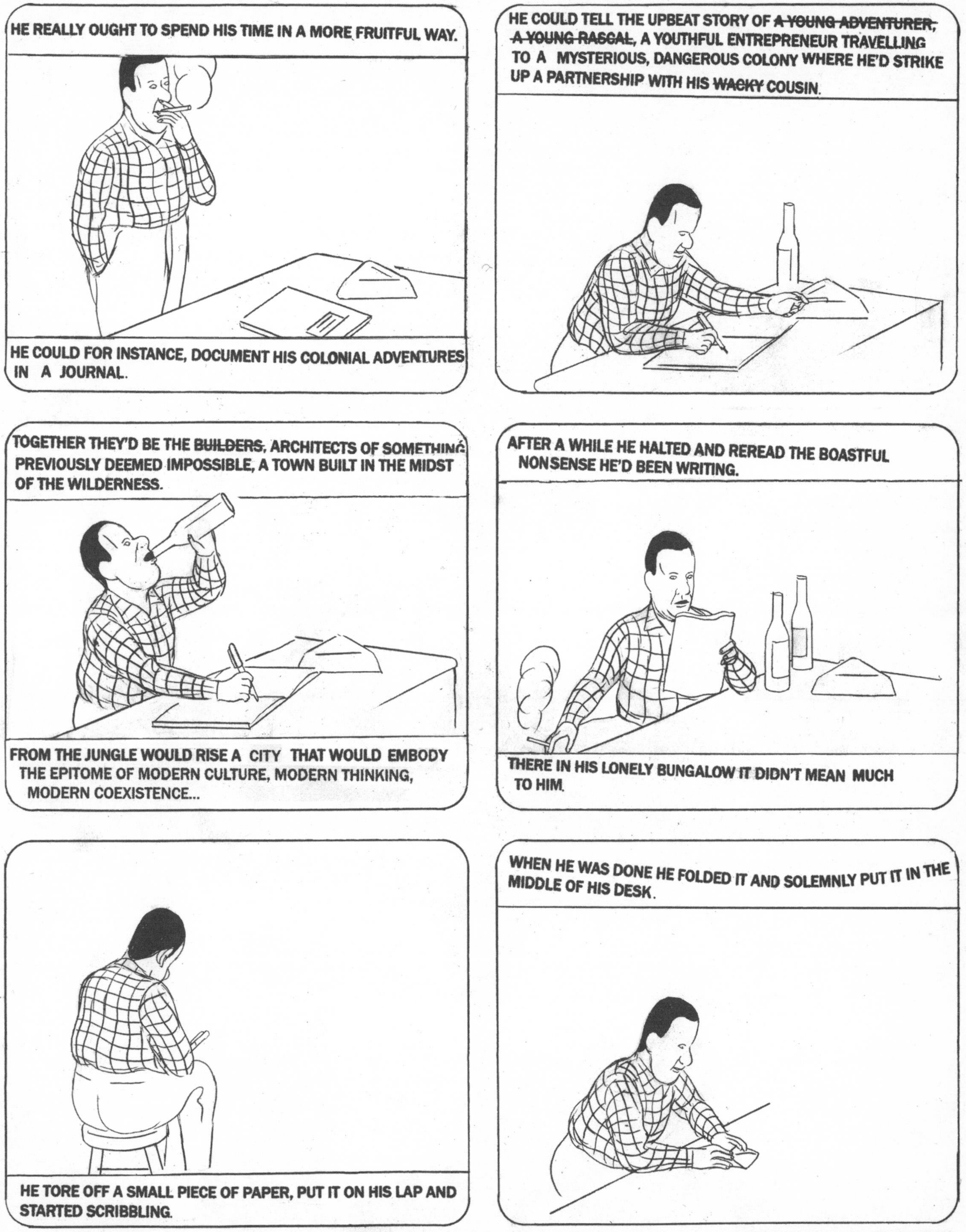
HE REALLY OUGHT TO SPEND HIS TIME IN A MORE FRUITFUL WAY.
HE COULD FOR INSTANCE, DOCUMENT HIS COLONIAL ADVENTURES IN A JOURNAL.
HE COULD TELL THE UPBEAT STORY OF ~~A YOUNG ADVENTURER, A YOUNG RASCAL,~~ A YOUTHFUL ENTREPRENEUR TRAVELLING TO A MYSTERIOUS, DANGEROUS COLONY WHERE HE'D STRIKE UP A PARTNERSHIP WITH HIS ~~WACKY~~ COUSIN.
TOGETHER THEY'D BE THE ~~BUILDERS,~~ ARCHITECTS OF SOMETHING PREVIOUSLY DEEMED IMPOSSIBLE, A TOWN BUILT IN THE MIDST OF THE WILDERNESS.
FROM THE JUNGLE WOULD RISE A CITY THAT WOULD EMBODY THE EPITOME OF MODERN CULTURE, MODERN THINKING, MODERN COEXISTENCE...
AFTER A WHILE HE HALTED AND REREAD THE BOASTFUL NONSENSE HE'D BEEN WRITING.
THERE IN HIS LONELY BUNGALOW IT DIDN'T MEAN MUCH TO HIM.
HE TORE OFF A SMALL PIECE OF PAPER, PUT IT ON HIS LAP AND STARTED SCRIBBLING.
WHEN HE WAS DONE HE FOLDED IT AND SOLEMNLY PUT IT IN THE MIDDLE OF HIS DESK.
THE NIGHT SET IN, GRADUALLY...

...YET SWIFTLY. IT TOOK GRANDPA COMPLETELY BY SURPRISE, AS IF HE WAS SUDDENLY DRIFTING THROUGH THE DARK DEPTHS OF SPACE.

HE TOOK A DEEP BREATH AND PRUDENTLY MOVED INTO THE **KITCHEN** WHERE HE GOT HOLD OF THE FLASHLIGHT.

IN THE SMALL SPHERE OF LIGHT, HE REGAINED HIS COMPOSURE.

...HE REMEMBERED HE PROMISED HIMSELF TO GO VISIT THE BOY.

FIREFLIES ZIGZAGGED THROUGH THE NIGHT; IT WAS QUITE MAGICAL.

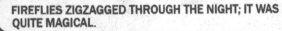

IN THE DISTANCE SHONE A DIM LIGHT... THAT'S WHERE HE WAS HEADING FOR.

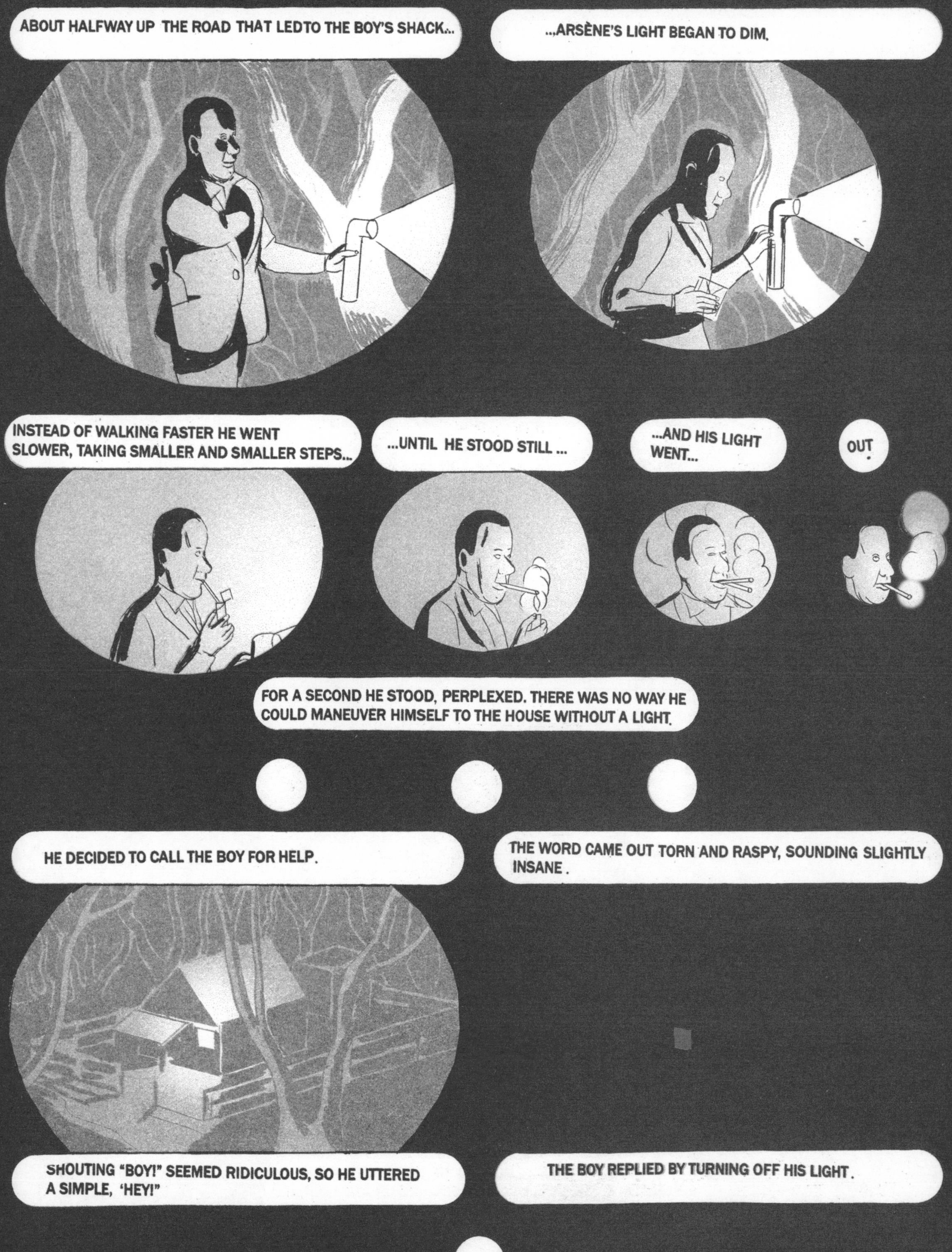
ABOUT HALFWAY UP THE ROAD THAT LED TO THE BOY'S SHACK...
...ARSÈNE'S LIGHT BEGAN TO DIM.
INSTEAD OF WALKING FASTER HE WENT SLOWER, TAKING SMALLER AND SMALLER STEPS...
...UNTIL HE STOOD STILL ...
...AND HIS LIGHT WENT...
OUT.
FOR A SECOND HE STOOD, PERPLEXED. THERE WAS NO WAY HE COULD MANEUVER HIMSELF TO THE HOUSE WITHOUT A LIGHT.
HE DECIDED TO CALL THE BOY FOR HELP.
THE WORD CAME OUT TORN AND RASPY, SOUNDING SLIGHTLY INSANE.
SHOUTING "BOY!" SEEMED RIDICULOUS, SO HE UTTERED A SIMPLE, 'HEY!"
THE BOY REPLIED BY TURNING OFF HIS LIGHT.

GRANDPA DECIDED TO WAIT UNTIL HIS EYES ACCUSTOMED TO THE DARK. AT WHICH POINT HE'D DECIDE EITHER TO GO FORWARD OR BACK.

I MUST NOTE THAT ARSÈNE WAS A THIS POINT SEVERELY DRUNK.

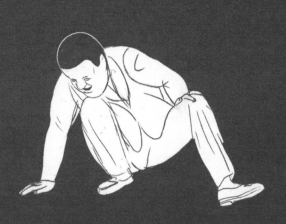

HE WATCHED A BUNCH OF FIREFLIES FLITTING ABOVE HIM, SPARKING LIKE SCRATCHES ON FILM.

NO PARTICULAR PATTERN EMERGED. HE JUST GAPED AT THE SPECTACLE, AT THE SMALL COMETS FLARING UP AND THEN DYING...

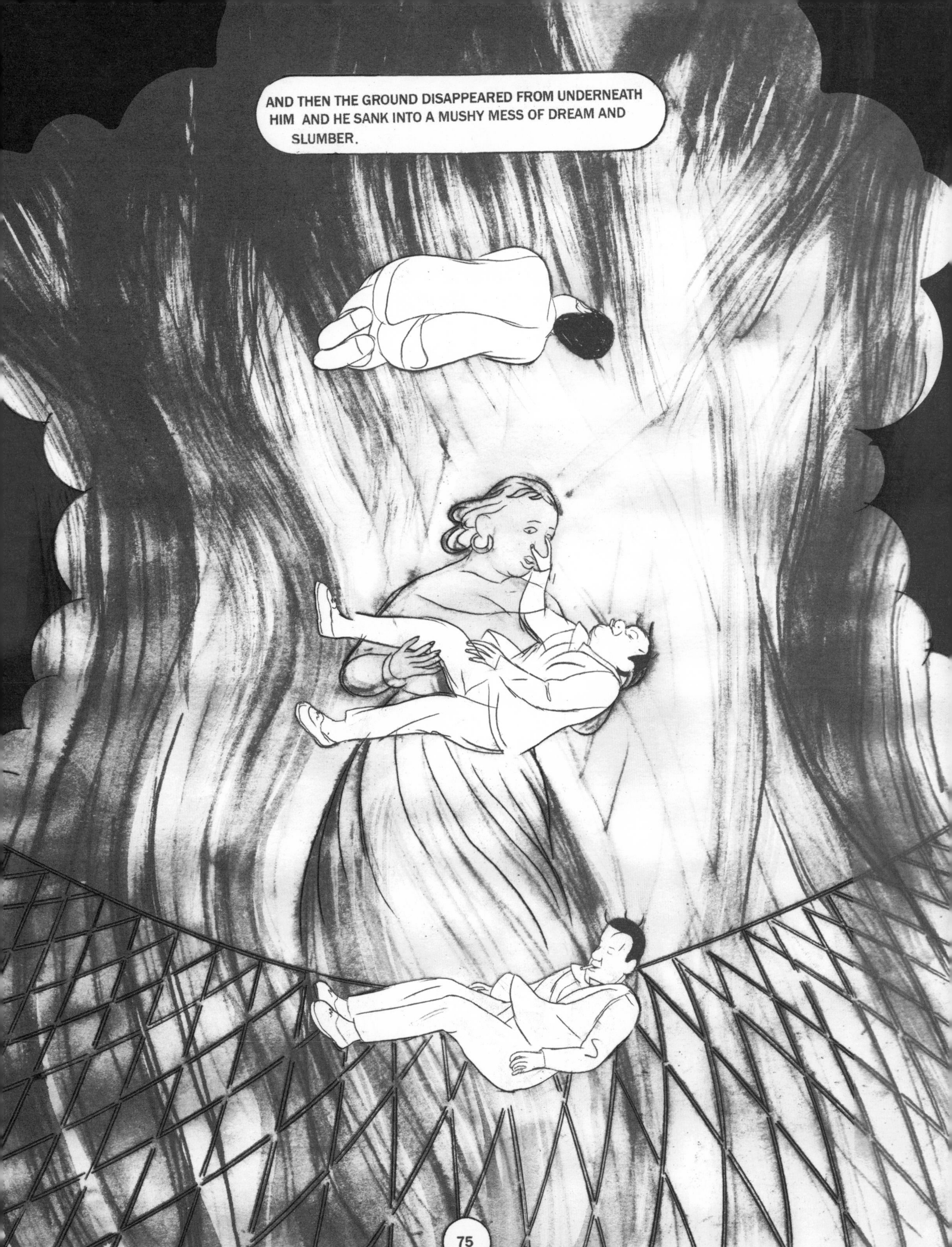
AND THEN THE GROUND DISAPPEARED FROM UNDERNEATH HIM AND HE SANK INTO A MUSHY MESS OF DREAM AND SLUMBER.

THAT MORNING SOMEONE WOKE HIM WITH A WOODEN MALLET.

"WHAT...?"

"HOW...?"

"THE BOY?!"

HAD THE BOY, — 'HIS' BOY — HELPED HIM TO HIS BED?!

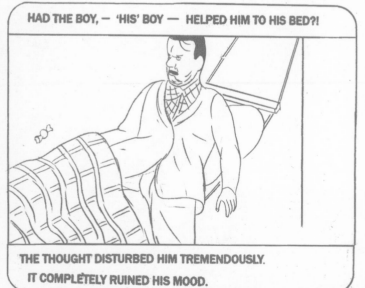

THE THOUGHT DISTURBED HIM TREMENDOUSLY.

IT COMPLETELY RUINED HIS MOOD.

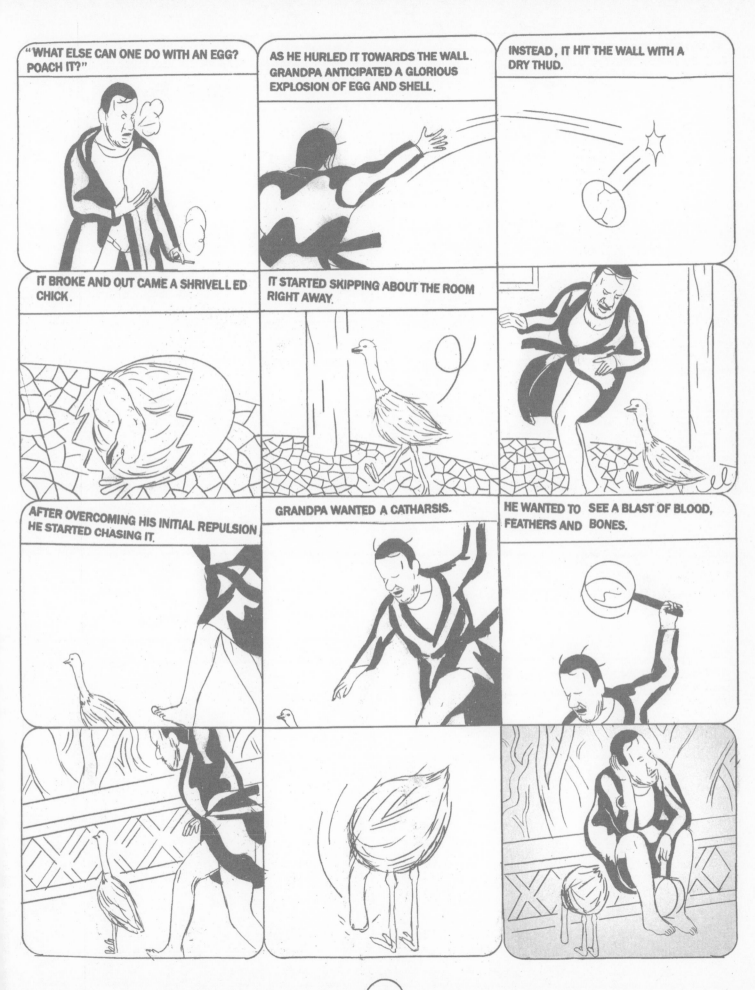

"WHAT ELSE CAN ONE DO WITH AN EGG? POACH IT?"

AS HE HURLED IT TOWARDS THE WALL. GRANDPA ANTICIPATED A GLORIOUS EXPLOSION OF EGG AND SHELL.

INSTEAD, IT HIT THE WALL WITH A DRY THUD.

IT BROKE AND OUT CAME A SHRIVELLED CHICK.

IT STARTED SKIPPING ABOUT THE ROOM RIGHT AWAY.

AFTER OVERCOMING HIS INITIAL REPULSION, HE STARTED CHASING IT.

GRANDPA WANTED A CATHARSIS.

HE WANTED TO SEE A BLAST OF BLOOD, FEATHERS AND BONES.

AS HE WAS GETTING READY TO (DRY) WASH HIMSELF, HE NOTICED THAT THE EGGSHELL HAD BEEN CLEANED UP.

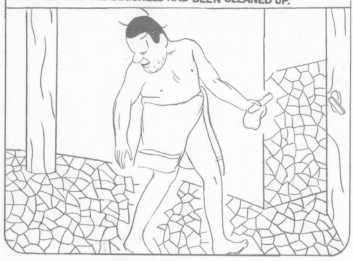

HIS DESK HAD BEEN ORDERED AND THE FOLDED PAPER HE'D LEFT IN THE MIDDLE OF THE TABLE WAS GONE.

AN UNPLEASANT WARM GLOW FILLED HIS BODY. HIS CHEEKS AND NOSE REDDENED.

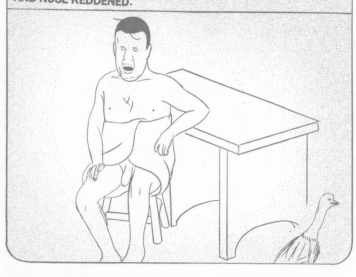

HAD THE BOY TAKEN IT? HAD HE READ IT?

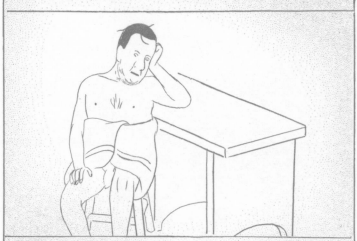

HE HAD TRUSTED HIS MOST TENDER FEELINGS TO THAT PIECE OF PAPER.

HE SHOULDN'T MAKE TOO MUCH OF IT, HE THOUGHT. AFTER ALL, HE'D EXPRESSED HIMSELF METAPHORICALLY.

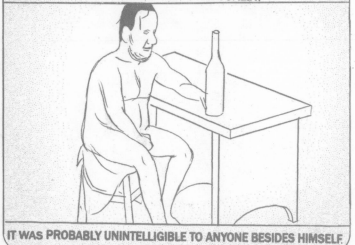

IT WAS PROBABLY UNINTELLIGIBLE TO ANYONE BESIDES HIMSELF.

(NO MORE CIGARETTES)

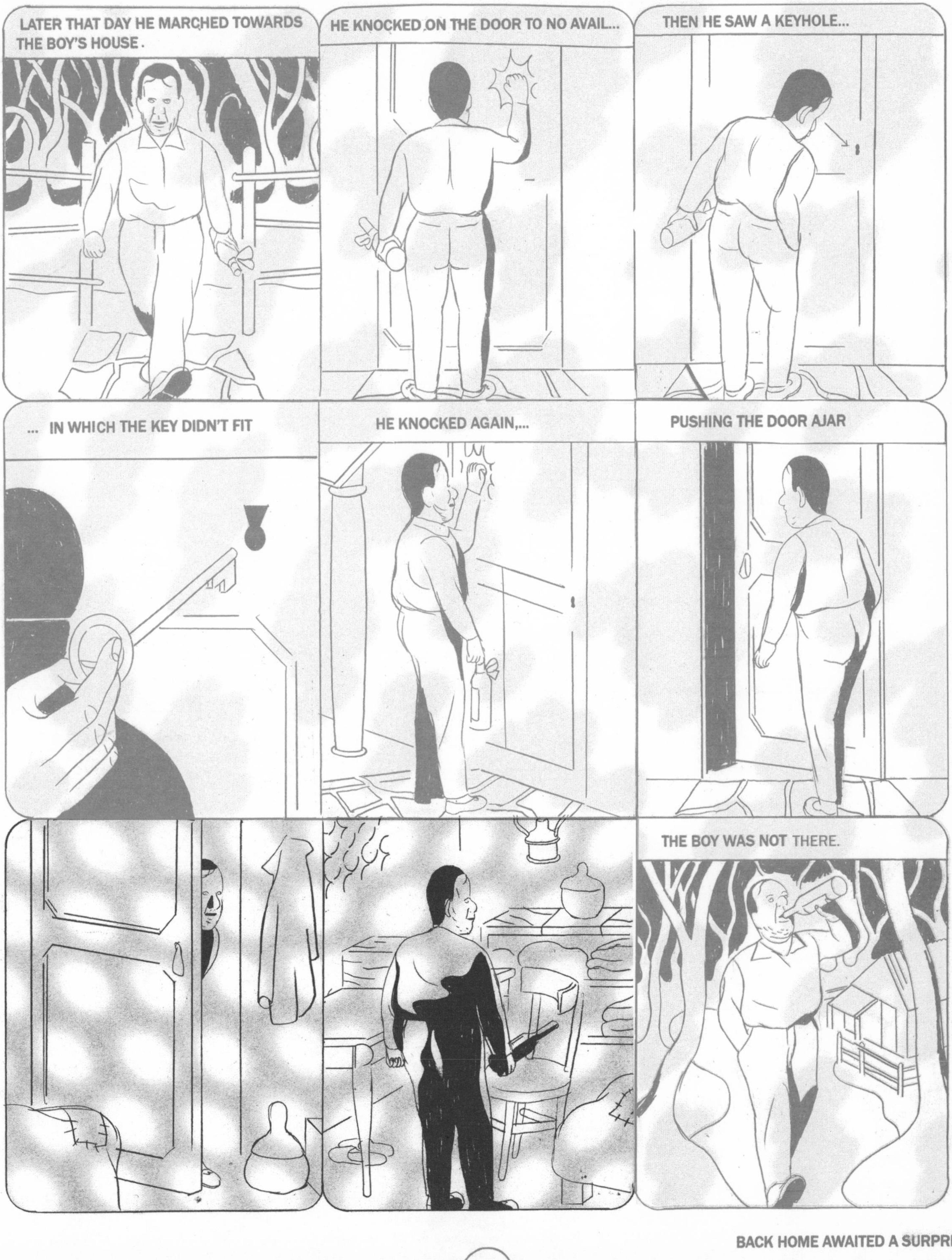
LATER THAT DAY HE MARCHED TOWARDS THE BOY'S HOUSE.
HE KNOCKED ON THE DOOR TO NO AVAIL...
THEN HE SAW A KEYHOLE...
... IN WHICH THE KEY DIDN'T FIT
HE KNOCKED AGAIN,...
PUSHING THE DOOR AJAR
THE BOY WAS NOT THERE.

BACK HOME AWAITED A SURPRISE...

IN THE MIDDLE OF THE DESK LAY A FLOWER.

BESIDE IT WAS A SMALL NOTE THAT READ:
"HOPE THIS IS SOMEWHAT SATISFACTORY"

FOR A WHILE HE WAS PERPLEXED...

...THEN HE REMEMBERED THE WORDS HE'D WRITTEN
THE DAY BEFORE:

If there is one thing I want in this world, it is to hold you, beautiful flower

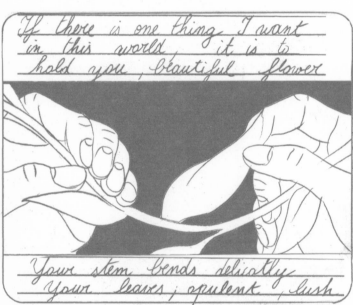

Your stem bends delicately
Your leaves, opulent, lush

The petals; like frozen sunshine
The lips and tongue; moist, welcoming

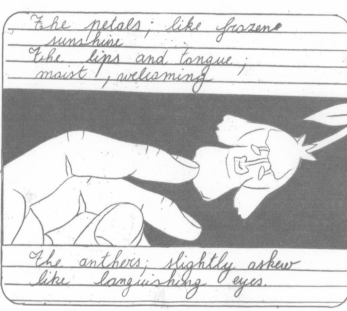

The anthers; slightly askew
like languishing eyes.

THE BOY HAD OUTDONE HIMSELF.

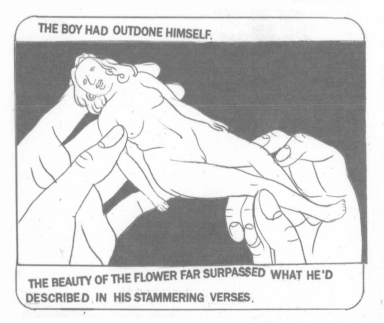

THE BEAUTY OF THE FLOWER FAR SURPASSED WHAT HE'D
DESCRIBED IN HIS STAMMERING VERSES.

GRANDPA TOOK A NEW PIECE OF PAPER.
NOW HE ASKED THE BOY FOR CIGARETTES. HE SPECIFIED THE
AMOUNT AND THE BRAND AND CONCLUDED BY THANKING HIM IN
ADVANCE.

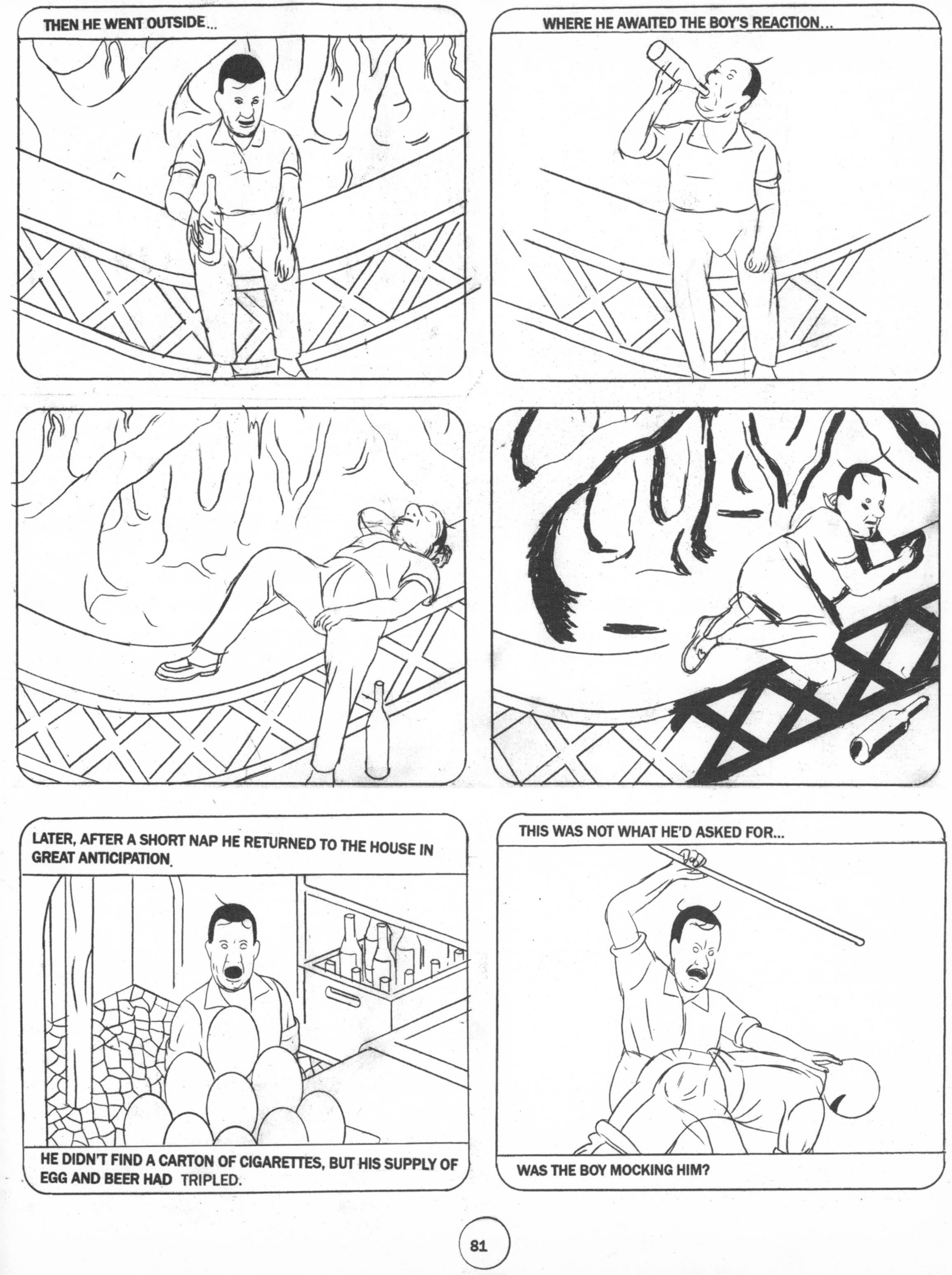
THEN HE WENT OUTSIDE...
WHERE HE AWAITED THE BOY'S REACTION...
LATER, AFTER A SHORT NAP HE RETURNED TO THE HOUSE IN GREAT ANTICIPATION.
HE DIDN'T FIND A CARTON OF CIGARETTES, BUT HIS SUPPLY OF EGG AND BEER HAD TRIPLED.
THIS WAS NOT WHAT HE'D ASKED FOR...
WAS THE BOY MOCKING HIM?

IF THE RELATIONSHIP BETWEEN ARSÈNE AND THE BOY COULD MATERIALIZE IN THE FORM OF A TIN TOY, IT WOULD LOOK SOMETHING LIKE THIS:

(WINDUP KEY MAKES BOTH FIGURES MOVE CLOCKWISE AT THE SAME SPEED)

THIS IDIOTIC MECHANISM NEEDED TO BE DISRUPTED.

THE NEXT DAY GRANDPA HID IN THE UNDERGROWTH BESIDE THE BUNGALOW, AND AWAITED THE BOY IN AMBUSH.

HE LAY QUITE COMFORTABLY BETWEEN TWO SMOOTH, FIRM BRANCHES.

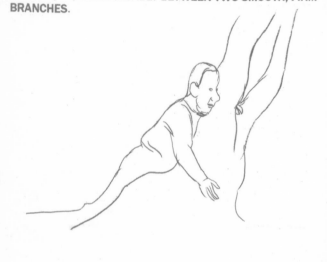

WHEN, AFTER ABOUT AN HOUR AND A HALF, HE BEGAN TO SUSPECT THAT THE BOY WOULDN'T SHOW...

YET HE REMAINED IN THE SAME SPOT, REFRESHING HIS GRIP ON THE BRANCHES, LOCKING HIMSELF ONTO THEM IN A QUIVERING EMBRACE.

HIS CROTCH FIT PERFECTLY IN A SHAFT BETWEEN THE FORKING TRUNKS.

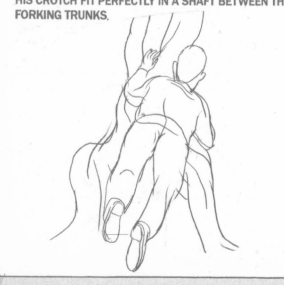

MY GRANDPA NEVER ONCE MASTURBATED IN HIS LIFE.

NOW AND THEN, THOUGH, HIS "SPERM-BLADDER" NEEDED TO BE EMPTIED, IN WHICH CASE HE WOULD ALWAYS TAKE CARE OF IT NEATLY AND DISCREETLY.

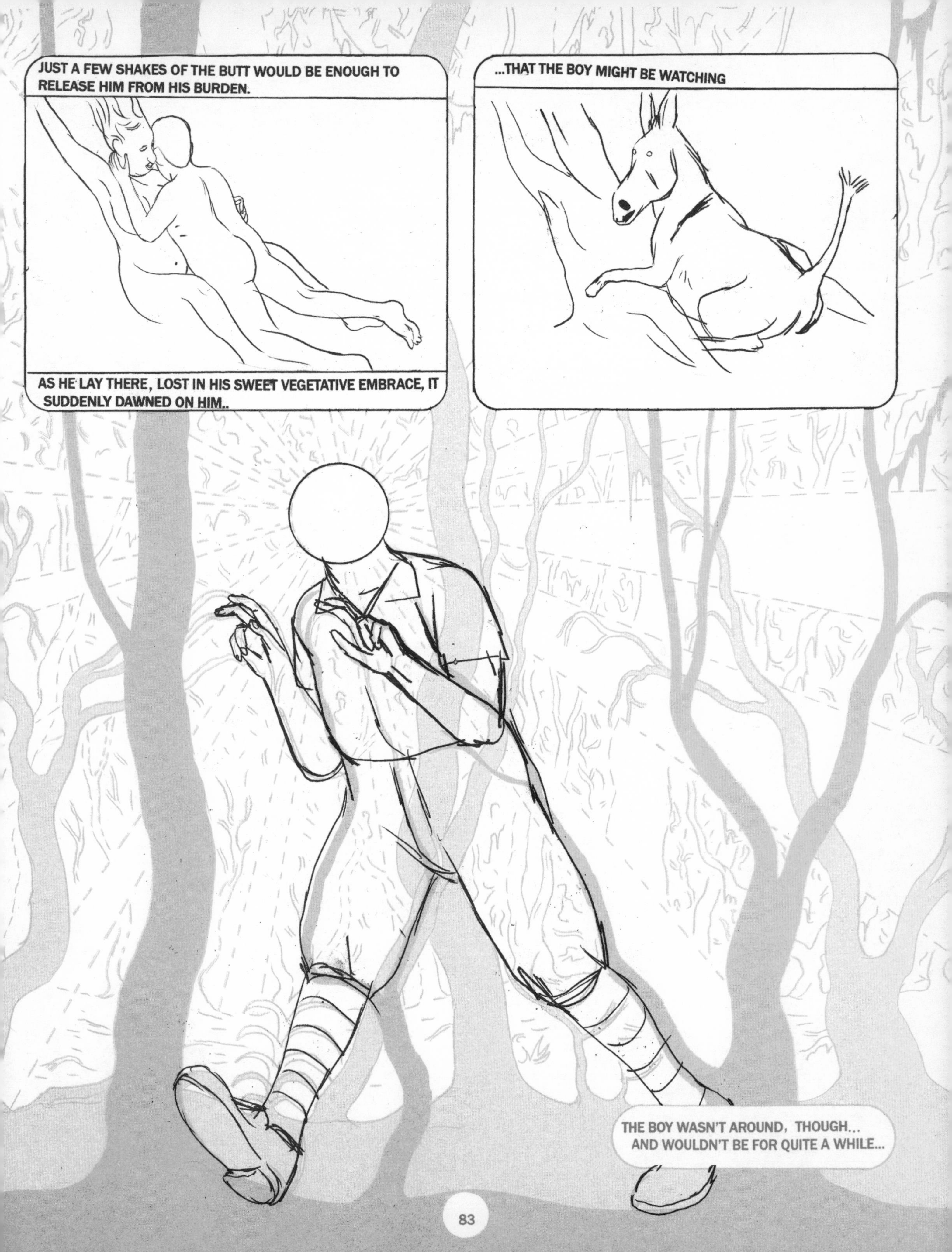
JUST A FEW SHAKES OF THE BUTT WOULD BE ENOUGH TO RELEASE HIM FROM HIS BURDEN.
AS HE LAY THERE, LOST IN HIS SWEET VEGETATIVE EMBRACE, IT SUDDENLY DAWNED ON HIM..
...THAT THE BOY MIGHT BE WATCHING
THE BOY WASN'T AROUND, THOUGH... AND WOULDN'T BE FOR QUITE A WHILE...

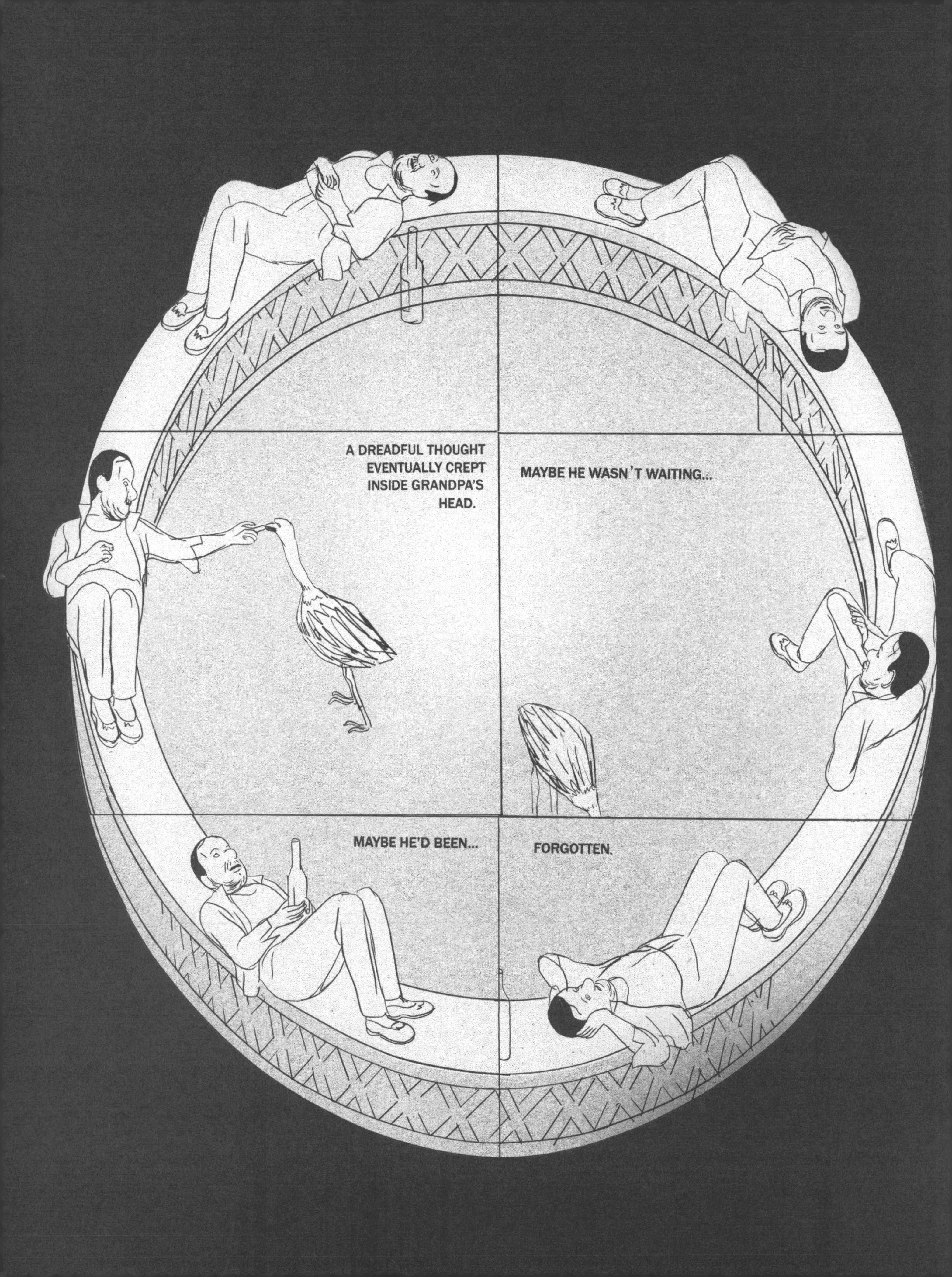
A DREADFUL THOUGHT EVENTUALLY CREPT INSIDE GRANDPA'S HEAD.
MAYBE HE WASN'T WAITING...
MAYBE HE'D BEEN...
FORGOTTEN.

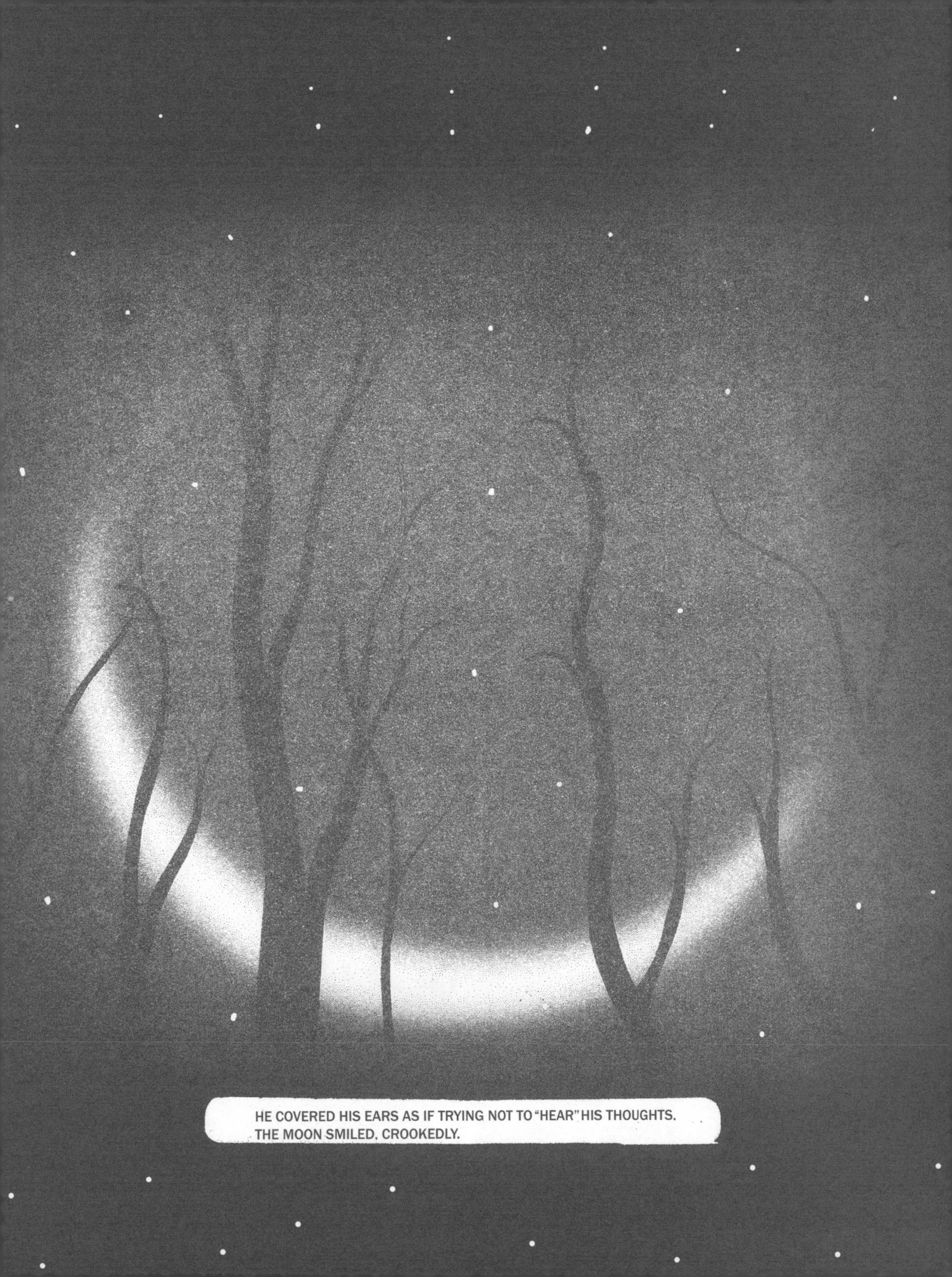
HE COVERED HIS EARS AS IF TRYING NOT TO "HEAR" HIS THOUGHTS.
THE MOON SMILED, CROOKEDLY.

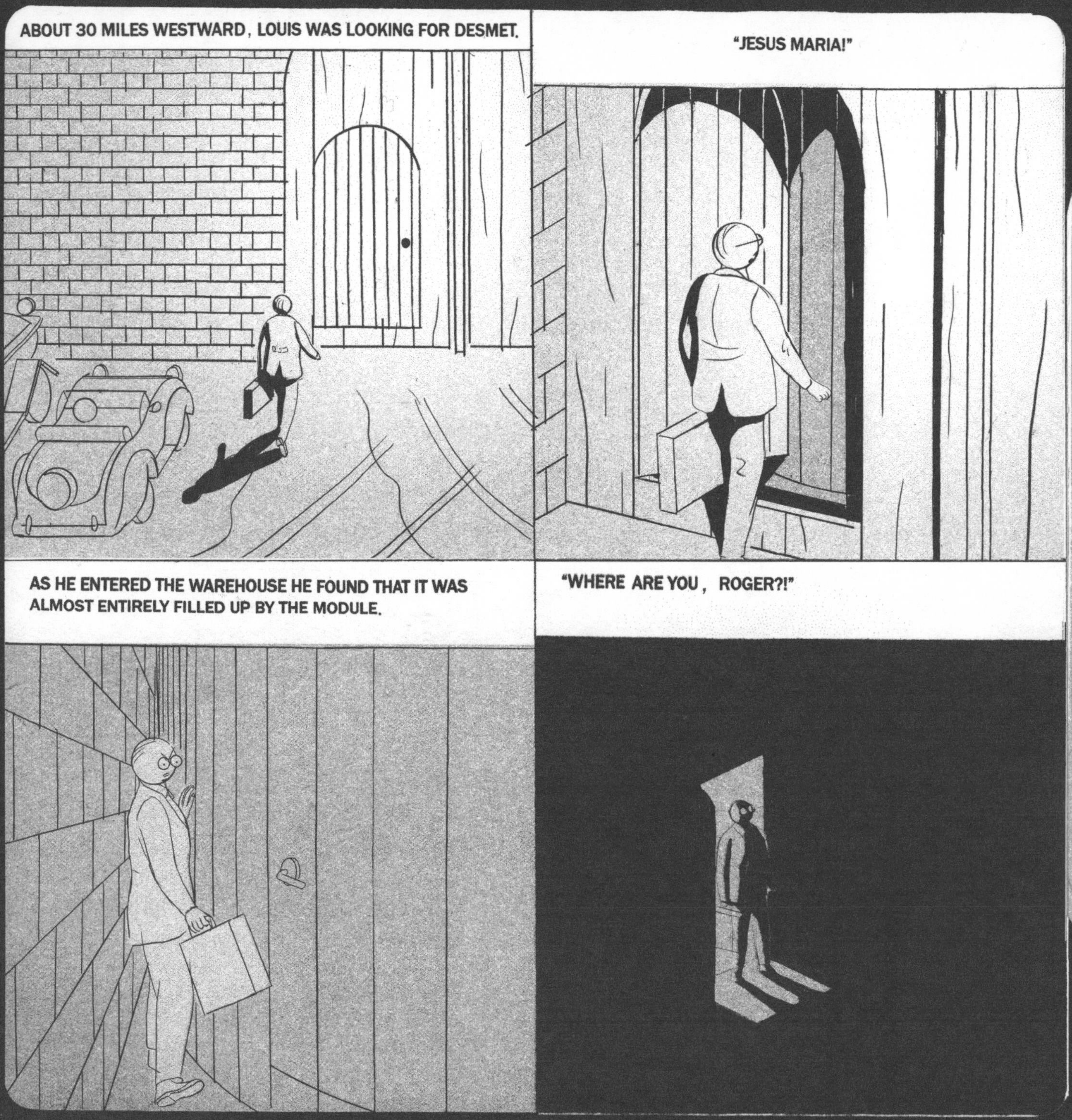
ABOUT 30 MILES WESTWARD, LOUIS WAS LOOKING FOR DESMET.
"JESUS MARIA!"
AS HE ENTERED THE WAREHOUSE HE FOUND THAT IT WAS ALMOST ENTIRELY FILLED UP BY THE MODULE.
"WHERE ARE YOU, ROGER?!"

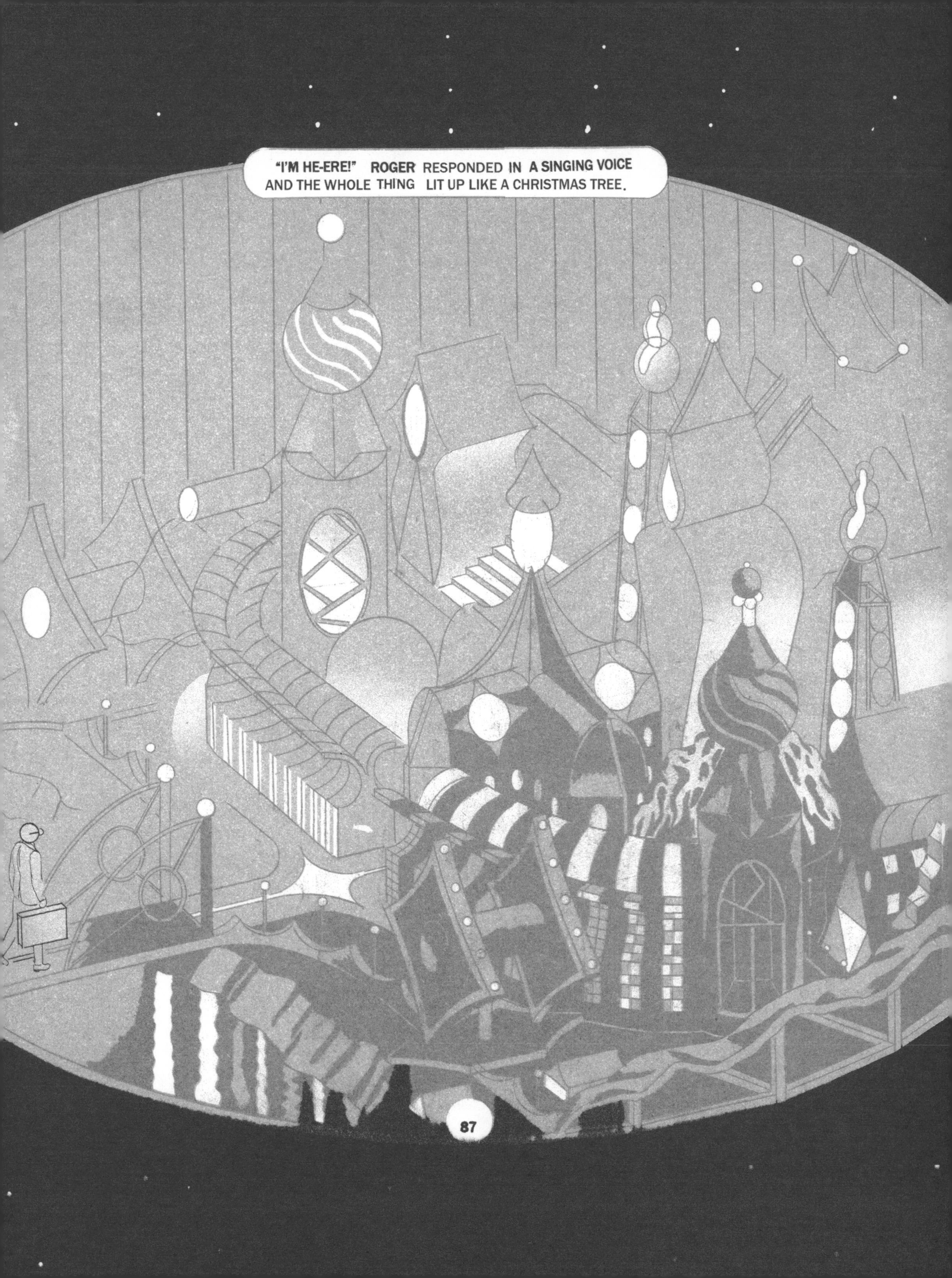
"I'M HE-ERE!" ROGER RESPONDED IN A SINGING VOICE AND THE WHOLE THING LIT UP LIKE A CHRISTMAS TREE.

LOUIS WAS HORRIFIED TO FIND MANY SCULPTURES IN THE "MINIATURE" NOW TOWERING A METER ABOVE HIS HEAD.

"WHERE THE HELL ARE YOU, DESMET?"

"RIGHT HERE!"

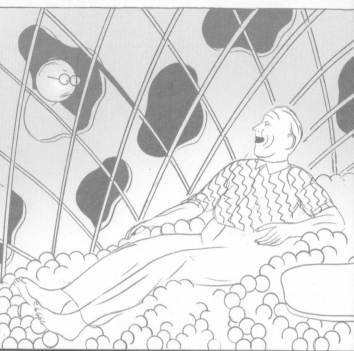

"SIT BACK AND RELAX! I'LL POUR YOU A TRAPPIST."

"FOR GOD'S SAKE, ROGER! I'VE URGED YOU TO DOWNSIZE AND YOU'VE DONE JUST THE OPPOSITE. THIS IS LUNACY!"

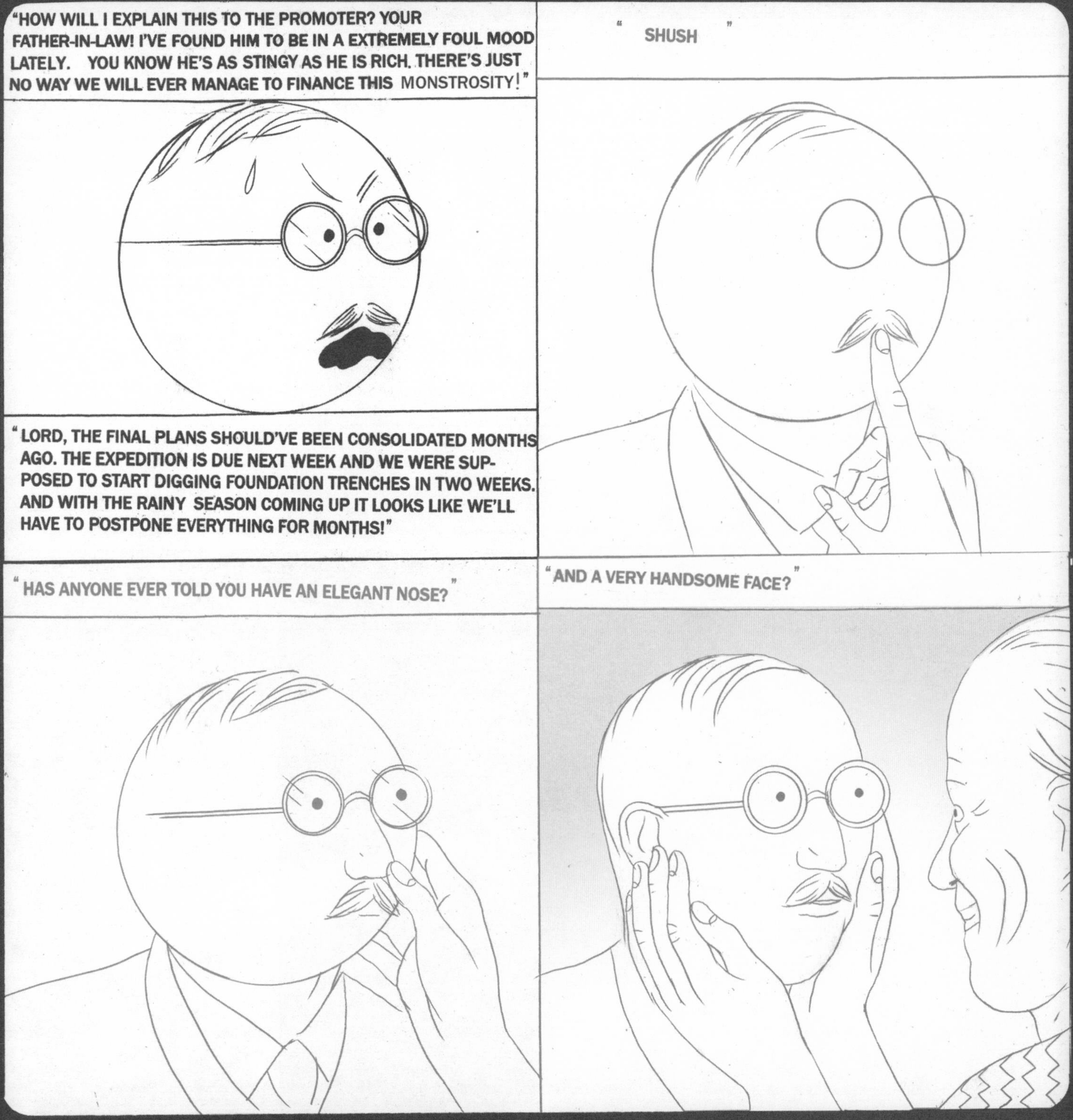
"HOW WILL I EXPLAIN THIS TO THE PROMOTER? YOUR FATHER-IN-LAW! I'VE FOUND HIM TO BE IN A EXTREMELY FOUL MOOD LATELY. YOU KNOW HE'S AS STINGY AS HE IS RICH. THERE'S JUST NO WAY WE WILL EVER MANAGE TO FINANCE THIS MONSTROSITY!"
"LORD, THE FINAL PLANS SHOULD'VE BEEN CONSOLIDATED MONTHS AGO. THE EXPEDITION IS DUE NEXT WEEK AND WE WERE SUPPOSED TO START DIGGING FOUNDATION TRENCHES IN TWO WEEKS. AND WITH THE RAINY SEASON COMING UP IT LOOKS LIKE WE'LL HAVE TO POSTPONE EVERYTHING FOR MONTHS!"
" SHUSH "
"HAS ANYONE EVER TOLD YOU HAVE AN ELEGANT NOSE?"
"AND A VERY HANDSOME FACE?"

"ROGER, PLEASE, CUT IT OUT.
SOMEONE MIGHT COME IN!"
"NOT TO WORRY..."

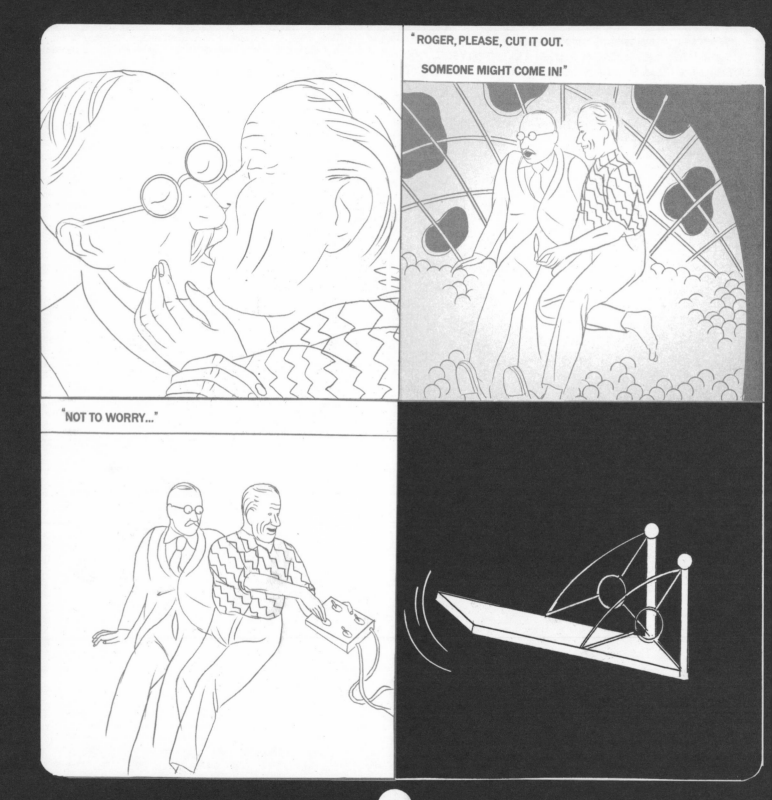

"HELLO MY LITTLE FRIEND!"

"BY THE WAY, HOW'S THAT COUSIN OF YOURS DOING?"

"OH LORD LOUIS, WHY WOULD YOU BRING THAT UP NOW?"

"I'M SURE HE'S DOING JUST FINE!
   ENJOYING HIS VACATION, DRINKING HIS TRAPPIST...

HAHAHA"

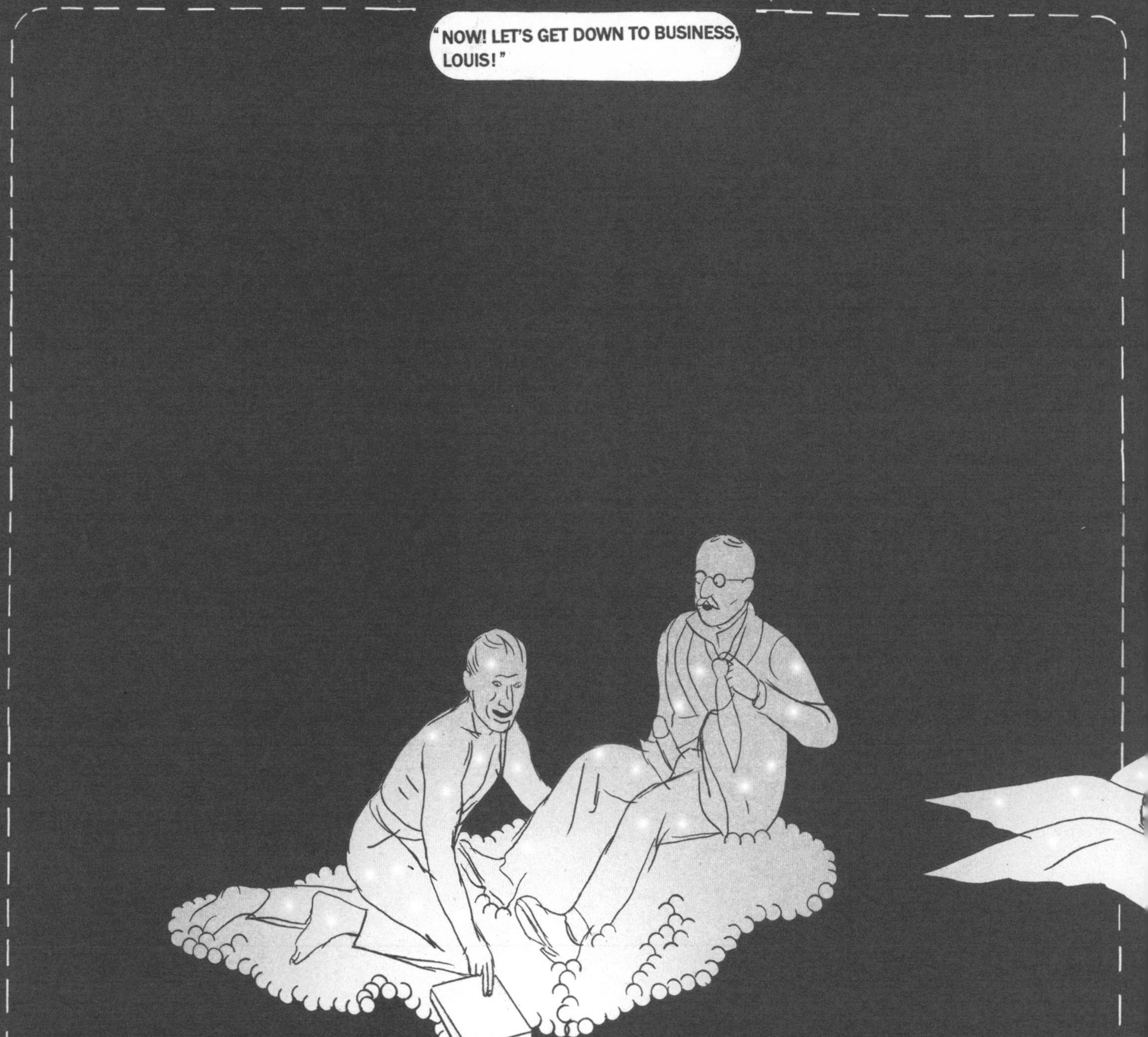
"NOW! LET'S GET DOWN TO BUSINESS, LOUIS!"

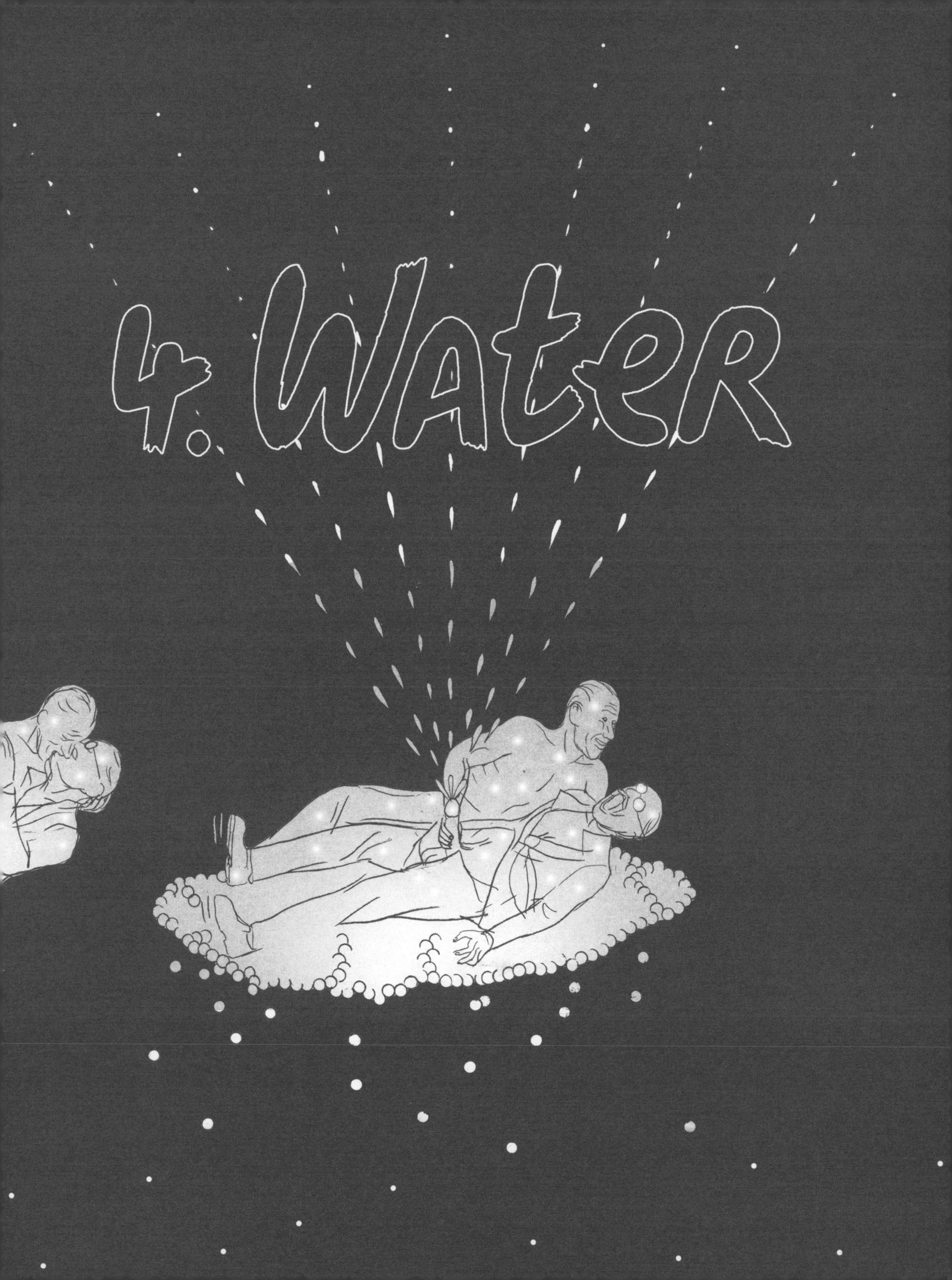
4. Water

AT SUNSET, WHEN THE SHADOWS OF THE TREES HAD STARTED TO WEAVE A NEST-LIKE PATTERN ON THE BUNGALOW, ARSENE DECIDED TO GO.

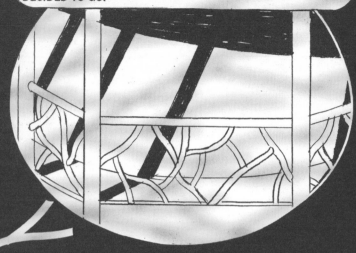

HE WOULD JUST...

GO

ESCAPE FROM THE DARNED HUT THAT HAD HELD HIM CAPTIVE FOR WEEKS.

HE DIDN'T EVEN BOTHER PACKING; HIS VALISE WOULD ONLY SLOW HIM DOWN.

HE WAS GASPING, FLAPPING HIS ARMS AROUND AS IF HE WAS TRYING TO TAKE OFF.

THEN A FAT RAINDROP FELL FROM THE SKY. HE FELT IT SQUASHING INTO THE CURLY HAIR OF HIS BEARD.

HE SHOOK IT OFF, JERKING HIS HEAD LIKE SOME BARN ANIMAL.

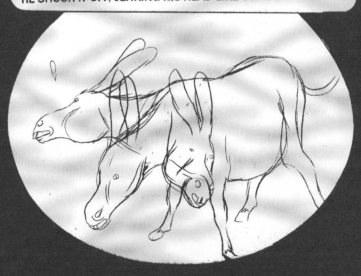

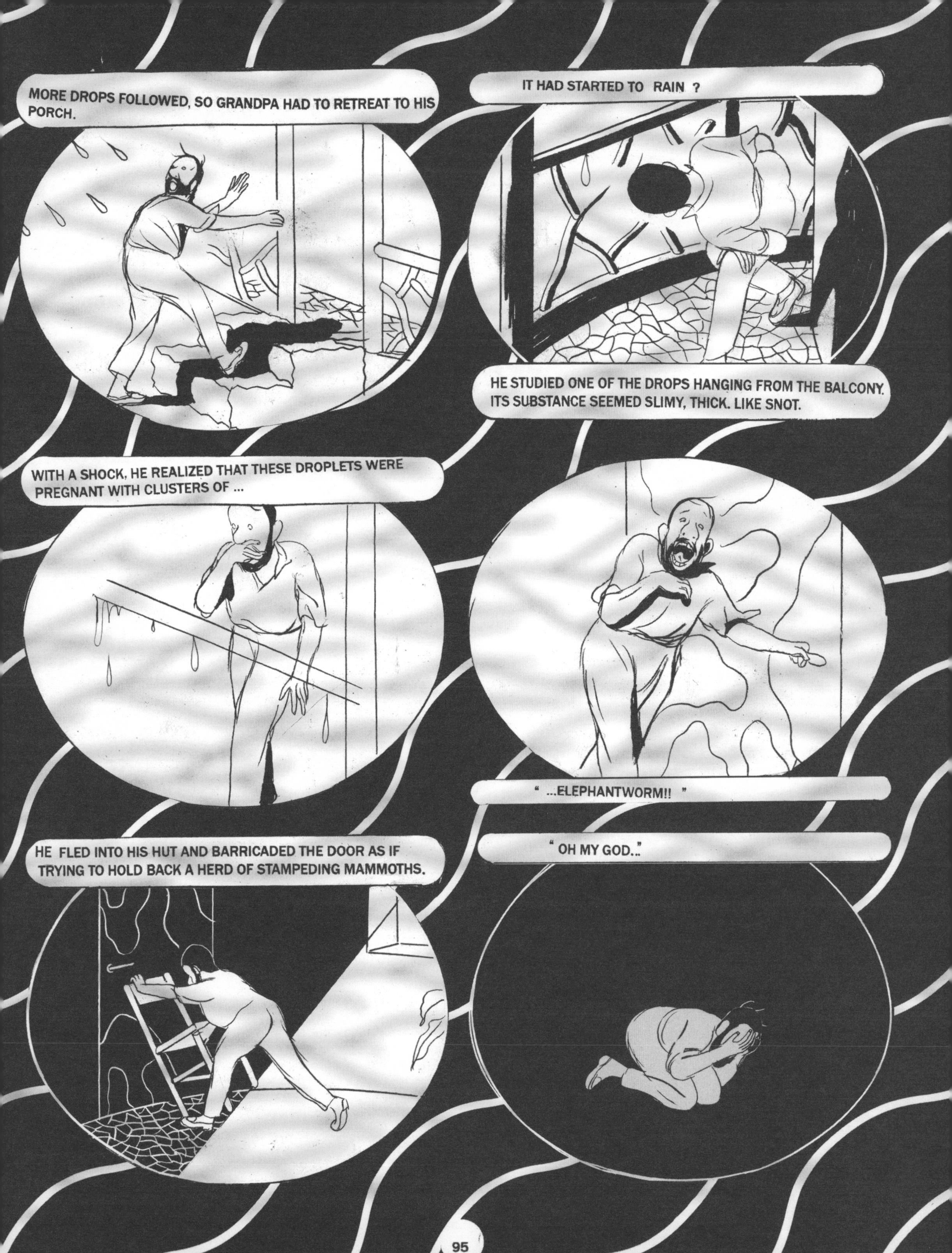

MORE DROPS FOLLOWED, SO GRANDPA HAD TO RETREAT TO HIS PORCH.

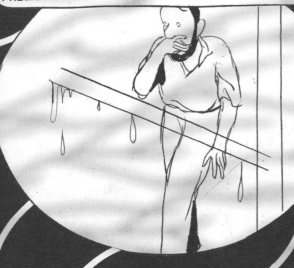

IT HAD STARTED TO RAIN ?

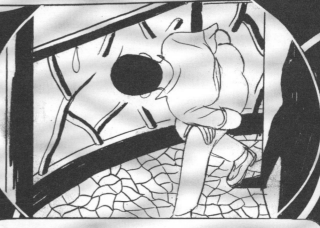

HE STUDIED ONE OF THE DROPS HANGING FROM THE BALCONY. ITS SUBSTANCE SEEMED SLIMY, THICK. LIKE SNOT.

WITH A SHOCK, HE REALIZED THAT THESE DROPLETS WERE PREGNANT WITH CLUSTERS OF ...

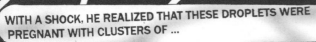

" ...ELEPHANTWORM!! "

HE FLED INTO HIS HUT AND BARRICADED THE DOOR AS IF TRYING TO HOLD BACK A HERD OF STAMPEDING MAMMOTHS.

" OH MY GOD.. "

WAS HE LOOSING HIS MIND?

HE HAD TO PULL HIMSELF TOGETHER.

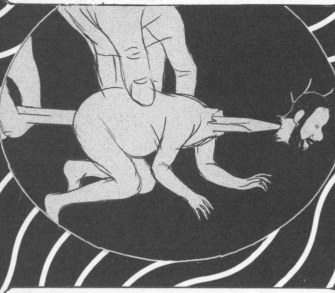

SURELY THIS ELEPHANTWORM BUSINESS WAS NONSENSE.

WHY, AS LONG AS HE KEPT HIS MOUTH SHUT, CLENCHED HIS BUTTOCKS AND PROTECTED HIS PEEHOLE, NO WORM WOULD ENTER HIS BODY.

IT WAS A BUNCH OF HORSESHIT SOLD TO HIM BY A BULLSHIT ARTIST.

IN THE NEXT DAYS, THE DOWNPOUR INTENSIFIED. AS THE WATER STARTED COMING DOWN HARDER, THE SOOTHING SOUND OF THE DRIZZLE SWELLED INTO A GLOOMY DRONE.

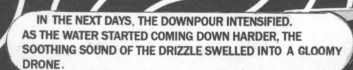

THE RAIN HAD COME IN DARK CLOUDS. THEY ENVELOPED THE BUNGALOW LIKE A SPONGE. INSIDE IT WAS NOW DARK, MOIST AND UNPLEASANTLY HOT.

IT WAS THE MOST AWFUL OF PRISON CELLS, AND ARSÈNE WAS CONDEMNED TO IT AS LONG AS THE RAIN CONTINUED.

STILL HE WENT ABOUT HIS DAILY DOINGS, TRYING TO KEEP IT TOGETHER.

HIS "DRY" WASHING HAD BECOME EVEN MORE USELESS NOW THAT HIS TOWELS AND WASHCLOTHS SMELLED LIKE SWISS CHEESE.

AND HE HAD TO USE HIS SHOELACES TO TIE UP HIS TRUNKS AS THE BAND-AIDS NO LONGER STUCK TO HIS SWEATING SKIN.

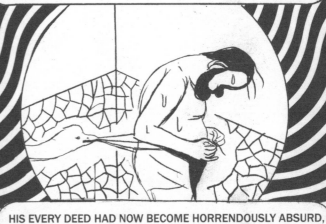

HIS EVERY DEED HAD NOW BECOME HORRENDOUSLY ABSURD, AS IF HE WERE A CHARACTER IN SOME SLAPSTICK PLAY.

HIS STAMINA WAS ADMIRABLE CONSIDERING THE SITUATION. SOON THE RAINWATER STARTED LEAKING THROUGH THE ROTTED ROOF.

HE IMAGINED IT TO BE THE ELEPHANTWORMS EATING THROUGH THE THIN MEMBRANE OF HIS SMALL WORLD.

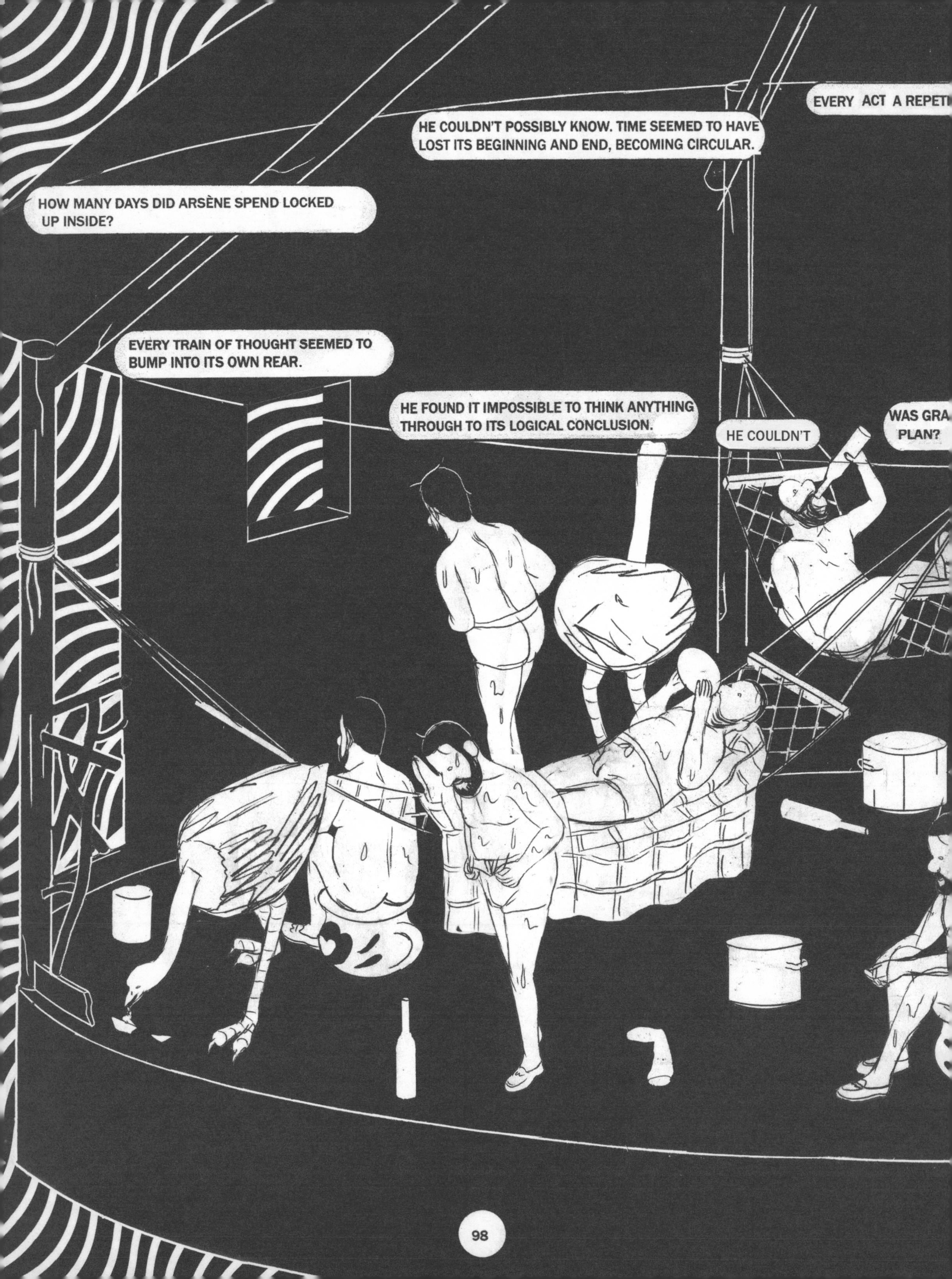
HOW MANY DAYS DID ARSÈNE SPEND LOCKED UP INSIDE?
HE COULDN'T POSSIBLY KNOW. TIME SEEMED TO HAVE LOST ITS BEGINNING AND END, BECOMING CIRCULAR.
EVERY ACT A REPETI
EVERY TRAIN OF THOUGHT SEEMED TO BUMP INTO ITS OWN REAR.
HE FOUND IT IMPOSSIBLE TO THINK ANYTHING THROUGH TO ITS LOGICAL CONCLUSION.
HE COULDN'T
WAS GRA
PLAN?

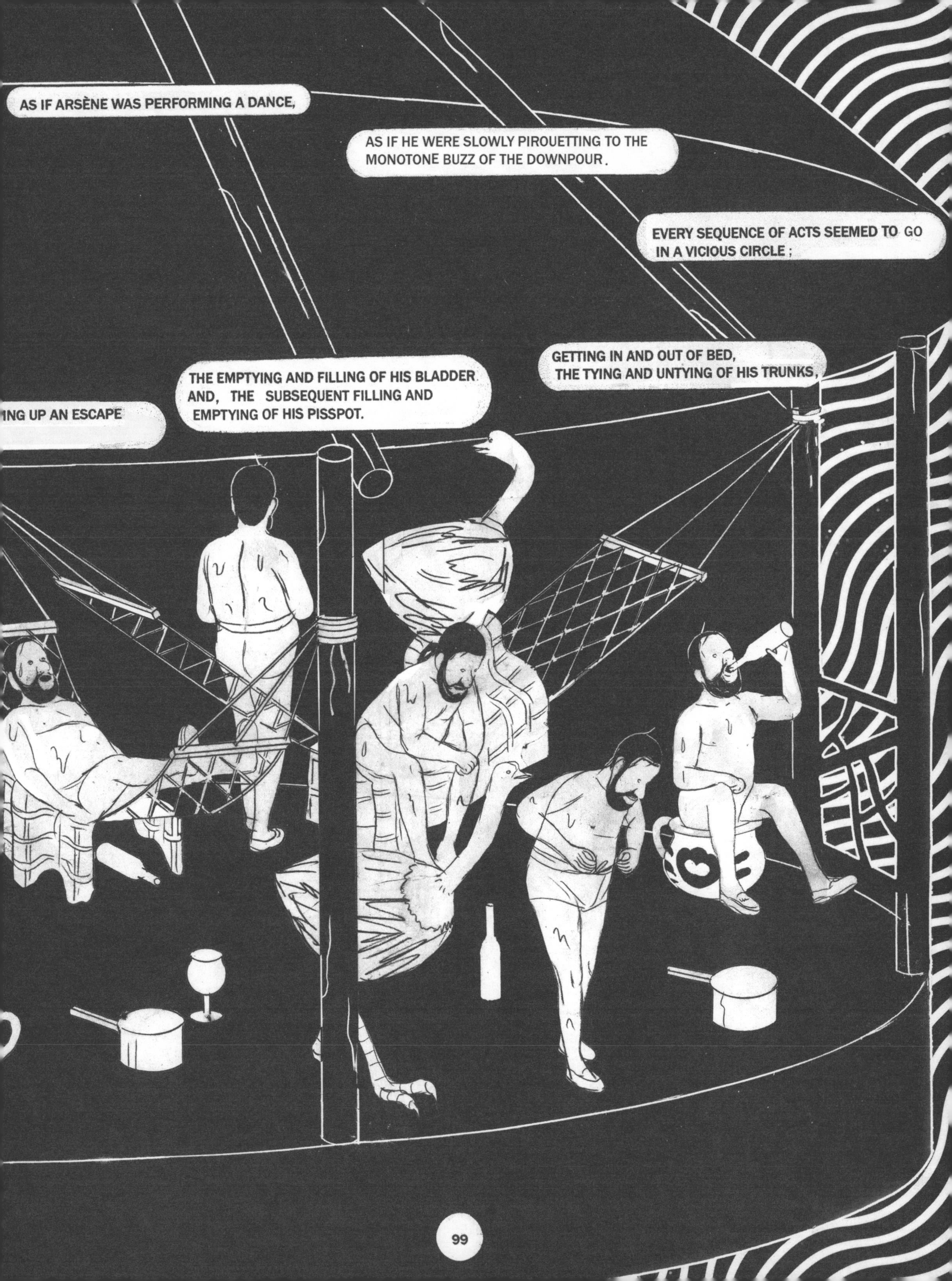
AS IF ARSÈNE WAS PERFORMING A DANCE,
AS IF HE WERE SLOWLY PIROUETTING TO THE MONOTONE BUZZ OF THE DOWNPOUR.
EVERY SEQUENCE OF ACTS SEEMED TO GO IN A VICIOUS CIRCLE ;
GETTING IN AND OUT OF BED, THE TYING AND UNTYING OF HIS TRUNKS,
THE EMPTYING AND FILLING OF HIS BLADDER AND, THE SUBSEQUENT FILLING AND EMPTYING OF HIS PISSPOT.
ING UP AN ESCAPE

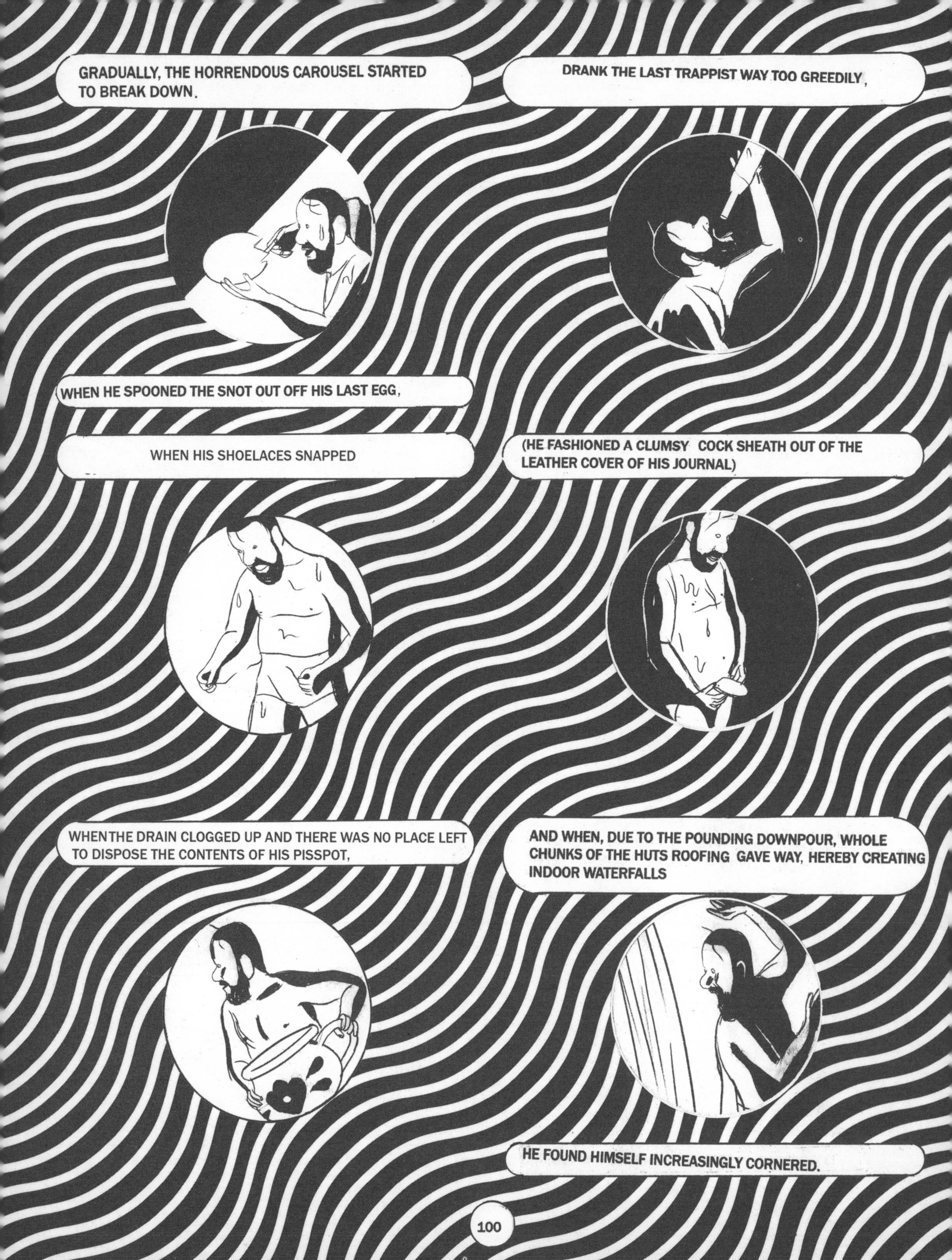
GRADUALLY, THE HORRENDOUS CAROUSEL STARTED TO BREAK DOWN.
DRANK THE LAST TRAPPIST WAY TOO GREEDILY,
WHEN HE SPOONED THE SNOT OUT OFF HIS LAST EGG,
WHEN HIS SHOELACES SNAPPED
(HE FASHIONED A CLUMSY COCK SHEATH OUT OF THE LEATHER COVER OF HIS JOURNAL)
WHENTHE DRAIN CLOGGED UP AND THERE WAS NO PLACE LEFT TO DISPOSE THE CONTENTS OF HIS PISSPOT,
AND WHEN, DUE TO THE POUNDING DOWNPOUR, WHOLE CHUNKS OF THE HUTS ROOFING GAVE WAY, HEREBY CREATING INDOOR WATERFALLS
HE FOUND HIMSELF INCREASINGLY CORNERED.

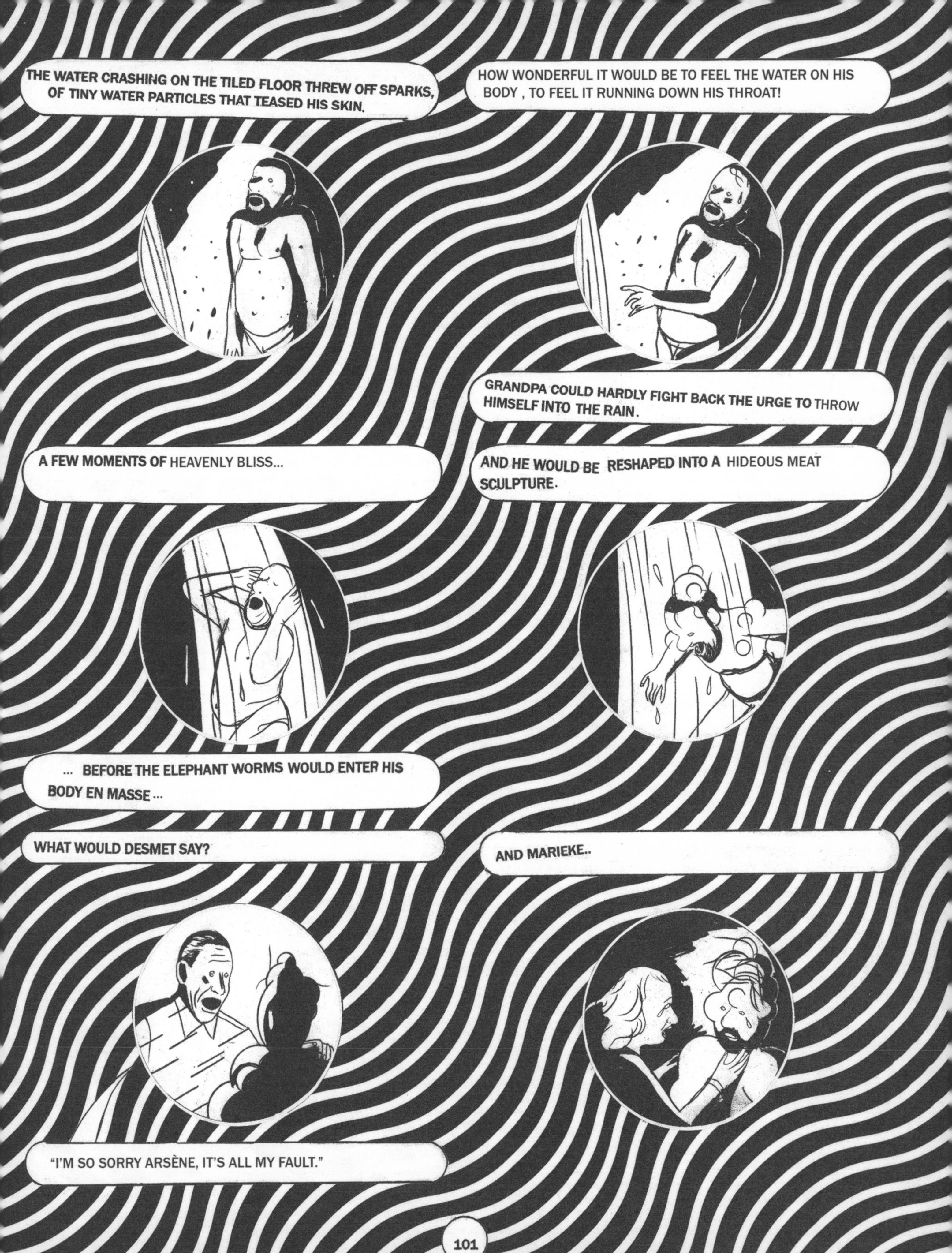
THE WATER CRASHING ON THE TILED FLOOR THREW OFF SPARKS, OF TINY WATER PARTICLES THAT TEASED HIS SKIN.
HOW WONDERFUL IT WOULD BE TO FEEL THE WATER ON HIS BODY , TO FEEL IT RUNNING DOWN HIS THROAT!
GRANDPA COULD HARDLY FIGHT BACK THE URGE TO THROW HIMSELF INTO THE RAIN.
A FEW MOMENTS OF HEAVENLY BLISS...
AND HE WOULD BE RESHAPED INTO A HIDEOUS MEAT SCULPTURE.
... BEFORE THE ELEPHANT WORMS WOULD ENTER HIS BODY EN MASSE ...
WHAT WOULD DESMET SAY?
AND MARIEKE..
"I'M SO SORRY ARSÈNE, IT'S ALL MY FAULT."

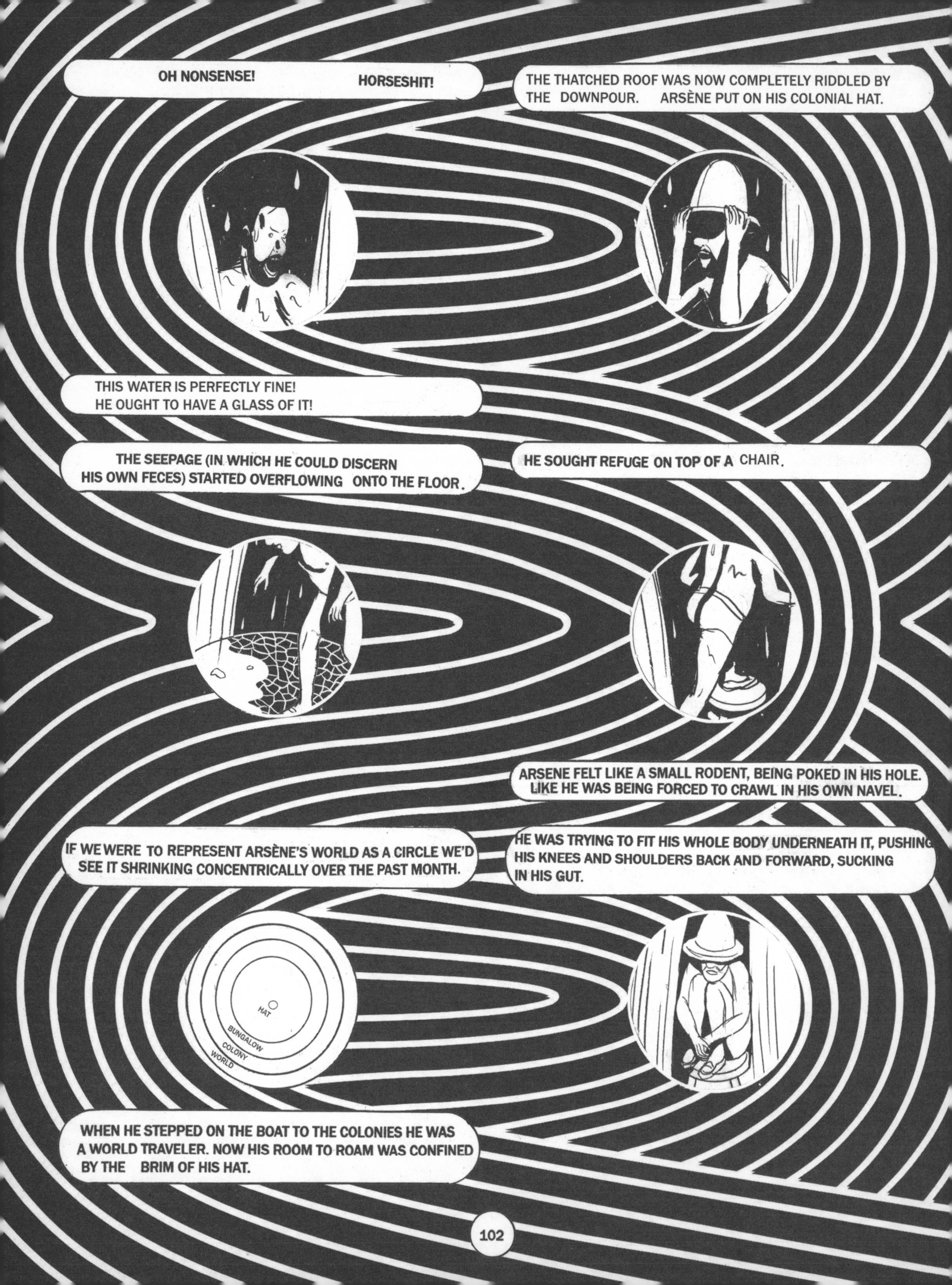
OH NONSENSE!
HORSESHIT!
THE THATCHED ROOF WAS NOW COMPLETELY RIDDLED BY THE DOWNPOUR. ARSÈNE PUT ON HIS COLONIAL HAT.
THIS WATER IS PERFECTLY FINE! HE OUGHT TO HAVE A GLASS OF IT!
THE SEEPAGE (IN WHICH HE COULD DISCERN HIS OWN FECES) STARTED OVERFLOWING ONTO THE FLOOR.
HE SOUGHT REFUGE ON TOP OF A CHAIR.
ARSENE FELT LIKE A SMALL RODENT, BEING POKED IN HIS HOLE. LIKE HE WAS BEING FORCED TO CRAWL IN HIS OWN NAVEL.
IF WE WERE TO REPRESENT ARSÈNE'S WORLD AS A CIRCLE WE'D SEE IT SHRINKING CONCENTRICALLY OVER THE PAST MONTH.
HE WAS TRYING TO FIT HIS WHOLE BODY UNDERNEATH IT, PUSHING HIS KNEES AND SHOULDERS BACK AND FORWARD, SUCKING IN HIS GUT.
HAT
BUNGALOW
COLONY
WORLD
WHEN HE STEPPED ON THE BOAT TO THE COLONIES HE WAS A WORLD TRAVELER. NOW HIS ROOM TO ROAM WAS CONFINED BY THE BRIM OF HIS HAT.

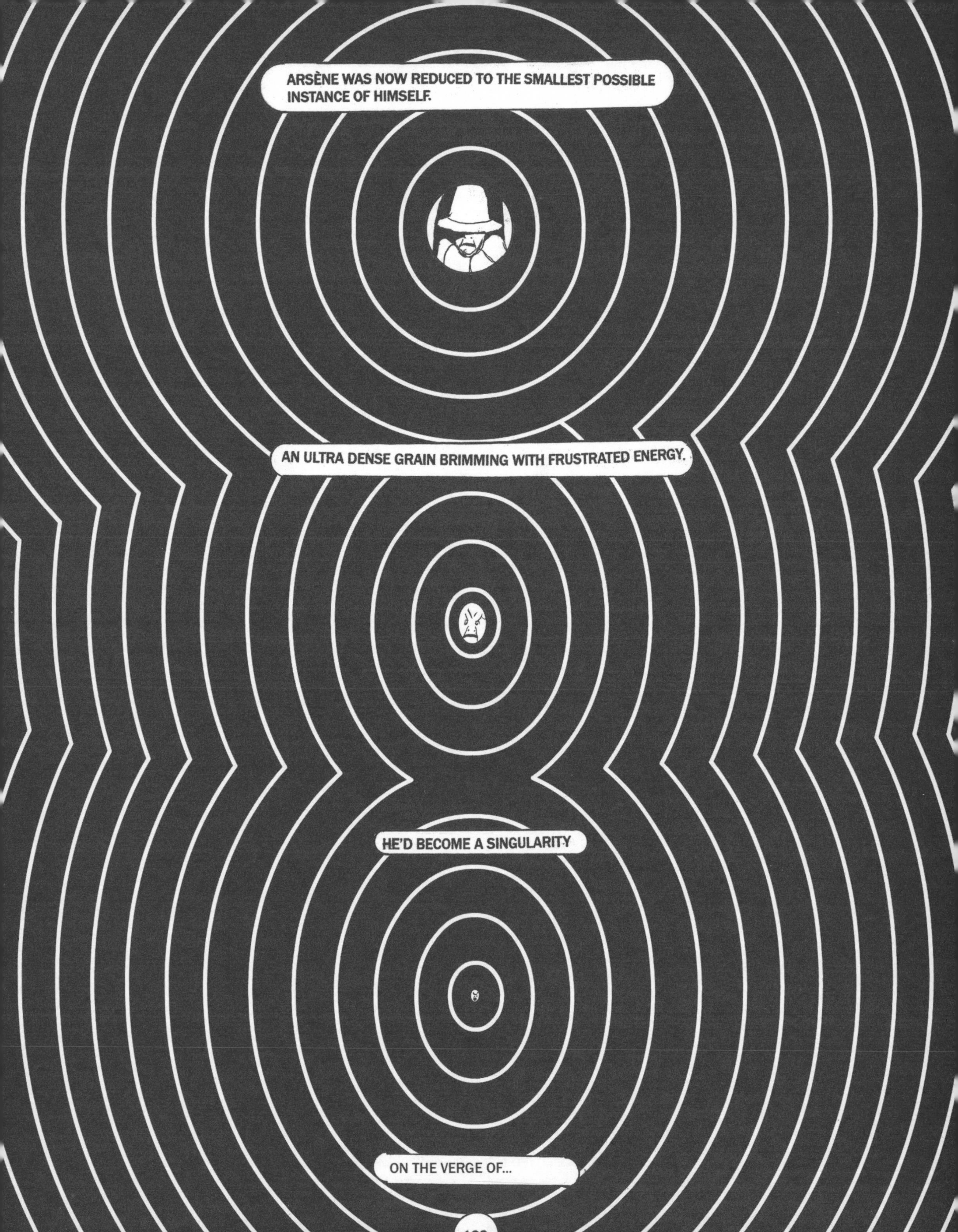
ARSÈNE WAS NOW REDUCED TO THE SMALLEST POSSIBLE INSTANCE OF HIMSELF.
AN ULTRA DENSE GRAIN BRIMMING WITH FRUSTRATED ENERGY.
HE'D BECOME A SINGULARITY
ON THE VERGE OF...

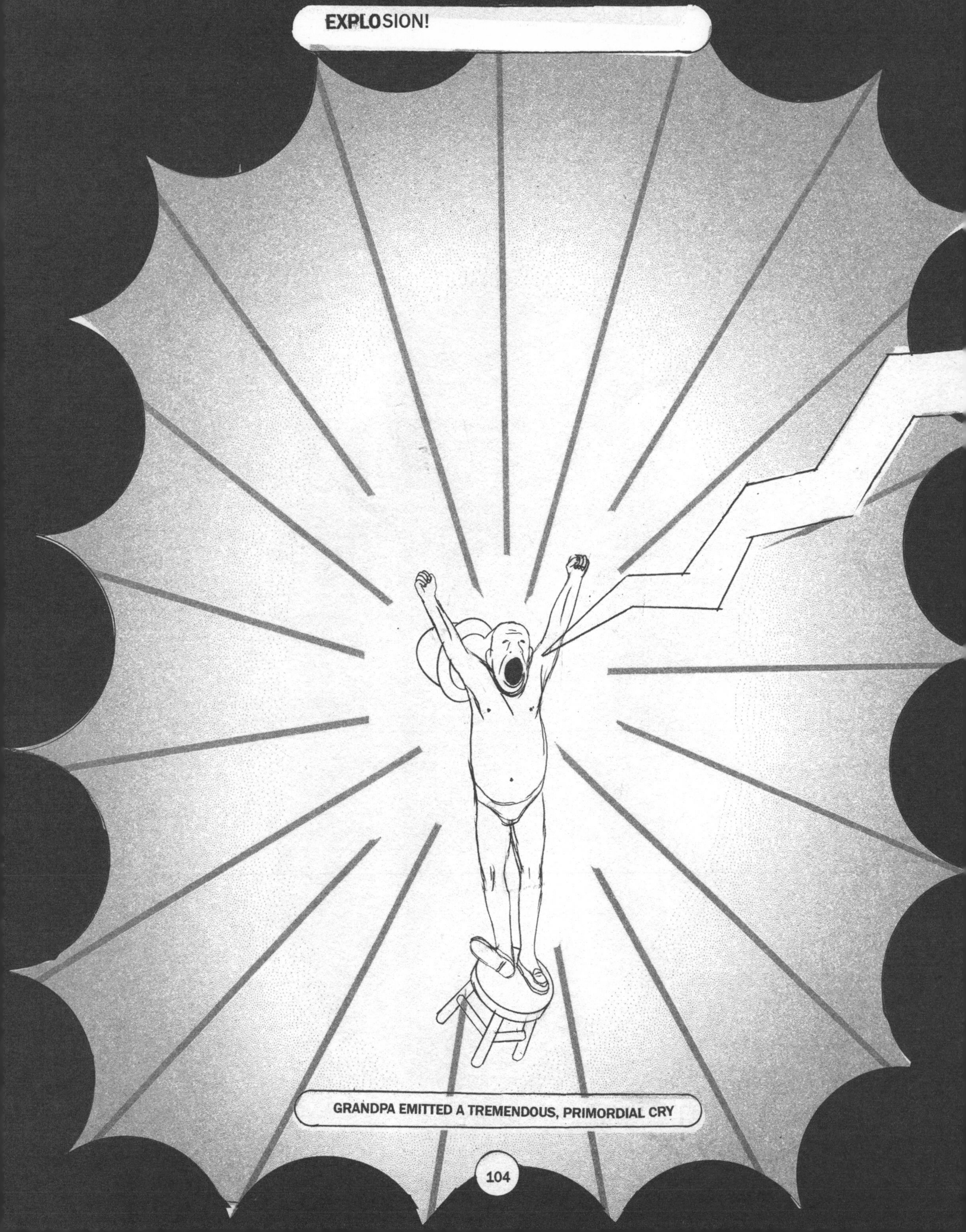
EXPLOSION!
GRANDPA EMITTED A TREMENDOUS, PRIMORDIAL CRY

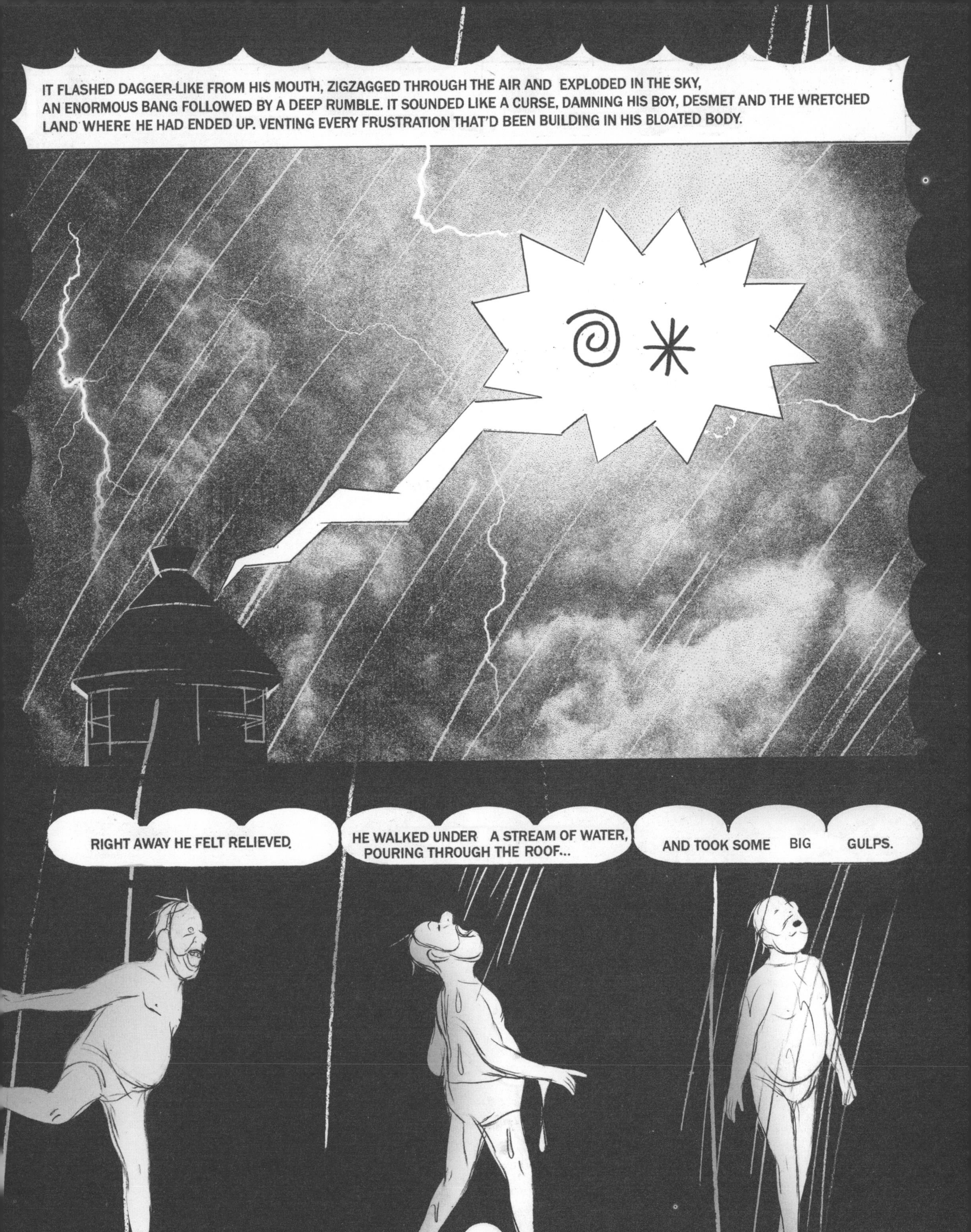
IT FLASHED DAGGER-LIKE FROM HIS MOUTH, ZIGZAGGED THROUGH THE AIR AND EXPLODED IN THE SKY, AN ENORMOUS BANG FOLLOWED BY A DEEP RUMBLE. IT SOUNDED LIKE A CURSE, DAMNING HIS BOY, DESMET AND THE WRETCHED LAND WHERE HE HAD ENDED UP. VENTING EVERY FRUSTRATION THAT'D BEEN BUILDING IN HIS BLOATED BODY.
RIGHT AWAY HE FELT RELIEVED.
HE WALKED UNDER A STREAM OF WATER, POURING THROUGH THE ROOF...
AND TOOK SOME BIG GULPS.

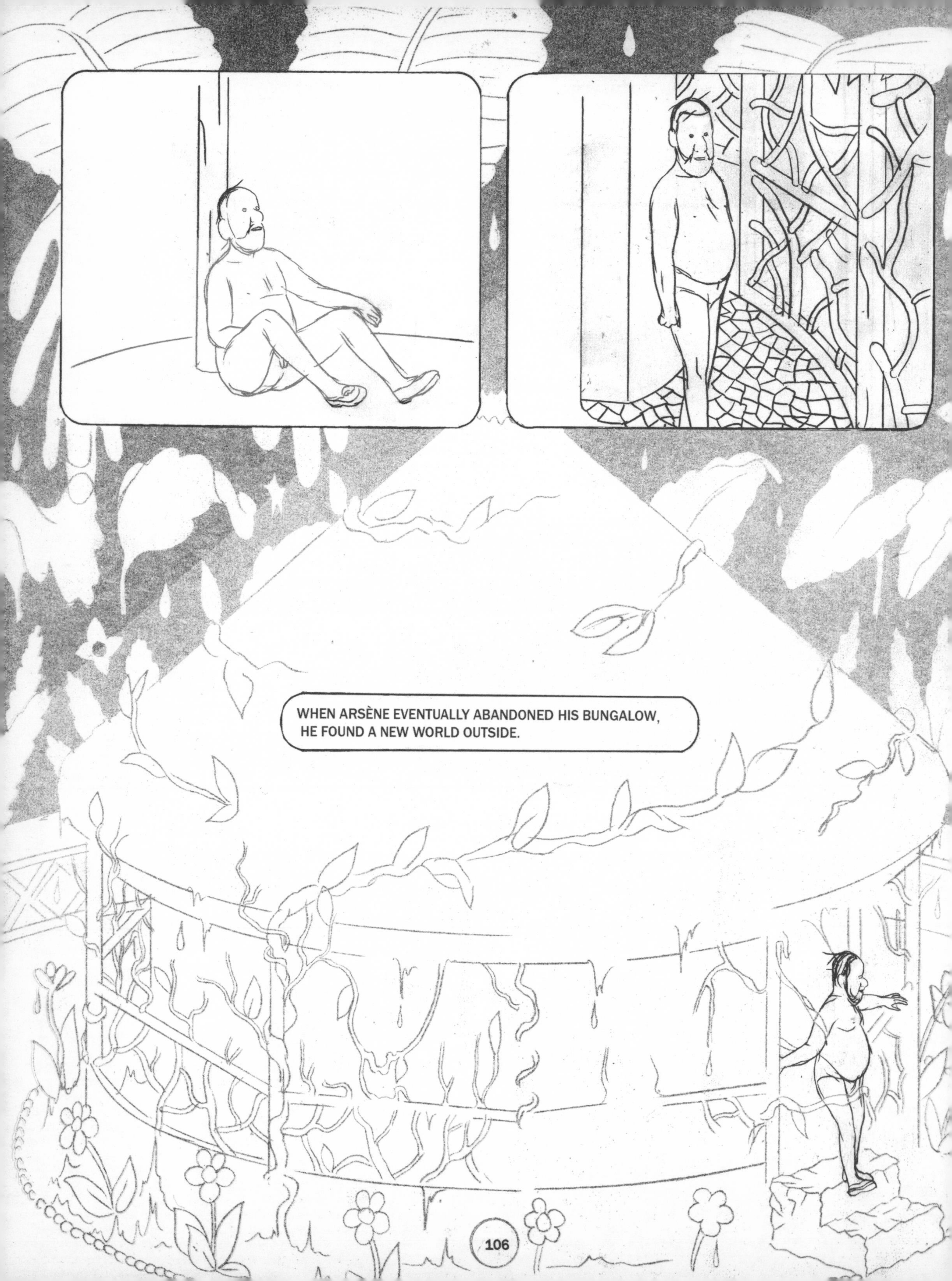
WHEN ARSÈNE EVENTUALLY ABANDONED HIS BUNGALOW, HE FOUND A NEW WORLD OUTSIDE.

EVERYTHING HAD COMPLETELY METAMORPHOSED.

THE BUNGALOW HAD ALTERED ITS OWN DESIGN, ITS PILLARS AND BALCONIES WHERE NOW ADORNED WITH A BAROQUE, FLORAL ORNAMENTATION.

AN ABUNDANCE OF BRIGHTLY COLORED BLADES AND PETALS HAD SPROUTED OUT OF THE BARREN UNDERGROWTH.

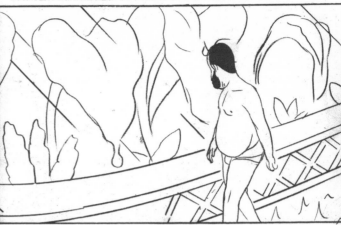

FAT LEAVES DANGLED DOWN LIKE TONGUES FROM DOGS' MOUTHS. FLOWER BUDS POUTED LIKE CHILDREN KISSING.

EVERYTHING WAS WET AND DRIPPING. RAINDROPS HUNG IN THE FRESH GREENERY LIKE JEWELRY; LIKE PEARLS TWINKLING IN THE BEAMING SUNLIGHT.

GRANDPA SAW A TINY BIRD ENTERING THE GAPING MOUTH OF A FLOWER, POKING ITS NEEDLE-LIKE BEAK IN THE FLOWER'S GENITALIA.

AS IT FLEW OFF IT WAS CAUGHT MID-AIR BY A GIANT BULLFROG.

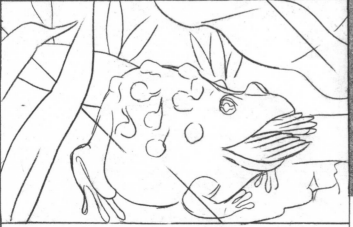

THE FROG TUCKED IT AWAY SEAMLESSLY, LIKE A SOCK IN A DRAWER.

AS THE BEAST LET ITSELF SINK IN A PUDDLE, IT'S "WARTS" CAME OFF, AND PROVED TO BE TADPOLES.

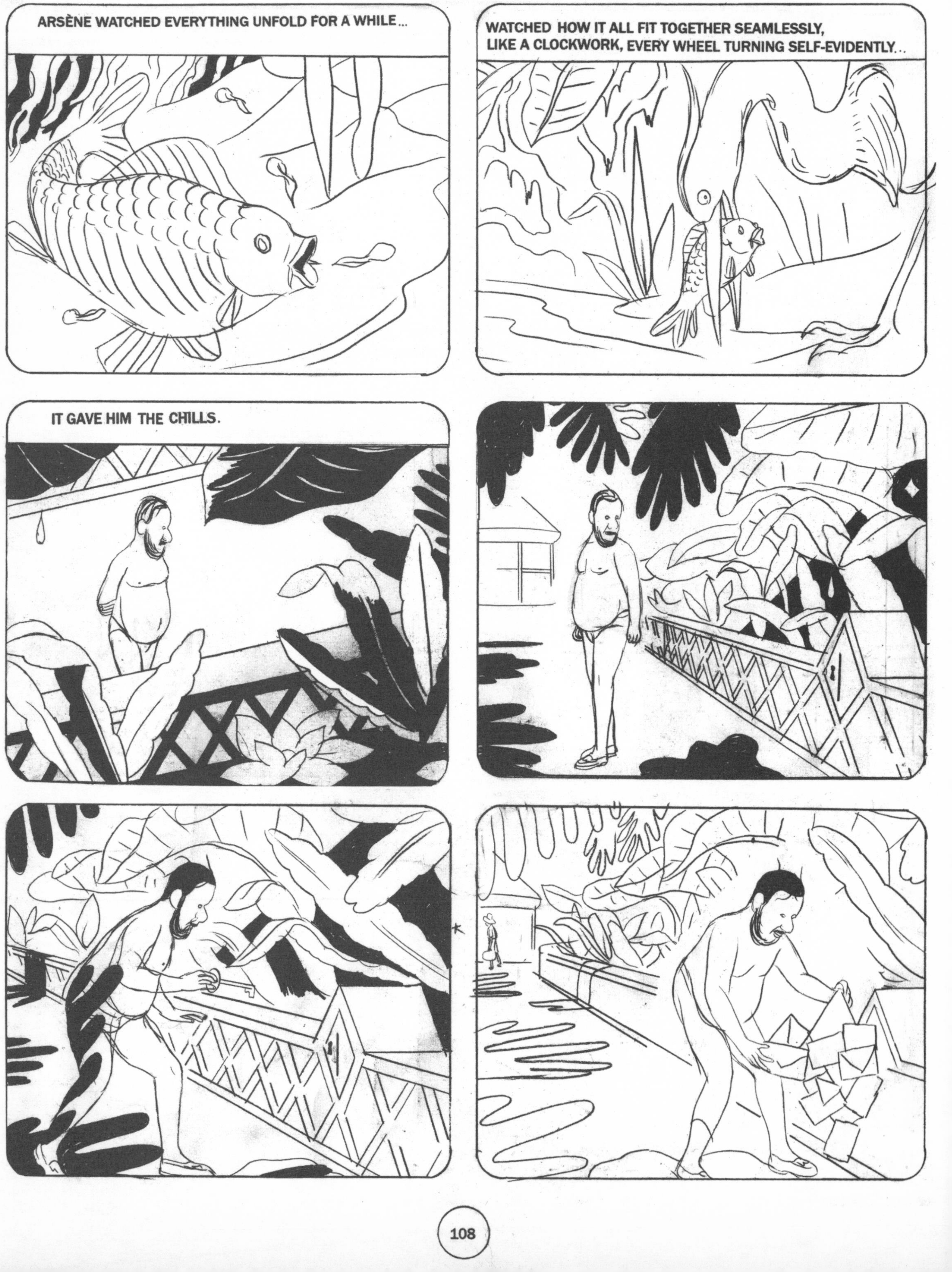
ARSÈNE WATCHED EVERYTHING UNFOLD FOR A WHILE...
WATCHED HOW IT ALL FIT TOGETHER SEAMLESSLY, LIKE A CLOCKWORK, EVERY WHEEL TURNING SELF-EVIDENTLY...
IT GAVE HIM THE CHILLS.

OUT OF THE MAILBOX CAME 25 LETTERS, ALL ADDRESSED TO HIM.

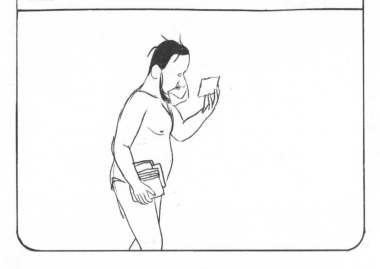

ON HIS DOORSTEP AWAITED ANOTHER SURPRISE.

(CONTENTS OF BASKET: CARTON OF CIGARETTES, 3 TRAPPISTS, A WHOLE CHICKEN, AND A NOTE).

THE NOTE CAME FROM THE BOY AND READ: "FORGIVE MY LATENESS. YOUR BRAND OF CIGARETTES WAS HARD TO COME BY. PLEASE EAT THE CHICKEN PROMPTLY."

THE LETTERS WERE ALL FROM...

MARIEKE!

NOW HIS HEART WAS BEATING TO THE KIND OF RHYTHM THAT SPURRED SLAVES IN A GALLEY.

HASTILY HE PUT THEM IN CHRONOLOGICAL ORDER.

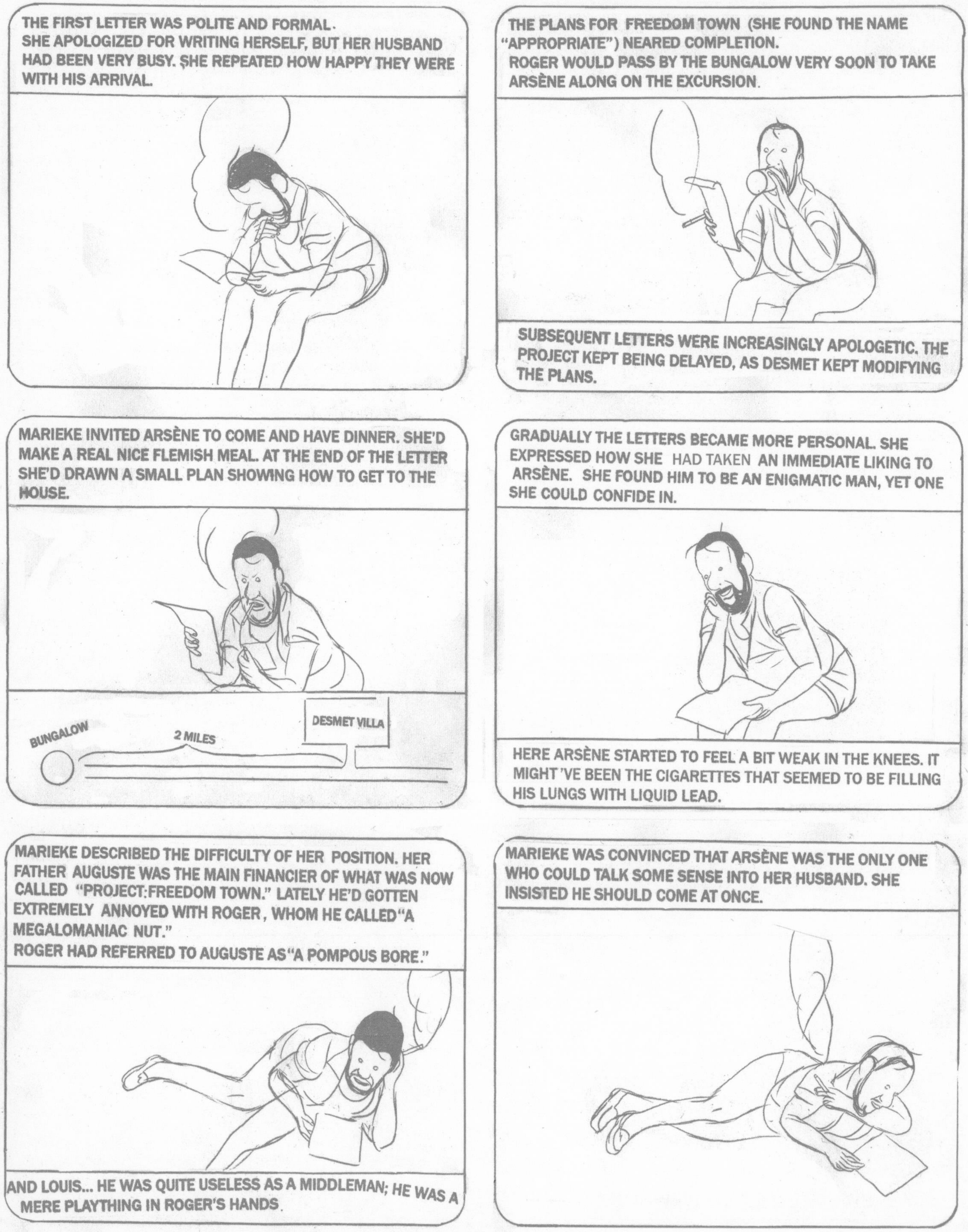
THE FIRST LETTER WAS POLITE AND FORMAL.
SHE APOLOGIZED FOR WRITING HERSELF, BUT HER HUSBAND HAD BEEN VERY BUSY. SHE REPEATED HOW HAPPY THEY WERE WITH HIS ARRIVAL.
THE PLANS FOR FREEDOM TOWN (SHE FOUND THE NAME "APPROPRIATE") NEARED COMPLETION.
ROGER WOULD PASS BY THE BUNGALOW VERY SOON TO TAKE ARSÈNE ALONG ON THE EXCURSION.
SUBSEQUENT LETTERS WERE INCREASINGLY APOLOGETIC. THE PROJECT KEPT BEING DELAYED, AS DESMET KEPT MODIFYING THE PLANS.
MARIEKE INVITED ARSÈNE TO COME AND HAVE DINNER. SHE'D MAKE A REAL NICE FLEMISH MEAL. AT THE END OF THE LETTER SHE'D DRAWN A SMALL PLAN SHOWING HOW TO GET TO THE HOUSE.
BUNGALOW
2 MILES
DESMET VILLA
GRADUALLY THE LETTERS BECAME MORE PERSONAL. SHE EXPRESSED HOW SHE HAD TAKEN AN IMMEDIATE LIKING TO ARSÈNE. SHE FOUND HIM TO BE AN ENIGMATIC MAN, YET ONE SHE COULD CONFIDE IN.
HERE ARSÈNE STARTED TO FEEL A BIT WEAK IN THE KNEES. IT MIGHT'VE BEEN THE CIGARETTES THAT SEEMED TO BE FILLING HIS LUNGS WITH LIQUID LEAD.
MARIEKE DESCRIBED THE DIFFICULTY OF HER POSITION. HER FATHER AUGUSTE WAS THE MAIN FINANCIER OF WHAT WAS NOW CALLED "PROJECT: FREEDOM TOWN." LATELY HE'D GOTTEN EXTREMELY ANNOYED WITH ROGER, WHOM HE CALLED "A MEGALOMANIAC NUT."
ROGER HAD REFERRED TO AUGUSTE AS "A POMPOUS BORE."
AND LOUIS... HE WAS QUITE USELESS AS A MIDDLEMAN; HE WAS A MERE PLAYTHING IN ROGER'S HANDS.
MARIEKE WAS CONVINCED THAT ARSÈNE WAS THE ONLY ONE WHO COULD TALK SOME SENSE INTO HER HUSBAND. SHE INSISTED HE SHOULD COME AT ONCE.

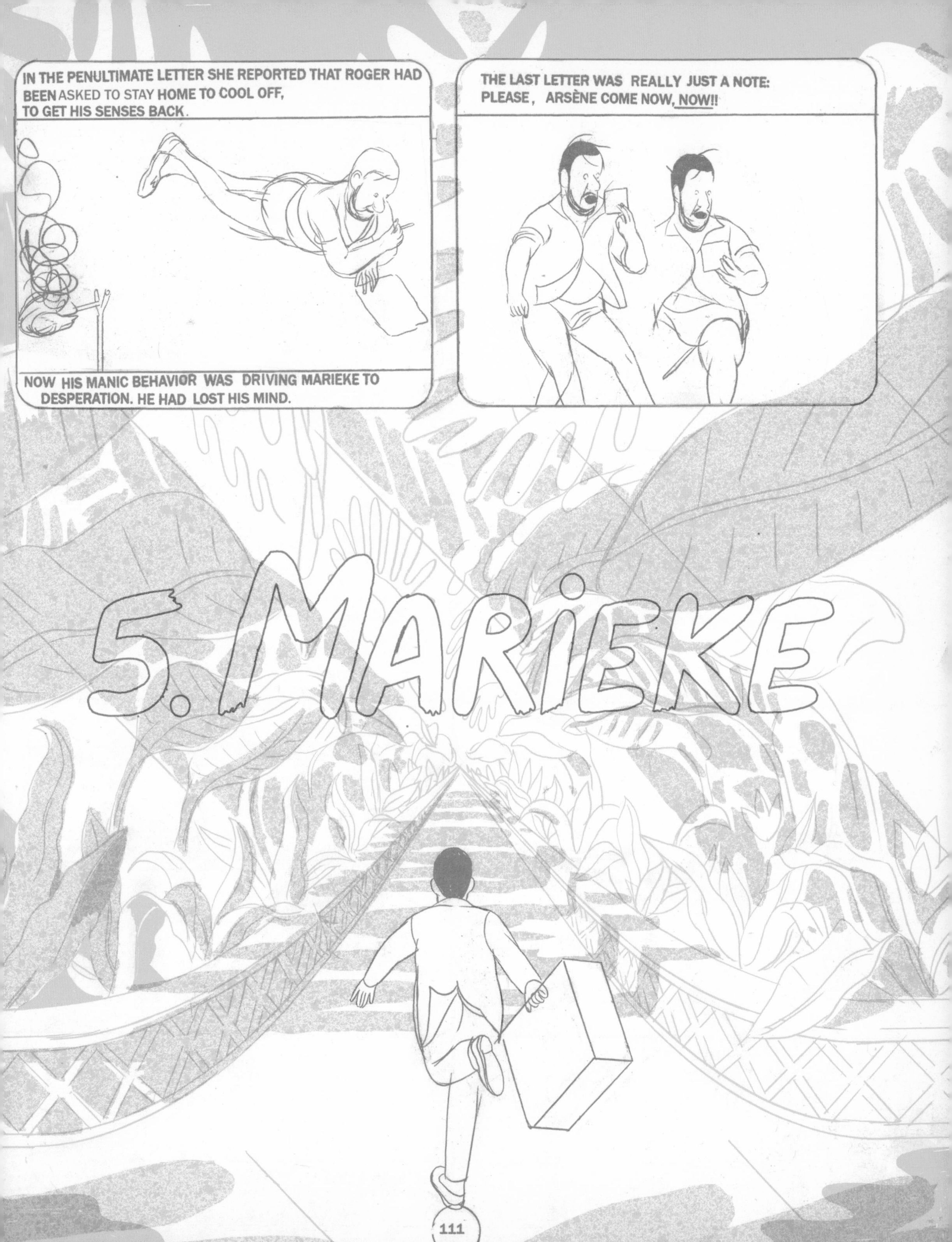
IN THE PENULTIMATE LETTER SHE REPORTED THAT ROGER HAD BEEN ASKED TO STAY HOME TO COOL OFF, TO GET HIS SENSES BACK.
NOW HIS MANIC BEHAVIOR WAS DRIVING MARIEKE TO DESPERATION. HE HAD LOST HIS MIND.
THE LAST LETTER WAS REALLY JUST A NOTE: PLEASE, ARSÈNE COME NOW, NOW!!
5. MARIEKE

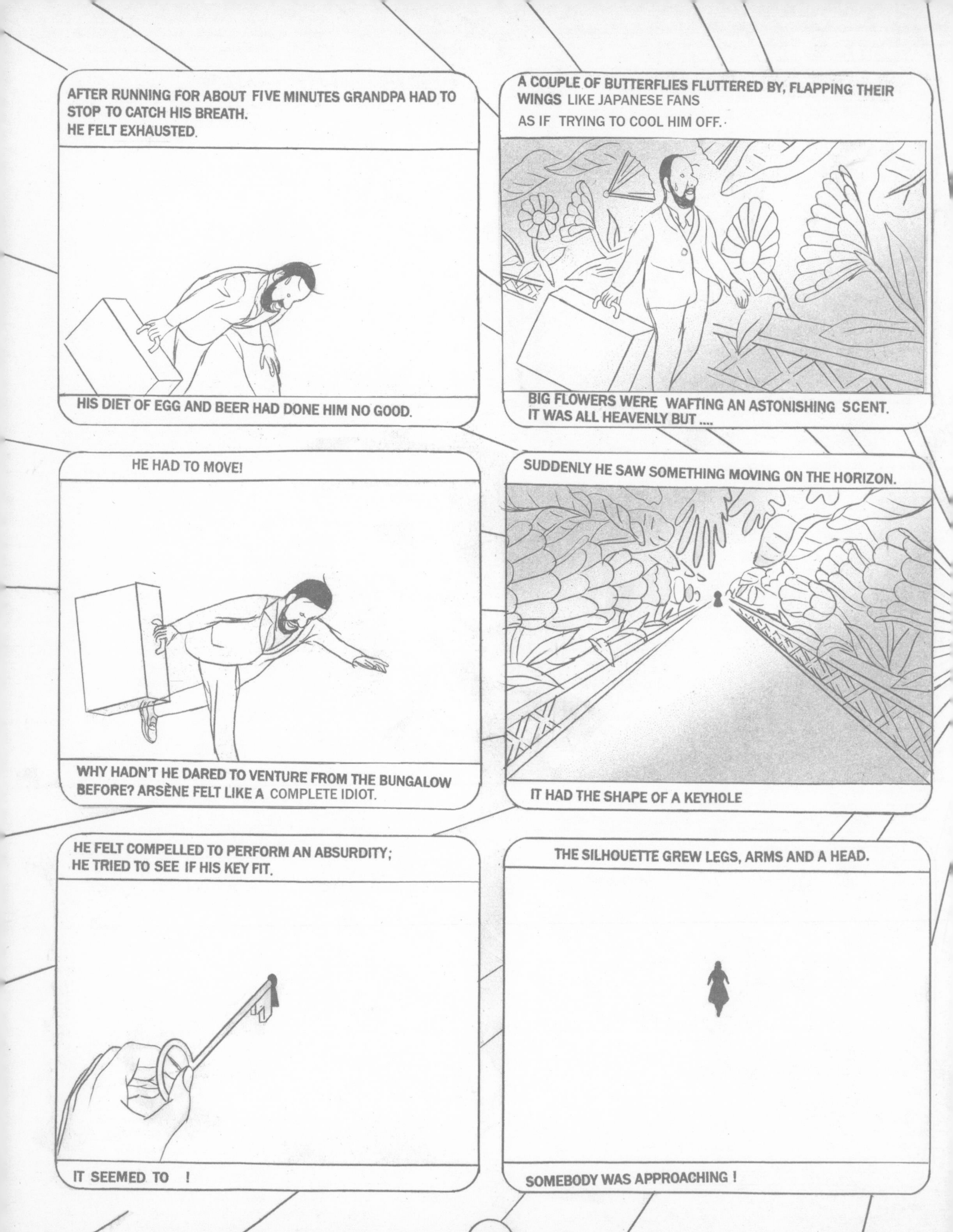
AFTER RUNNING FOR ABOUT FIVE MINUTES GRANDPA HAD TO STOP TO CATCH HIS BREATH.
HE FELT EXHAUSTED.
HIS DIET OF EGG AND BEER HAD DONE HIM NO GOOD.
A COUPLE OF BUTTERFLIES FLUTTERED BY, FLAPPING THEIR WINGS LIKE JAPANESE FANS
AS IF TRYING TO COOL HIM OFF.
BIG FLOWERS WERE WAFTING AN ASTONISHING SCENT.
IT WAS ALL HEAVENLY BUT ....
HE HAD TO MOVE!
WHY HADN'T HE DARED TO VENTURE FROM THE BUNGALOW BEFORE? ARSÈNE FELT LIKE A COMPLETE IDIOT.
SUDDENLY HE SAW SOMETHING MOVING ON THE HORIZON.
IT HAD THE SHAPE OF A KEYHOLE
HE FELT COMPELLED TO PERFORM AN ABSURDITY;
HE TRIED TO SEE IF HIS KEY FIT.
IT SEEMED TO !
THE SILHOUETTE GREW LEGS, ARMS AND A HEAD.
SOMEBODY WAS APPROACHING !

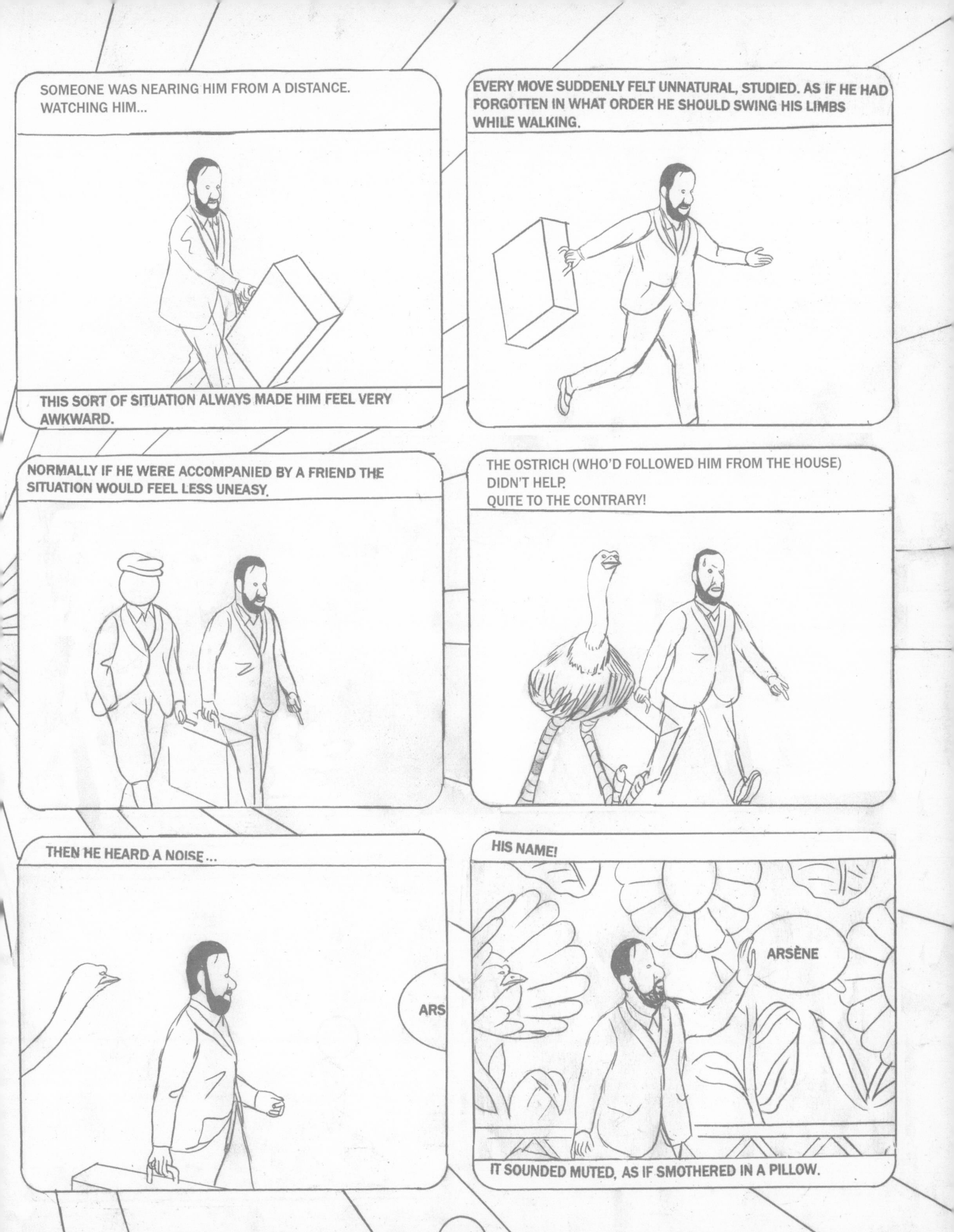
SOMEONE WAS NEARING HIM FROM A DISTANCE. WATCHING HIM...
THIS SORT OF SITUATION ALWAYS MADE HIM FEEL VERY AWKWARD.
EVERY MOVE SUDDENLY FELT UNNATURAL, STUDIED. AS IF HE HAD FORGOTTEN IN WHAT ORDER HE SHOULD SWING HIS LIMBS WHILE WALKING.
NORMALLY IF HE WERE ACCOMPANIED BY A FRIEND THE SITUATION WOULD FEEL LESS UNEASY.
THE OSTRICH (WHO'D FOLLOWED HIM FROM THE HOUSE) DIDN'T HELP. QUITE TO THE CONTRARY!
THEN HE HEARD A NOISE...
ARS
HIS NAME!
ARSÈNE
IT SOUNDED MUTED, AS IF SMOTHERED IN A PILLOW.

"MARIEKE"

THOUGH HE FELT CLOSE TO COLLAPSING, ARSENE STARTED RUNNING

THEIR EMBRACE WAS UNRESTRAINED, WHOLEHEARTED.

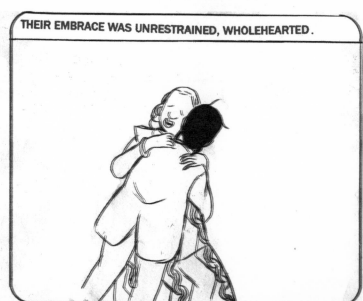

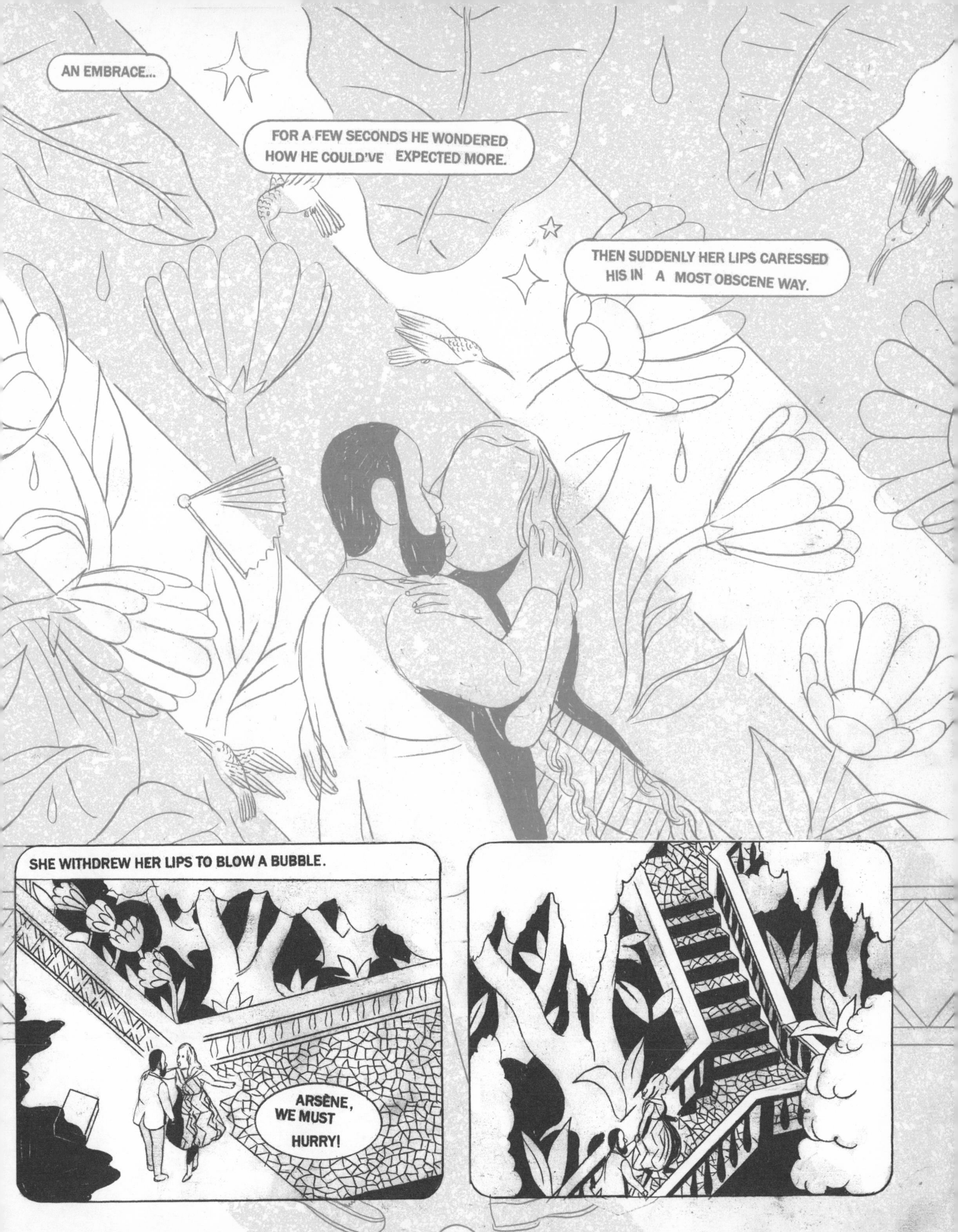

AN EMBRACE...
FOR A FEW SECONDS HE WONDERED HOW HE COULD'VE EXPECTED MORE.
THEN SUDDENLY HER LIPS CARESSED HIS IN A MOST OBSCENE WAY.
SHE WITHDREW HER LIPS TO BLOW A BUBBLE.
ARSÈNE, WE MUST HURRY!

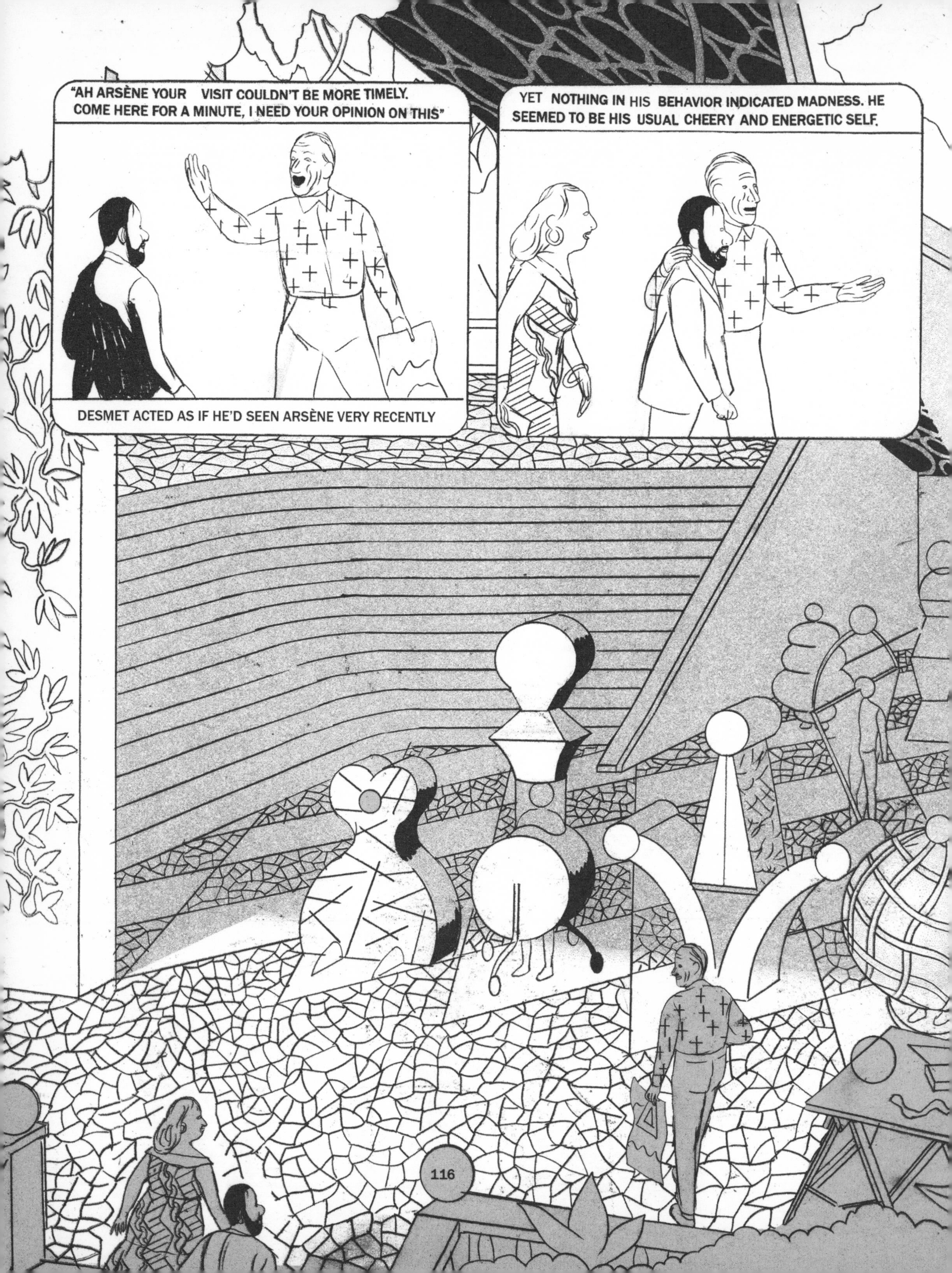
"AH ARSÈNE YOUR VISIT COULDN'T BE MORE TIMELY. COME HERE FOR A MINUTE, I NEED YOUR OPINION ON THIS"
DESMET ACTED AS IF HE'D SEEN ARSÈNE VERY RECENTLY
YET NOTHING IN HIS BEHAVIOR INDICATED MADNESS. HE SEEMED TO BE HIS USUAL CHEERY AND ENERGETIC SELF.

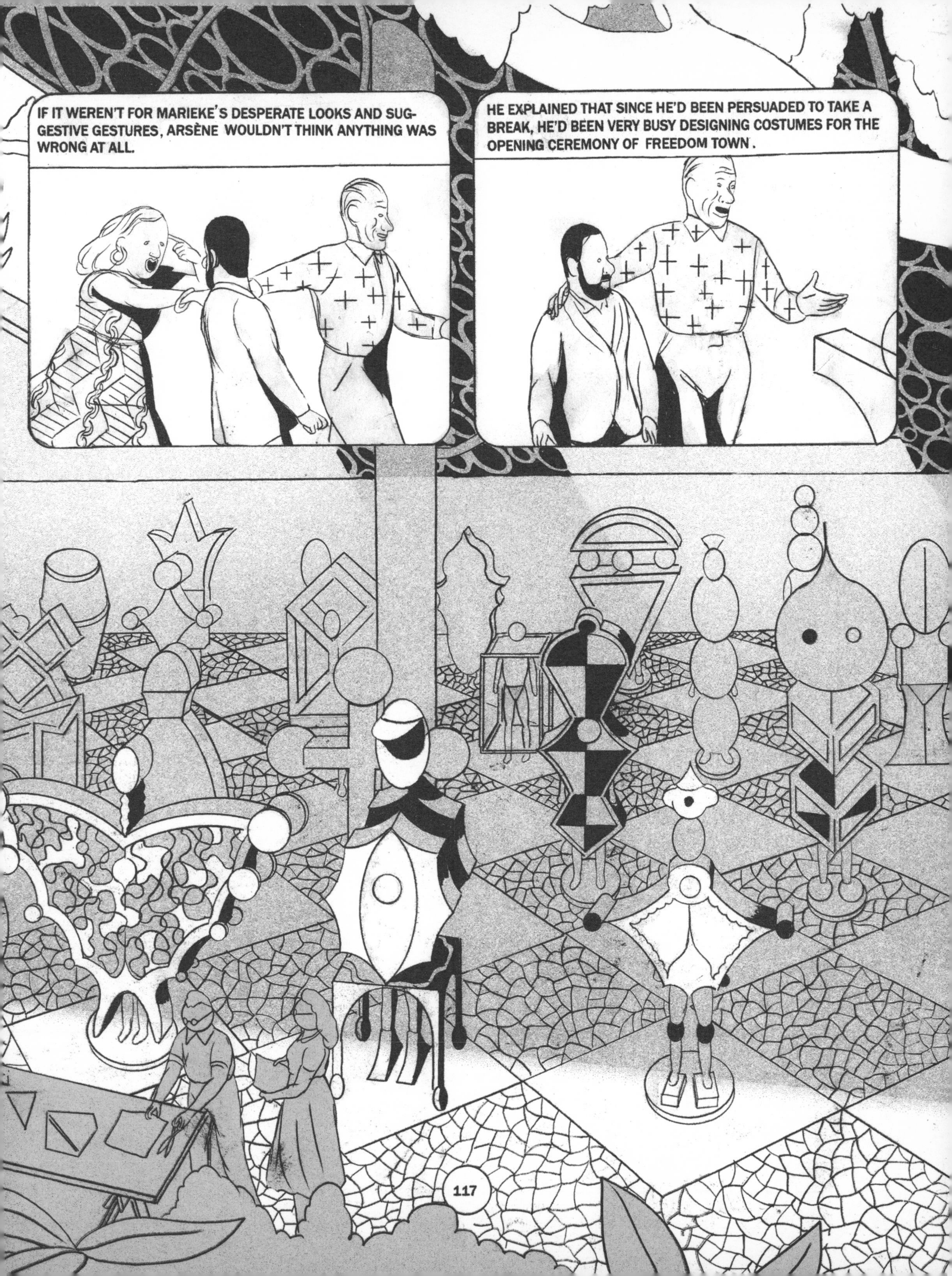
IF IT WEREN'T FOR MARIEKE'S DESPERATE LOOKS AND SUGGESTIVE GESTURES, ARSÈNE WOULDN'T THINK ANYTHING WAS WRONG AT ALL.
HE EXPLAINED THAT SINCE HE'D BEEN PERSUADED TO TAKE A BREAK, HE'D BEEN VERY BUSY DESIGNING COSTUMES FOR THE OPENING CEREMONY OF FREEDOM TOWN.

ROGER GUIDED GRANDPA ALONG A ROW OF FUNNY LOOKING COSTUMES.

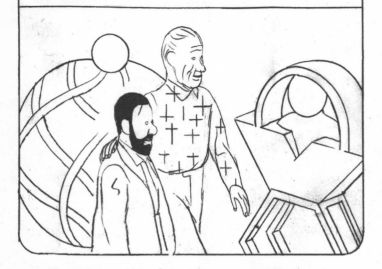

SUDDENLY HE TURNED TO ARSÈNE, LOOKING AS IF HE'D JUST BEEN FED A SPOONFUL OF COD LIVER OIL.

"MY GOD ARSÈNE, I HOPE YOU WEREN'T TOO BORED IN THAT BUNGALOW?!"
"HAS THE BOY TAKEN GOOD CARE OF YOU?"

THE QUESTIONS WERE RHETORICAL; BEFORE ARSÈNE COULD COME UP WITH AN ANSWER, ROGER COMPLEMENTED GRANDPA ON HIS BEARD AND TURNED HIS ATTENTION BACK TO THE COSTUMES.

ARSÈNE, YOU'RE A MAN OF TASTE; GIVE ME YOUR UNCENSORED OPINION...

"I FEEL THERE'S SOMETHING MISSING, A CERTAIN 'JE NE SAIS QUOI', A CERTAIN..."

"THAT'S AN EXCELLENT IDEA."

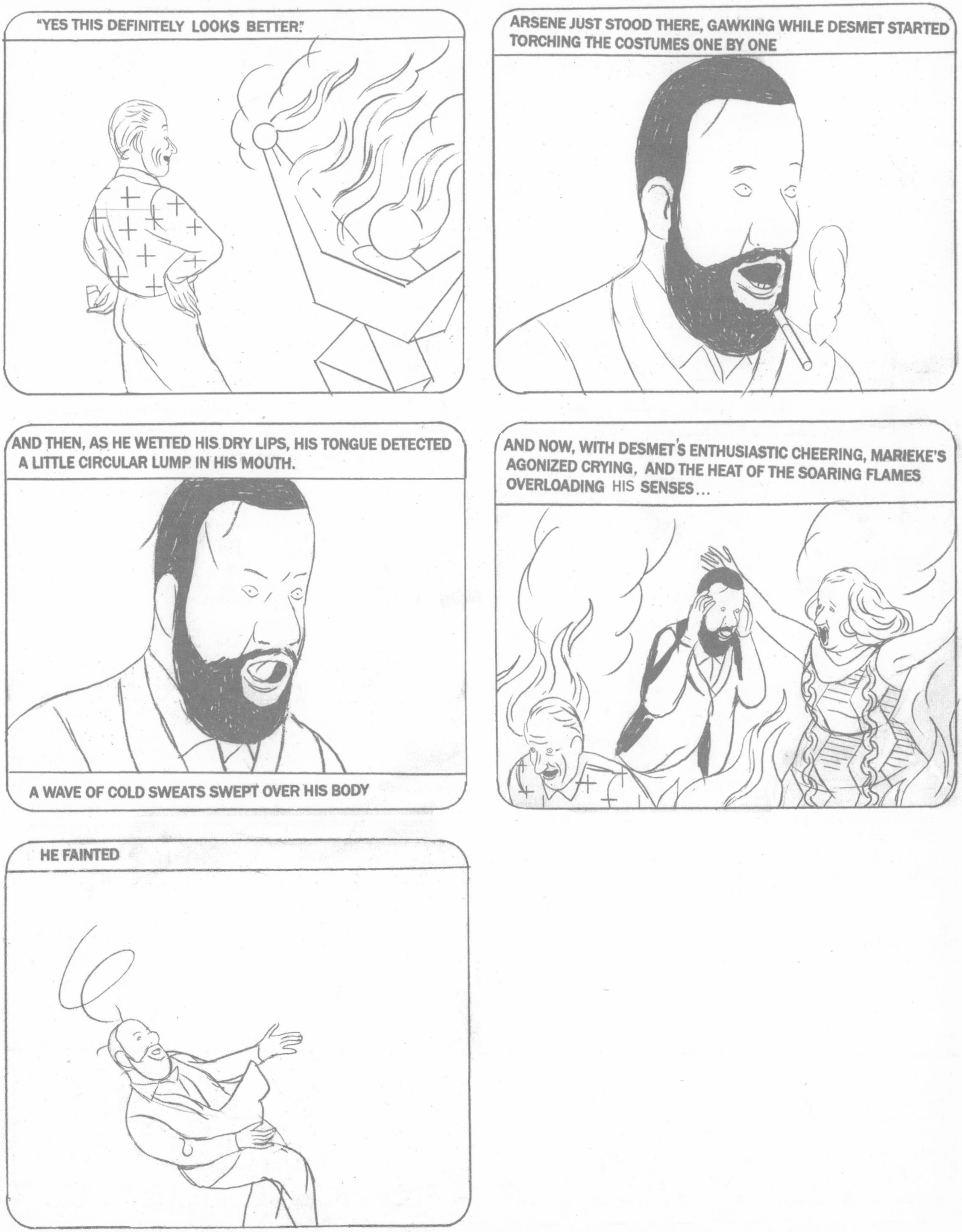
"YES THIS DEFINITELY LOOKS BETTER."
ARSENE JUST STOOD THERE, GAWKING WHILE DESMET STARTED TORCHING THE COSTUMES ONE BY ONE
AND THEN, AS HE WETTED HIS DRY LIPS, HIS TONGUE DETECTED A LITTLE CIRCULAR LUMP IN HIS MOUTH.
A WAVE OF COLD SWEATS SWEPT OVER HIS BODY
AND NOW, WITH DESMET'S ENTHUSIASTIC CHEERING, MARIEKE'S AGONIZED CRYING, AND THE HEAT OF THE SOARING FLAMES OVERLOADING HIS SENSES...
HE FAINTED

WHEN HE WOKE UP, HE WAS NO LONGER IN HELL

...OR AT LEAST NO LONGER IN DESMET'S HOUSE.

HE SEEMED TO BE IN SOME KIND OF PALACE.

LIGHT BOUNCED OFF THE MARBLE FLOORS AND WALLS OF THE ROOM. IT SEEMED TO BE EARLY MORNING

HE WAS IN A LARGE BED, BUTT-NAKED.

HIS MOUTH WAS NOW FULL OF LITTLE BUMPS, IT FELT LIKE THE INSIDE OF A POMEGRANATE.

THE SHEETS FELT COOL AND CLEAN ON HIS SKIN. AS HE TRIED TO PULL THEM OVER HIS CHEST, HE FELT SOMETHING WEIGHING DOWN ON THEM.

IT WAS THE PLUMP BODY OF MARIEKE SLEEPING AT THE EDGE OF THE BED.

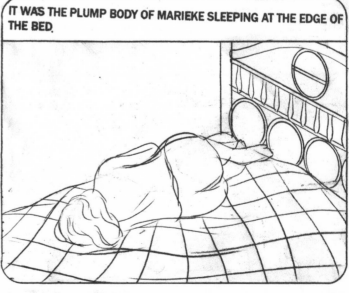

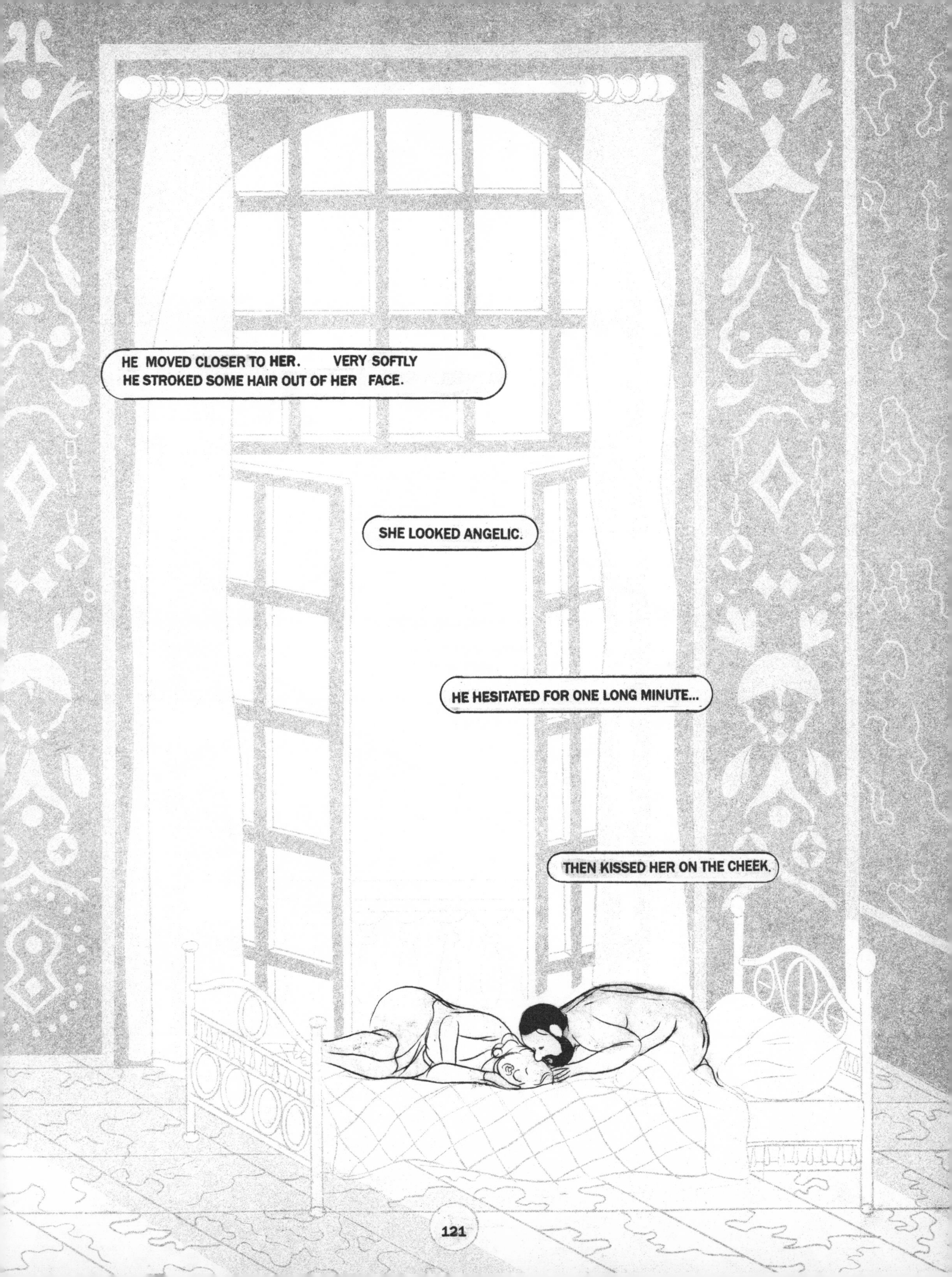
HE MOVED CLOSER TO HER. VERY SOFTLY HE STROKED SOME HAIR OUT OF HER FACE.
SHE LOOKED ANGELIC.
HE HESITATED FOR ONE LONG MINUTE...
THEN KISSED HER ON THE CHEEK.

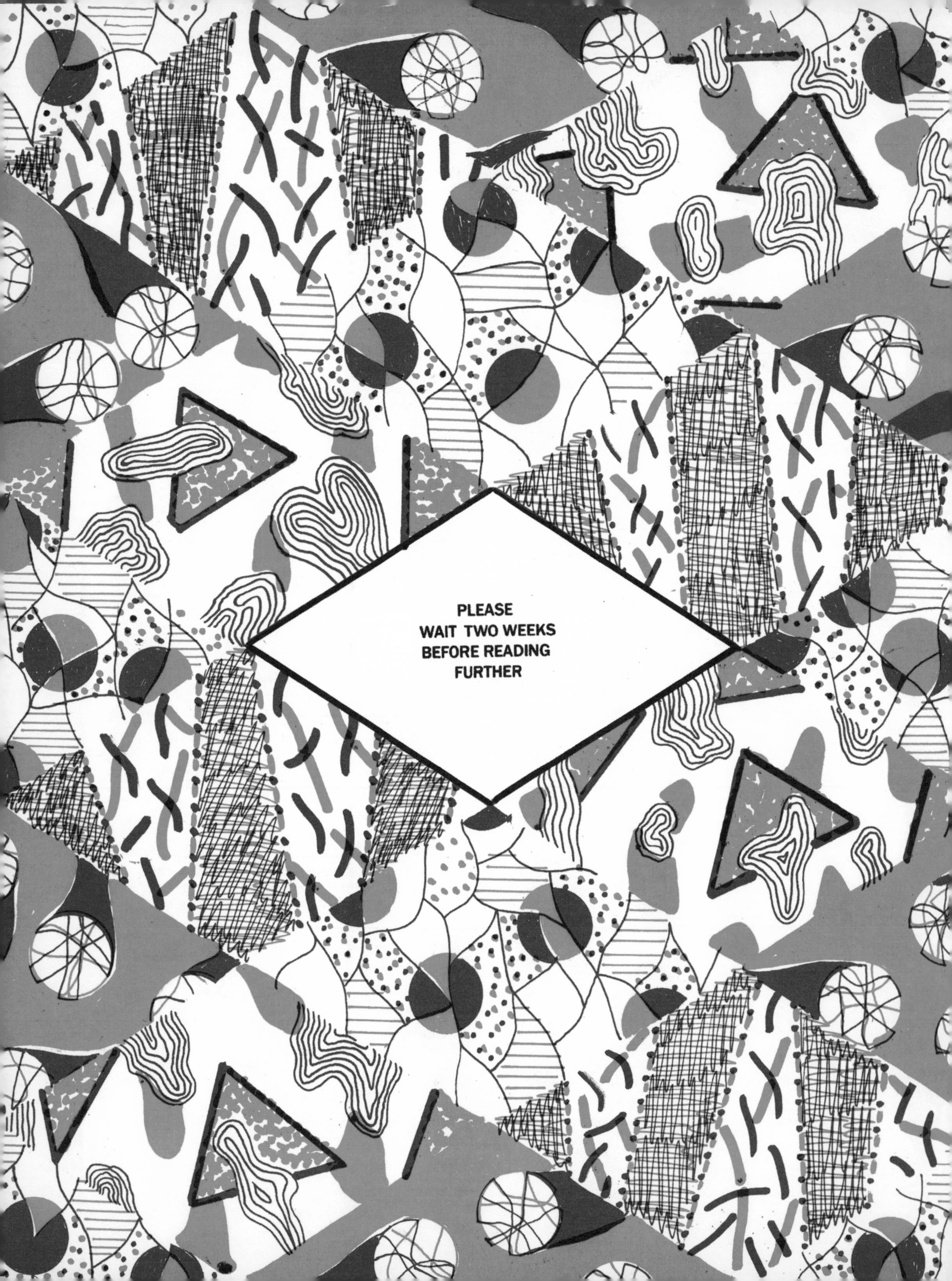
PLEASE
WAIT TWO WEEKS
BEFORE READING
FURTHER

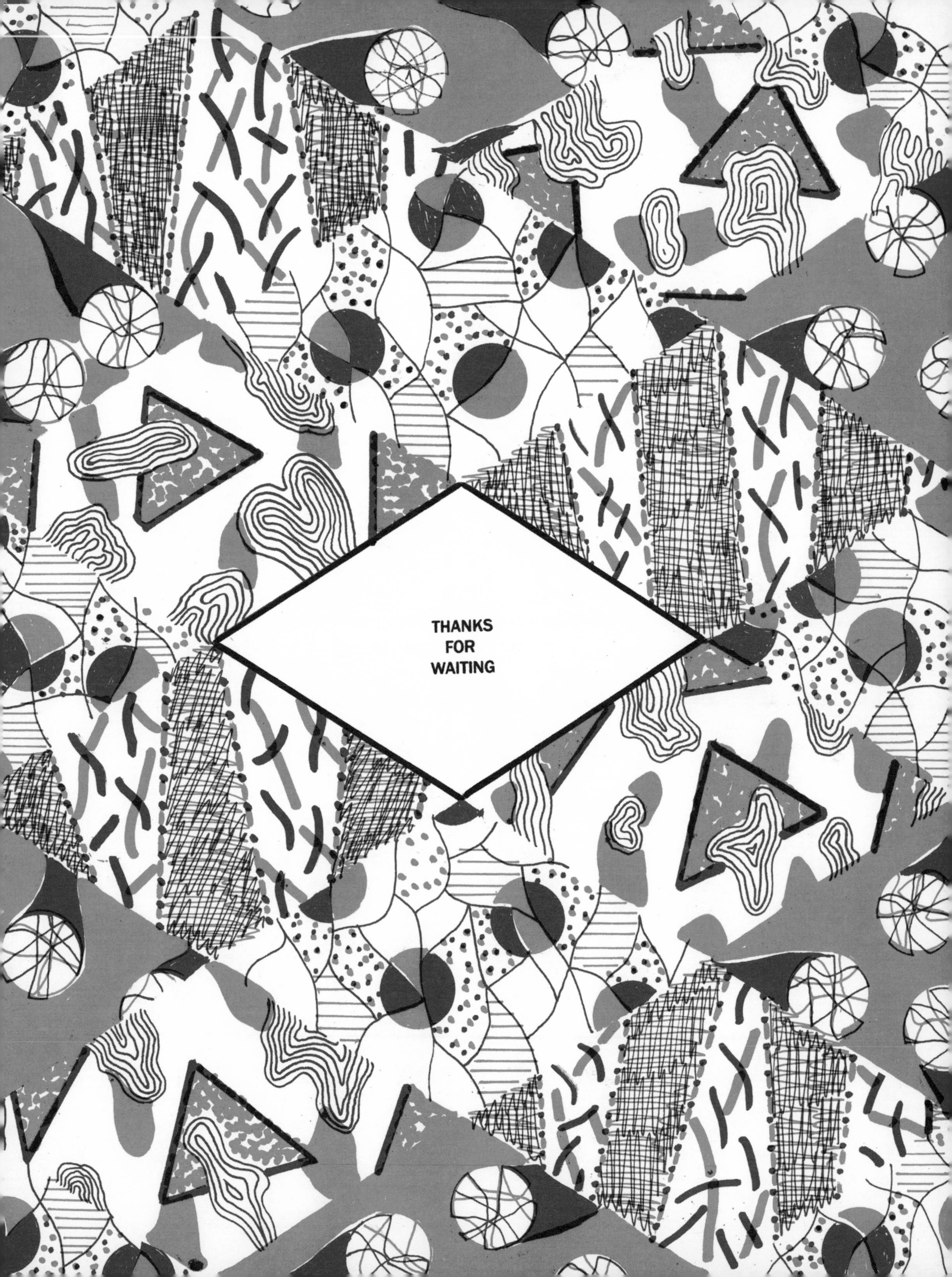
THANKS
FOR
WAITING

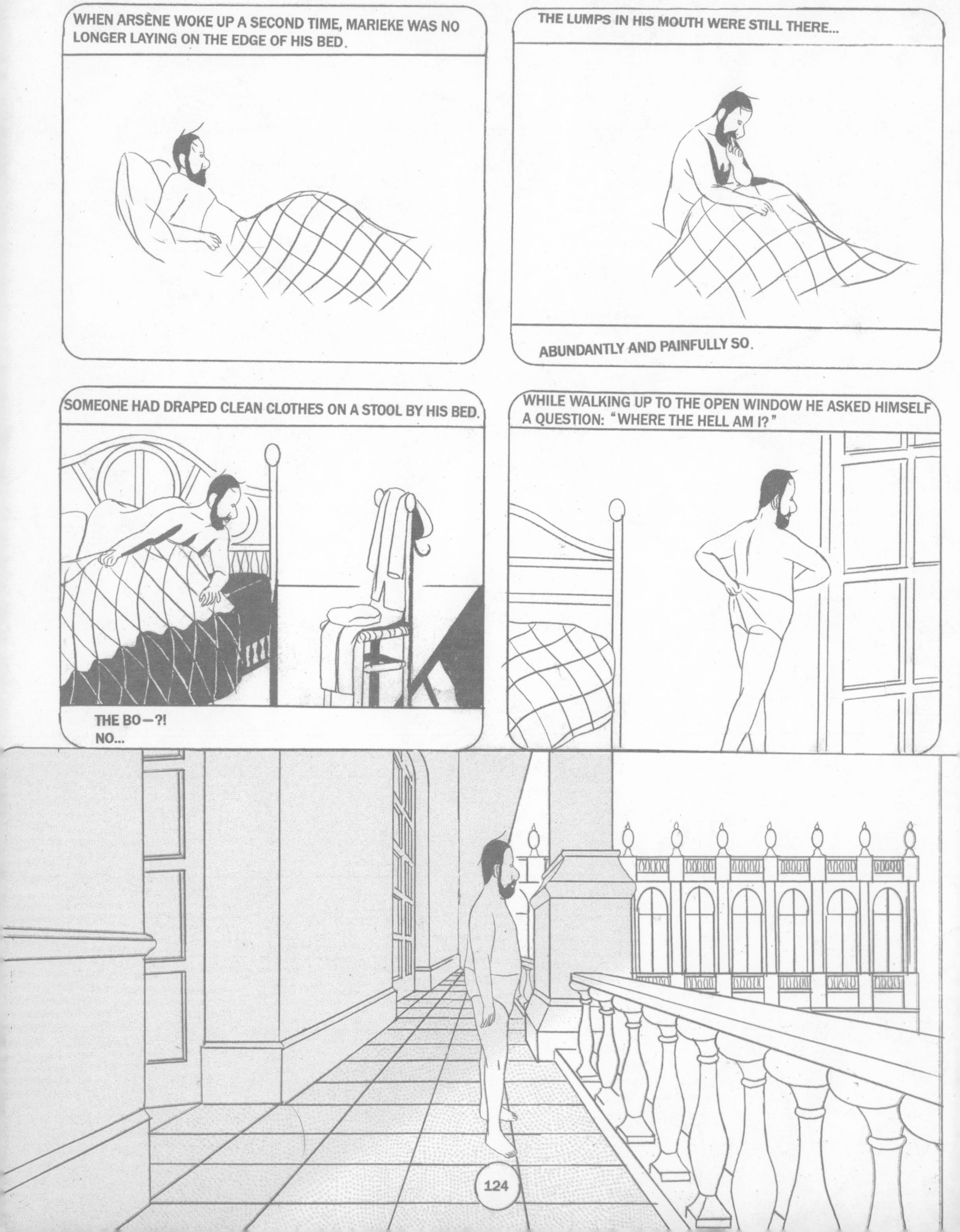
WHEN ARSÈNE WOKE UP A SECOND TIME, MARIEKE WAS NO LONGER LAYING ON THE EDGE OF HIS BED.
THE LUMPS IN HIS MOUTH WERE STILL THERE...
ABUNDANTLY AND PAINFULLY SO.
SOMEONE HAD DRAPED CLEAN CLOTHES ON A STOOL BY HIS BED.
THE BO—?!
NO...
WHILE WALKING UP TO THE OPEN WINDOW HE ASKED HIMSELF A QUESTION: "WHERE THE HELL AM I?"

"WELL..."

SINCE HIS BODY WAS ALREADY FESTERING WITH ELEPHANTWORMS...

CAN I COME IN?

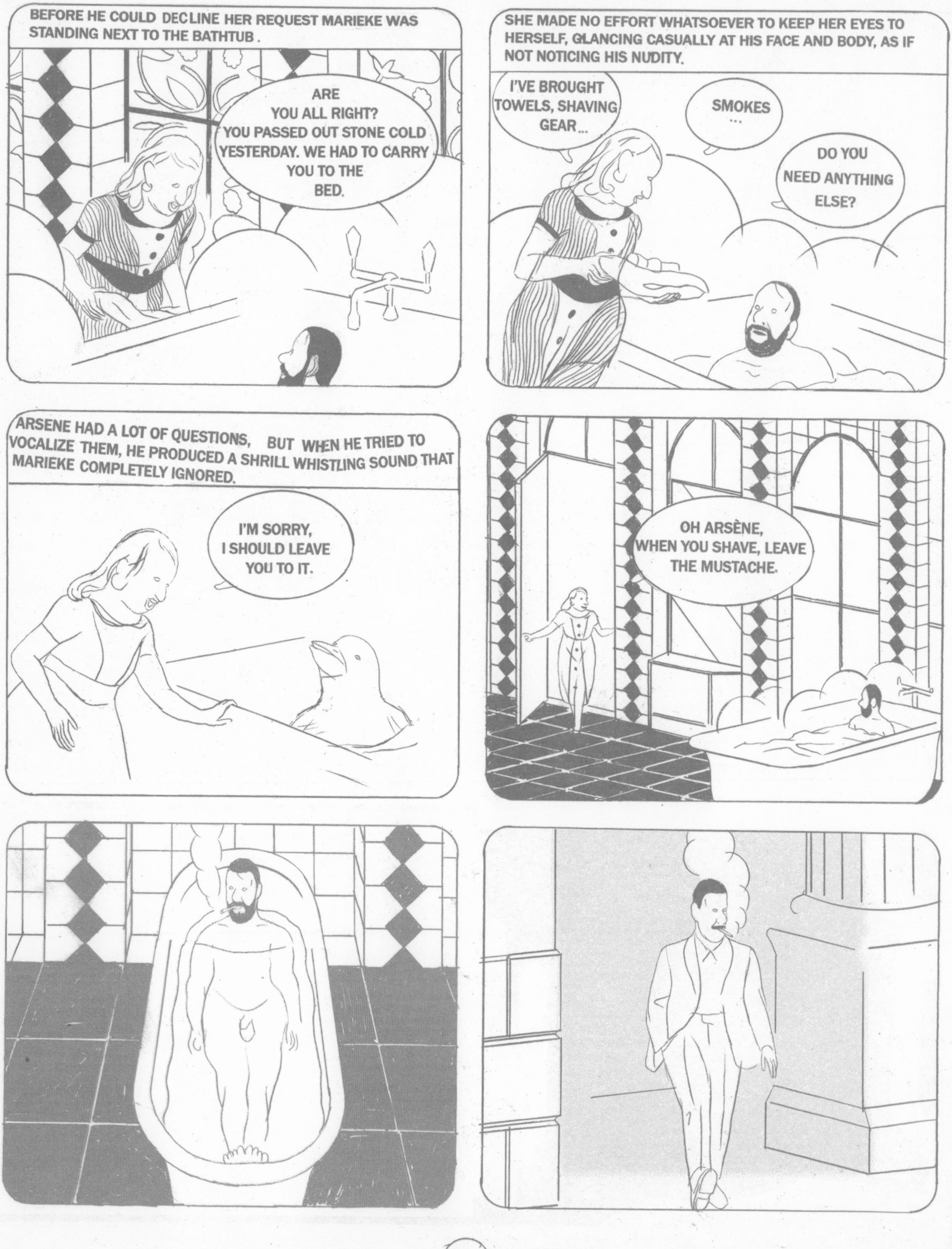
BEFORE HE COULD DECLINE HER REQUEST MARIEKE WAS STANDING NEXT TO THE BATHTUB.
ARE YOU ALL RIGHT? YOU PASSED OUT STONE COLD YESTERDAY. WE HAD TO CARRY YOU TO THE BED.
SHE MADE NO EFFORT WHATSOEVER TO KEEP HER EYES TO HERSELF, GLANCING CASUALLY AT HIS FACE AND BODY, AS IF NOT NOTICING HIS NUDITY.
I'VE BROUGHT TOWELS, SHAVING GEAR...
SMOKES ...
DO YOU NEED ANYTHING ELSE?
ARSENE HAD A LOT OF QUESTIONS, BUT WHEN HE TRIED TO VOCALIZE THEM, HE PRODUCED A SHRILL WHISTLING SOUND THAT MARIEKE COMPLETELY IGNORED.
I'M SORRY, I SHOULD LEAVE YOU TO IT.
OH ARSÈNE, WHEN YOU SHAVE, LEAVE THE MUSTACHE.

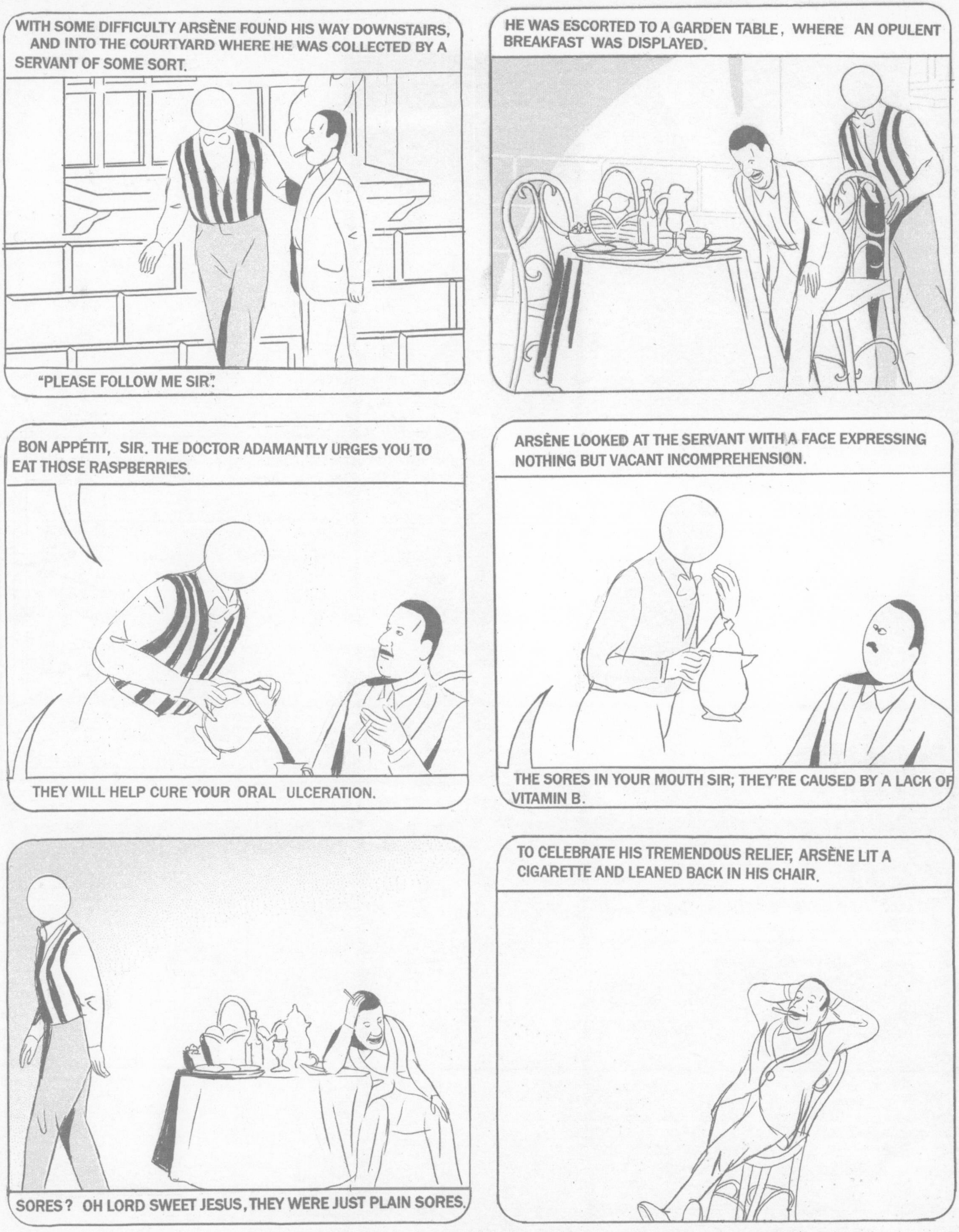
WITH SOME DIFFICULTY ARSÈNE FOUND HIS WAY DOWNSTAIRS, AND INTO THE COURTYARD WHERE HE WAS COLLECTED BY A SERVANT OF SOME SORT.
"PLEASE FOLLOW ME SIR".
HE WAS ESCORTED TO A GARDEN TABLE, WHERE AN OPULENT BREAKFAST WAS DISPLAYED.
BON APPÉTIT, SIR. THE DOCTOR ADAMANTLY URGES YOU TO EAT THOSE RASPBERRIES.
THEY WILL HELP CURE YOUR ORAL ULCERATION.
ARSÈNE LOOKED AT THE SERVANT WITH A FACE EXPRESSING NOTHING BUT VACANT INCOMPREHENSION.
THE SORES IN YOUR MOUTH SIR; THEY'RE CAUSED BY A LACK OF VITAMIN B.
SORES? OH LORD SWEET JESUS, THEY WERE JUST PLAIN SORES.
TO CELEBRATE HIS TREMENDOUS RELIEF, ARSÈNE LIT A CIGARETTE AND LEANED BACK IN HIS CHAIR.

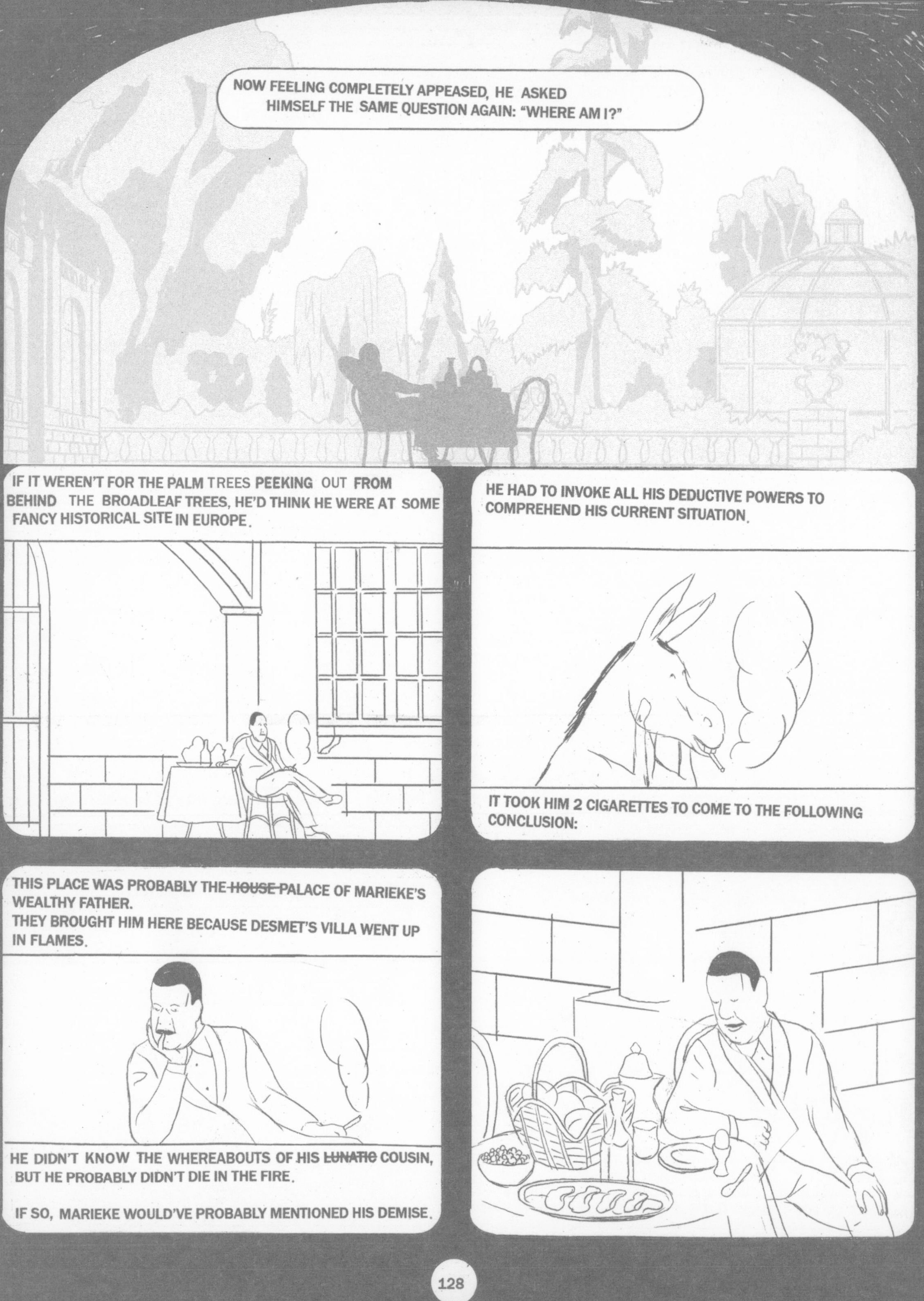
NOW FEELING COMPLETELY APPEASED, HE ASKED HIMSELF THE SAME QUESTION AGAIN: "WHERE AM I?"
IF IT WEREN'T FOR THE PALM TREES PEEKING OUT FROM BEHIND THE BROADLEAF TREES, HE'D THINK HE WERE AT SOME FANCY HISTORICAL SITE IN EUROPE.
HE HAD TO INVOKE ALL HIS DEDUCTIVE POWERS TO COMPREHEND HIS CURRENT SITUATION.
IT TOOK HIM 2 CIGARETTES TO COME TO THE FOLLOWING CONCLUSION:
THIS PLACE WAS PROBABLY THE ~~HOUSE~~ PALACE OF MARIEKE'S WEALTHY FATHER.
THEY BROUGHT HIM HERE BECAUSE DESMET'S VILLA WENT UP IN FLAMES.
HE DIDN'T KNOW THE WHEREABOUTS OF HIS ~~LUNATIC~~ COUSIN, BUT HE PROBABLY DIDN'T DIE IN THE FIRE.
IF SO, MARIEKE WOULD'VE PROBABLY MENTIONED HIS DEMISE.

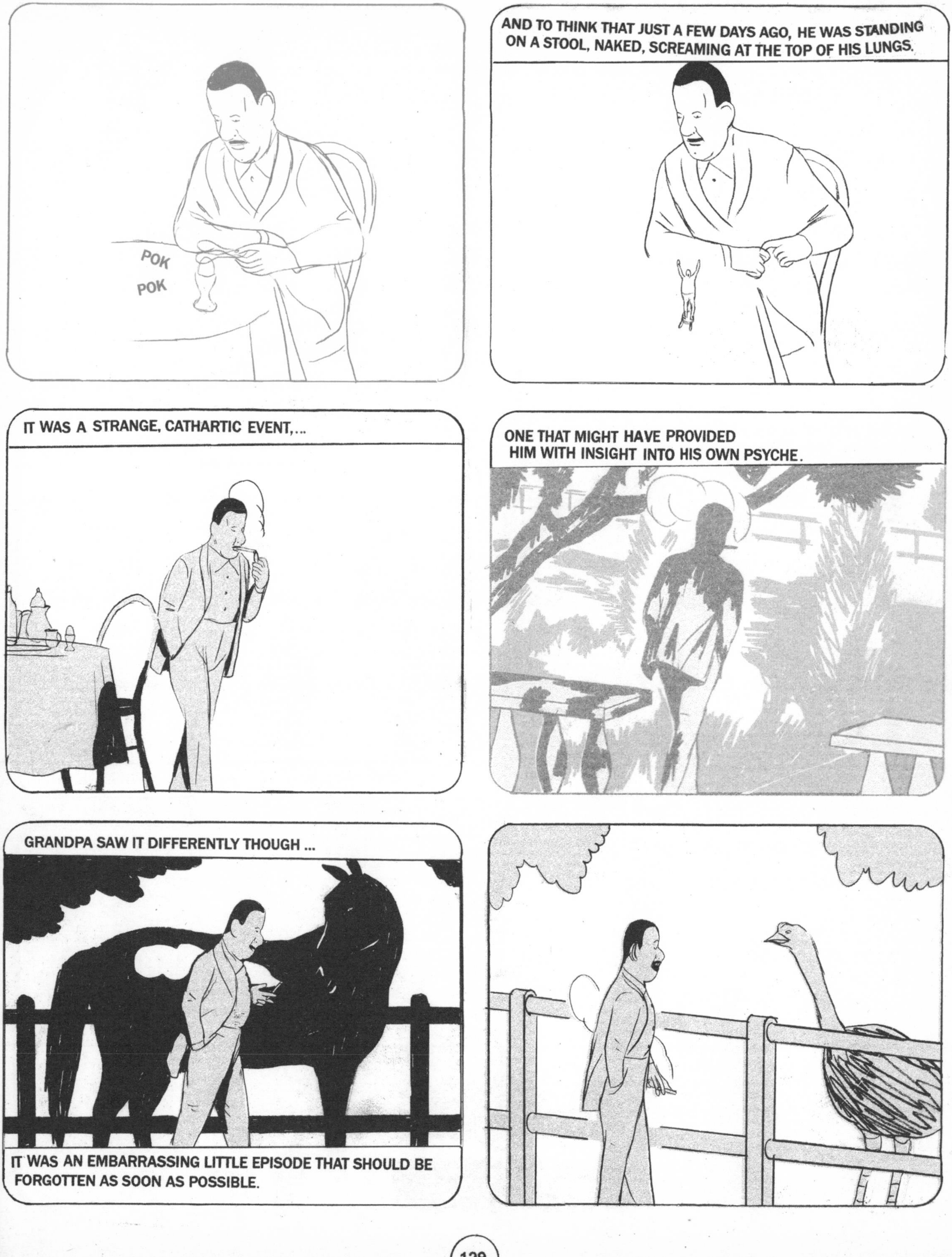
POK
POK
AND TO THINK THAT JUST A FEW DAYS AGO, HE WAS STANDING ON A STOOL, NAKED, SCREAMING AT THE TOP OF HIS LUNGS.
IT WAS A STRANGE, CATHARTIC EVENT,...
ONE THAT MIGHT HAVE PROVIDED HIM WITH INSIGHT INTO HIS OWN PSYCHE.
GRANDPA SAW IT DIFFERENTLY THOUGH ...
IT WAS AN EMBARRASSING LITTLE EPISODE THAT SHOULD BE FORGOTTEN AS SOON AS POSSIBLE.

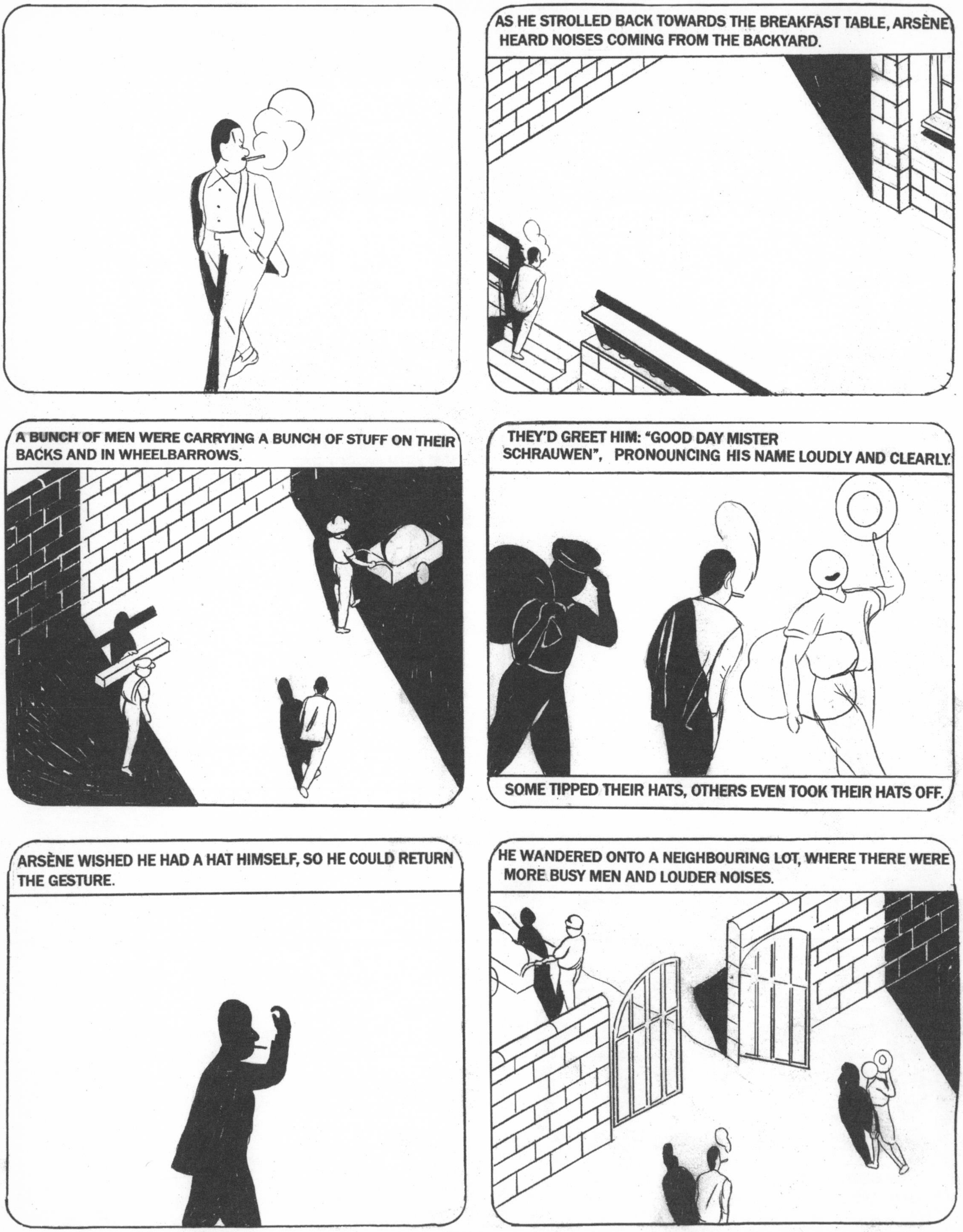

AS HE STROLLED BACK TOWARDS THE BREAKFAST TABLE, ARSÈNE HEARD NOISES COMING FROM THE BACKYARD.
A BUNCH OF MEN WERE CARRYING A BUNCH OF STUFF ON THEIR BACKS AND IN WHEELBARROWS.
THEY'D GREET HIM: "GOOD DAY MISTER SCHRAUWEN", PRONOUNCING HIS NAME LOUDLY AND CLEARLY.
SOME TIPPED THEIR HATS, OTHERS EVEN TOOK THEIR HATS OFF.
ARSÈNE WISHED HE HAD A HAT HIMSELF, SO HE COULD RETURN THE GESTURE.
HE WANDERED ONTO A NEIGHBOURING LOT, WHERE THERE WERE MORE BUSY MEN AND LOUDER NOISES.

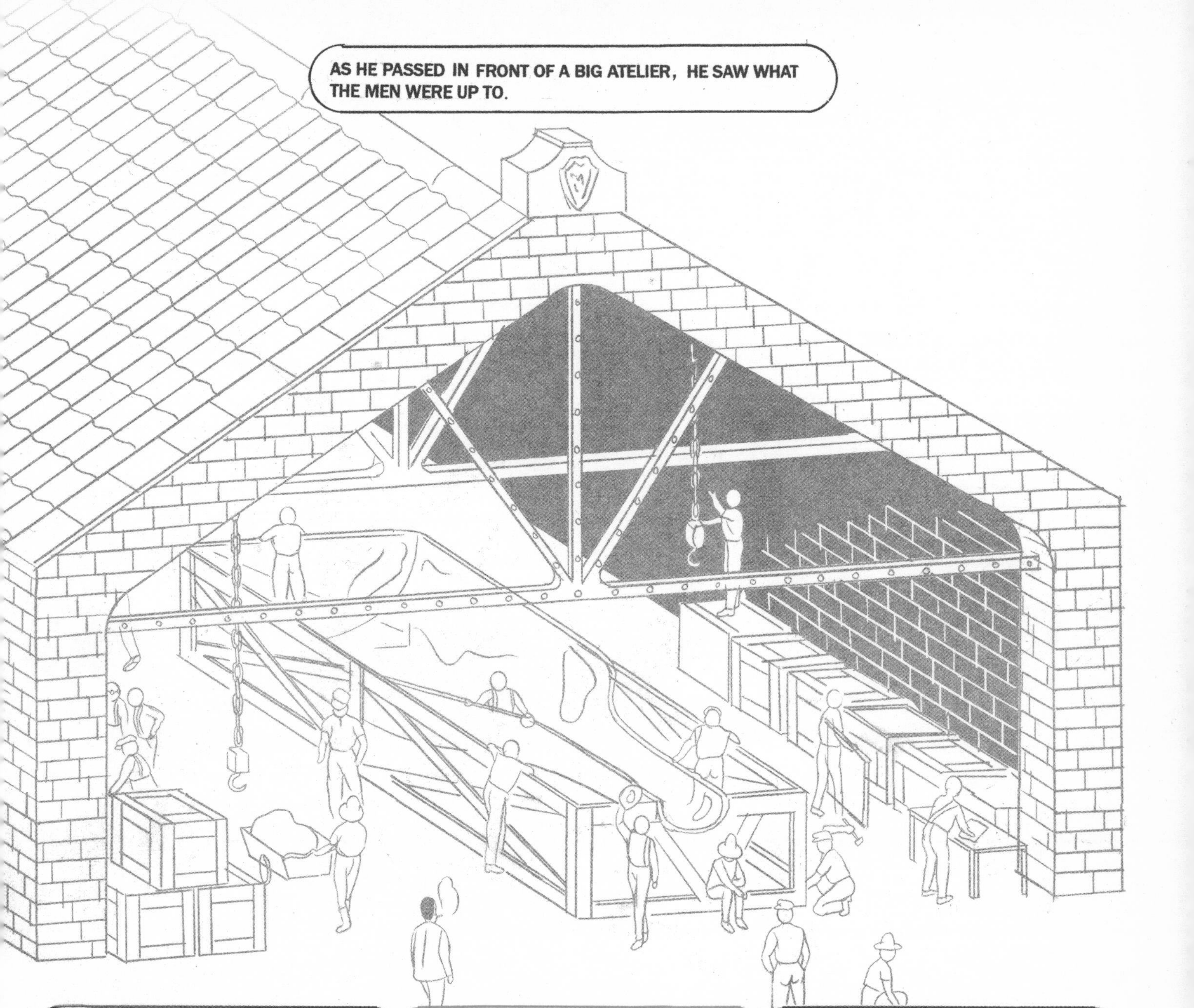
AS HE PASSED IN FRONT OF A BIG ATELIER, HE SAW WHAT THE MEN WERE UP TO.

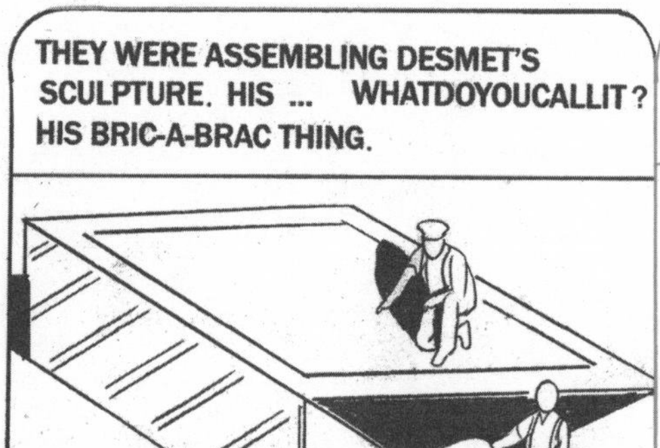
THEY WERE ASSEMBLING DESMET'S SCULPTURE. HIS ... WHATDOYOUCALLIT? HIS BRIC-A-BRAC THING.

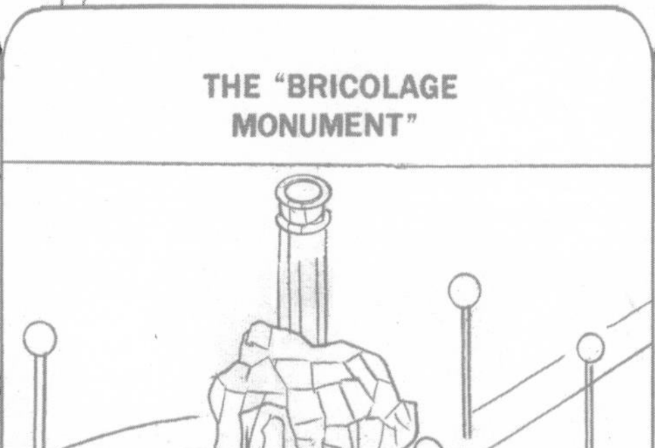
THE "BRICOLAGE MONUMENT"

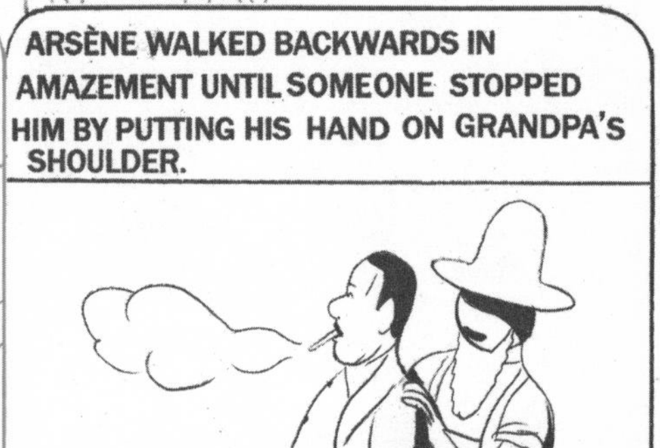
ARSÈNE WALKED BACKWARDS IN AMAZEMENT UNTIL SOMEONE STOPPED HIM BY PUTTING HIS HAND ON GRANDPA'S SHOULDER.
"WATCH YOUR STEP MISTER SCHRAUWEN."

ARSÈNE WANTED TO REMOVE HIMSELF FROM THE MAN, BUT HE WAS KEPT IN PLACE BY A WRENCH-LIKE GRIP.

GRANDPA DID NOT DARE LOOK THE MAN IN THE EYES; INSTEAD, HE LOOKED AT HIS LIPLESS MOUTH.

SIR, WE'RE SO HAPPY A WISE AND STEADFAST MAN SUCH AS YOURSELF IS OVERTAKING THIS OPERATION.

A ROTTEN BREATH EMANATED FROM IN BETWEEN HIS SPARSE TEETH, LIKE FUMES FROM A SEWER.

WITH ALL DUE RESPECT SIR, BUT MOST MEN HERE DEEM YOUR COUSIN CRAZY IN THE COCONUT.

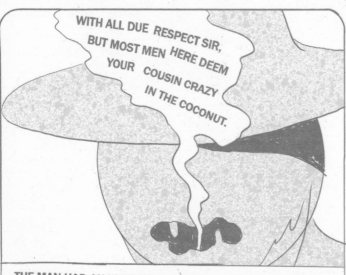

THE MAN HAD AN UNSTEADY VOICE; HIS WORDS DRIFTING LIKE LETTERS ON SOUP.

AND LORD BEHOLD WE CAN'T HAVE HIS MISSES BOSSING US AROUND! NO SIR, WE'RE VERY HAPPY TO HAVE A LEVEL-HEADED MAN HANDLING THE BUSINESS.

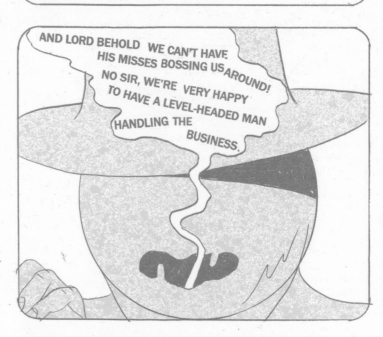

IT'S GOOD TO KNOW THAT WE'RE NOT JUST WASTING OUR TIME HERE, IN THIS MISERABLE FUCKING HELLHOLE.

DO EXCUSE MY GUTTERMOUTH SIR, I DON'T WANT TO OFFEND YOUR DELICATE SENSIBILITIES.

WHEN THE MAN FINALLY LOOSENED HIS GRIP, ARSÈNE WALKED AWAY FROM HIM WITH AN URGENT STEP.

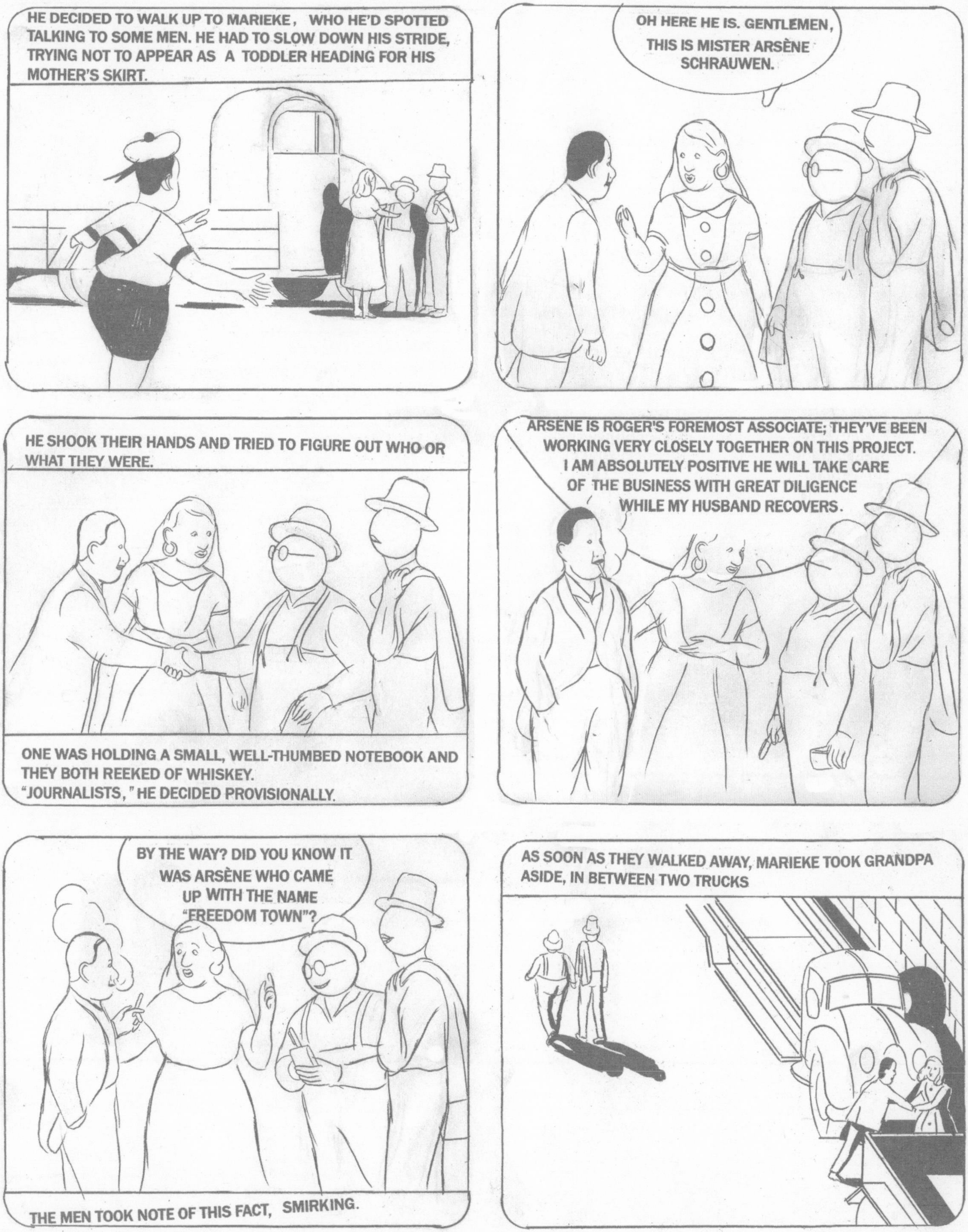
HE DECIDED TO WALK UP TO MARIEKE, WHO HE'D SPOTTED TALKING TO SOME MEN. HE HAD TO SLOW DOWN HIS STRIDE, TRYING NOT TO APPEAR AS A TODDLER HEADING FOR HIS MOTHER'S SKIRT.
OH HERE HE IS. GENTLEMEN, THIS IS MISTER ARSÈNE SCHRAUWEN.
HE SHOOK THEIR HANDS AND TRIED TO FIGURE OUT WHO OR WHAT THEY WERE.
ONE WAS HOLDING A SMALL, WELL-THUMBED NOTEBOOK AND THEY BOTH REEKED OF WHISKEY.
"JOURNALISTS," HE DECIDED PROVISIONALLY.
ARSÈNE IS ROGER'S FOREMOST ASSOCIATE; THEY'VE BEEN WORKING VERY CLOSELY TOGETHER ON THIS PROJECT. I AM ABSOLUTELY POSITIVE HE WILL TAKE CARE OF THE BUSINESS WITH GREAT DILIGENCE WHILE MY HUSBAND RECOVERS.
BY THE WAY? DID YOU KNOW IT WAS ARSÈNE WHO CAME UP WITH THE NAME "FREEDOM TOWN"?
THE MEN TOOK NOTE OF THIS FACT, SMIRKING.
AS SOON AS THEY WALKED AWAY, MARIEKE TOOK GRANDPA ASIDE, IN BETWEEN TWO TRUCKS

I'M SORRY TO THROW YOU IN HOT WATER LIKE THIS, ARSÈNE. I OWE YOU AN EXPLANATION.

ARSÈNE HAD HIS BACK AGAINST THE WALL NOW, AND AS SHE STARTED TALKING, HE FELT HER CHEST PUMPING ON HIS.

SHE EXPLAINED HOW AFTER ROGER'S MELTDOWN, HIS FIT OF ACUTE PYROMANIA OR WHATEVER IT WAS THAT MADE HIM BURN DOWN THE ENTIRE NORTH WING OF THEIR VILLA, HE'D BEEN COLLECTED BY LOCAL LAW ENFORCEMENT AND BROUGHT TO THE CLINIC.

HIS CONVALESCENCE THERE WAS OF THE HIGHEST PRIORITY, AND MARIEKE WAS SURE THAT ROGER WOULD BE BACK IN THE SADDLE IN NO TIME.

IN THE MEANTIME THE MACHINERY OF "PROJECT: FREEDOM TOWN" HAD BEEN SET IN MOTION AND THERE WAS NO WAY TO SLOW OR HALT THIS TITANIC UNDERTAKING NOW.

IT SEEMED MOST CONVENIENT THAT, FOR THE TIME BEING, ARSÈNE WOULD ASSUME LEADERSHIP, ALBEIT MOSTLY PRO FORMA.

IN ANY CASE, HE OUGHT NOT TO UTTER A SINGLE WORD ABOUT THE TROUBLES HAUNTING THE PROJECT TO ANYONE. HE SHOULD KEEP HIS LIPS SEALED.

AS IF TO ILLUSTRATE HER POINT, SHE STAMPED HIS LIPS WITH A HARD, WET KISS.

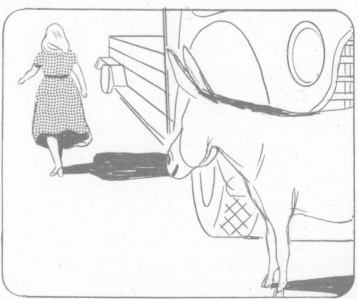

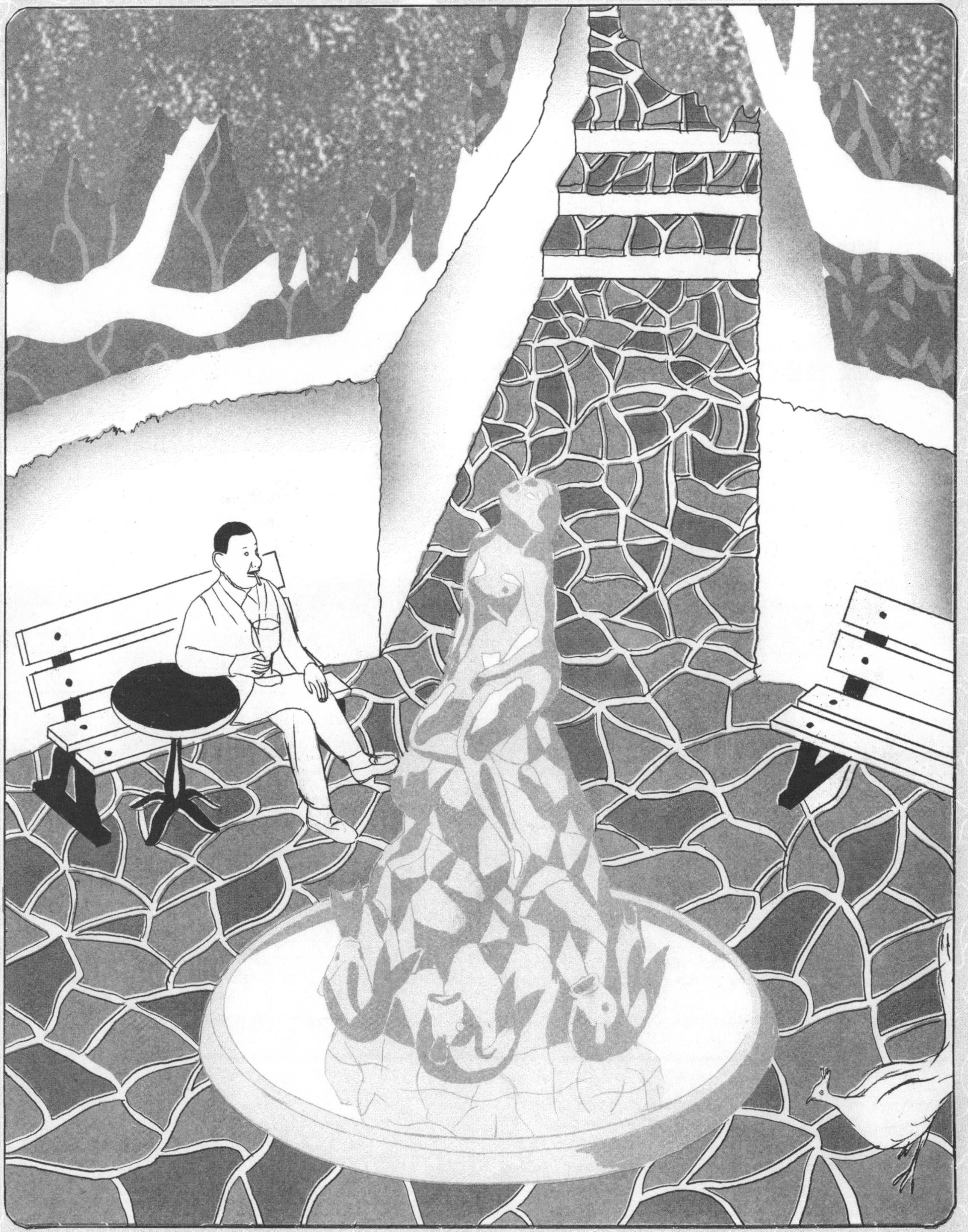

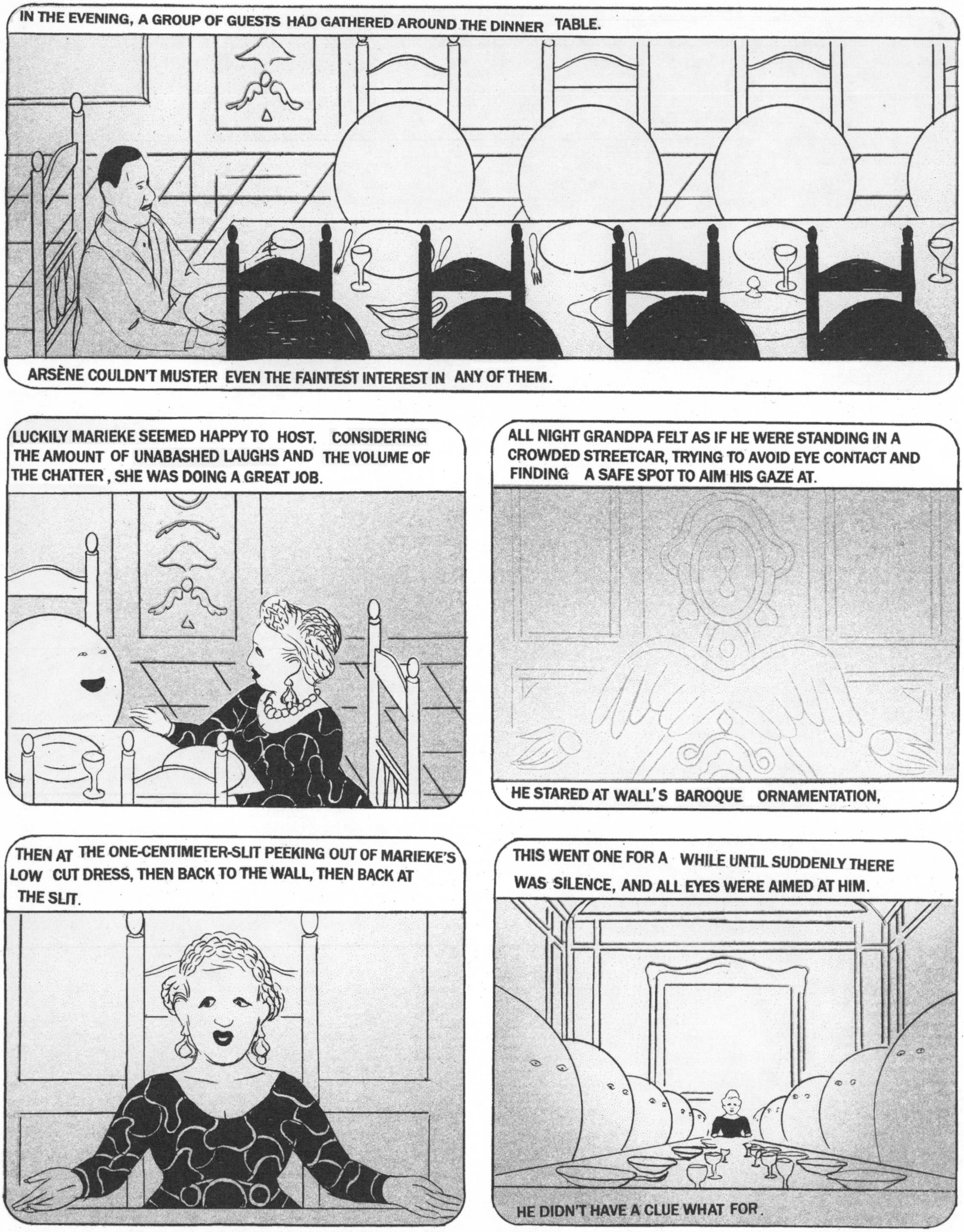
IN THE EVENING, A GROUP OF GUESTS HAD GATHERED AROUND THE DINNER TABLE.
ARSÈNE COULDN'T MUSTER EVEN THE FAINTEST INTEREST IN ANY OF THEM.
LUCKILY MARIEKE SEEMED HAPPY TO HOST. CONSIDERING THE AMOUNT OF UNABASHED LAUGHS AND THE VOLUME OF THE CHATTER, SHE WAS DOING A GREAT JOB.
ALL NIGHT GRANDPA FELT AS IF HE WERE STANDING IN A CROWDED STREETCAR, TRYING TO AVOID EYE CONTACT AND FINDING A SAFE SPOT TO AIM HIS GAZE AT.
HE STARED AT WALL'S BAROQUE ORNAMENTATION,
THEN AT THE ONE-CENTIMETER-SLIT PEEKING OUT OF MARIEKE'S LOW CUT DRESS, THEN BACK TO THE WALL, THEN BACK AT THE SLIT.
THIS WENT ONE FOR A WHILE UNTIL SUDDENLY THERE WAS SILENCE, AND ALL EYES WERE AIMED AT HIM.
HE DIDN'T HAVE A CLUE WHAT FOR.

LUCKILY, MARIEKE WAS KIND ENOUGH TO PUT HIM OUT OF HIS MISERY.

I WAS JUST TELLING THEM THAT IT WAS YOU WHO CAME UP WITH THE NAME "FREEDOM TOWN"...

ARSÈNE CONFIRMED THAT THIS WAS INDEED THE CASE.

A SILENCE FOLLOWED, IN WHICH HE COULD'VE FIT A WITTY REMARK.

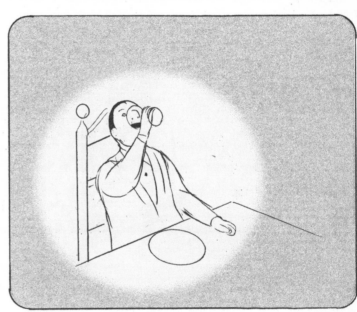

SUCH A THING DID NOT OCCUR.

LATER, THE PARTY RELOCATED TO THE SALON.

THE CHATTER AND LAUGHTER CONTINUED, YET GRANDPA WAS NOT ENGAGED IN ANY OF IT. HE DECIDED TO SNEAK OUT...

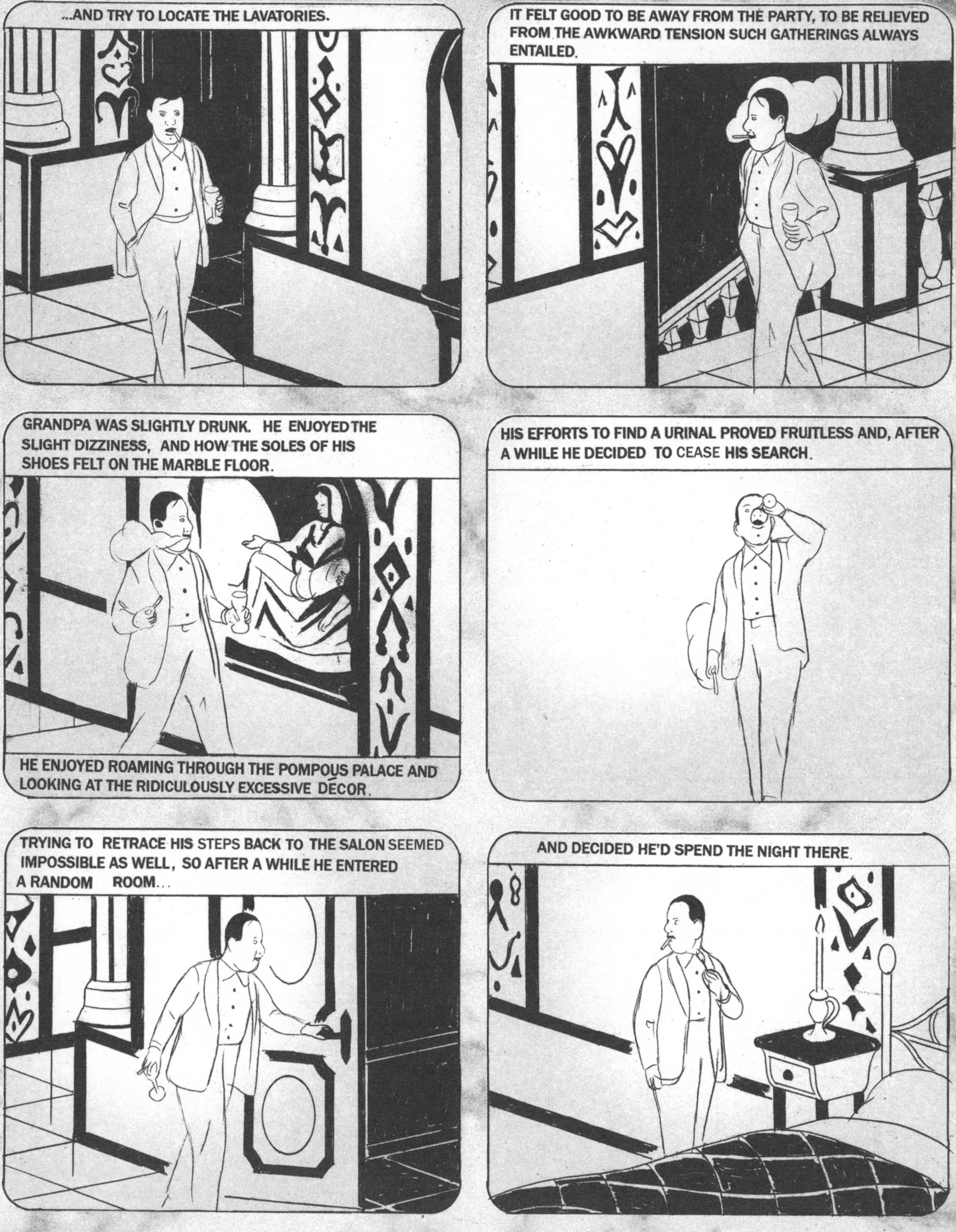
...AND TRY TO LOCATE THE LAVATORIES.
IT FELT GOOD TO BE AWAY FROM THE PARTY, TO BE RELIEVED FROM THE AWKWARD TENSION SUCH GATHERINGS ALWAYS ENTAILED.
GRANDPA WAS SLIGHTLY DRUNK. HE ENJOYED THE SLIGHT DIZZINESS, AND HOW THE SOLES OF HIS SHOES FELT ON THE MARBLE FLOOR.
HE ENJOYED ROAMING THROUGH THE POMPOUS PALACE AND LOOKING AT THE RIDICULOUSLY EXCESSIVE DÉCOR.
HIS EFFORTS TO FIND A URINAL PROVED FRUITLESS AND, AFTER A WHILE HE DECIDED TO CEASE HIS SEARCH.
TRYING TO RETRACE HIS STEPS BACK TO THE SALON SEEMED IMPOSSIBLE AS WELL, SO AFTER A WHILE HE ENTERED A RANDOM ROOM...
AND DECIDED HE'D SPEND THE NIGHT THERE.

IN THE PRIVACY OF THE ROOM, ARSÈNE ACTED OUT A LITTLE PANTOMIME.

THE EXACT NARRATIVE OF THIS PLAY, WORDLESS AND STIFFLY ACTED , WOULD LEAVE ANY SPECTATOR GUESSING.

I CAN TELL YOU IT INVOLVED MARIEKE.

HOW HE'D BOLDLY APPROACH HER,

THROW HER ON THE BED,

AND SMOOTHER HER IN CARESSES AND KISSES.

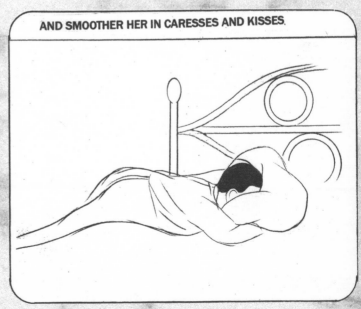

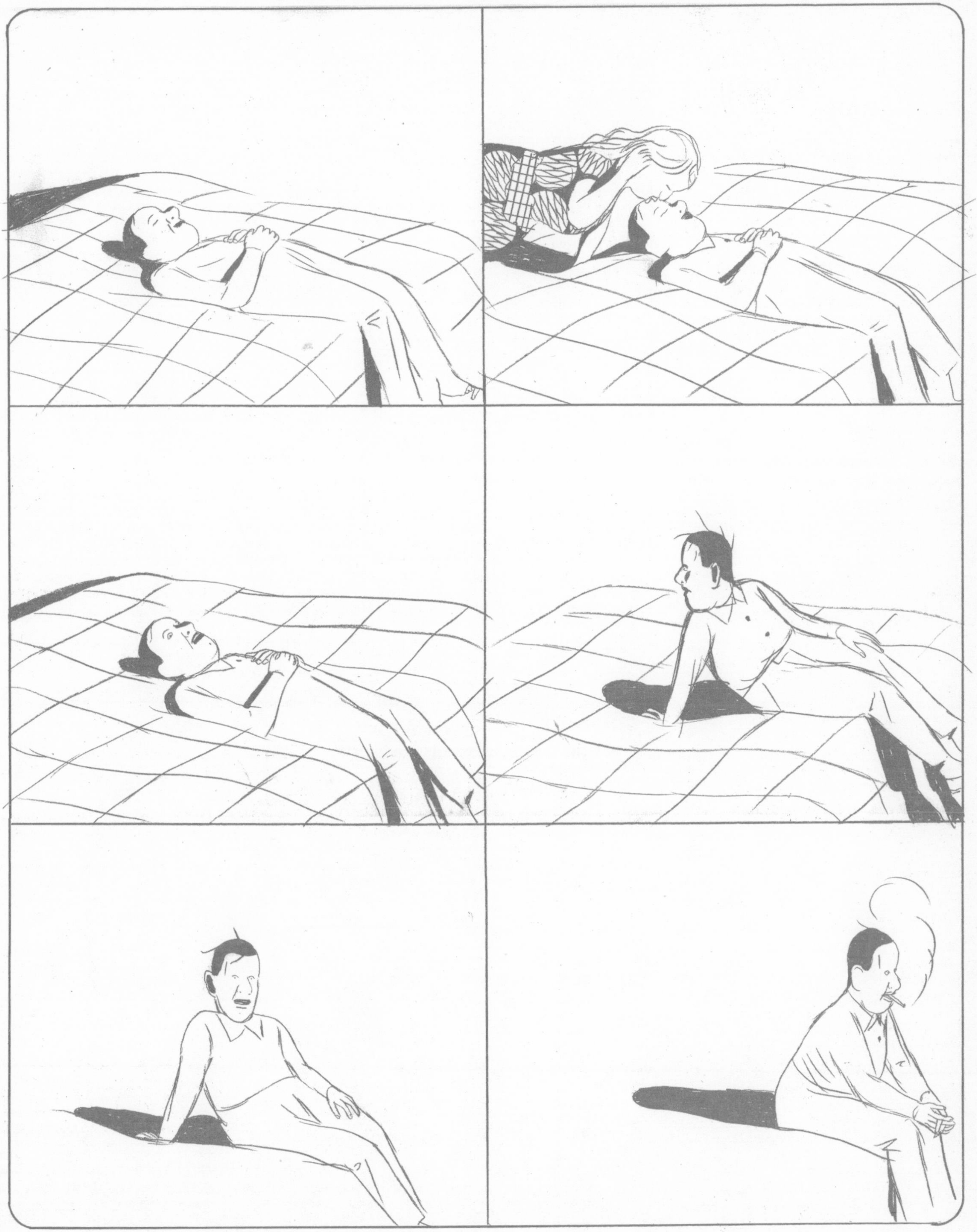

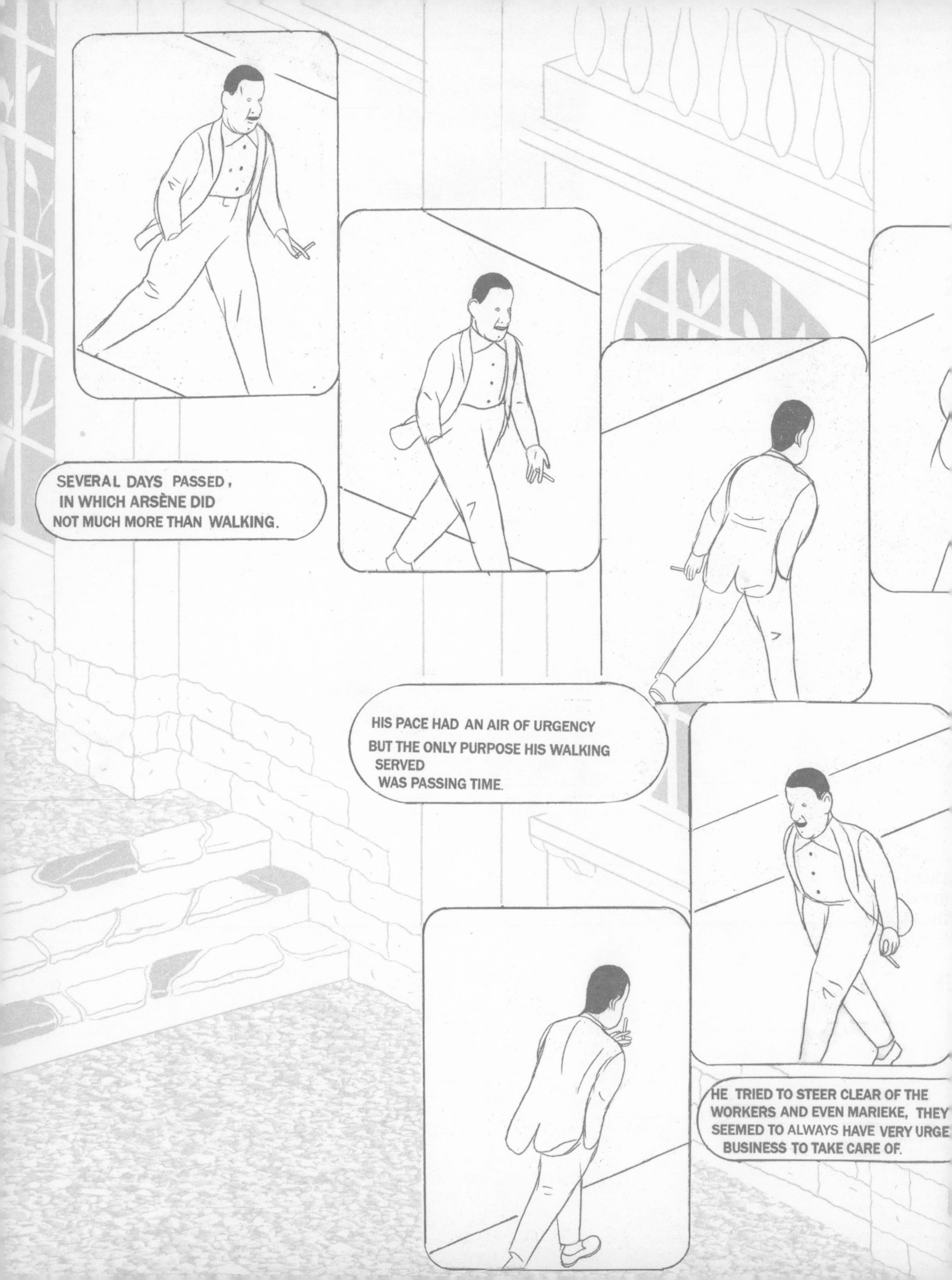
SEVERAL DAYS PASSED, IN WHICH ARSÈNE DID NOT MUCH MORE THAN WALKING.
HIS PACE HAD AN AIR OF URGENCY BUT THE ONLY PURPOSE HIS WALKING SERVED WAS PASSING TIME.
HE TRIED TO STEER CLEAR OF THE WORKERS AND EVEN MARIEKE, THEY SEEMED TO ALWAYS HAVE VERY URGE BUSINESS TO TAKE CARE OF.

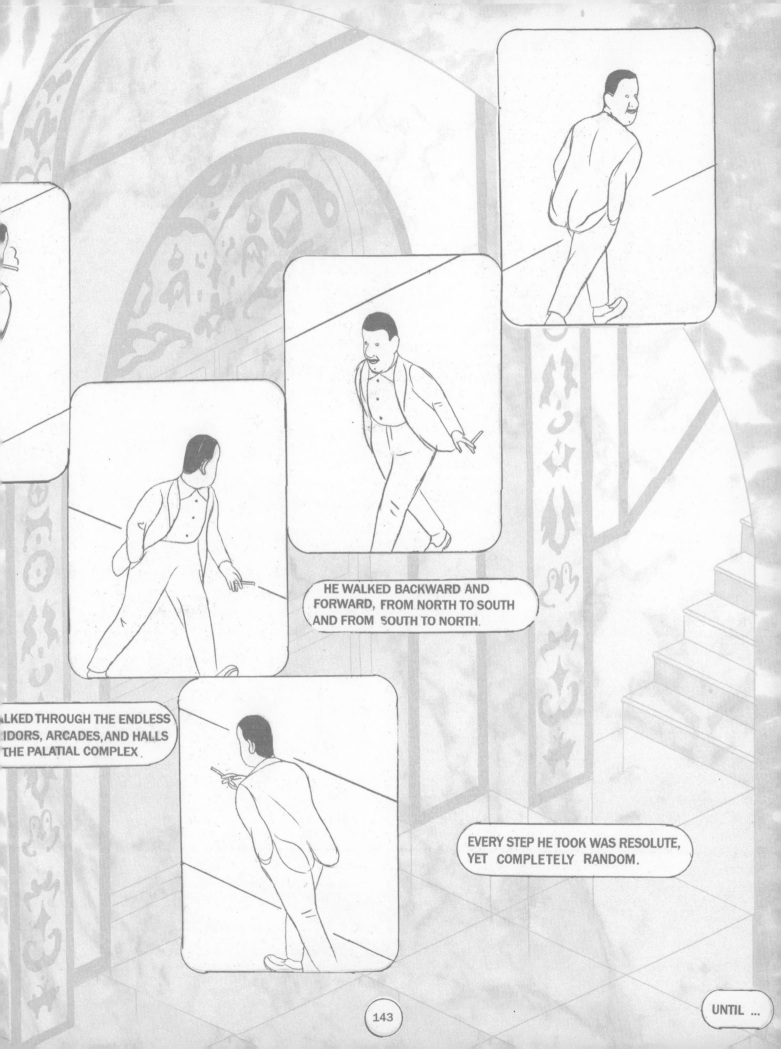

HE WALKED BACKWARD AND FORWARD, FROM NORTH TO SOUTH AND FROM SOUTH TO NORTH.

...LKED THROUGH THE ENDLESS ...IDORS, ARCADES, AND HALLS ...THE PALATIAL COMPLEX.

EVERY STEP HE TOOK WAS RESOLUTE, YET COMPLETELY RANDOM.

UNTIL ...

ONE MORNING ARSENE WAS WOKEN BY THE SOUNDS OF PEOPLE HEADING TOWARDS THE INNER COURTYARD. HE HAD NO IDEA WHAT WAS GOING ON.

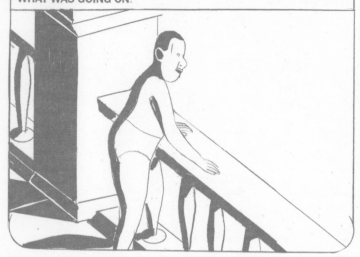

A PECULIAR GET-UP HAD BEEN LAID OUT FOR HIM.

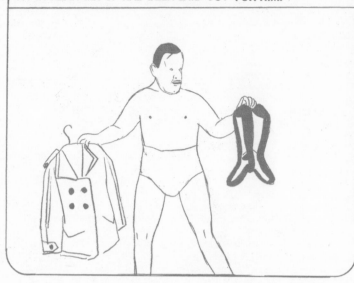

AS HE PUT IT ON, IT FELT LIKE HE WAS DRESSING UP FOR SOME THEATER SHOW . . .

BUT HE DIDN'T EVEN KNOW WHAT PART THEY WANTED HIM TO PLAY.

THEN A GLORIOUS-LOOKING MARIEKE CAME RUSHING INTO HIS ROOM.

ARSÈNE, TRY THIS HAT ON...

SHE GAVE HIM BACK SOME OF HIS CONFIDENCE.

OH YOU LOOK GREAT! REALLY MANLY!

THEY WENT DOWN TO THE COURTYARD...

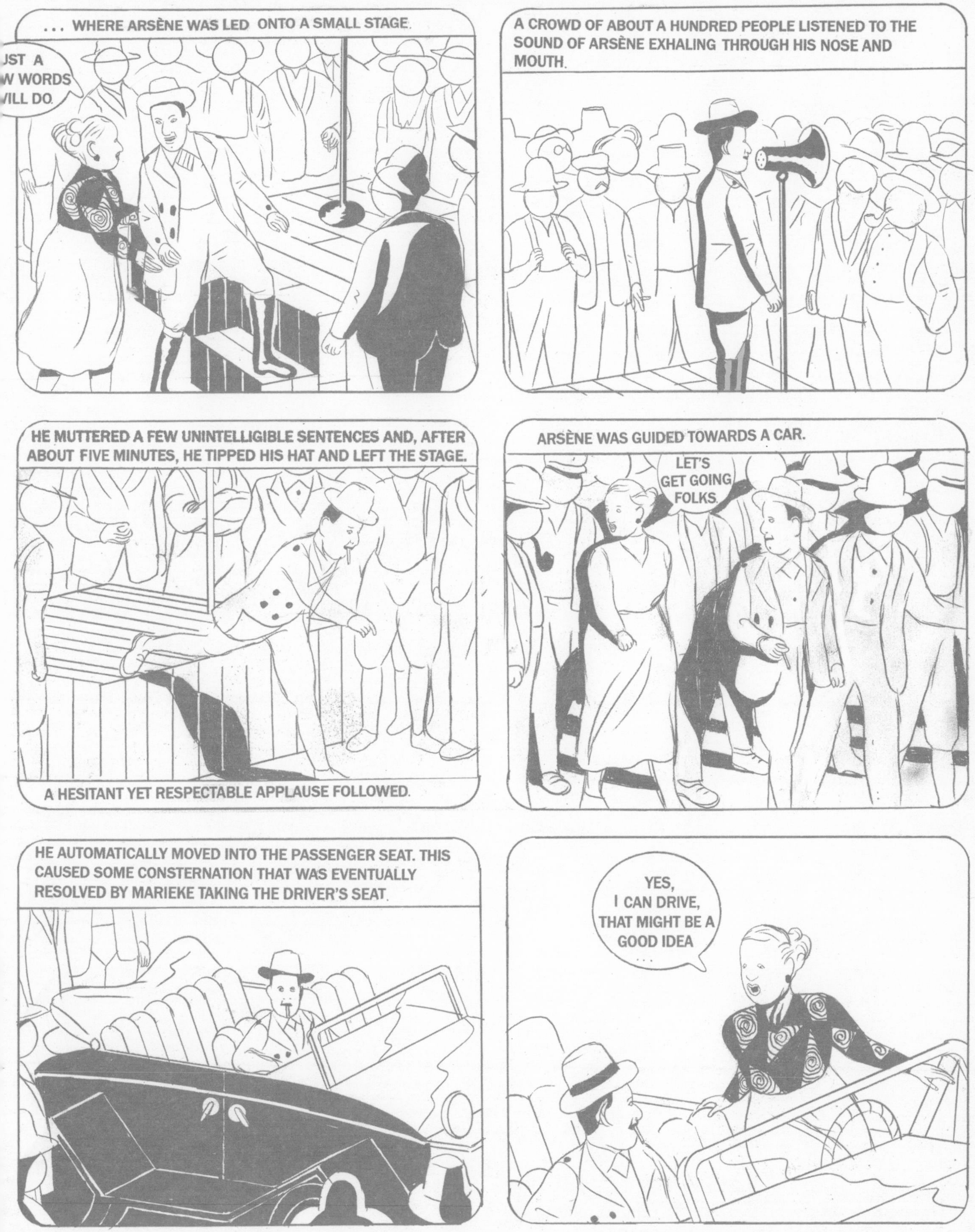
. . . WHERE ARSÈNE WAS LED ONTO A SMALL STAGE.
UST A W WORDS VILL DO.
A CROWD OF ABOUT A HUNDRED PEOPLE LISTENED TO THE SOUND OF ARSÈNE EXHALING THROUGH HIS NOSE AND MOUTH.
HE MUTTERED A FEW UNINTELLIGIBLE SENTENCES AND, AFTER ABOUT FIVE MINUTES, HE TIPPED HIS HAT AND LEFT THE STAGE.
A HESITANT YET RESPECTABLE APPLAUSE FOLLOWED.
ARSÈNE WAS GUIDED TOWARDS A CAR.
LET'S GET GOING FOLKS.
HE AUTOMATICALLY MOVED INTO THE PASSENGER SEAT. THIS CAUSED SOME CONSTERNATION THAT WAS EVENTUALLY RESOLVED BY MARIEKE TAKING THE DRIVER'S SEAT.
YES, I CAN DRIVE, THAT MIGHT BE A GOOD IDEA . . .

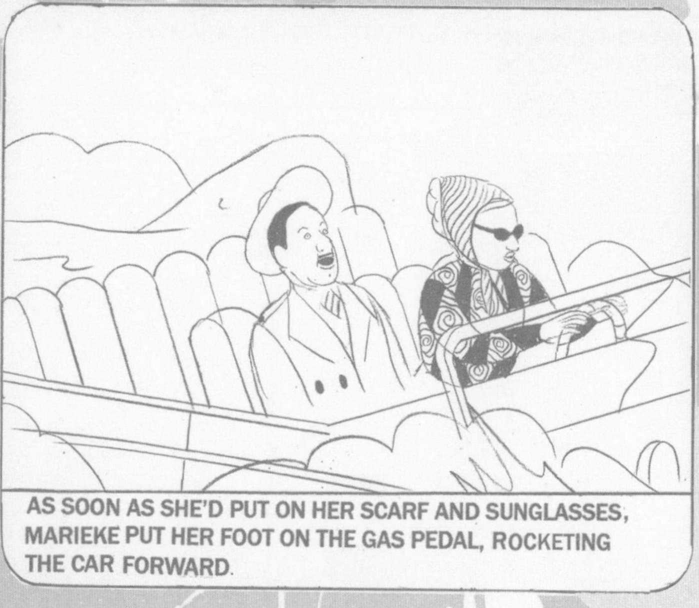
AS SOON AS SHE'D PUT ON HER SCARF AND SUNGLASSES, MARIEKE PUT HER FOOT ON THE GAS PEDAL, ROCKETING THE CAR FORWARD.

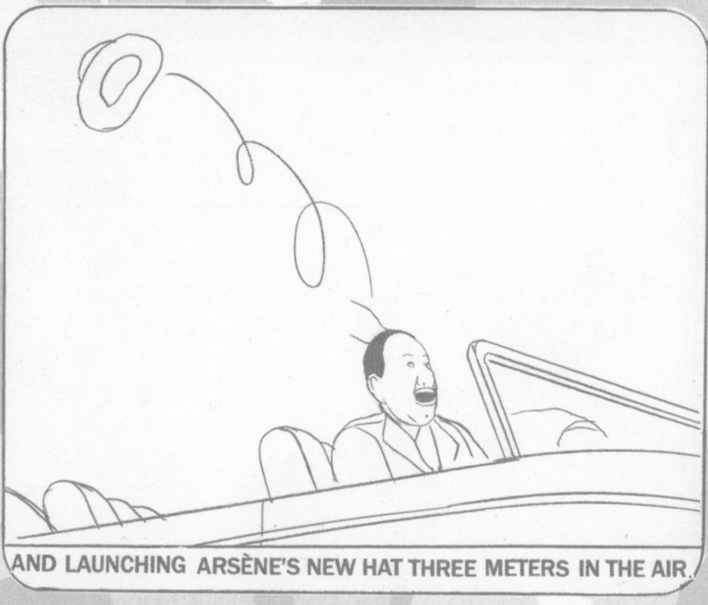
AND LAUNCHING ARSÈNE'S NEW HAT THREE METERS IN THE AIR.

6. VENTURE

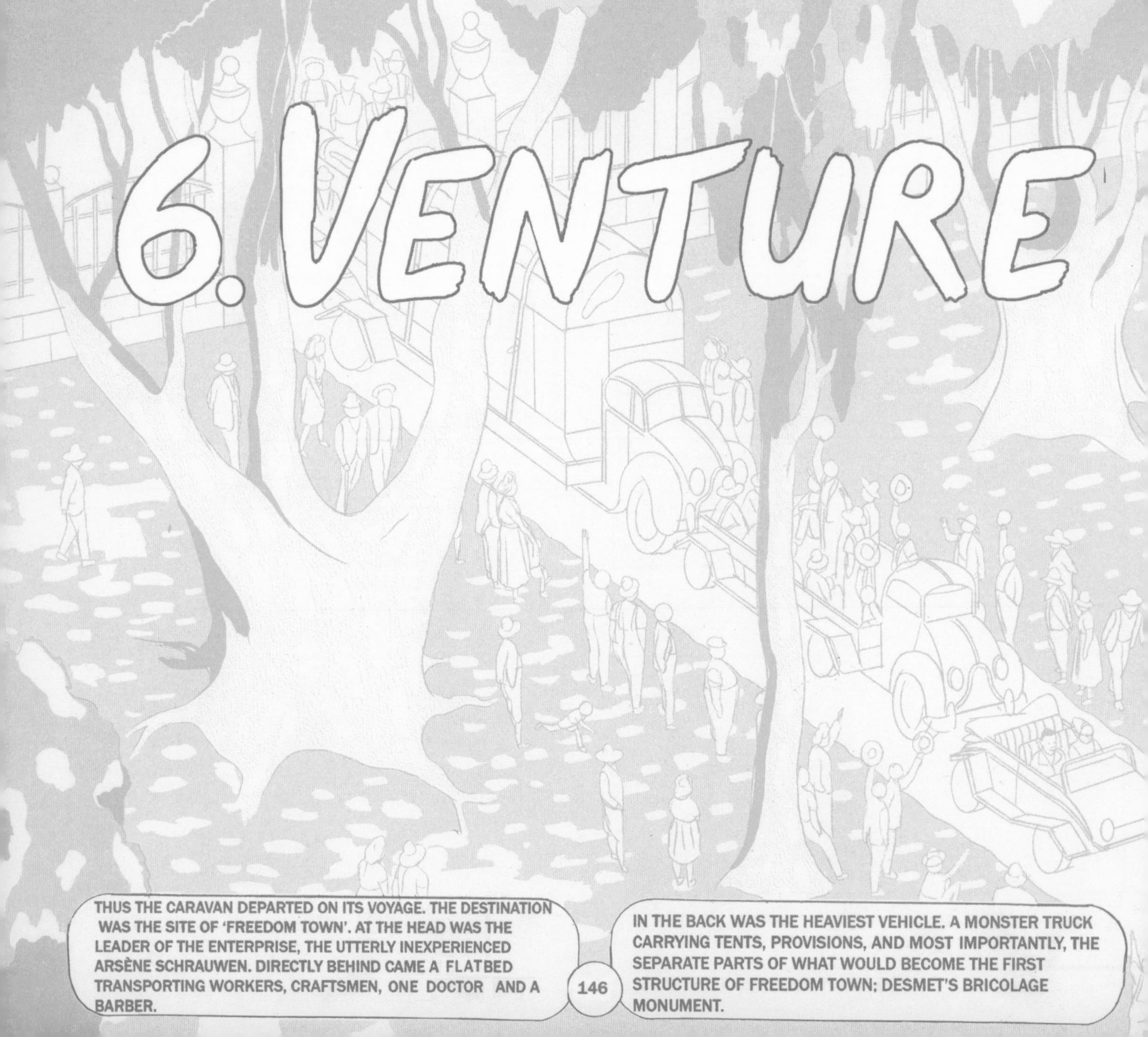
THUS THE CARAVAN DEPARTED ON ITS VOYAGE. THE DESTINATION WAS THE SITE OF 'FREEDOM TOWN'. AT THE HEAD WAS THE LEADER OF THE ENTERPRISE, THE UTTERLY INEXPERIENCED ARSÈNE SCHRAUWEN. DIRECTLY BEHIND CAME A FLATBED TRANSPORTING WORKERS, CRAFTSMEN, ONE DOCTOR AND A BARBER.
IN THE BACK WAS THE HEAVIEST VEHICLE. A MONSTER TRUCK CARRYING TENTS, PROVISIONS, AND MOST IMPORTANTLY, THE SEPARATE PARTS OF WHAT WOULD BECOME THE FIRST STRUCTURE OF FREEDOM TOWN; DESMET'S BRICOLAGE MONUMENT.

BY THE SIDE OF THE ROAD PEOPLE WERE WAVING AND KIDS WERE RUNNING, TRYING TO KEEP UP WITH THE VEHICLES. IT HAD THE AIR OF A ROYAL PARADE, SO GRANDPA REACTED APPROPRIATELY, WITH A MEASURED WAVE.

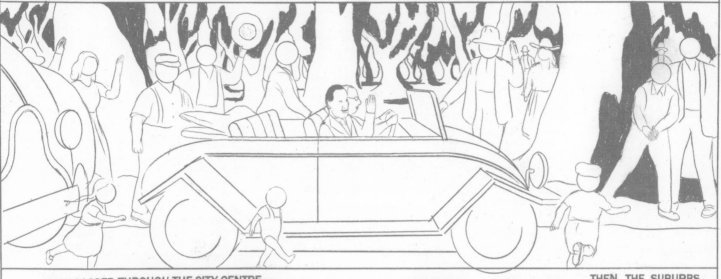

THEY PASSED THROUGH THE CITY CENTRE,   THEN THE SUBURBS,

AND EVENTUALLY PAST AN ENDLESS ROW OF TINY HOUSES. ARSÈNE GUESSED THEY WERE FOR LABORERS OR NATIVES OR NATIVE LABORERS.

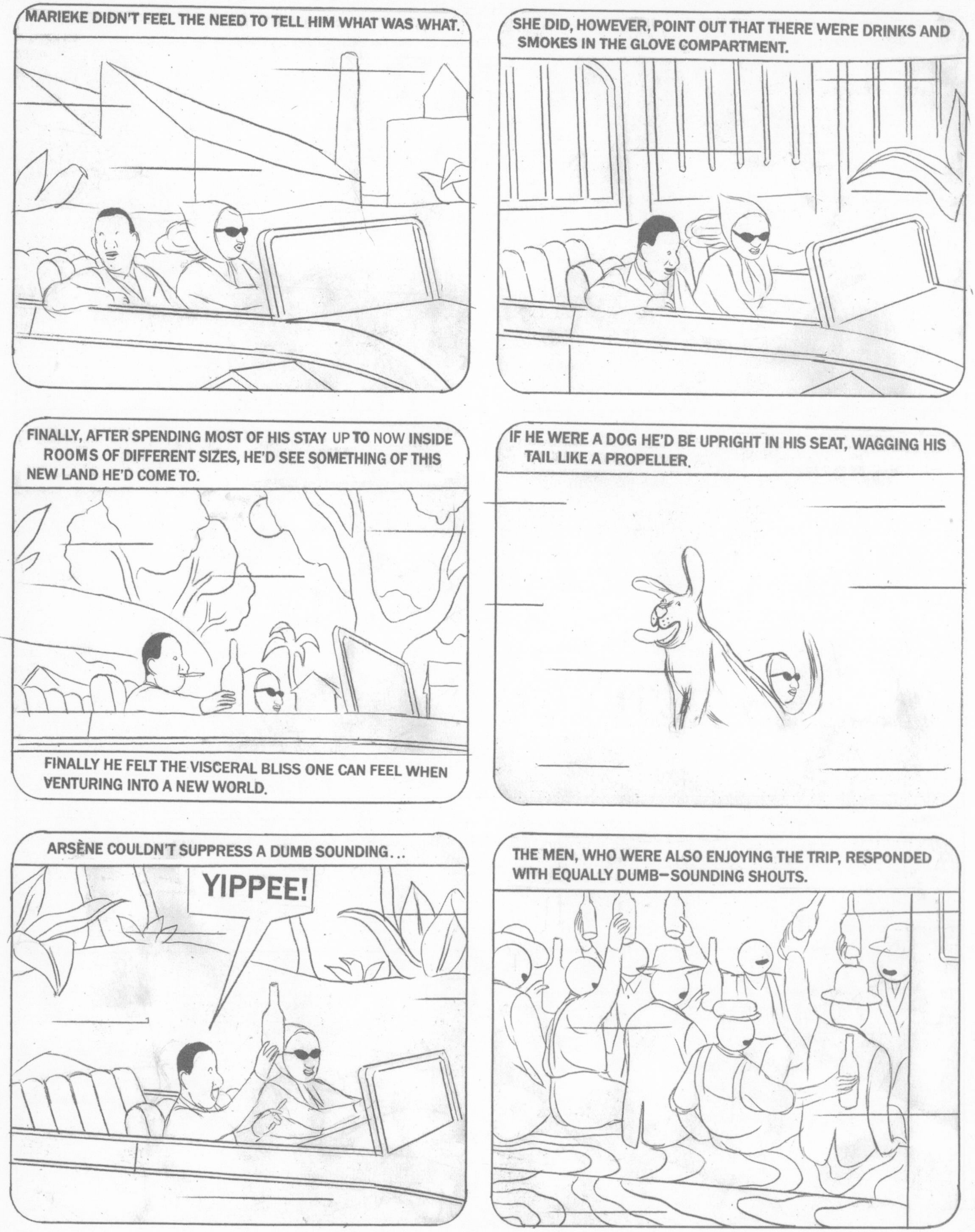
MARIEKE DIDN'T FEEL THE NEED TO TELL HIM WHAT WAS WHAT.
SHE DID, HOWEVER, POINT OUT THAT THERE WERE DRINKS AND SMOKES IN THE GLOVE COMPARTMENT.
FINALLY, AFTER SPENDING MOST OF HIS STAY UP TO NOW INSIDE ROOMS OF DIFFERENT SIZES, HE'D SEE SOMETHING OF THIS NEW LAND HE'D COME TO.
FINALLY HE FELT THE VISCERAL BLISS ONE CAN FEEL WHEN VENTURING INTO A NEW WORLD.
IF HE WERE A DOG HE'D BE UPRIGHT IN HIS SEAT, WAGGING HIS TAIL LIKE A PROPELLER.
ARSÈNE COULDN'T SUPPRESS A DUMB SOUNDING...
YIPPEE!
THE MEN, WHO WERE ALSO ENJOYING THE TRIP, RESPONDED WITH EQUALLY DUMB–SOUNDING SHOUTS.

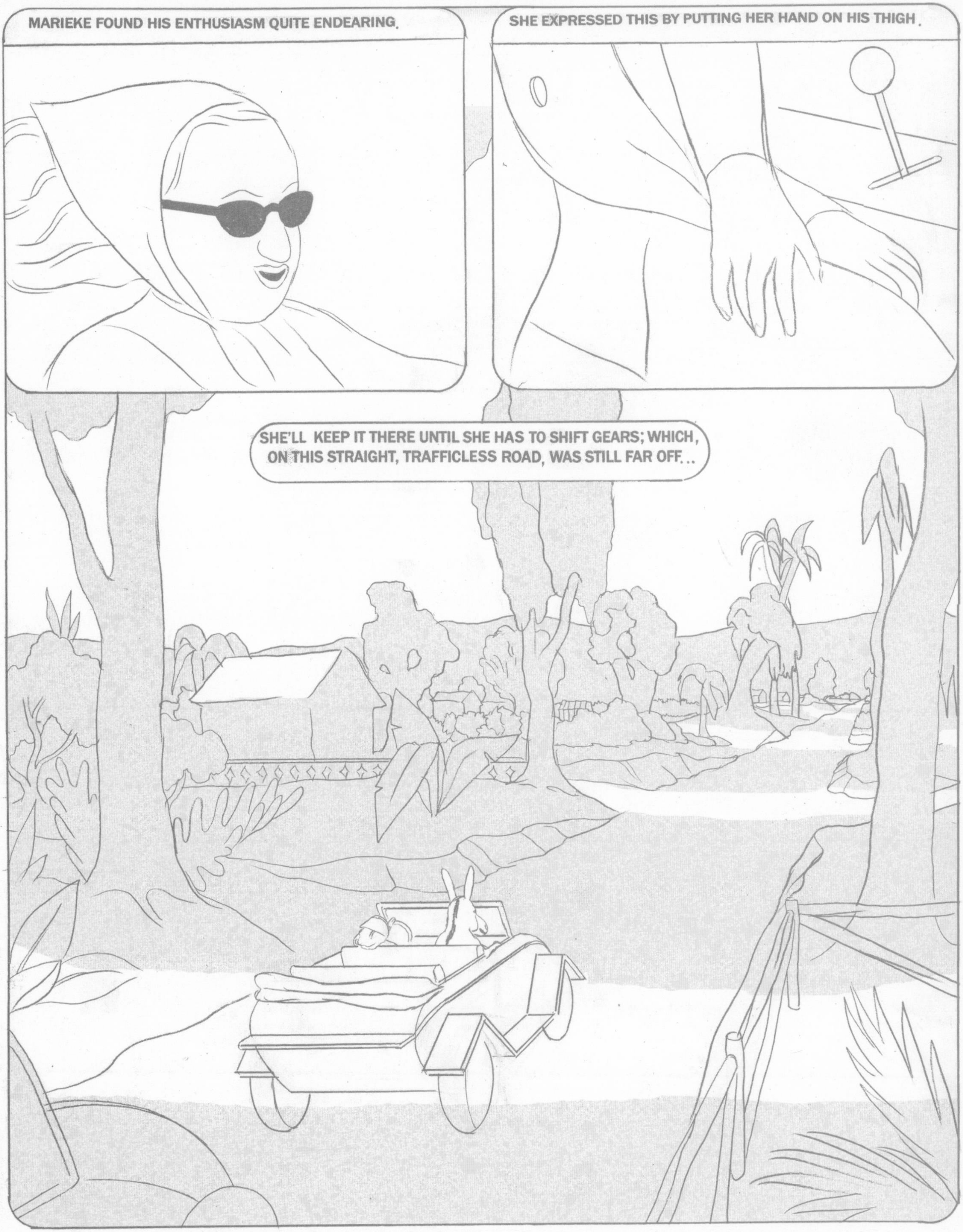
MARIEKE FOUND HIS ENTHUSIASM QUITE ENDEARING.
SHE EXPRESSED THIS BY PUTTING HER HAND ON HIS THIGH.
SHE'LL KEEP IT THERE UNTIL SHE HAS TO SHIFT GEARS; WHICH, ON THIS STRAIGHT, TRAFFICLESS ROAD, WAS STILL FAR OFF...

AT THAT VERY MOMENT, ROGER WAS IN A SEASIDE HOSPITAL.

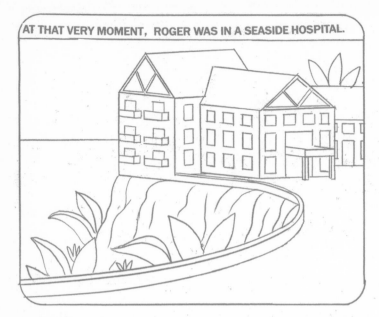

HE WAS SITTING ON THE BALCONY OF A FAIRLY PLEASANT ROOM, VERY MUCH ANNOYED WITH HIS CAPTIVITY.

ROGER?

LOUIS, IS THAT YOU?

THANK GOODNESS YOU'RE HERE! YOU MUST GO TO THE HOSPITAL DIRECTOR AT ONCE, AND HAVE HIM RELEASE ME. I'M PERFECTLY FINE.

YOU TRIED TO BURN DOWN YOUR HOUSE!

OH PLEASE LOUIS, DON'T EVEN BRING THAT UP. I JUST GOT CARRIED AWAY THERE. YOU KNOW MY "FIERY ENTHUSIASM", HAHA!

SERIOUSLY, THERE IS NOTHING WRONG WITH ME. THE ONLY THING I'M SUFFERING FROM HERE IS TERMINAL BOREDOM.

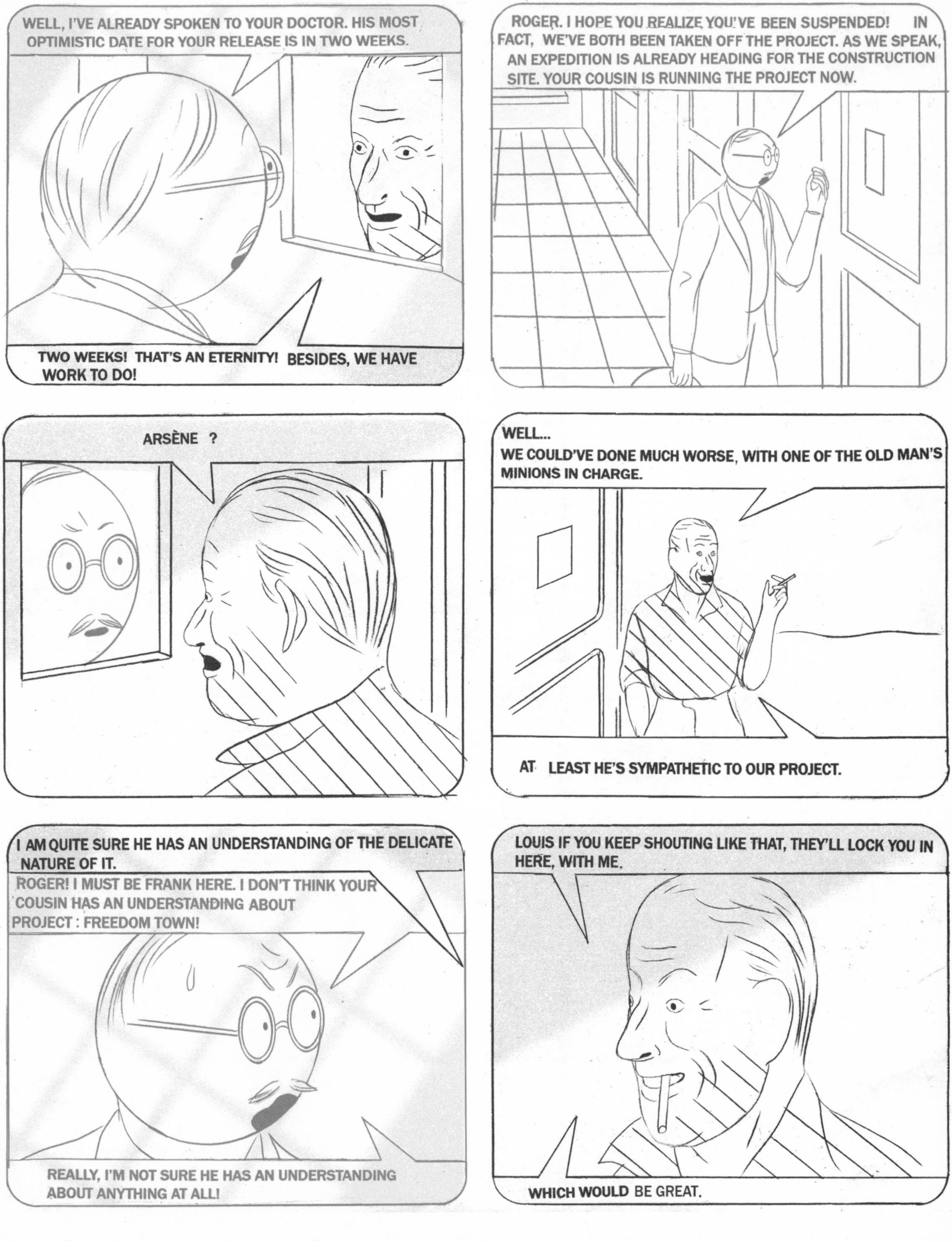
WELL, I'VE ALREADY SPOKEN TO YOUR DOCTOR. HIS MOST OPTIMISTIC DATE FOR YOUR RELEASE IS IN TWO WEEKS.
TWO WEEKS! THAT'S AN ETERNITY! BESIDES, WE HAVE WORK TO DO!
ROGER. I HOPE YOU REALIZE YOU'VE BEEN SUSPENDED! IN FACT, WE'VE BOTH BEEN TAKEN OFF THE PROJECT. AS WE SPEAK, AN EXPEDITION IS ALREADY HEADING FOR THE CONSTRUCTION SITE. YOUR COUSIN IS RUNNING THE PROJECT NOW.
ARSÈNE ?
WELL...
WE COULD'VE DONE MUCH WORSE, WITH ONE OF THE OLD MAN'S MINIONS IN CHARGE.
AT LEAST HE'S SYMPATHETIC TO OUR PROJECT.
I AM QUITE SURE HE HAS AN UNDERSTANDING OF THE DELICATE NATURE OF IT.
ROGER! I MUST BE FRANK HERE. I DON'T THINK YOUR COUSIN HAS AN UNDERSTANDING ABOUT PROJECT : FREEDOM TOWN!
REALLY, I'M NOT SURE HE HAS AN UNDERSTANDING ABOUT ANYTHING AT ALL!
LOUIS IF YOU KEEP SHOUTING LIKE THAT, THEY'LL LOCK YOU IN HERE, WITH ME.
WHICH WOULD BE GREAT.

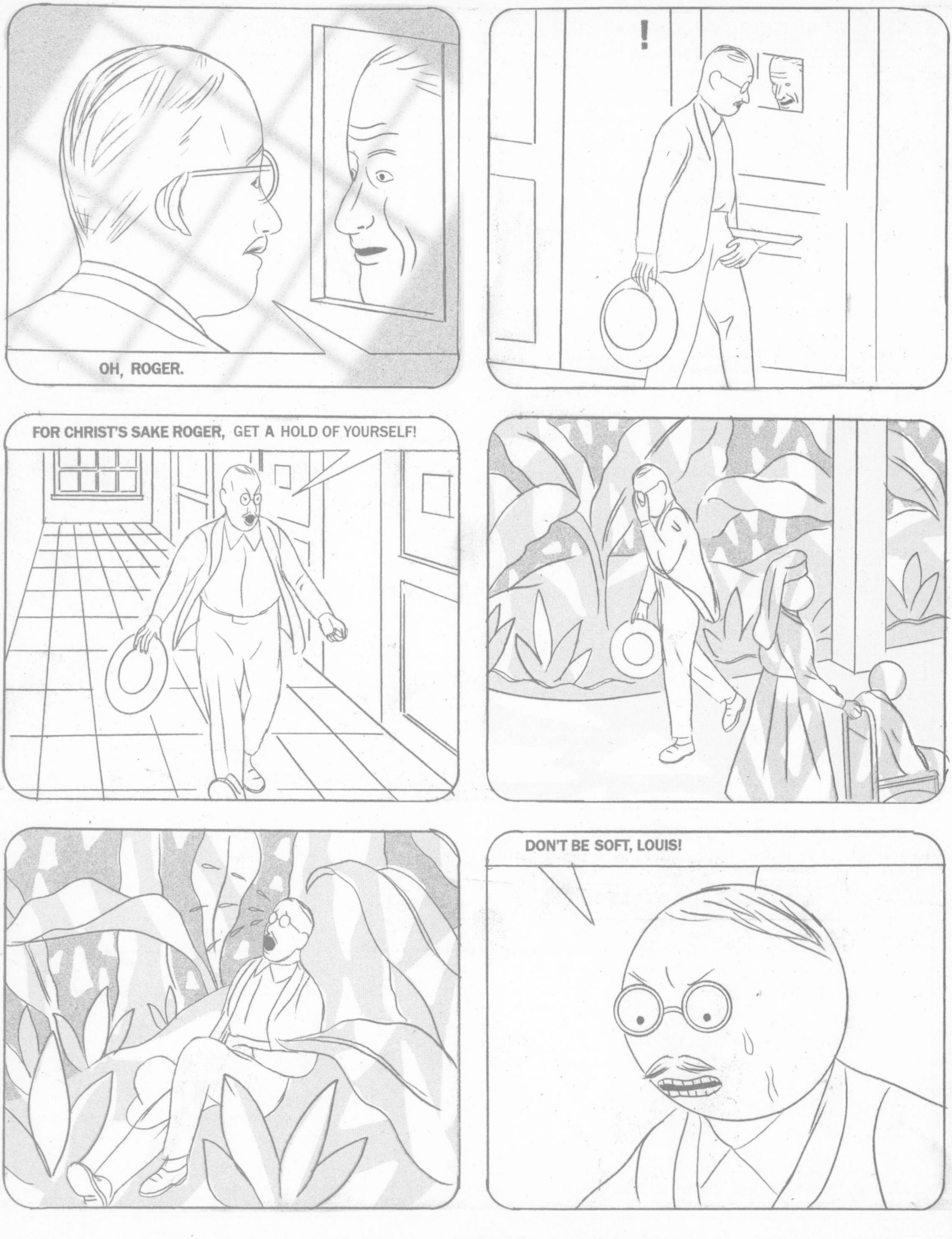
OH, ROGER.
!
FOR CHRIST'S SAKE ROGER, GET A HOLD OF YOURSELF!
DON'T BE SOFT, LOUIS!

BACK INSIDE THE HOSPITAL TWO DOCTORS WERE PASSING BY ROGER'S ROOM.

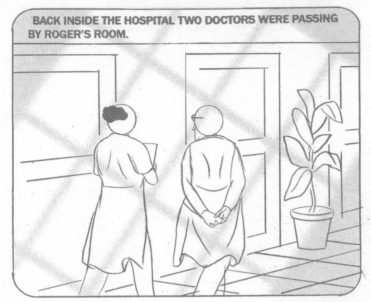

IN HERE WE'VE GOT MISTER DESMET. HE'S BEEN WITH US FOR A WEEK.

OH YES, DESMET, HE MUST BE HANDLED WITH THE UTMOST CARE.

'WE OUGHT NOT FORGET THAT, WITHOUT HIS FATHER-IN-LAW THIS HOSPITAL WOULDN'T HAVE A LEFT WING.

INDEED, AND HIS PAPA HAS ALSO PROVIDED US WITH A BEAUTIFUL NEW MACHINE THAT IS EXCEPTIONALLY WELL SUITED FOR HIS TREATMENT.

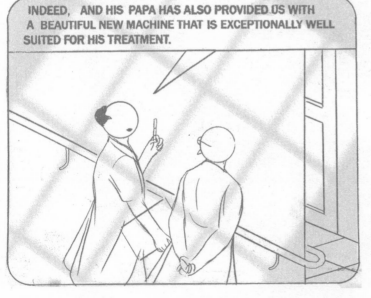

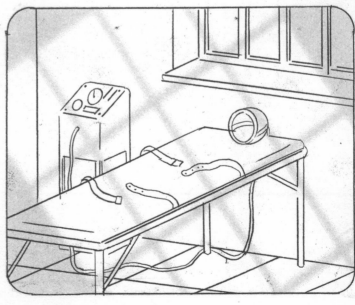

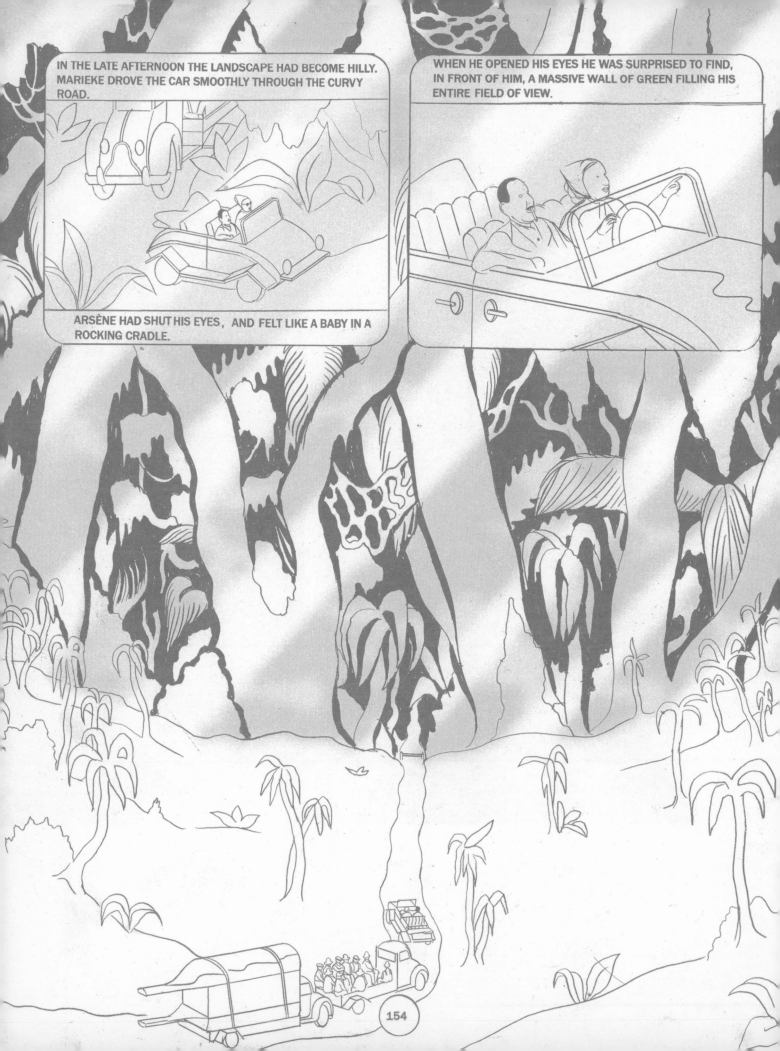

IN THE LATE AFTERNOON THE LANDSCAPE HAD BECOME HILLY. MARIEKE DROVE THE CAR SMOOTHLY THROUGH THE CURVY ROAD.

WHEN HE OPENED HIS EYES HE WAS SURPRISED TO FIND, IN FRONT OF HIM, A MASSIVE WALL OF GREEN FILLING HIS ENTIRE FIELD OF VIEW.

ARSÈNE HAD SHUT HIS EYES, AND FELT LIKE A BABY IN A ROCKING CRADLE.

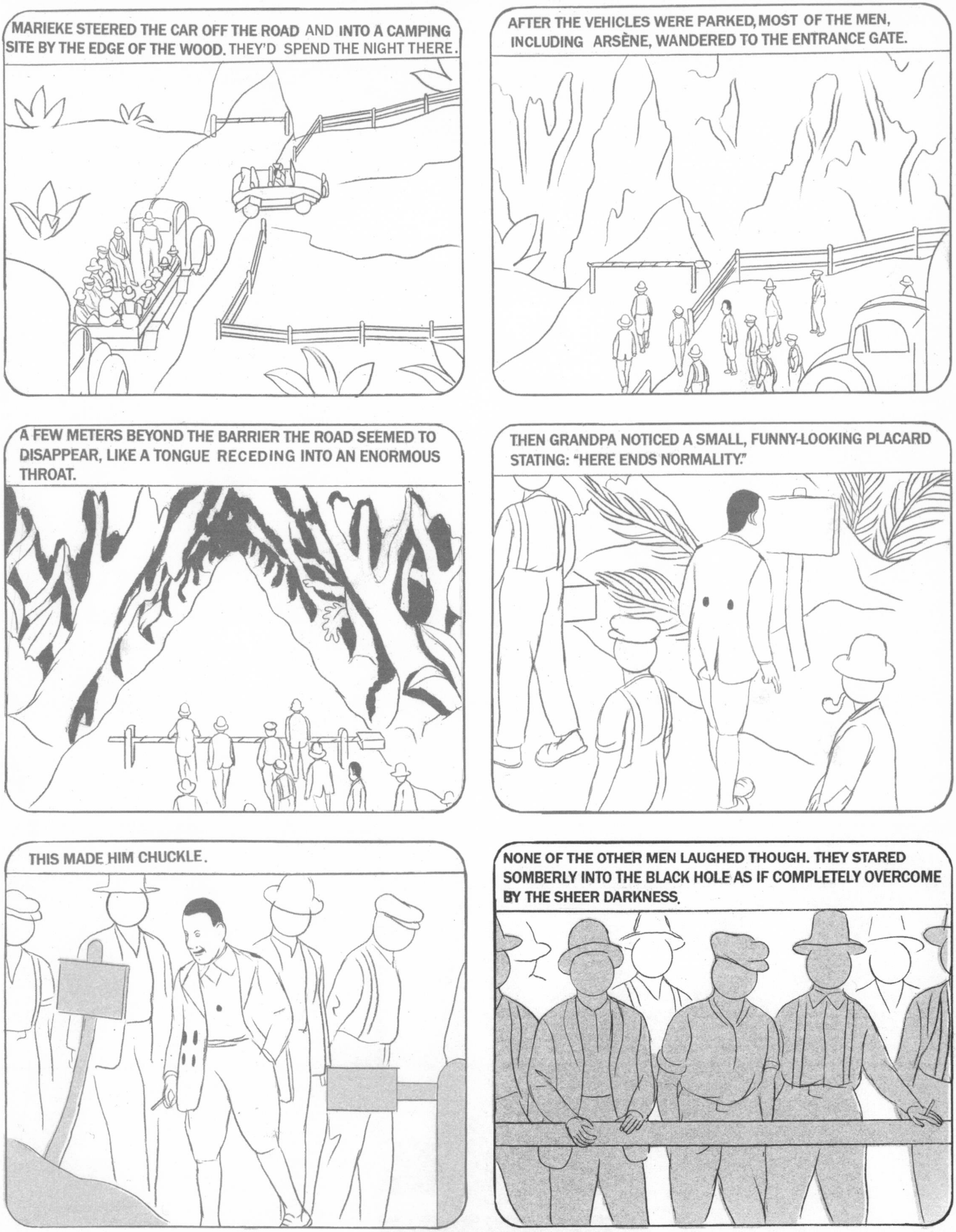
MARIEKE STEERED THE CAR OFF THE ROAD AND INTO A CAMPING SITE BY THE EDGE OF THE WOOD. THEY'D SPEND THE NIGHT THERE.
AFTER THE VEHICLES WERE PARKED, MOST OF THE MEN, INCLUDING ARSÈNE, WANDERED TO THE ENTRANCE GATE.
A FEW METERS BEYOND THE BARRIER THE ROAD SEEMED TO DISAPPEAR, LIKE A TONGUE RECEDING INTO AN ENORMOUS THROAT.
THEN GRANDPA NOTICED A SMALL, FUNNY-LOOKING PLACARD STATING: "HERE ENDS NORMALITY."
THIS MADE HIM CHUCKLE.
NONE OF THE OTHER MEN LAUGHED THOUGH. THEY STARED SOMBERLY INTO THE BLACK HOLE AS IF COMPLETELY OVERCOME BY THE SHEER DARKNESS.

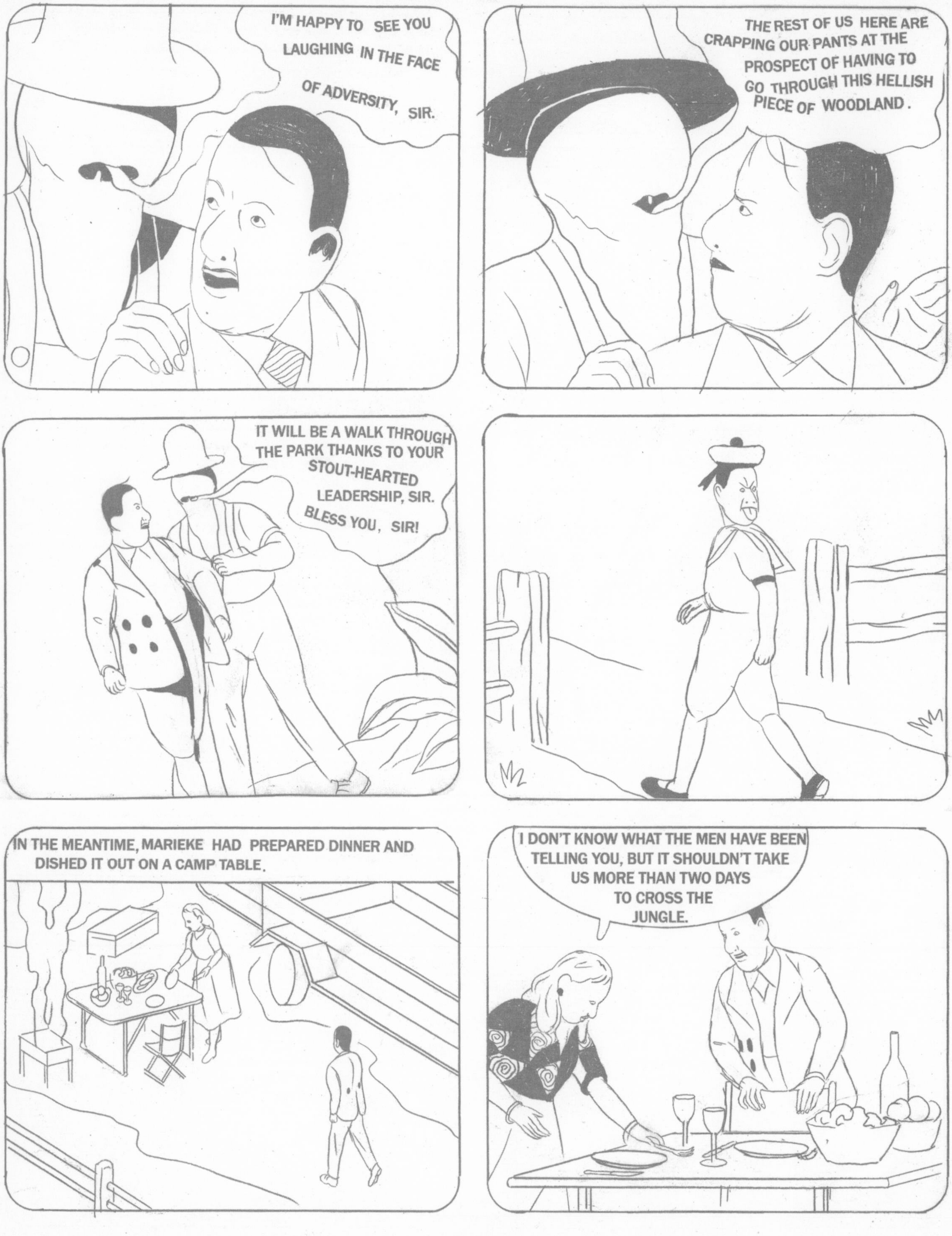
I'M HAPPY TO SEE YOU LAUGHING IN THE FACE OF ADVERSITY, SIR.
THE REST OF US HERE ARE CRAPPING OUR PANTS AT THE PROSPECT OF HAVING TO GO THROUGH THIS HELLISH PIECE OF WOODLAND.
IT WILL BE A WALK THROUGH THE PARK THANKS TO YOUR STOUT-HEARTED LEADERSHIP, SIR. BLESS YOU, SIR!
IN THE MEANTIME, MARIEKE HAD PREPARED DINNER AND DISHED IT OUT ON A CAMP TABLE.
I DON'T KNOW WHAT THE MEN HAVE BEEN TELLING YOU, BUT IT SHOULDN'T TAKE US MORE THAN TWO DAYS TO CROSS THE JUNGLE.

AS LONG AS WE FOLLOW THE RIGHT ROUTE WE'LL BE FINE.

MARIEKE'S WORDS REASSURED HIM AND WHILE HE WAS CONSUMING HER RATHER DELICIOUS MEAL, HE WATCHED A PRETTY BIRD GLIDE THROUGH THE AIR.

IT FLEW LEISURELY, CARRIED BY THE AIR CURRENT'S GENTLY UNDULATING CURVES.

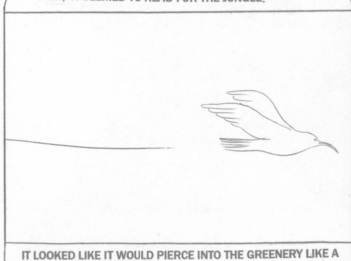

THEN, IT SEEMED TO HEAD FOR THE JUNGLE.

IT LOOKED LIKE IT WOULD PIERCE INTO THE GREENERY LIKE A KNIFE INTO A FAT BELLY.

BUT RIGHT BEFORE ENTERING, IT MADE A VERY AWKWARD LOOKING MANEUVER...

...AND FLEW IN THE OPPOSITE DIRECTION.

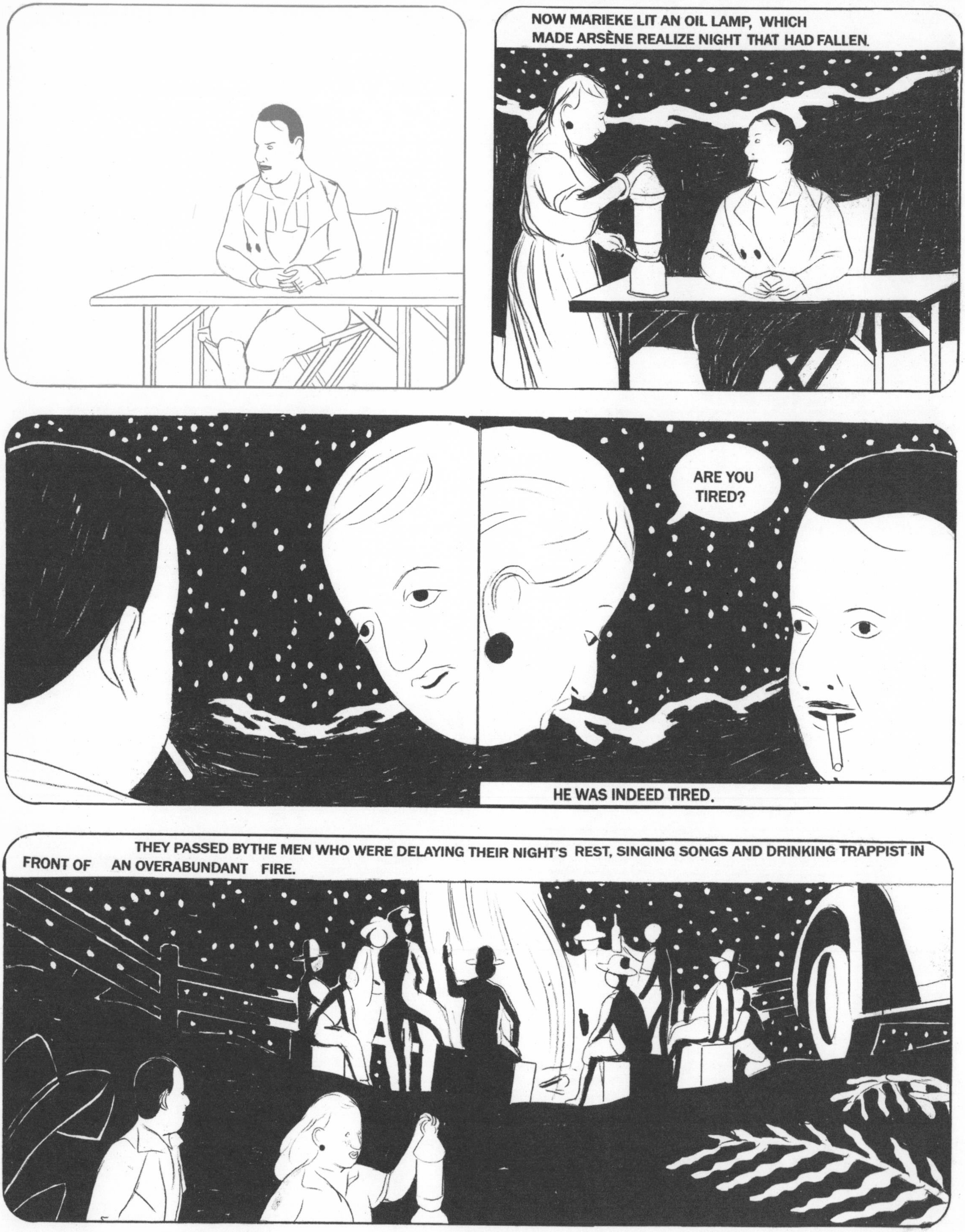
NOW MARIEKE LIT AN OIL LAMP, WHICH MADE ARSÈNE REALIZE NIGHT THAT HAD FALLEN.
ARE YOU TIRED?
HE WAS INDEED TIRED.
THEY PASSED BYTHE MEN WHO WERE DELAYING THEIR NIGHT'S REST, SINGING SONGS AND DRINKING TRAPPIST IN FRONT OF AN OVERABUNDANT FIRE.

THE TRAILER OF THE BIG TRUCK WASN'T ENTIRELY FILLED WITH CARGO. DESMET HAD PREPARED AN EMPTY COMPARTMENT THAT COULD SERVE AS A SHELTER OR A SLEEPING PLACE.

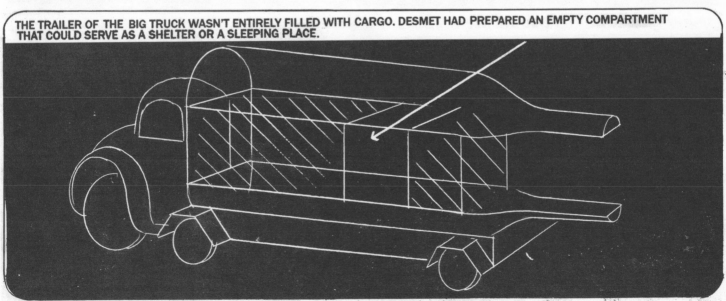

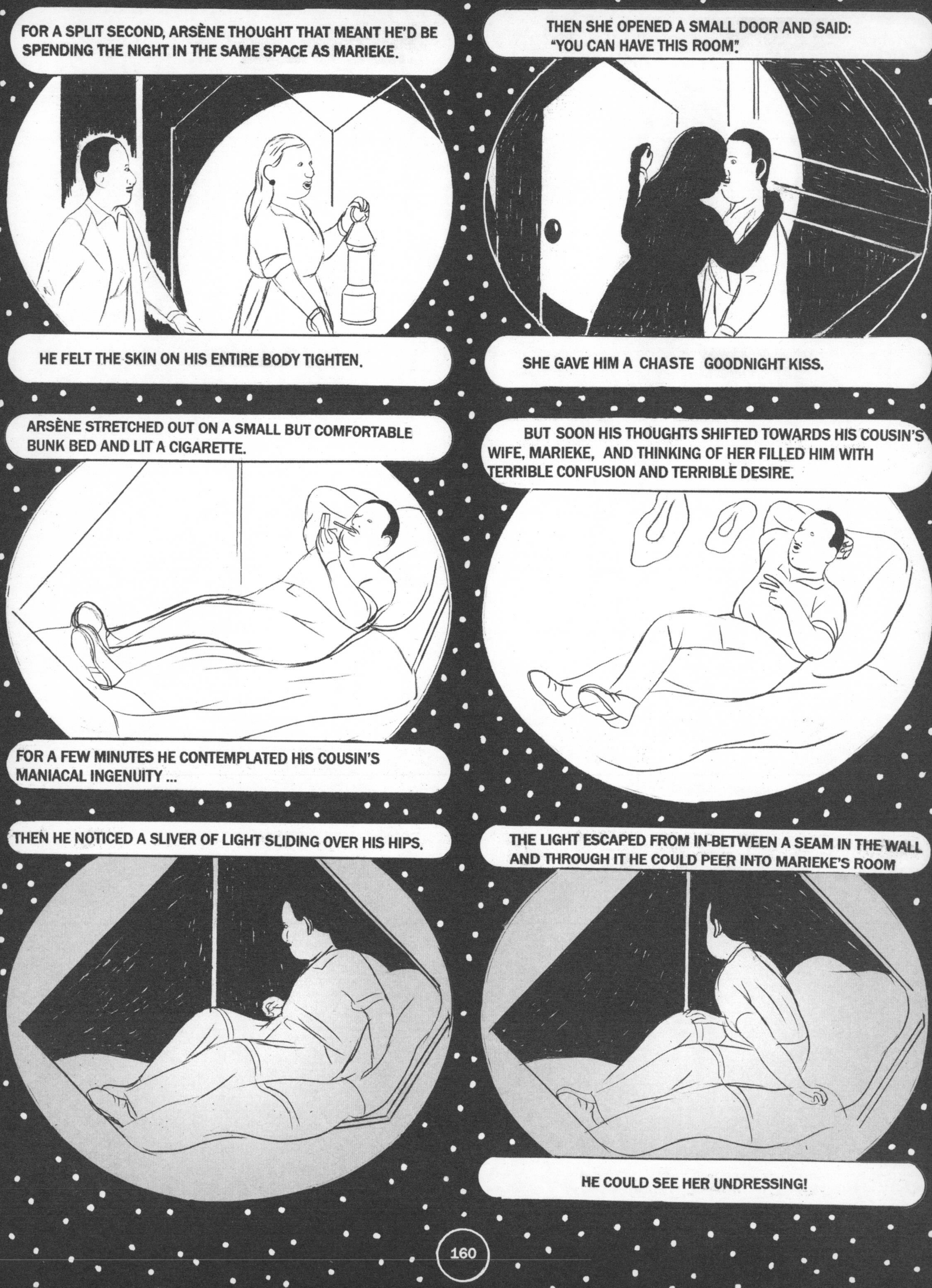
FOR A SPLIT SECOND, ARSÈNE THOUGHT THAT MEANT HE'D BE SPENDING THE NIGHT IN THE SAME SPACE AS MARIEKE.
HE FELT THE SKIN ON HIS ENTIRE BODY TIGHTEN.
THEN SHE OPENED A SMALL DOOR AND SAID: "YOU CAN HAVE THIS ROOM".
SHE GAVE HIM A CHASTE GOODNIGHT KISS.
ARSÈNE STRETCHED OUT ON A SMALL BUT COMFORTABLE BUNK BED AND LIT A CIGARETTE.
FOR A FEW MINUTES HE CONTEMPLATED HIS COUSIN'S MANIACAL INGENUITY ...
BUT SOON HIS THOUGHTS SHIFTED TOWARDS HIS COUSIN'S WIFE, MARIEKE, AND THINKING OF HER FILLED HIM WITH TERRIBLE CONFUSION AND TERRIBLE DESIRE.
THEN HE NOTICED A SLIVER OF LIGHT SLIDING OVER HIS HIPS.
THE LIGHT ESCAPED FROM IN-BETWEEN A SEAM IN THE WALL AND THROUGH IT HE COULD PEER INTO MARIEKE'S ROOM
HE COULD SEE HER UNDRESSING!

IT WAS A TANTALIZING YET FRUSTRATING SIGHT,

HE COULD ONLY SEE SLICES OF HER AND HIS MIND COULDN'T QUITE ADD THEM UP INTO A SATISFYING WHOLE.

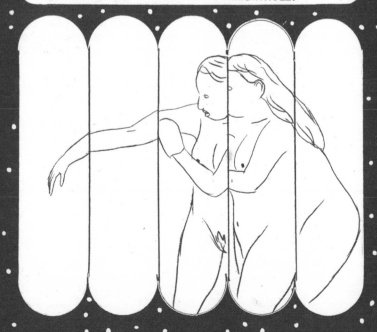

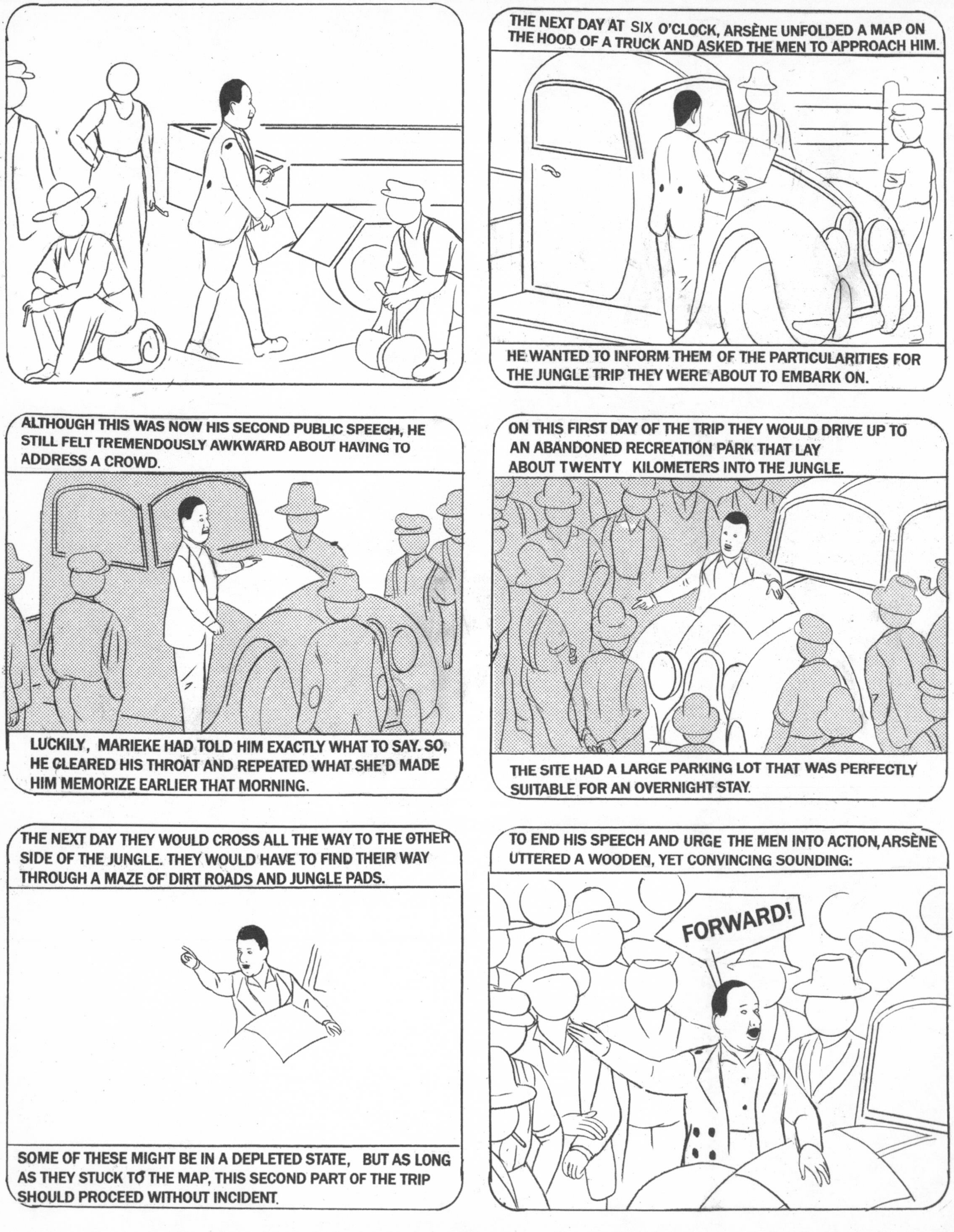
THE NEXT DAY AT SIX O'CLOCK, ARSÈNE UNFOLDED A MAP ON THE HOOD OF A TRUCK AND ASKED THE MEN TO APPROACH HIM.
HE WANTED TO INFORM THEM OF THE PARTICULARITIES FOR THE JUNGLE TRIP THEY WERE ABOUT TO EMBARK ON.
ALTHOUGH THIS WAS NOW HIS SECOND PUBLIC SPEECH, HE STILL FELT TREMENDOUSLY AWKWARD ABOUT HAVING TO ADDRESS A CROWD.
LUCKILY, MARIEKE HAD TOLD HIM EXACTLY WHAT TO SAY. SO, HE CLEARED HIS THROAT AND REPEATED WHAT SHE'D MADE HIM MEMORIZE EARLIER THAT MORNING.
ON THIS FIRST DAY OF THE TRIP THEY WOULD DRIVE UP TO AN ABANDONED RECREATION PARK THAT LAY ABOUT TWENTY KILOMETERS INTO THE JUNGLE.
THE SITE HAD A LARGE PARKING LOT THAT WAS PERFECTLY SUITABLE FOR AN OVERNIGHT STAY.
THE NEXT DAY THEY WOULD CROSS ALL THE WAY TO THE OTHER SIDE OF THE JUNGLE. THEY WOULD HAVE TO FIND THEIR WAY THROUGH A MAZE OF DIRT ROADS AND JUNGLE PADS.
SOME OF THESE MIGHT BE IN A DEPLETED STATE, BUT AS LONG AS THEY STUCK TO THE MAP, THIS SECOND PART OF THE TRIP SHOULD PROCEED WITHOUT INCIDENT.
TO END HIS SPEECH AND URGE THE MEN INTO ACTION, ARSÈNE UTTERED A WOODEN, YET CONVINCING SOUNDING:
FORWARD!

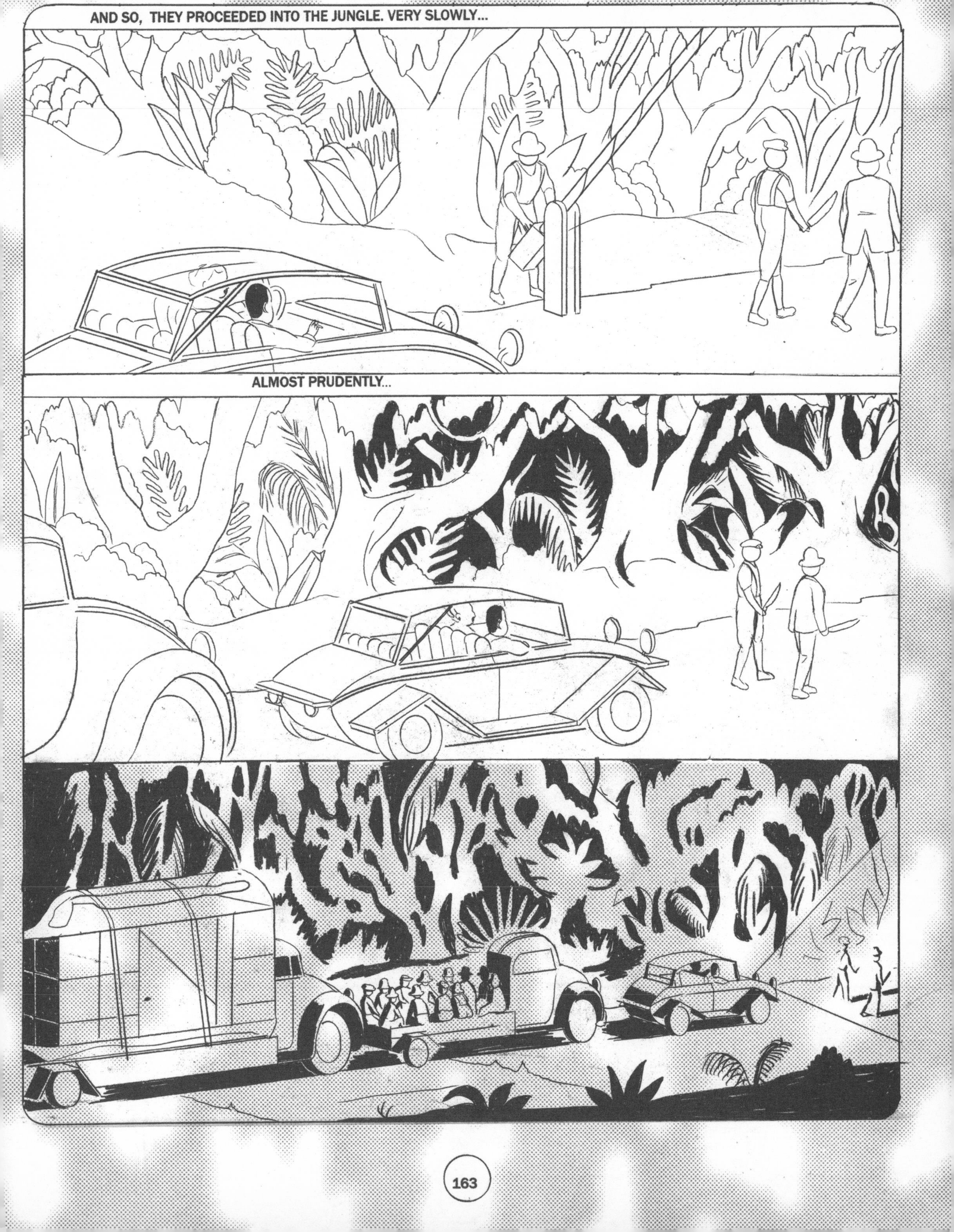
AND SO, THEY PROCEEDED INTO THE JUNGLE. VERY SLOWLY...
ALMOST PRUDENTLY...

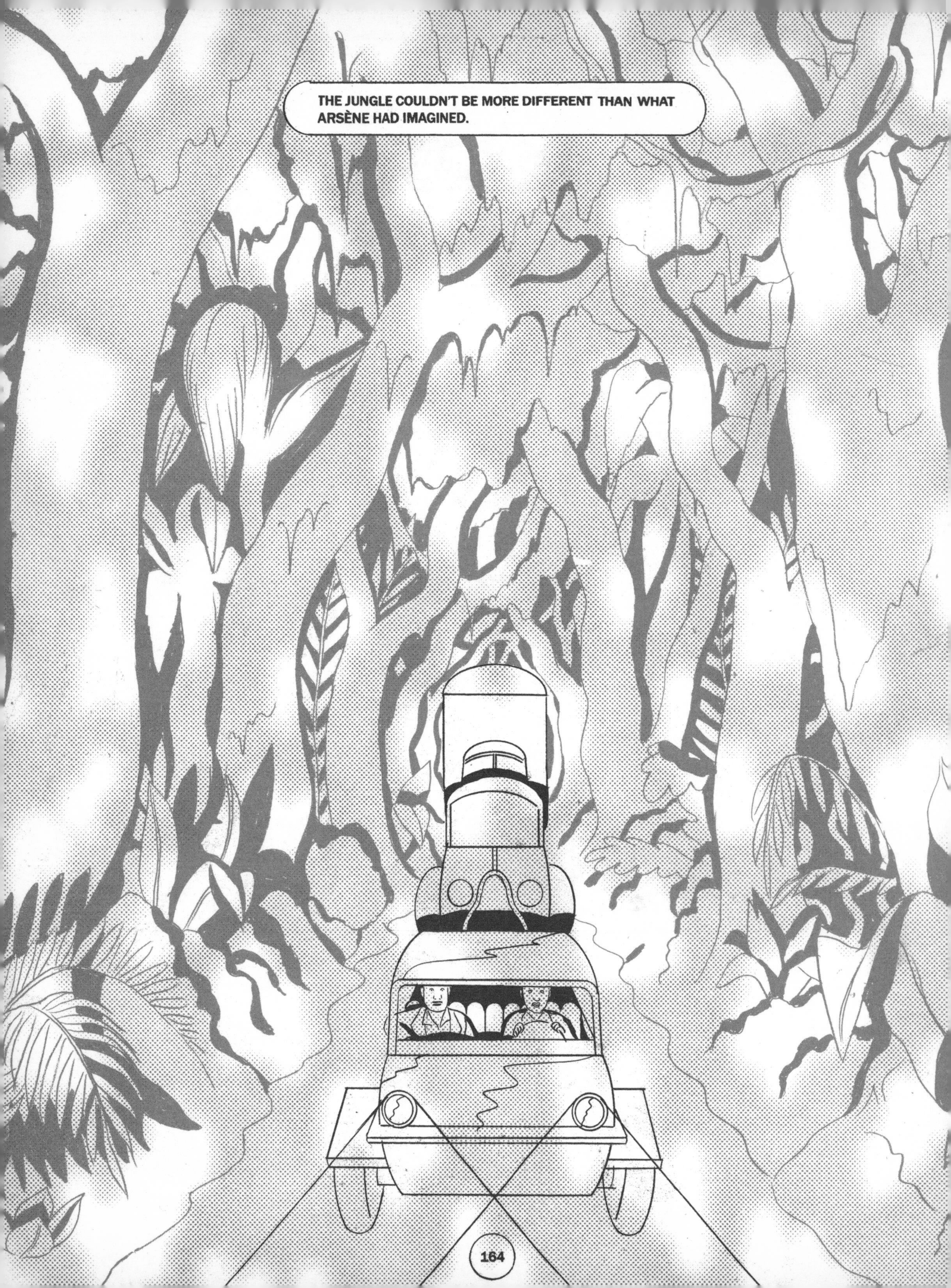
THE JUNGLE COULDN'T BE MORE DIFFERENT THAN WHAT ARSÈNE HAD IMAGINED.

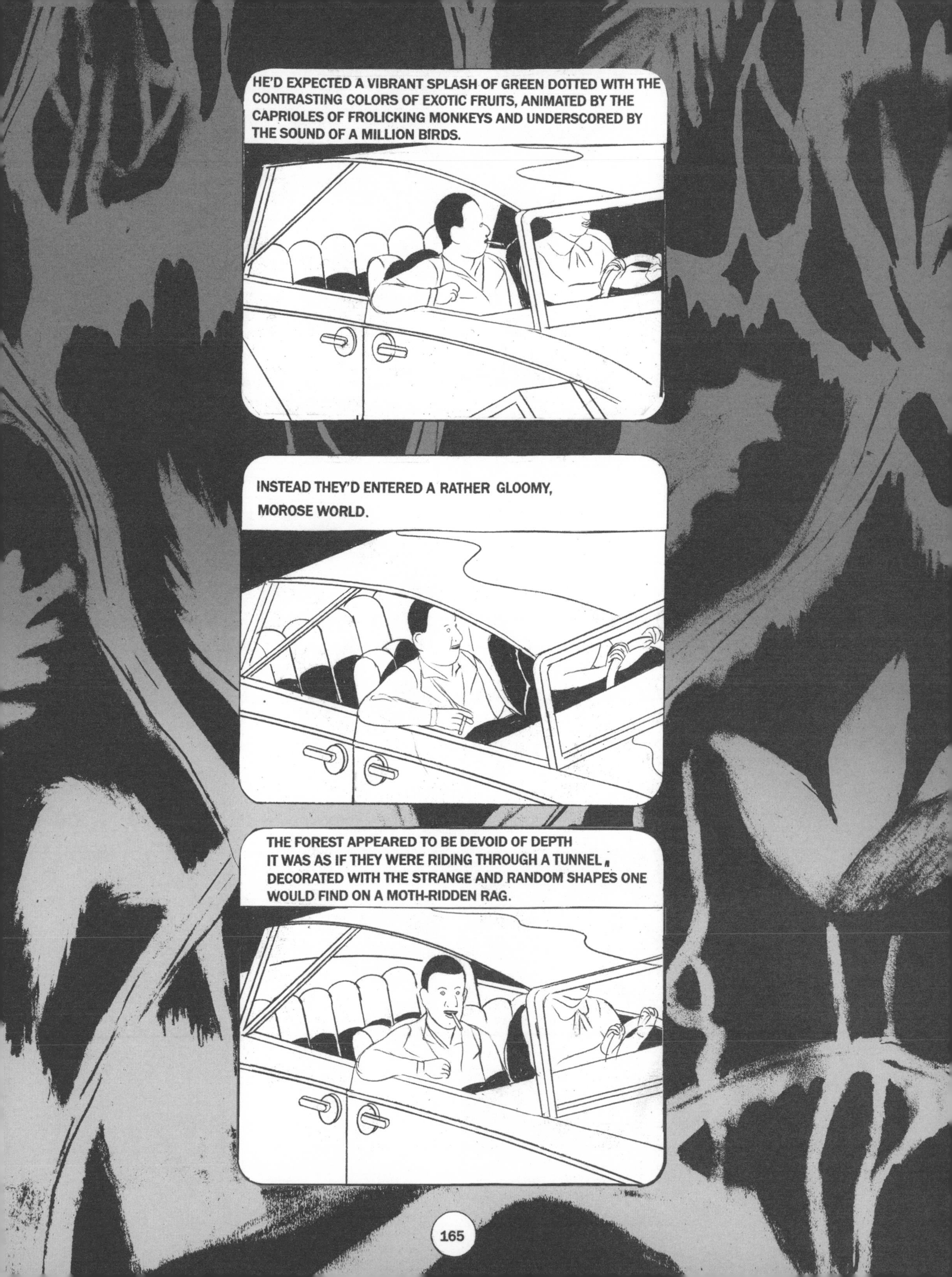
HE'D EXPECTED A VIBRANT SPLASH OF GREEN DOTTED WITH THE CONTRASTING COLORS OF EXOTIC FRUITS, ANIMATED BY THE CAPRIOLES OF FROLICKING MONKEYS AND UNDERSCORED BY THE SOUND OF A MILLION BIRDS.
INSTEAD THEY'D ENTERED A RATHER GLOOMY, MOROSE WORLD.
THE FOREST APPEARED TO BE DEVOID OF DEPTH
IT WAS AS IF THEY WERE RIDING THROUGH A TUNNEL, DECORATED WITH THE STRANGE AND RANDOM SHAPES ONE WOULD FIND ON A MOTH-RIDDEN RAG.

FOR THE ENTIRE MORNING ARSENE GLANCED ALTERNATELY AT MARIEKE

(WHO WAS THE EPITOME OF CALM),

THE MEN IN FRONT OF THE CAR

(WHO WERE LAZILY SWINGING THEIR MACHETES AT OBSTRUCTIVE SHRUBS AND OVERHANGING LIANAS),

AND THE MAP ON HIS LAP

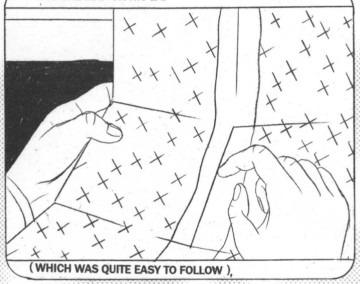

(WHICH WAS QUITE EASY TO FOLLOW),

HE LOOKED IN TURN AT MARIEKE

(WHO'D OCCASIONALLY LOOK BACK, FAINTLY SMILING),

AT THE MEN

(WHO SEEMED TO BE SWIMMING IN A TAR-PIT),

AND THE MAP

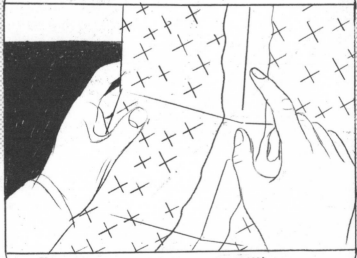

(WHICH COULDN'T CONFUSE A BLIND MAN).

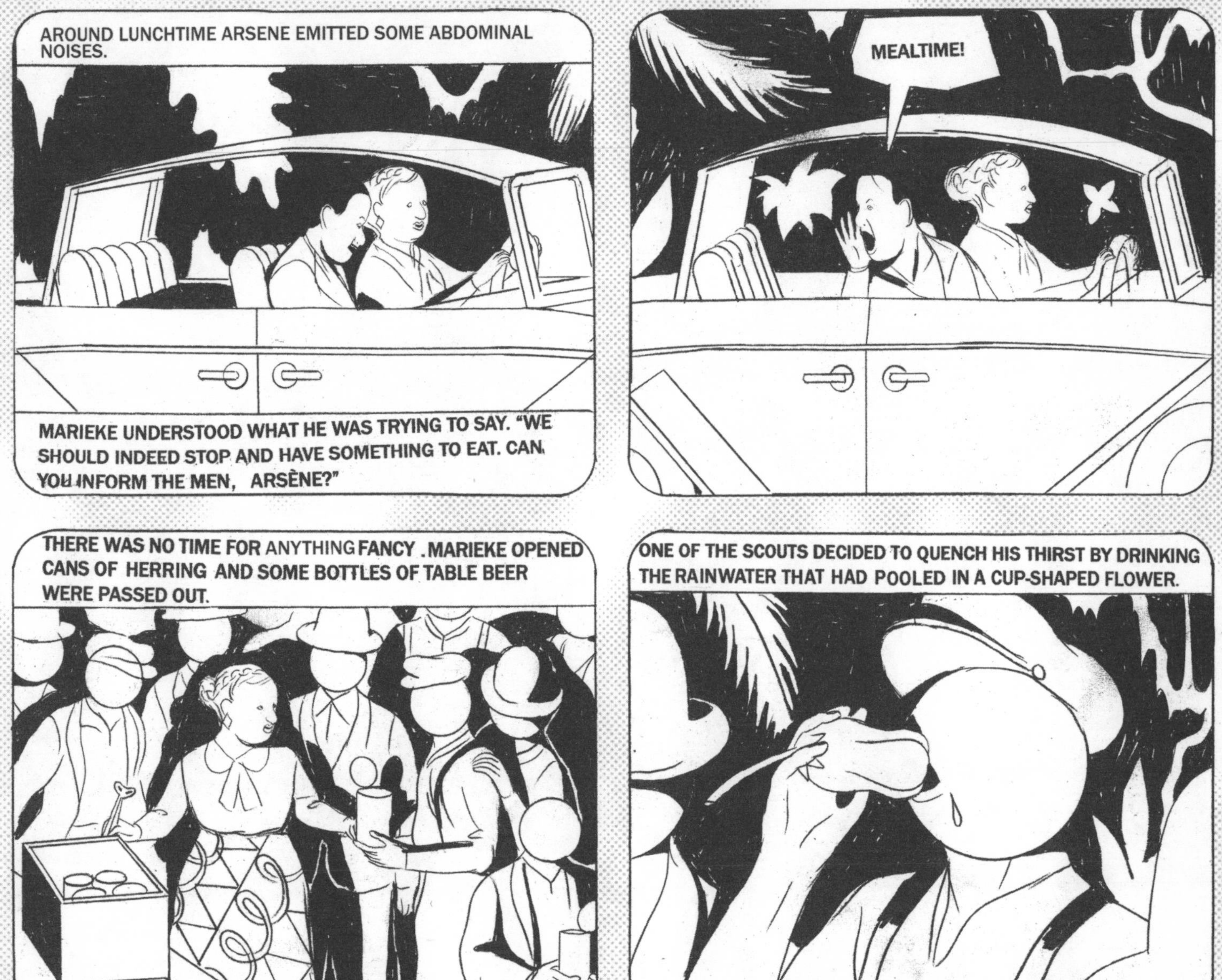
AROUND LUNCHTIME ARSENE EMITTED SOME ABDOMINAL NOISES.
MARIEKE UNDERSTOOD WHAT HE WAS TRYING TO SAY. "WE SHOULD INDEED STOP AND HAVE SOMETHING TO EAT. CAN YOU INFORM THE MEN, ARSÈNE?"
MEALTIME!
THERE WAS NO TIME FOR ANYTHING FANCY. MARIEKE OPENED CANS OF HERRING AND SOME BOTTLES OF TABLE BEER WERE PASSED OUT.
ONE OF THE SCOUTS DECIDED TO QUENCH HIS THIRST BY DRINKING THE RAINWATER THAT HAD POOLED IN A CUP-SHAPED FLOWER.
"SWEET AND REFRESHING," HE REMARKED ENTHUSIASTICALLY.
WHY NOT? WHEN ONE IS THIRSTY, ONE OUGHT TO DRINK.
THAT'S JUST COMMON SENSE.
INSPIRED BY THIS COMMONSENSICAL BEHAVIOR, ARSÈNE DECIDED TO VENTURE INTO THE BERM.
HE NEEDED TO DISPOSE OF THE HERRING, AS WELL AS THE CONTENT OFF HIS BOWELS.

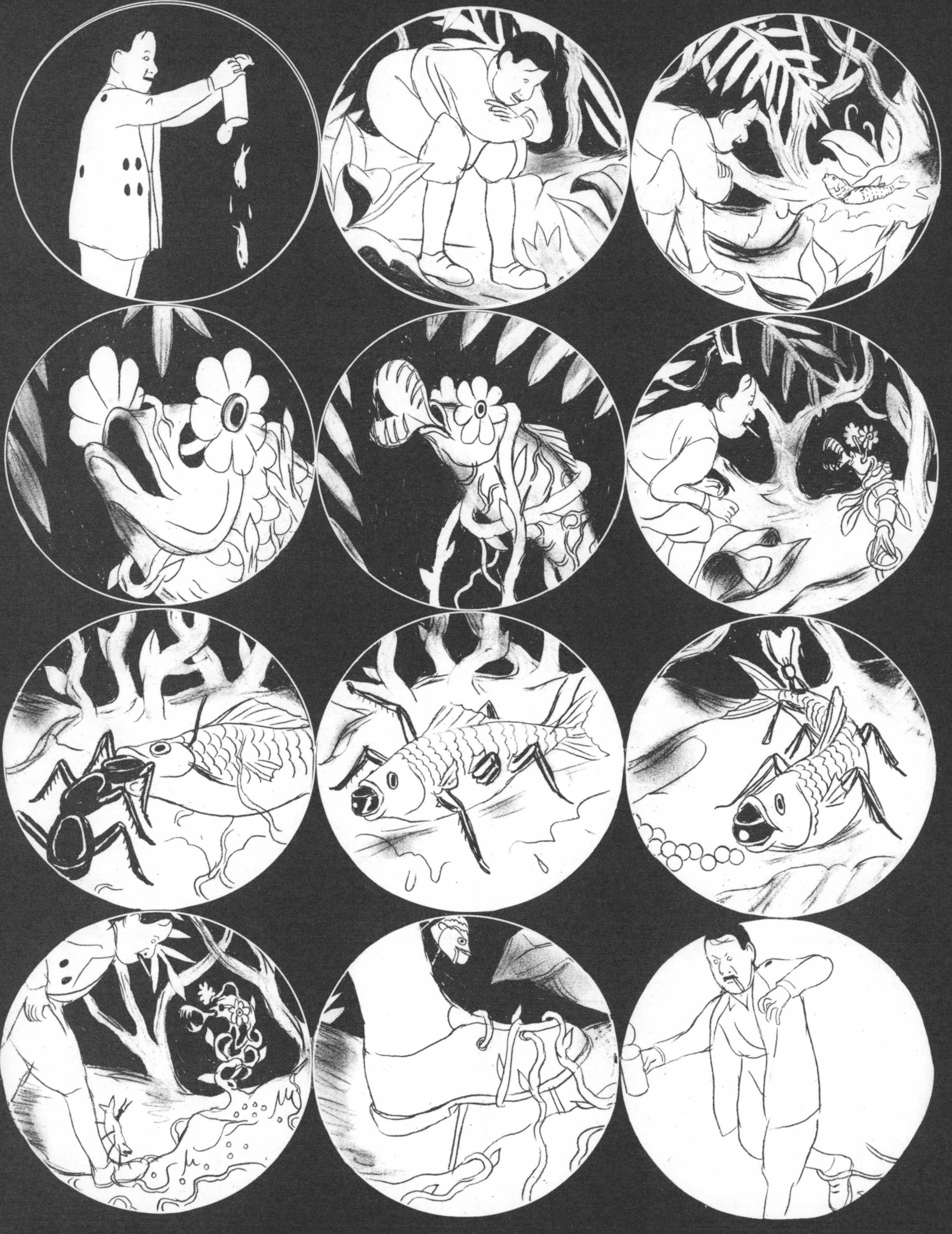

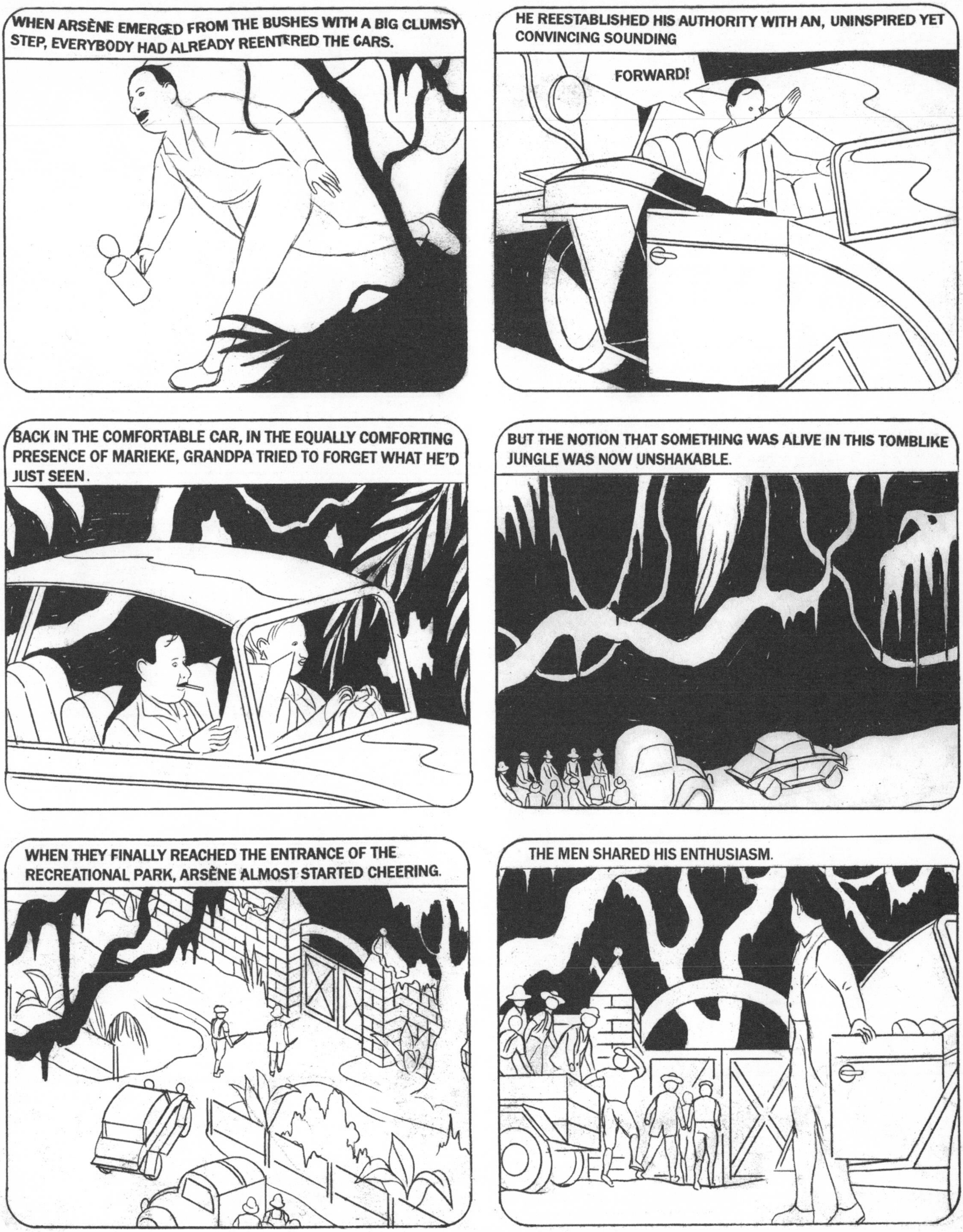
WHEN ARSÈNE EMERGED FROM THE BUSHES WITH A BIG CLUMSY STEP, EVERYBODY HAD ALREADY REENTERED THE CARS.
HE REESTABLISHED HIS AUTHORITY WITH AN, UNINSPIRED YET CONVINCING SOUNDING
FORWARD!
BACK IN THE COMFORTABLE CAR, IN THE EQUALLY COMFORTING PRESENCE OF MARIEKE, GRANDPA TRIED TO FORGET WHAT HE'D JUST SEEN.
BUT THE NOTION THAT SOMETHING WAS ALIVE IN THIS TOMBLIKE JUNGLE WAS NOW UNSHAKABLE.
WHEN THEY FINALLY REACHED THE ENTRANCE OF THE RECREATIONAL PARK, ARSÈNE ALMOST STARTED CHEERING.
THE MEN SHARED HIS ENTHUSIASM.

THEY RAN UP TO THE ENTRANCE GATE OF THE "PLEASURE GARDEN" EN MASSE.

ONE GUY WAS BRANDISHING OVERSIZED PLIERS AND WAS ABOUT TO ATTACK THE CHAINS ON THE FENCE

ARSÈNE TOO, WAS CURIOUS TO SEE WHAT LAY BEYOND THE GATE WHEN HE HEARD MARIEKE'S SOFT VOICE.

ARSÈNE YOU HAVE TO TAKE A LOOK AT THIS.

MARIEKE TOOK HIM IN-BETWEEN TWO VEHICLES, WHERE THEY FOUND A SMALL MAN PIPE-SMOKING MAN BENDING OVER ANOTHER MAN, WHOM GRANDPA IDENTIFIED AS THE COMMON-SENSICAL SCOUT.

THE PIPE-SMOKING MAN INTRODUCED HIMSELF WITH A PREOC-CUPIED NONCHALANCE: "JULES PEETERS".

HE'D COME ALONG THE TRIP SERVING BOTH AS A DOCTOR AND BARBER.

NOW HE WAS FINGERING A CLUSTER OF GRAPE-SIZED ABSCESSES SURROUNDING THE SCOUT'S MOUTH.

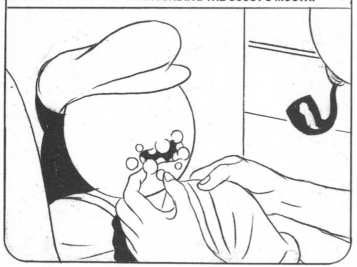

AS IF SUDDENLY OVERCOME BY NAUSEA THE SCOUT'S BODY WENT LIMP AND SLID ONTO THE GROUND.

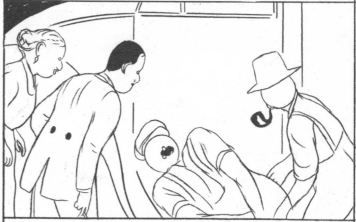

"WE MUST PUT THIS MAN TO BED," SAID PEETERS. "HE CAN HAVE MINE," PROPOSED ARSÈNE.

AFTER THEY'D MOVED HIM TO THE BUNK, PEETERS EXAMINED HIS FACE ANEW. FRESH PUSTULES WERE SPREADING OUT FROM HIS MOUTH INTO HIS FACE.

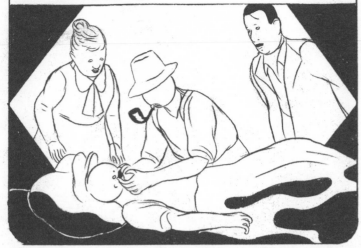

PEETERS PULLED THE BLANKET UP TO THE MAN'S NOSE AND SUGGESTED THEY SHOULD LET HIM HAVE HIS REST.

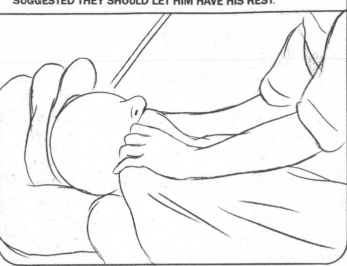

WHAT CAN YOU DO FOR THIS MAN, DOCTOR?

I CAN GIVE HIM A HAIRCUT.

THEN ARSÈNE LET A WORD SLIP FROM HIS MOUTH:

ELEPHANTWORM

IT SOUNDED COMPLETELY INAPPROPRIATE, AS IF IT HAD BEEN THRUST INTO REALITY FROM THE REALM OF BULLSHIT.

FOR A WHILE, THE WORD SEEMED TO HOVER ABOVE THEIR HEADS, NO ONE WANTED TO ALLOW IT INTO THEIR EARS.

ELEPHANT WORM

HAHAHA, THE MAN JUST NEEDS A GOOD NIGHT'S SLEEP. THAT'S ALL.

YOU MIGHT WANT REMIND THE MEN THAT THEY NEED THEIR REST, TOO.

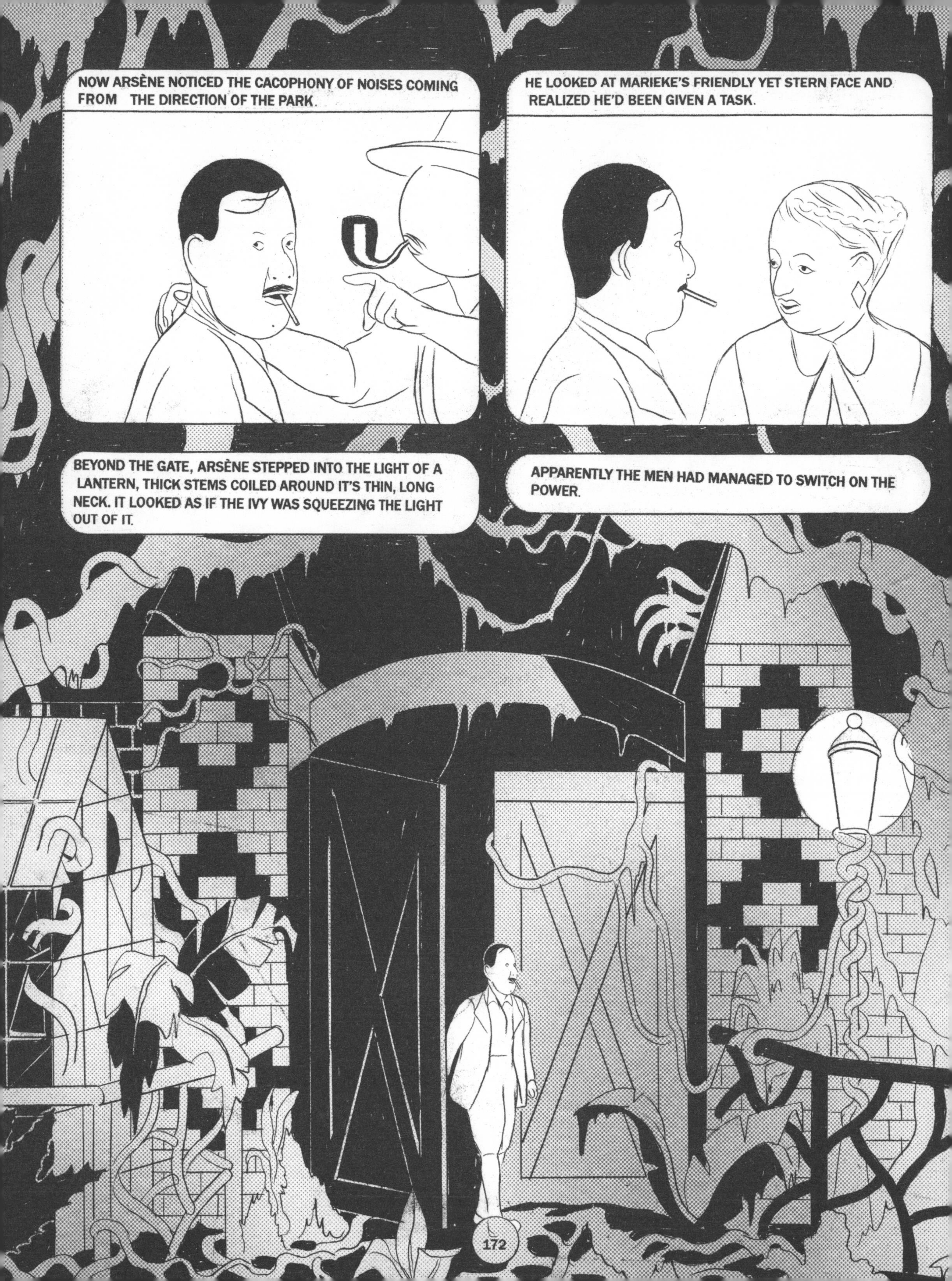
NOW ARSÈNE NOTICED THE CACOPHONY OF NOISES COMING FROM THE DIRECTION OF THE PARK.
HE LOOKED AT MARIEKE'S FRIENDLY YET STERN FACE AND REALIZED HE'D BEEN GIVEN A TASK.
BEYOND THE GATE, ARSÈNE STEPPED INTO THE LIGHT OF A LANTERN, THICK STEMS COILED AROUND IT'S THIN, LONG NECK. IT LOOKED AS IF THE IVY WAS SQUEEZING THE LIGHT OUT OF IT.
APPARENTLY THE MEN HAD MANAGED TO SWITCH ON THE POWER.

A LOUDSPEAKER MOUNTED ON A POLE EMITTED A VAGUELY FAMILIAR TUNE. IT SOUNDED EERIE; MUTED AND DELAYED.

AS HE PROCEEDED INTO THE PARK THE SOUND SEEMED TO DETERIORATE, AS IF THE TAPE-PLAYER WAS SINKING INTO A PUDDLE OF MUD.

ARSÈNE WONDERED WHAT FUNNYMAN HAD THOUGHT OF BUILDING A BELGIAN THEME PARK IN THIS TROPICAL SETTING?

AND WHY HAD HE BUILT IT SO DEEP IN THE JUNGLE, AS IF IT WERE AN EMBARRASSMENT. LIKE SOME SENTIMENTAL ARTIFACT ONE HIDES IN THE CORNER OF A CLOSET.

IN FACT THE PARK HAD BEEN CONCEIVED AS A REFUGE FOR BELGIAN COLONIST FAMILIES OUT ON A SUNDAY OUTING. THE LOCATION HAD SEEMED IDEAL FOR A RECREATION OF THE HOMELAND.

THE FOREST ROOF OFFERED SHELTER FOR THE PUNISHING SUNLIGHT. THE TEMPERATURE WAS MODERATE AND THERE WAS THE OCCASIONAL PLEASANT DRIZZLE.

THERE WAS A VEGETABLE GARDEN WHICH ONCE SPROUTED BRUSSELS SPROUTS, CHICORY AND RED CABBAGE.

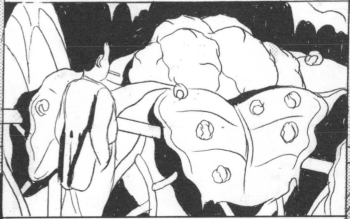

THE VEGETABLES WHERE STILL THERE, BUT PLAGUED BY GIGANTISM AND FUSED TOGETHER IN THE MOST INCONGRUOUS HYBRIDS.

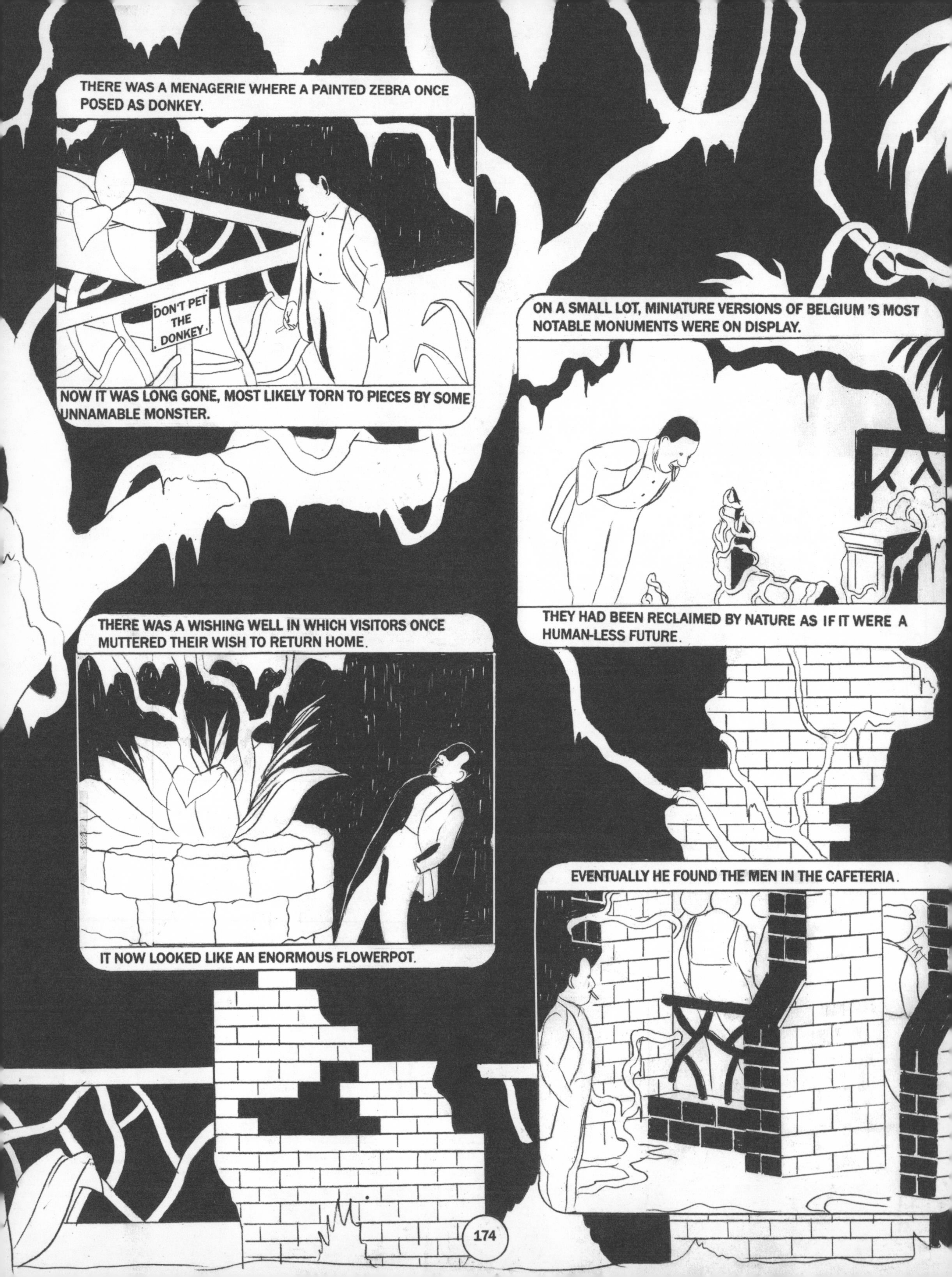
THERE WAS A MENAGERIE WHERE A PAINTED ZEBRA ONCE POSED AS DONKEY.
DON'T PET THE DONKEY.
NOW IT WAS LONG GONE, MOST LIKELY TORN TO PIECES BY SOME UNNAMABLE MONSTER.
ON A SMALL LOT, MINIATURE VERSIONS OF BELGIUM 'S MOST NOTABLE MONUMENTS WERE ON DISPLAY.
THEY HAD BEEN RECLAIMED BY NATURE AS IF IT WERE A HUMAN-LESS FUTURE.
THERE WAS A WISHING WELL IN WHICH VISITORS ONCE MUTTERED THEIR WISH TO RETURN HOME.
IT NOW LOOKED LIKE AN ENORMOUS FLOWERPOT.
EVENTUALLY HE FOUND THE MEN IN THE CAFETERIA.

THE NEON LIGHTING WAS FLASHING ON AND OFF, CUTTING THEIR UNRULY MOVEMENTS INTO BITS.

THE MEN DIDN'T SEEM TO NOTICE, THEY'D FOUND A BEER KEG AND HAD MANAGED TO CONNECT IT TO THE TAP.

THEY WERE DRINKING, DANCING AND SINGING IN A COMPLETELY ARTLESS FASHION

AS SOON AS THEY NOTICED ARSÈNE'S PRESENCE, THEIR RACKET LESSENED AND THEY FORMED A HUMAN CORRIDOR ALLOWING HIM TO GO UP TO THE BAR.

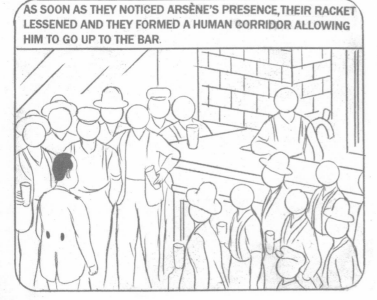

HE LAID HIS ARMS ON THE COUNTER AND A MAN CAME FORWARD TO TAKE UP THE BARTENDING DUTIES.

HE ASKED ARSÈNE: "WHAT SHALL IT BE, SIR?"

A BURST OF LAUGHTER ENSUED.

I'LL HAVE A BEER.

HERE YOU GO, SIR.

ARSÈNE EMPTIED THE GLASS IN ONE GULP.

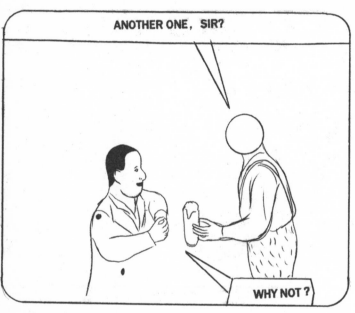

ANOTHER ONE, SIR?

WHY NOT?

AGAIN, HE DOWNED THE DRINK IN THE BLINK OF AN EYE.

(LAUGHTER AND APPLAUSE)

IF HE CONTINUED LIKE THIS, HIS COMMAND OVER THE SITUATION WOULD SURELY WEAKEN.

SO, AFTER FOUR BEERS GRANDPA TURNED AROUND AND WALKED OUT OF THE CAFETERIA.

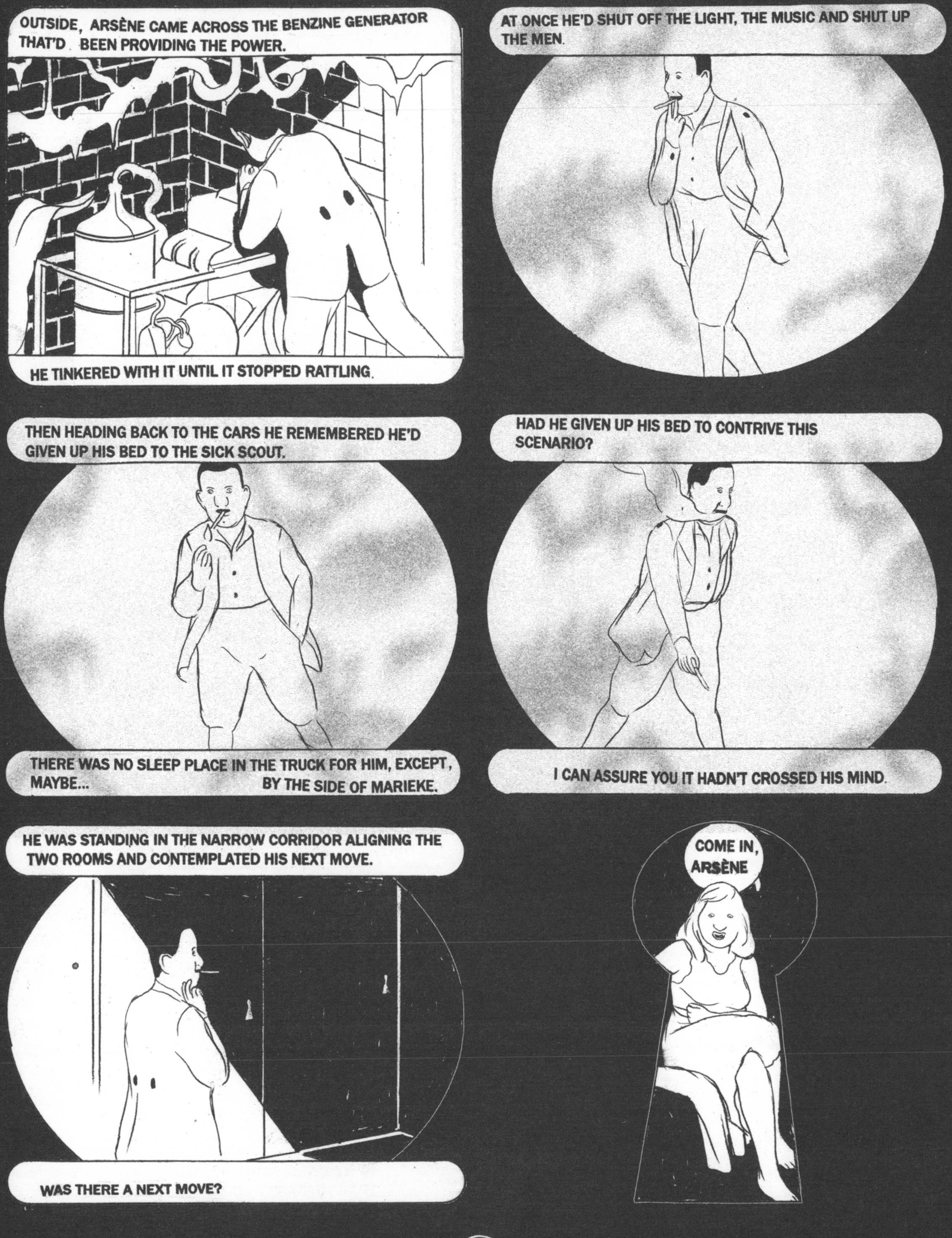
OUTSIDE, ARSÈNE CAME ACROSS THE BENZINE GENERATOR THAT'D BEEN PROVIDING THE POWER.
HE TINKERED WITH IT UNTIL IT STOPPED RATTLING.
AT ONCE HE'D SHUT OFF THE LIGHT, THE MUSIC AND SHUT UP THE MEN.
THEN HEADING BACK TO THE CARS HE REMEMBERED HE'D GIVEN UP HIS BED TO THE SICK SCOUT.
THERE WAS NO SLEEP PLACE IN THE TRUCK FOR HIM, EXCEPT, MAYBE... BY THE SIDE OF MARIEKE.
HAD HE GIVEN UP HIS BED TO CONTRIVE THIS SCENARIO?
I CAN ASSURE YOU IT HADN'T CROSSED HIS MIND.
HE WAS STANDING IN THE NARROW CORRIDOR ALIGNING THE TWO ROOMS AND CONTEMPLATED HIS NEXT MOVE.
WAS THERE A NEXT MOVE?
COME IN, ARSÈNE

SHE PUT HER FINGER ON HER LIPS, SIGNIFYING HIM TO BE QUIET. (AN UNNECESSARY GESTURE, AS HE WAS ENTIRELY SPEECHLESS)

SHE POINTED TOWARDS THE ADJOINING ROOM, WHERE A MAN WAS QUIETLY SUFFERING.

THEN SHE LEANED DOWN AND GESTURED AT HIM TO COME AND LAY NEXT TO HER IN THE TINY BUNK BED.

NOW MARIEKE—A 36 YEAR OLD MARRIED WOMAN— FACED MY GRANDFATHER, A MANCHILD WHO WAS ALMOST TEN YEARS HER JUNIOR.

SHE LOOKED HIM STRAIGHT IN THE EYES, PATIENTLY ANTICIPATING HIS ADVANCES.

WATCHING HIS EVERY MOVE...

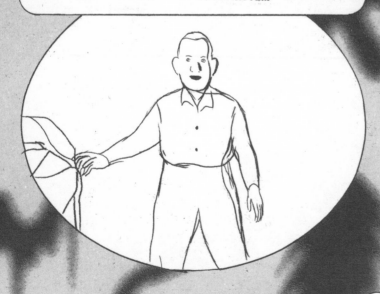

HE APPROACHED HER PRUDENTLY.

AT A CERTAIN POINT SHE SIGHED LIGHTLY, IT MOMENTARILY DEFLATED HIS COURAGE.

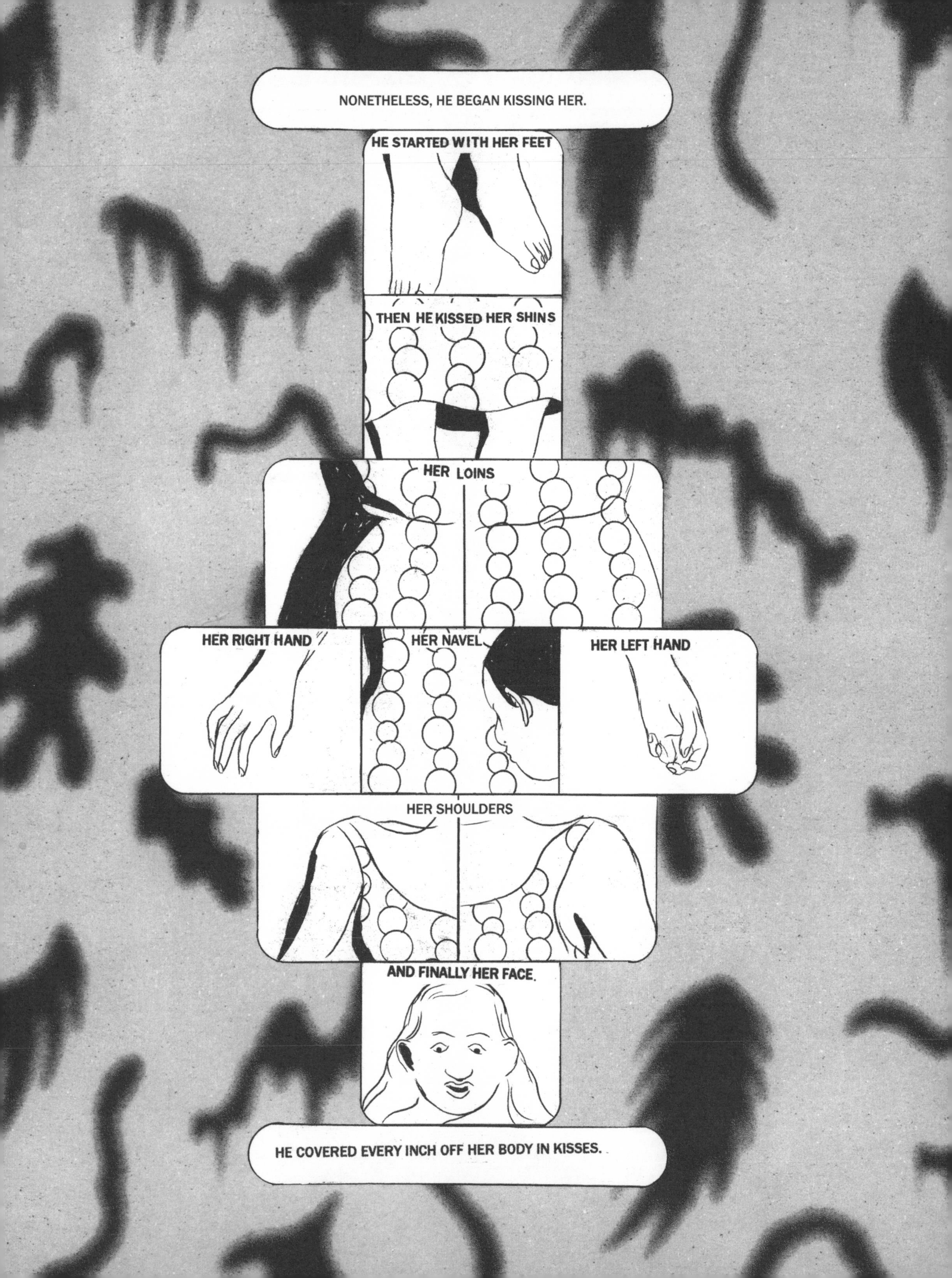

NONETHELESS, HE BEGAN KISSING HER.

HE STARTED WITH HER FEET

THEN HE KISSED HER SHINS

HER LOINS

HER RIGHT HAND

HER NAVEL

HER LEFT HAND

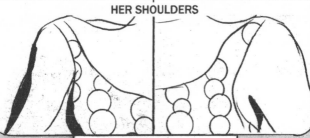

HER SHOULDERS

AND FINALLY HER FACE.

HE COVERED EVERY INCH OFF HER BODY IN KISSES.

EVENTUALLY, MARIEKE PUT AN END TO GRANDPA'S EXPANSIVE KISSING BY OPENING HIS PANTS.

HIS GENITALS LAY FORMLESS, BALLED UP BETWEEN HIS UPPER THIGHS.

SHE KISSED HIM ON THE EAR AND HIS MEMBER STARTED MOVING.

IT UNFOLDED ITSELF SLOWLY, QUIVERING LIKE A BIRD HATCHING OUT OF AN EGG

SLOWLY ITS STICKY FLESH UNFOLDED FORMING A PERFECT YOUNG PENIS.

AND THEN, ALTHOUGH NEVER PRACTICED, HE INSTINCTIVELY KNEW WHAT TO DO NEXT...

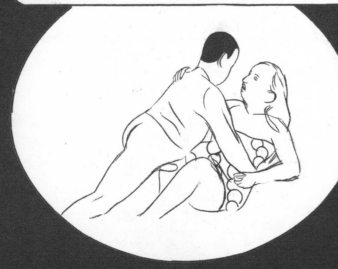

WITH A LITTLE HELP.

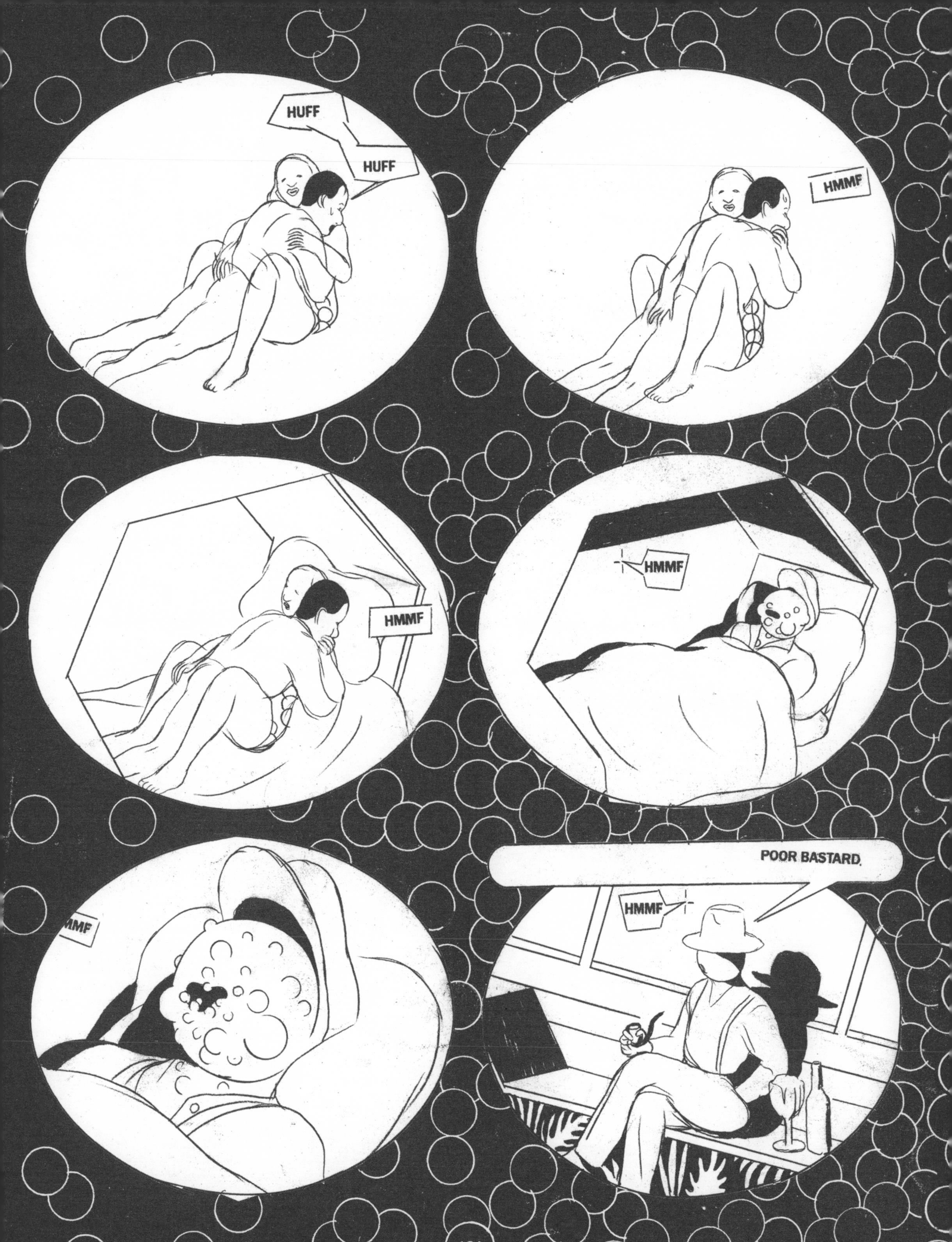
HUFF
HUFF
HMMF
HMMF
HMMF
MMF
POOR BASTARD.
HMMF

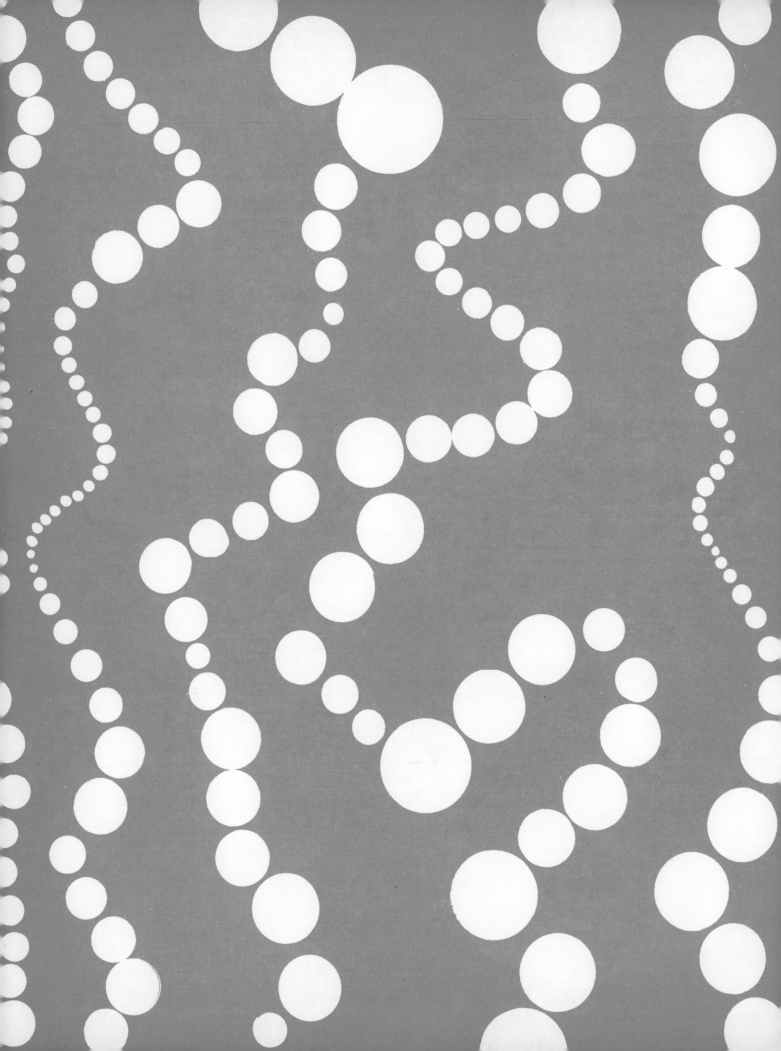

THAT MORNING MARIEKE AWOKE ARSÈNE BY CRAWLING OVER HIM.

WHEN HE OPENED HIS EYES SHE'D SLIPPED OUT OF THE ROOM BUT HER SCENT WAS STILL THERE.

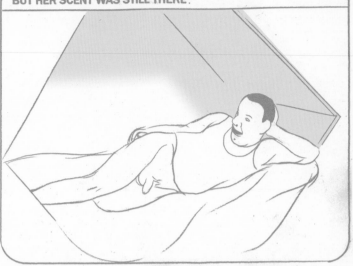

HE SHOVED HIS FACE IN HER PILLOW AND INHALED HER SWEET AROMA.

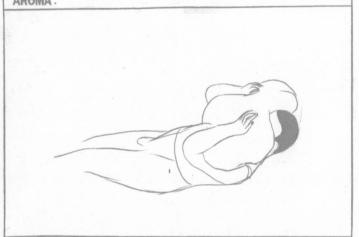

IT FILLED HIS TRACHEA, HIS LUNGS AND THEN HIS ENTIRE BODY.

HE FELT HIMSELF BECOMING WEIGHTLESS, THEN ASCENDING ABOUT FIVE CENTIMETERS ABOVE THE BED.

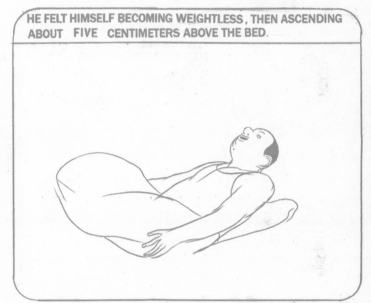

HE GLIDED OUT OF THE VEHICLE.

IN A STATE OF BLISS HE FLOATED OVER THE CAR PARK, MOVING SILENTLY BETWEEN THE BODIES OF THE SLEEPING MEN.

HIS PENIS FELT PLEASANTLY UNFAMILIAR THAT MORNING,

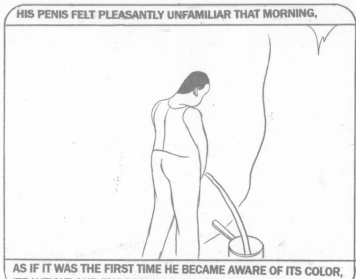

AS IF IT WAS THE FIRST TIME HE BECAME AWARE OF ITS COLOR, ITS WEIGHT AND THE PECULIAR FOLDS IN ITS FORESKIN.

AS HE WAS PISSING THROUGH HIS NEW PENIS HE NOTICED MARIEKE, RUSHING INTO THE BUSHES.

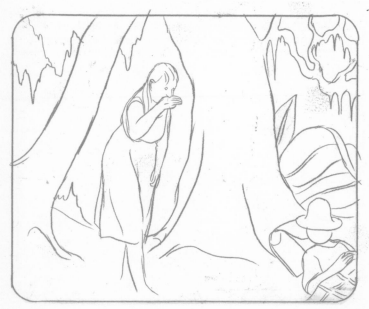

MR PEETERS WAKE UP!

HE'S IN A TERRIBLE STATE!

184

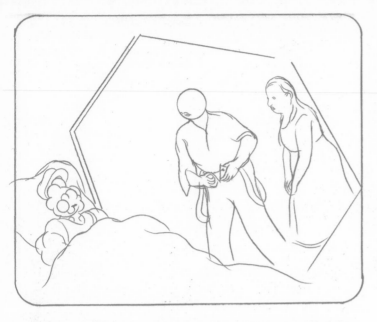

He must be be attended to. He can't eat or drink or do anything independently.

Listen, madame, I'm a doctor, a barber, and a pipe smoker. I have no desire to add nurse to that list.

Arsène, you'll have to drive the car today while I watch over this poor man. It is important you follow the map very closely.

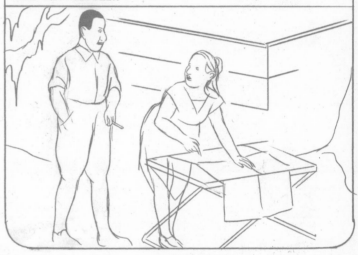

While she was explaining the specifics of the route Grandpa was watching her lips and her chubby finger, and then the arm, shoulder and chin connecting both.

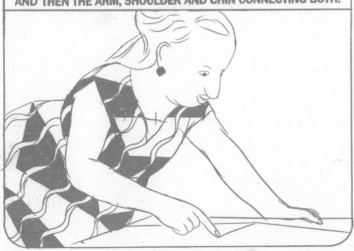

He watched the curly hair on her back, how it seemed to intertwine with the pattern of her dress.

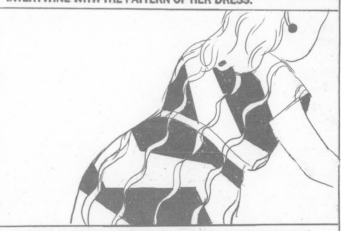

How the shapes on the textile where altered by the curves of her body.

AFTER MARIEKE'S EXPOSITION GRANDPA WALKED, OR RATHER, SWAGGERED UP TO THE AMPHIBIAN VEHICLE.

HE SHOUTED THIS PHRASE: **LET'S GET GOING, FELLAS!**

IT WAS MET WITH SOME RESISTANCE, AS MOST MEN HADN'T EVEN HAD THE CHANCE TO HAVE THEIR MORNING COFFEE YET.

BUT ARSÈNE'S CONFIDENCE, HIS USE OF THE SOMEWHAT OVER-FAMILIAR "FELLAS", DID ENCOURAGE THEM TO GET MOVING.

TEN MINUTES LATER THE CARAVAN WAS MOVING OFF THE PARKING LOT.

ARSÈNE LAUNCHED INTO IT WITH ZEST. TODAY THE TEMPO WOULD BE A LITTLE FASTER.

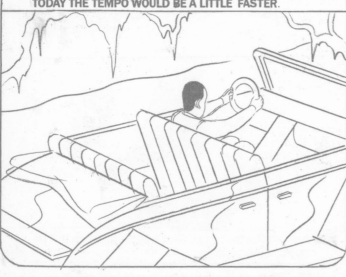

THE MAN IN FRONT OF THE CAR, NOW WORKING ALONE, WAS SWINGING HIS MACHETE AS IF HE WERE IN A SWORD FIGHT.

HE HAD TO MAINTAIN A STEADY CLIP IF HE DIDN'T WANT THE CAR TO BUMP HIM IN THE BEHIND.

ABOUT A HUNDRED METERS BEYOND THE PARK, THE ROAD SUDDENLY CHANGED.
AS IF, UNTIL NOW, IT BEEN DRAWN OUT WITH A RULER WHILE THIS WAS NOW RENDERED IN A SLOPPY FREEHAND.
THE PATH LED THEM UPWARDS AND AS THEY WERE CLIMBING THE FOLIAGE BECAME THINNER.
THE STABBING SUNLIGHT THREW MESSY, IRREGULAR SHADES EVERYWHERE.
ARSÈNE WAS HAPPY TO HAVE THE CLEAR, CLEAN LINES OF THE MAP SHOWING HIM THE WAY.
ROCKY ROAD
BUSH
MUDDY ROAD
A LITTLE FURTHER, THOUGH, THE ROUTE BECAME ROCKY...
...AND THE MAP UNREADABLE.
SEEMS LIKE WE'VE HIT A BUMPY PATCH.

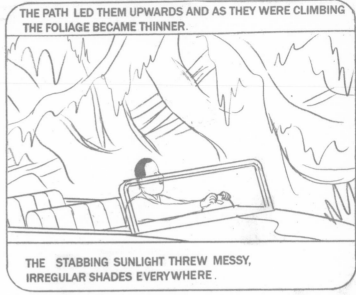

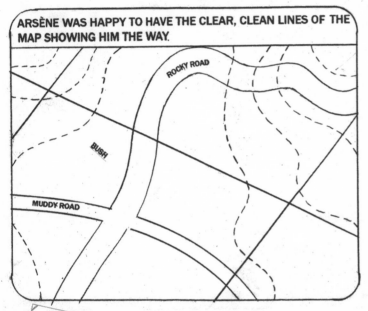

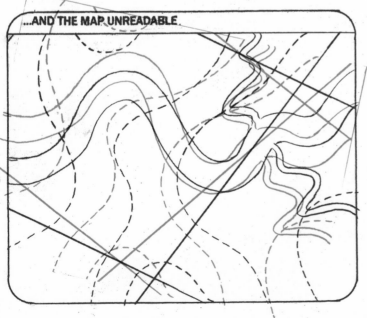

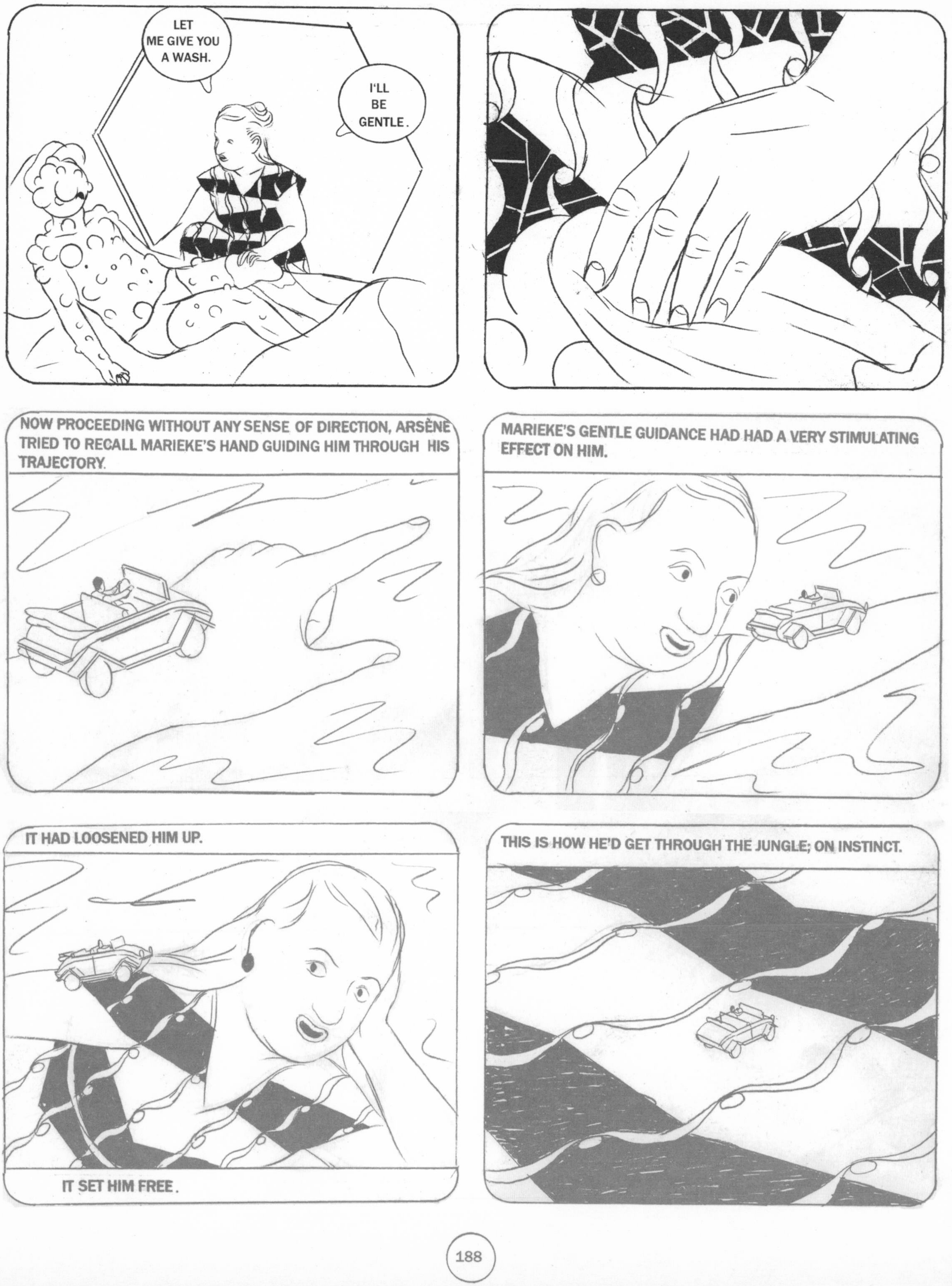
LET ME GIVE YOU A WASH.
I'LL BE GENTLE.
NOW PROCEEDING WITHOUT ANY SENSE OF DIRECTION, ARSÈNE TRIED TO RECALL MARIEKE'S HAND GUIDING HIM THROUGH HIS TRAJECTORY.
MARIEKE'S GENTLE GUIDANCE HAD HAD A VERY STIMULATING EFFECT ON HIM.
IT HAD LOOSENED HIM UP.
IT SET HIM FREE.
THIS IS HOW HE'D GET THROUGH THE JUNGLE; ON INSTINCT.

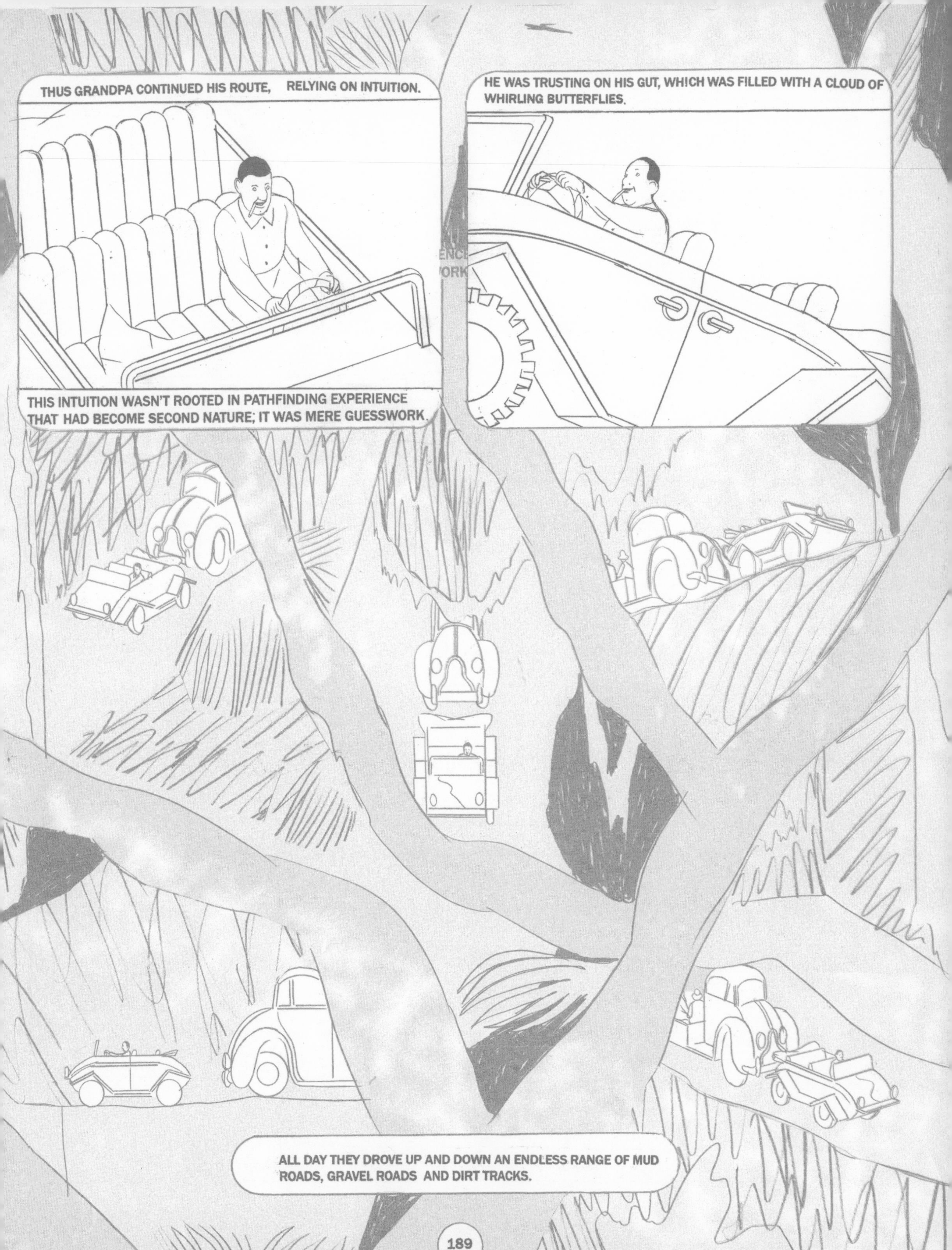
THUS GRANDPA CONTINUED HIS ROUTE, RELYING ON INTUITION.
THIS INTUITION WASN'T ROOTED IN PATHFINDING EXPERIENCE THAT HAD BECOME SECOND NATURE; IT WAS MERE GUESSWORK.
HE WAS TRUSTING ON HIS GUT, WHICH WAS FILLED WITH A CLOUD OF WHIRLING BUTTERFLIES.
ALL DAY THEY DROVE UP AND DOWN AN ENDLESS RANGE OF MUD ROADS, GRAVEL ROADS AND DIRT TRACKS.

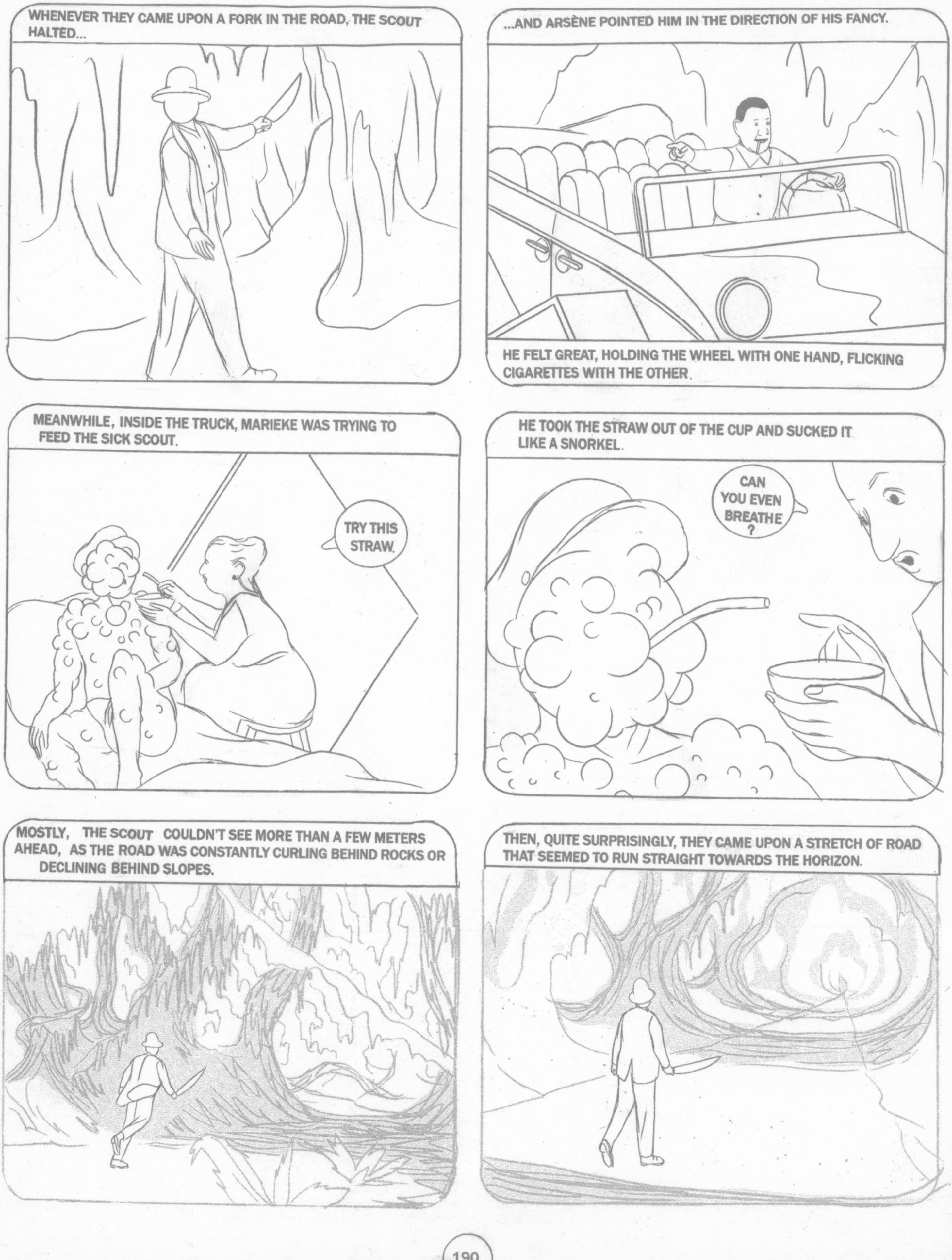
WHENEVER THEY CAME UPON A FORK IN THE ROAD, THE SCOUT HALTED...
...AND ARSÈNE POINTED HIM IN THE DIRECTION OF HIS FANCY.
HE FELT GREAT, HOLDING THE WHEEL WITH ONE HAND, FLICKING CIGARETTES WITH THE OTHER.
MEANWHILE, INSIDE THE TRUCK, MARIEKE WAS TRYING TO FEED THE SICK SCOUT.
TRY THIS STRAW.
HE TOOK THE STRAW OUT OF THE CUP AND SUCKED IT LIKE A SNORKEL.
CAN YOU EVEN BREATHE ?
MOSTLY, THE SCOUT COULDN'T SEE MORE THAN A FEW METERS AHEAD, AS THE ROAD WAS CONSTANTLY CURLING BEHIND ROCKS OR DECLINING BEHIND SLOPES.
THEN, QUITE SURPRISINGLY, THEY CAME UPON A STRETCH OF ROAD THAT SEEMED TO RUN STRAIGHT TOWARDS THE HORIZON.

THE SCOUT STARTED RUNNING AS IF HE'D FIND THE END OF THE JUNGLE AT THE VANISHING POINT.

HE FOUND THE END OF THE ROAD QUITE FAST.

AFTER A FEW METERS IT NARROWED INTO A POINT.

BEHIND IT THE LAND DROPPED OFF DRAMATICALLY.

TO GRANDPA IT HAD LOOKED AS IF THE SCOUT HAD GROWN INTO A GIANT.

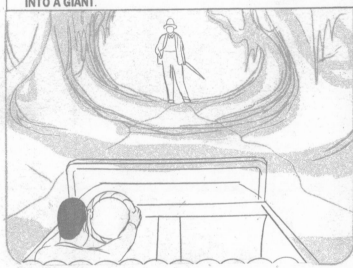

HE WAS QUITE HAPPY TO FIND OUT IT WAS JUST AN OPTICAL ILLUSION.

THE MEN WHO'D BEEN DENIED BOTH BREAKFAST AND LUNCH CAME OFF THE TRUCK.

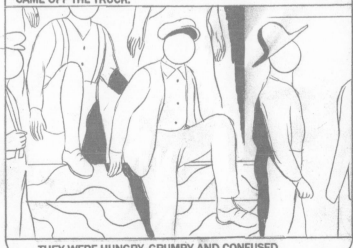

THEY WERE HUNGRY, GRUMPY AND CONFUSED.

ARSÈNE HAD SOME EXPLAINING TO DO.

HE EXPRESSED HIMSELF IN SIMPLE, ROBUST SENTENCES:

LISTEN, MEN!

WE HAVE COME UPON AN UNFORESEEN SINKHOLE.

WE'LL CEASE OR TRIP FOR TODAY AND SET UP CAMP HERE.

TOMORROW, WE'LL TAKE A SMALL DETOUR TO GET BACK ON TRACK.

THAT'S ALL.

HIS EXPLANATION SEEMED ACCEPTABLE AND THEY DWINDLED OFF, HAPPY TO FINALLY BE ABLE TO EAT.

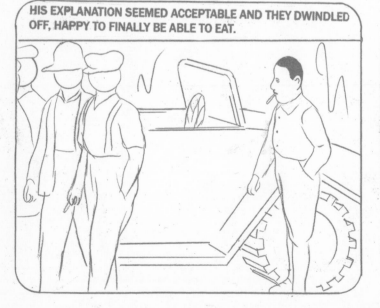

THE WORDS HAD COME EASILY.

THEY'D BEEN WHISPERED IN HIS EAR BY MARIEKE WHO HAD BEEN STANDING DISCREETLY BEHIND HIM.

SO HOW FAR OFF TRACK ARE WE?

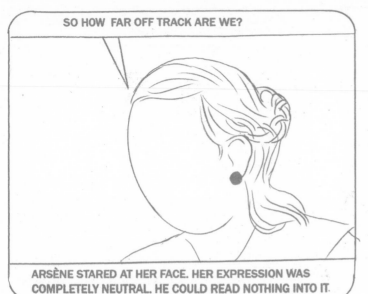

ARSÈNE STARED AT HER FACE. HER EXPRESSION WAS COMPLETELY NEUTRAL. HE COULD READ NOTHING INTO IT.

NOT TOO FAR.

"NOT TOO FAR." HE SAID IT TWICE, AND IT ALREADY SOUNDED LESS CONVINCING THE SECOND TIME.

HE WANTED TO KISS HER, BUT THAT SEEMED TOTALLY IMPOSSIBLE NOW.

EVENTUALLY, SHE WENT BACK TO RESUME HER NURSING DUTIES.

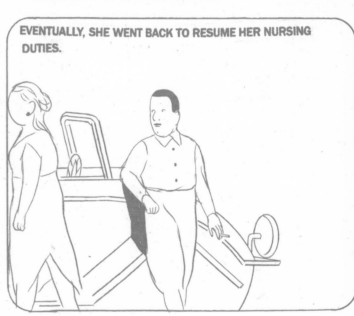

HE SPREAD OUT THE MAP ON THE HOOD OF THE CAR AND STUDIED IT...

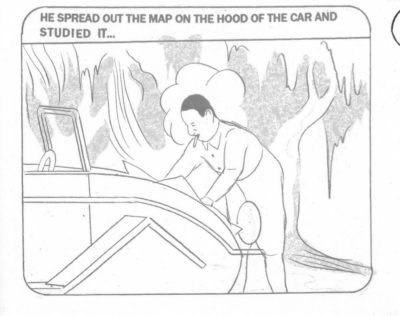

UNTIL HE NEEDED A LANTERN TO SEE IT.

193

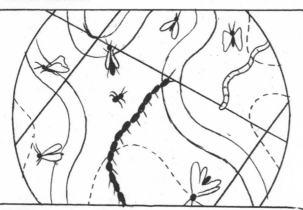

HE STARED AT THE MAP UNTIL THE LINES STARTED MOVING.

A VARIETY OF INSECTS WERE NOW REDRAWING THE MAP, MARKING IT WITH THEIR DROPPINGS AND SUGGESTING NEW BY-WAYS WITH THEIR BODIES.

AS ARSENE SMASHED HIS FIST ONTO THE MAP TO CHASE THEM OFF, ONE OF THE MEN APPROACHED HIM.

SIR, WOULD YOU LIKE TO JOIN US? WE'VE ROASTED SOME MEAT AND THERE IS BEER.

HE DECLINED THE PROPOSAL, FOLDED UP HIS MAP AND WALKED OFF

HE WALKED OFF JUST TO DISAPPEAR OUT OF SIGHT, NOT QUITE KNOWING WHERE TO GO.

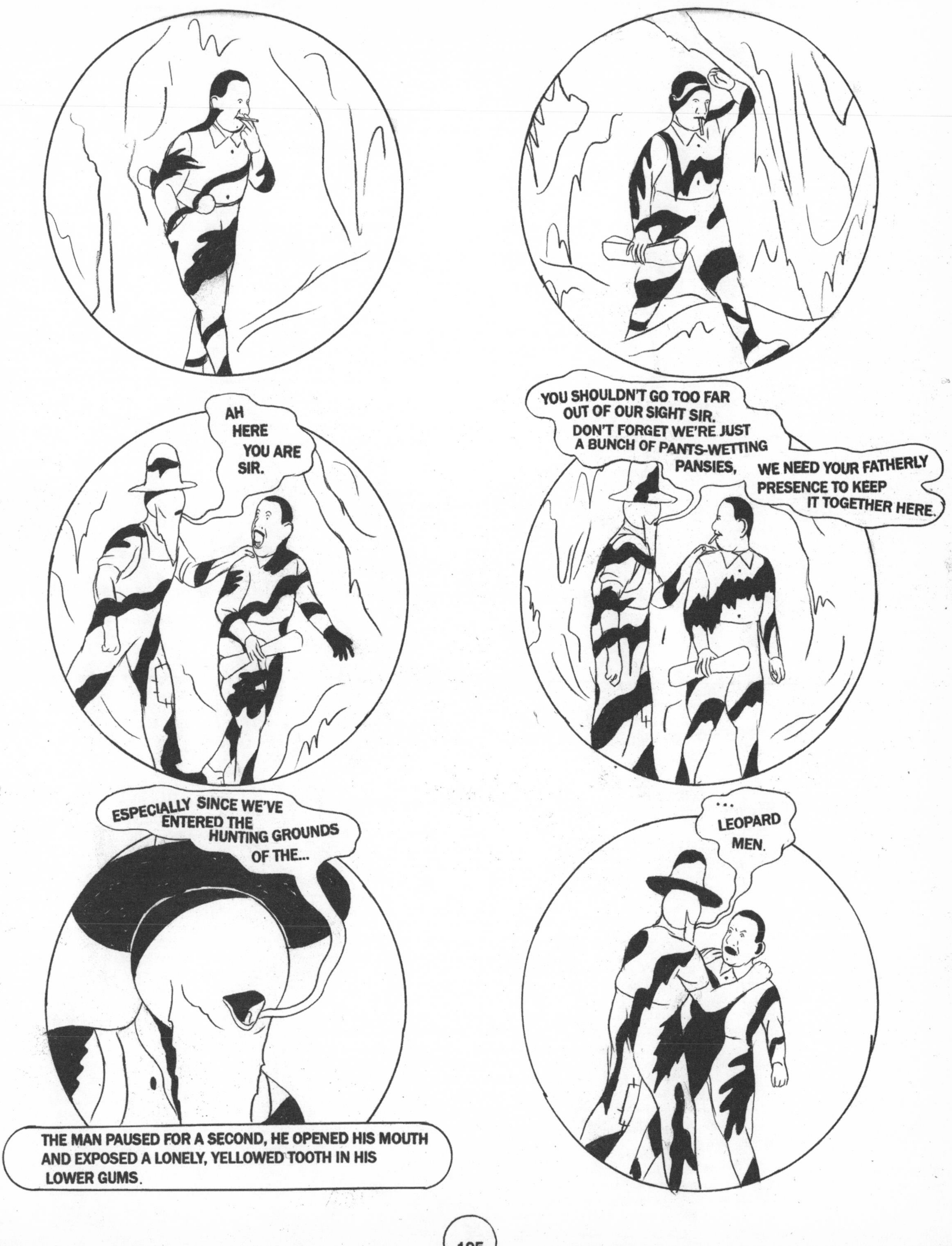
AH HERE YOU ARE SIR.
YOU SHOULDN'T GO TOO FAR OUT OF OUR SIGHT SIR. DON'T FORGET WE'RE JUST A BUNCH OF PANTS-WETTING PANSIES,
WE NEED YOUR FATHERLY PRESENCE TO KEEP IT TOGETHER HERE.
ESPECIALLY SINCE WE'VE ENTERED THE HUNTING GROUNDS OF THE...
THE MAN PAUSED FOR A SECOND, HE OPENED HIS MOUTH AND EXPOSED A LONELY, YELLOWED TOOTH IN HIS LOWER GUMS.
... LEOPARD MEN.

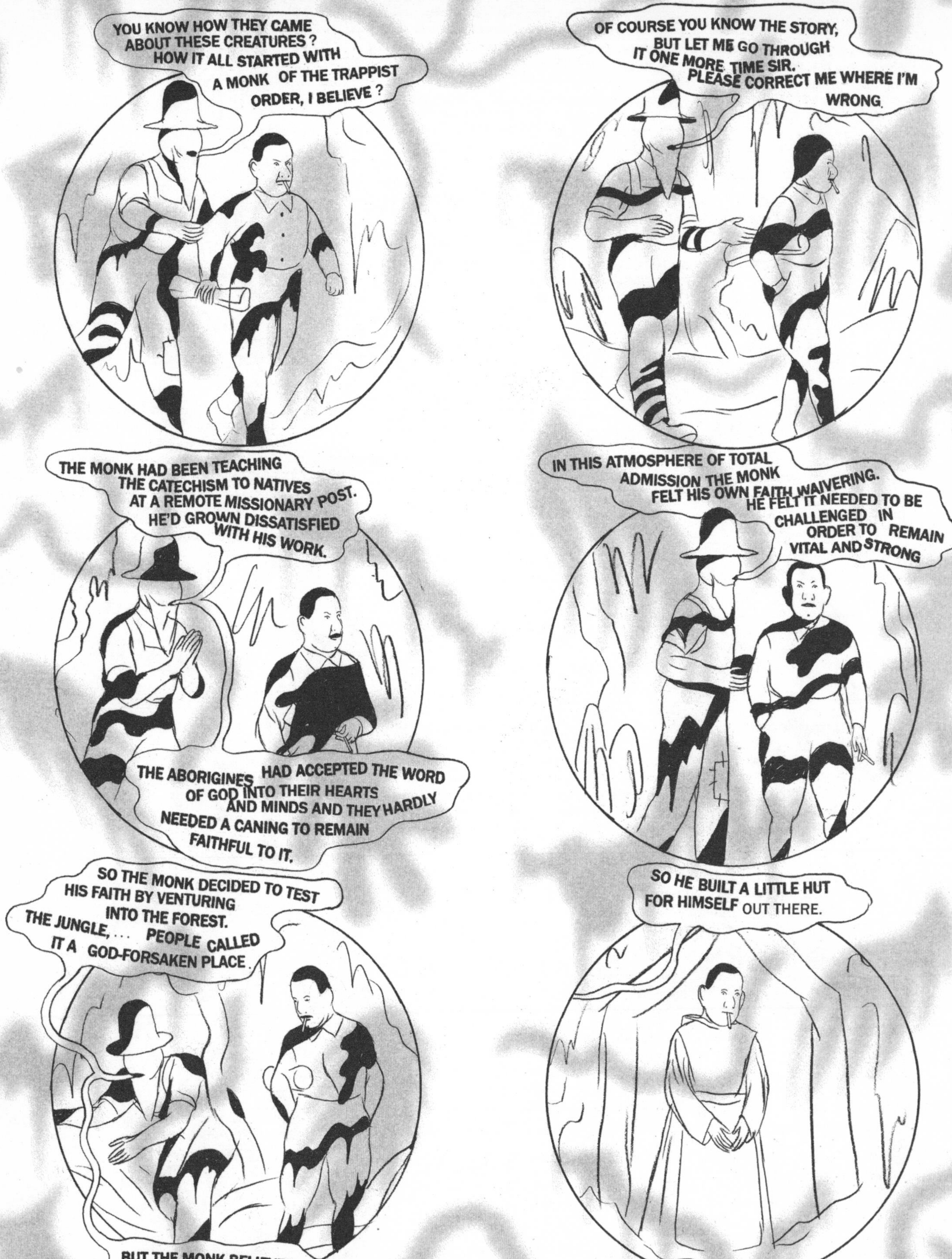
YOU KNOW HOW THEY CAME ABOUT THESE CREATURES? HOW IT ALL STARTED WITH A MONK OF THE TRAPPIST ORDER, I BELIEVE?
OF COURSE YOU KNOW THE STORY, BUT LET ME GO THROUGH IT ONE MORE TIME SIR. PLEASE CORRECT ME WHERE I'M WRONG.
THE MONK HAD BEEN TEACHING THE CATECHISM TO NATIVES AT A REMOTE MISSIONARY POST. HE'D GROWN DISSATISFIED WITH HIS WORK.
THE ABORIGINES HAD ACCEPTED THE WORD OF GOD INTO THEIR HEARTS AND MINDS AND THEY HARDLY NEEDED A CANING TO REMAIN FAITHFUL TO IT.
IN THIS ATMOSPHERE OF TOTAL ADMISSION THE MONK FELT HIS OWN FAITH WAIVERING. HE FELT IT NEEDED TO BE CHALLENGED IN ORDER TO REMAIN VITAL AND STRONG
SO THE MONK DECIDED TO TEST HIS FAITH BY VENTURING INTO THE FOREST. THE JUNGLE, ... PEOPLE CALLED IT A GOD-FORSAKEN PLACE.
BUT THE MONK BELIEVED THAT GOD WAS EVERYWHERE.
SO HE BUILT A LITTLE HUT FOR HIMSELF OUT THERE.

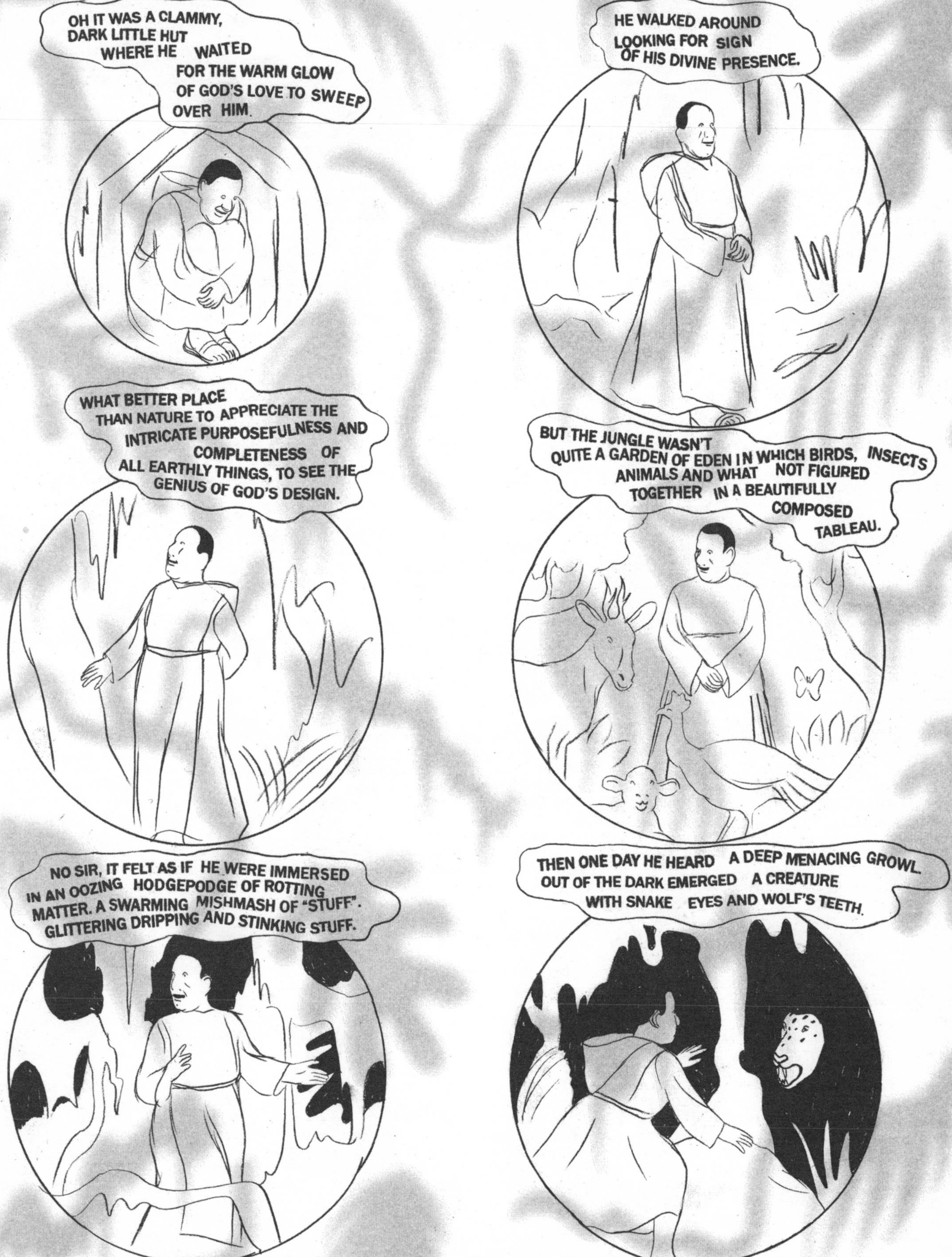
OH IT WAS A CLAMMY, DARK LITTLE HUT WHERE HE WAITED FOR THE WARM GLOW OF GOD'S LOVE TO SWEEP OVER HIM.
HE WALKED AROUND LOOKING FOR SIGN OF HIS DIVINE PRESENCE.
WHAT BETTER PLACE THAN NATURE TO APPRECIATE THE INTRICATE PURPOSEFULNESS AND COMPLETENESS OF ALL EARTHLY THINGS, TO SEE THE GENIUS OF GOD'S DESIGN.
BUT THE JUNGLE WASN'T QUITE A GARDEN OF EDEN IN WHICH BIRDS, INSECTS ANIMALS AND WHAT NOT FIGURED TOGETHER IN A BEAUTIFULLY COMPOSED TABLEAU.
NO SIR, IT FELT AS IF HE WERE IMMERSED IN AN OOZING HODGEPODGE OF ROTTING MATTER. A SWARMING MISHMASH OF "STUFF". GLITTERING DRIPPING AND STINKING STUFF.
THEN ONE DAY HE HEARD A DEEP MENACING GROWL. OUT OF THE DARK EMERGED A CREATURE WITH SNAKE EYES AND WOLF'S TEETH.

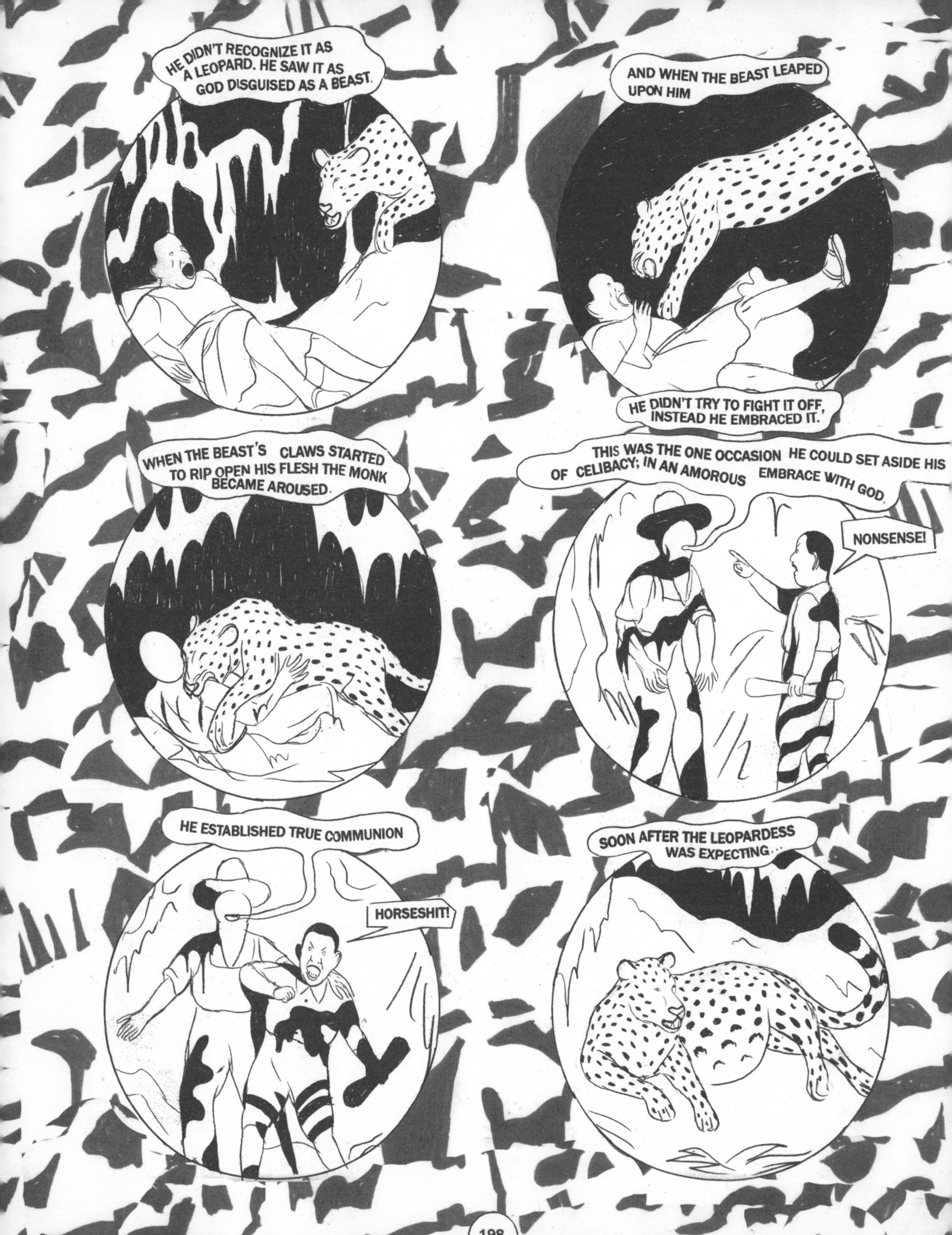
HE DIDN'T RECOGNIZE IT AS A LEOPARD. HE SAW IT AS GOD DISGUISED AS A BEAST.
AND WHEN THE BEAST LEAPED UPON HIM
HE DIDN'T TRY TO FIGHT IT OFF, INSTEAD HE EMBRACED IT.'
WHEN THE BEAST'S CLAWS STARTED TO RIP OPEN HIS FLESH THE MONK BECAME AROUSED.
THIS WAS THE ONE OCCASION HE COULD SET ASIDE HIS OF CELIBACY; IN AN AMOROUS EMBRACE WITH GOD.
NONSENSE!
HE ESTABLISHED TRUE COMMUNION
HORSESHIT!
SOON AFTER THE LEOPARDESS WAS EXPECTING...

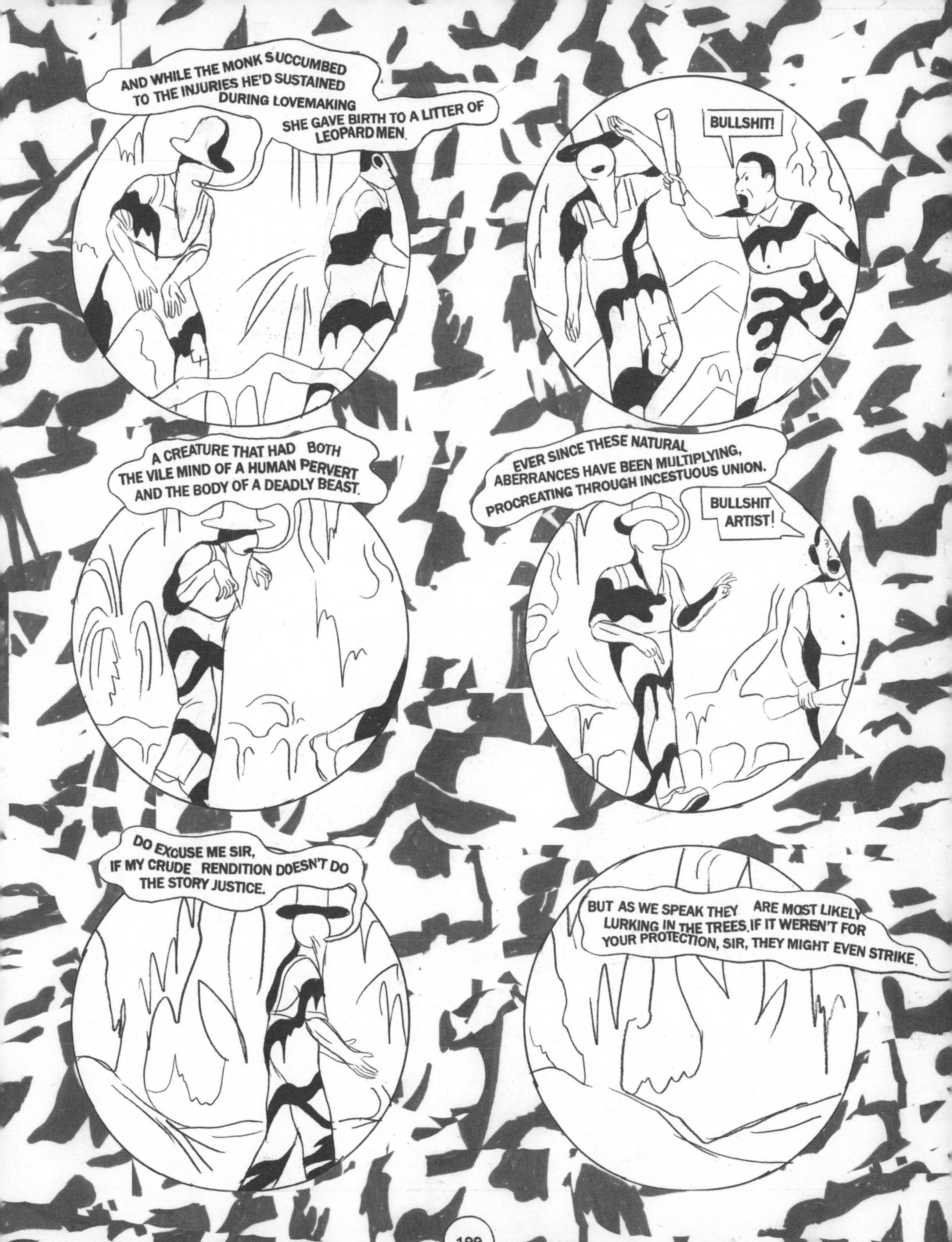
AND WHILE THE MONK SUCCUMBED TO THE INJURIES HE'D SUSTAINED DURING LOVEMAKING
SHE GAVE BIRTH TO A LITTER OF LEOPARD MEN.
BULLSHIT!
A CREATURE THAT HAD BOTH THE VILE MIND OF A HUMAN PERVERT AND THE BODY OF A DEADLY BEAST.
EVER SINCE THESE NATURAL ABERRANCES HAVE BEEN MULTIPLYING, PROCREATING THROUGH INCESTUOUS UNION.
BULLSHIT ARTIST!
DO EXCUSE ME SIR, IF MY CRUDE RENDITION DOESN'T DO THE STORY JUSTICE.
BUT AS WE SPEAK THEY ARE MOST LIKELY LURKING IN THE TREES. IF IT WEREN'T FOR YOUR PROTECTION, SIR, THEY MIGHT EVEN STRIKE.

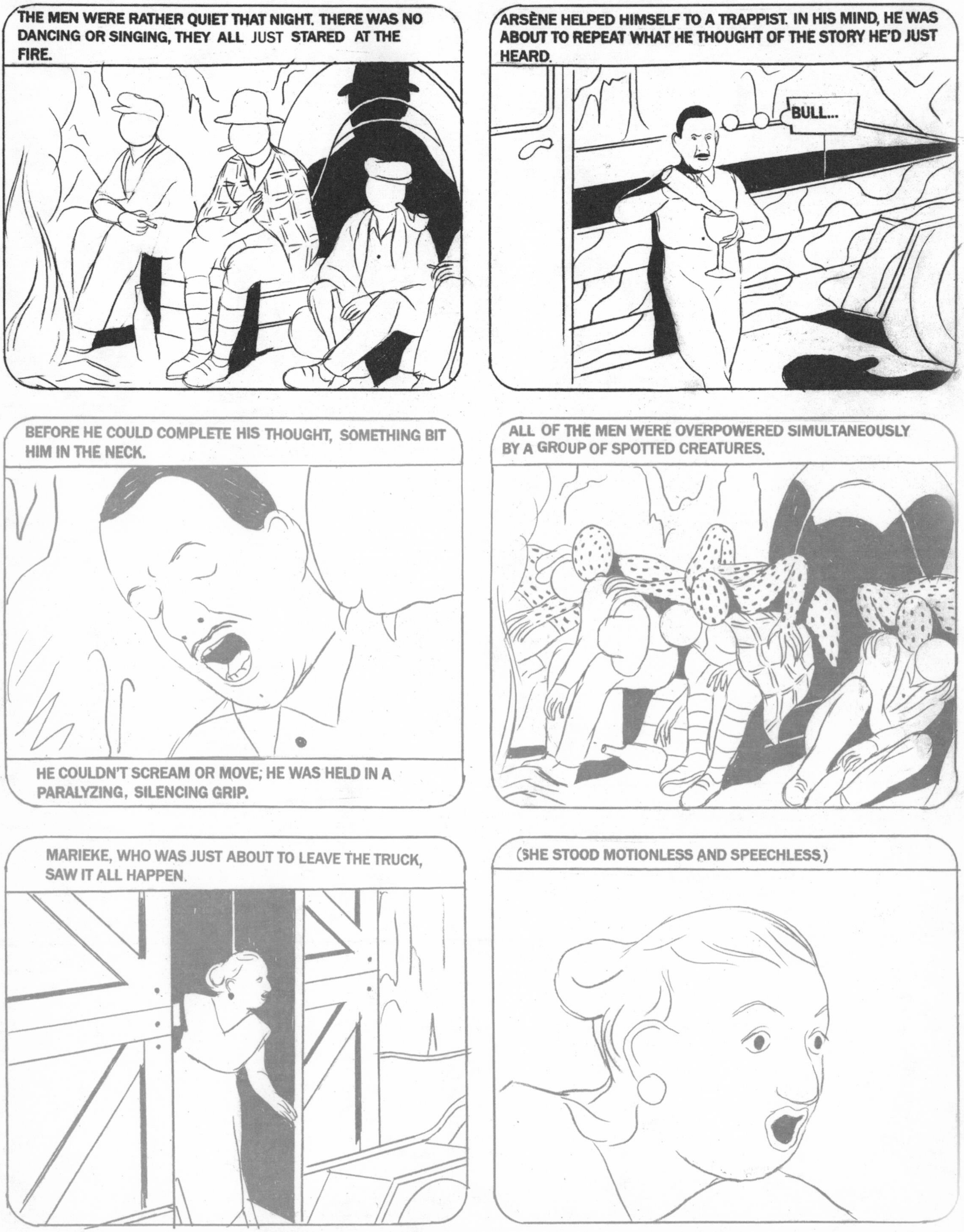
THE MEN WERE RATHER QUIET THAT NIGHT. THERE WAS NO DANCING OR SINGING, THEY ALL JUST STARED AT THE FIRE.
ARSÈNE HELPED HIMSELF TO A TRAPPIST. IN HIS MIND, HE WAS ABOUT TO REPEAT WHAT HE THOUGHT OF THE STORY HE'D JUST HEARD.
BULL...
BEFORE HE COULD COMPLETE HIS THOUGHT, SOMETHING BIT HIM IN THE NECK.
HE COULDN'T SCREAM OR MOVE; HE WAS HELD IN A PARALYZING, SILENCING GRIP.
ALL OF THE MEN WERE OVERPOWERED SIMULTANEOUSLY BY A GROUP OF SPOTTED CREATURES.
MARIEKE, WHO WAS JUST ABOUT TO LEAVE THE TRUCK, SAW IT ALL HAPPEN.
(SHE STOOD MOTIONLESS AND SPEECHLESS.)

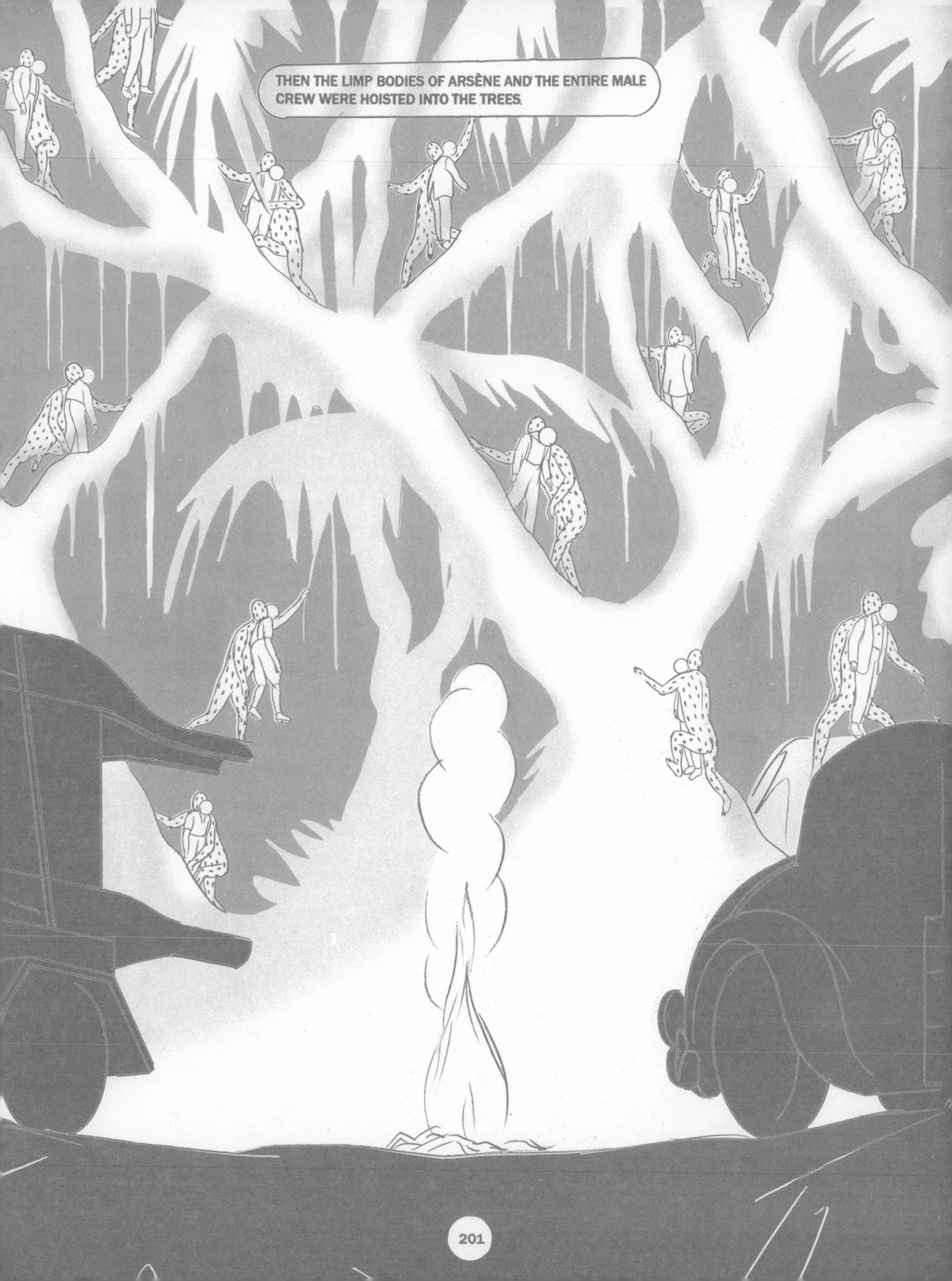
THEN THE LIMP BODIES OF ARSÈNE AND THE ENTIRE MALE CREW WERE HOISTED INTO THE TREES.

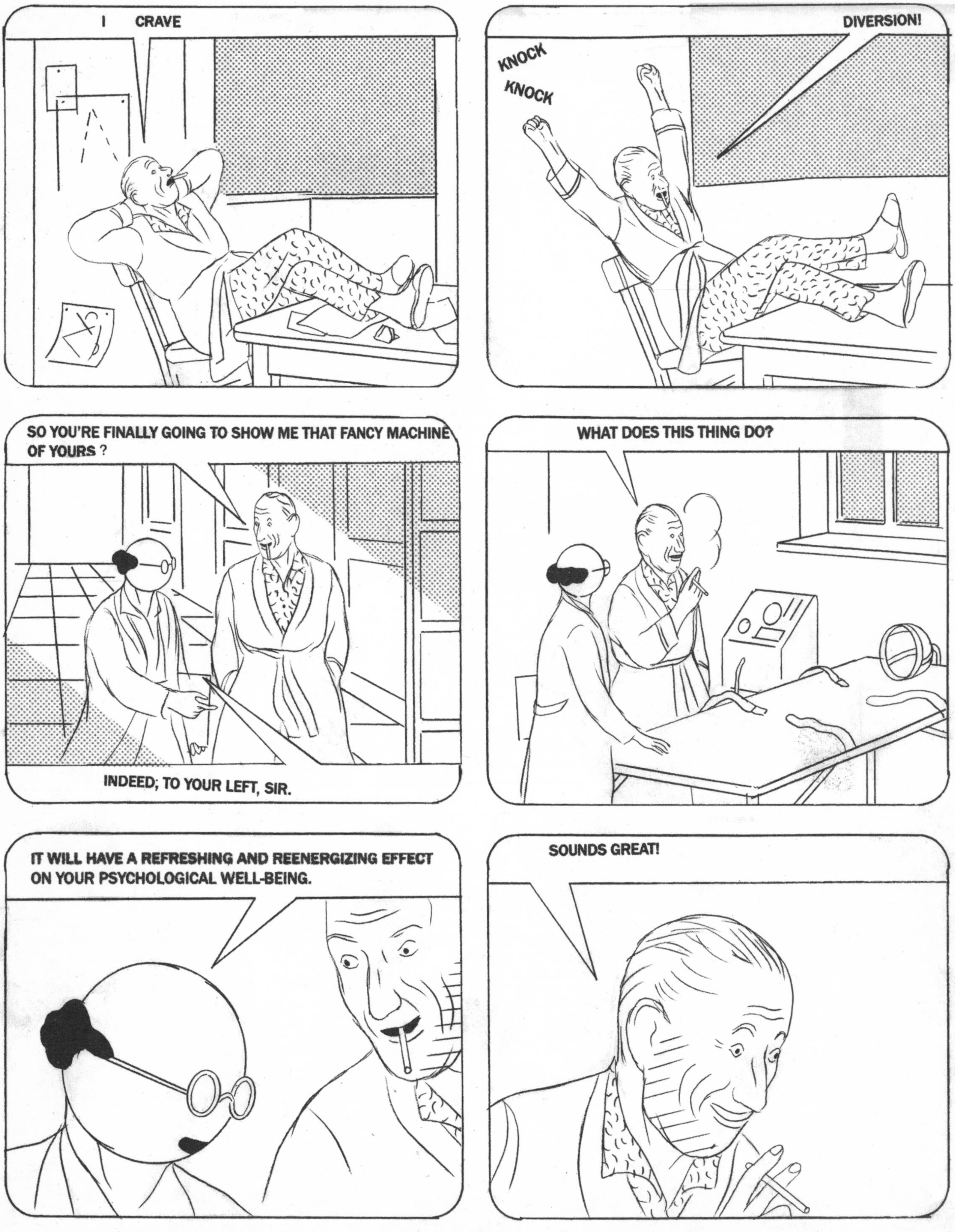
I CRAVE
DIVERSION!
KNOCK
KNOCK
SO YOU'RE FINALLY GOING TO SHOW ME THAT FANCY MACHINE OF YOURS ?
INDEED; TO YOUR LEFT, SIR.
WHAT DOES THIS THING DO?
IT WILL HAVE A REFRESHING AND REENERGIZING EFFECT ON YOUR PSYCHOLOGICAL WELL-BEING.
SOUNDS GREAT!

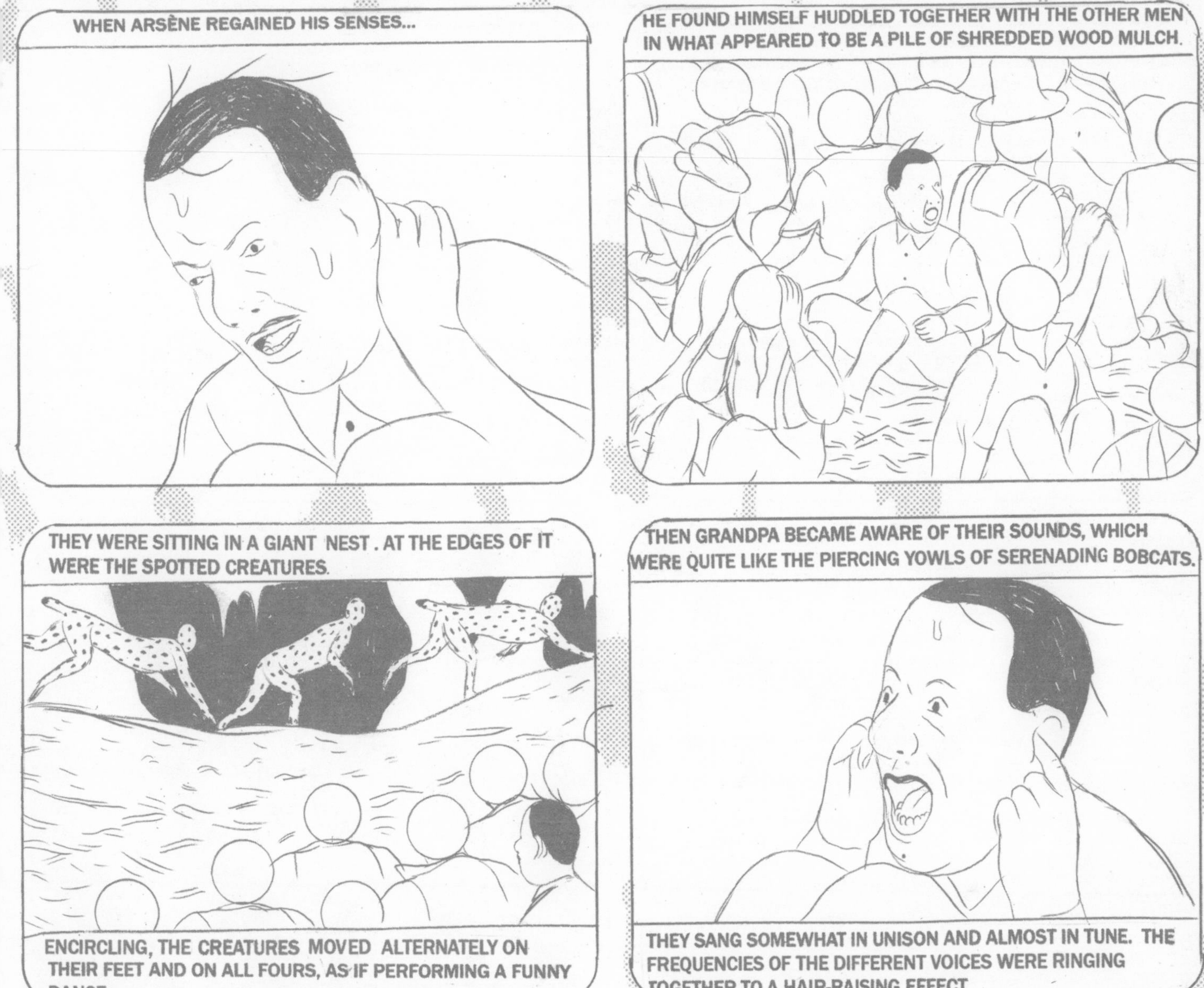
WHEN ARSÈNE REGAINED HIS SENSES...
HE FOUND HIMSELF HUDDLED TOGETHER WITH THE OTHER MEN IN WHAT APPEARED TO BE A PILE OF SHREDDED WOOD MULCH.
THEY WERE SITTING IN A GIANT NEST . AT THE EDGES OF IT WERE THE SPOTTED CREATURES.
ENCIRCLING, THE CREATURES MOVED ALTERNATELY ON THEIR FEET AND ON ALL FOURS, AS IF PERFORMING A FUNNY DANCE.
THEN GRANDPA BECAME AWARE OF THEIR SOUNDS, WHICH WERE QUITE LIKE THE PIERCING YOWLS OF SERENADING BOBCATS.
THEY SANG SOMEWHAT IN UNISON AND ALMOST IN TUNE. THE FREQUENCIES OF THE DIFFERENT VOICES WERE RINGING TOGETHER TO A HAIR-RAISING EFFECT.
AS THE CREATURES SLOWLY CLOSED IN ON THE GROUP OF MEN, ARSÈNE COULD SEE THEIR FACES.
NO CARNIVAL MASK COULD POSSIBLY REPLICATE THOSE GROTESQUE FEATURES. EVERY FACIAL MUSCLE SEEMED TO MOVE INDEPENDENTLY, AS IF THERE WAS A CLUSTER OF SQUIRMING SNAKES BENEATH THE SKIN.

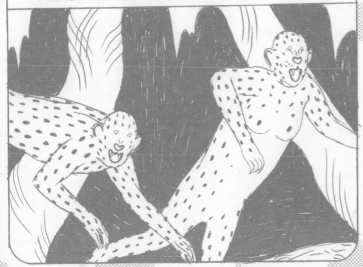

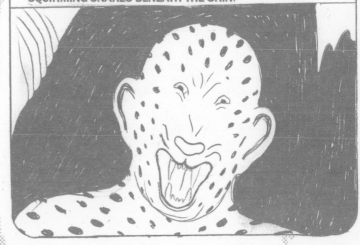

THERE WERE SMALL DIFFERENCES BETWEEN THE INDIVIDUALS. SOME WERE TAILLESS, OTHERS HAD SHORT APPENDAGES THAT WHERE ONLY PARTLY COVERED IN HAIR. AT THE TIP WAS A HAIRLESS, BULGING KNOB.

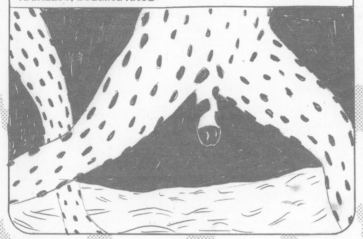

LOOK AT THOSE COCK- TAILS

OH, THIS IS MOST UNFORTUNATE SIR. WE'RE COMPLETELY OVERPOWERED. WE CANNOT POSSIBLY EXPECT YOU TO DO ANYTHING ABOUT IT. WE'RE AT MERCY OF THESE MONSTERS.

THEN THE GUTTER-MOUTHED MAN WAS TAKEN OUT OF THE GROUP BY THREE LEOPARD-MEN.

THE SCENE LOOKED PERFECTLY INNOCENT AT FIRST. THEY SEEMED TO BE FOOLING AROUND WITH HIM; MOCK-FIGHTING, LIKE CATS WITH A BALL OF WOOL.

THEN THEY STRIPPED HIM OFF HIS CLOTHES WITH SURPRISING EASE, USING THEIR RAZOR-SHARP CLAWS.

WHAT WERE THEY GOING TO DO WITH THE POOR BASTARD? WERE THEY GOING TO RIP HIM TO SHREDS?

ARSENE DIDN'T DARE LOOK BUT HE ALSO DAREN'T NOT TO LOOK.

THE MAN, NOW COMPLETELY DISROBED, WAS HOISTED AGAINST A TREE TRUNK. HE WAS HELD IN PLACE BY TWO LEOPARDS. ANOTHER ONE APPROACHED HIM WITH EXTENDED CLAWS.

IN ONE SWIFT MOTION IT SCRATCHED A SYMMETRICAL PATTERN IN THE MAN'S FACE, CHEST AND UPPER LEGS.

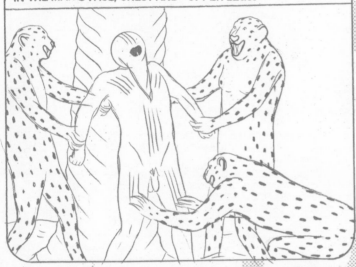

THE CUTS APPEARED TO BE SUPERFICIAL, YET NONETHELESS THE MAN SANK TO HIS KNEES WHILE THE LEOPARDS WERE LAPPING HIS BLOOD WITH THEIR TONGUES.

GRANDPA HAD NEVER PAID MUCH ATTENTION TO THE MAN'S APPEARANCE BUT NOW, AS HE WAS BEING TORTURED, HE NOTICED HIS CHISELED FEATURES, HIS COARSE RED BEARD, AND DARK BLACK EYES.

THE LICKING WASN'T PURELY MEDICINAL; AFTER THEY'D DABBED THE BLOOD, THEY DIVERTED THEIR ATTENTION TO THE MAN'S NIPPLES AND GENITALS.

CAN I HAVE YOUR ROBE, SIR?

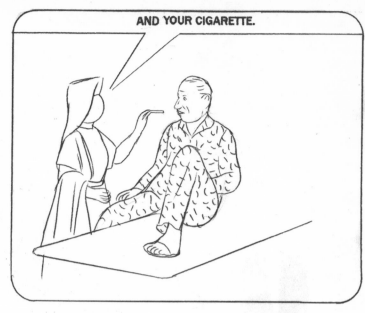

AND YOUR CIGARETTE.

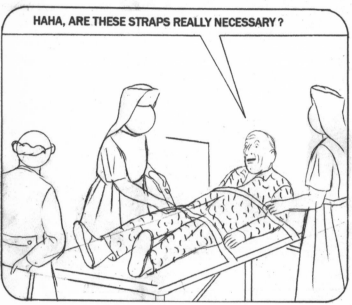

HAHA, ARE THESE STRAPS REALLY NECESSARY?

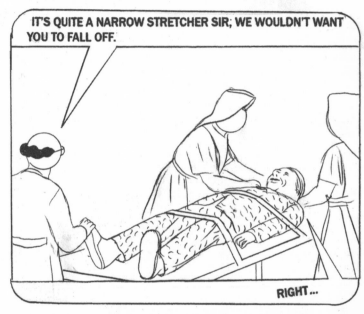

IT'S QUITE A NARROW STRETCHER SIR; WE WOULDN'T WANT YOU TO FALL OFF.

RIGHT...

WHILE ONE LEOPARD WAS WORKING THE MAN'S GENITALS WITH A LARGE, COARSE-LOOKING TONGUE...

...ANOTHER LEOPARD WAS SQUATTING ABOVE HIS FACE, PRESENTING ITS VAGINA (CLOACA?) LOOKING EXPECTANT.

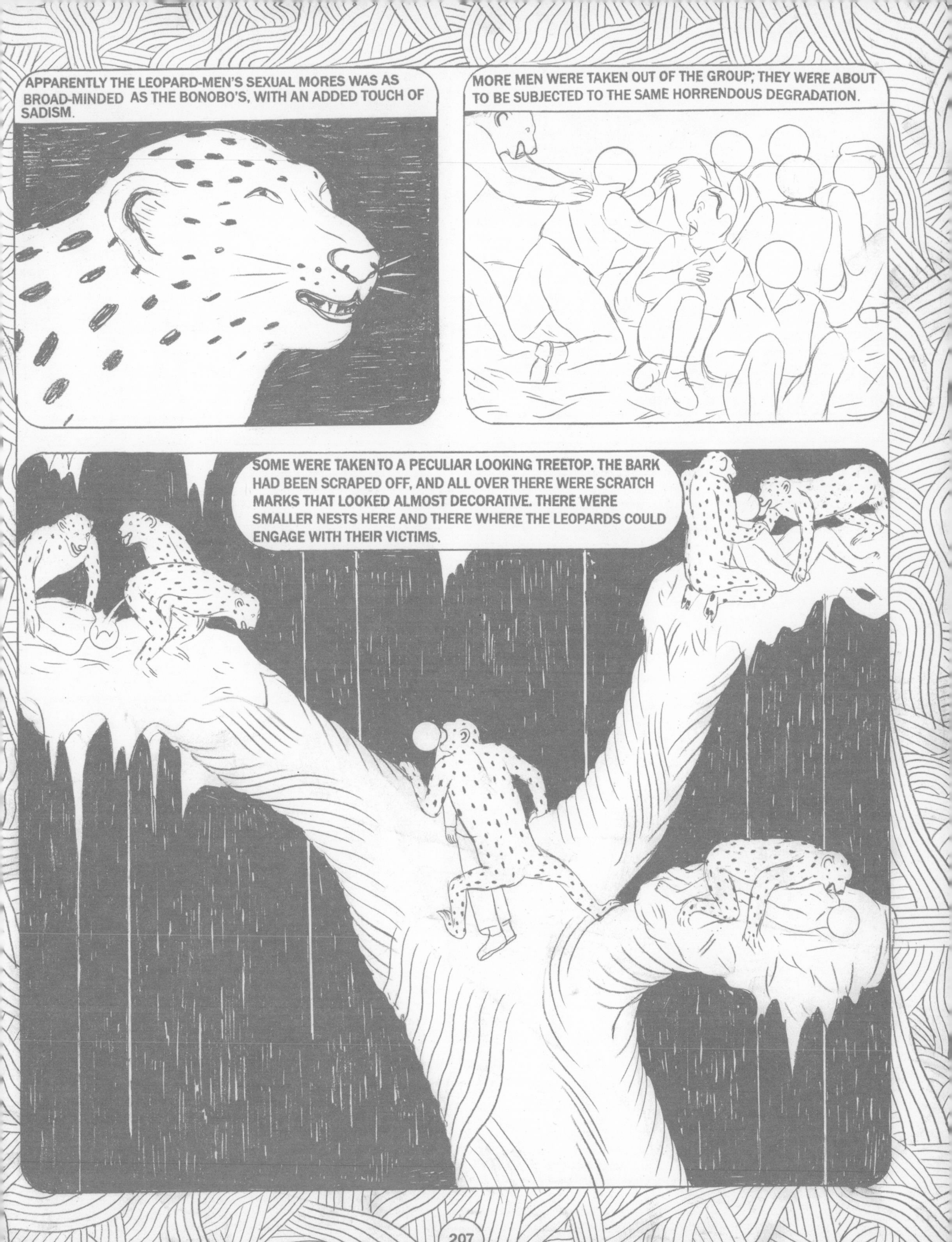

APPARENTLY THE LEOPARD-MEN'S SEXUAL MORES WAS AS BROAD-MINDED AS THE BONOBO'S, WITH AN ADDED TOUCH OF SADISM.
MORE MEN WERE TAKEN OUT OF THE GROUP; THEY WERE ABOUT TO BE SUBJECTED TO THE SAME HORRENDOUS DEGRADATION.
SOME WERE TAKEN TO A PECULIAR LOOKING TREETOP. THE BARK HAD BEEN SCRAPED OFF, AND ALL OVER THERE WERE SCRATCH MARKS THAT LOOKED ALMOST DECORATIVE. THERE WERE SMALLER NESTS HERE AND THERE WHERE THE LEOPARDS COULD ENGAGE WITH THEIR VICTIMS.

THE FOUL-MOUTHED MAN WAS STILL BEING "PLEASURED" AGAINST HIS WILL

WHILE VORACIOUSLY LICKING HIS PENIS, ONE OF THE LEOPARDS DECIDED TO CURL A CLAW INSIDE THE ANUS OF THE MAN.

THE MAN RESPONDED WITH A VOCAL CORD RIPPING YELL.

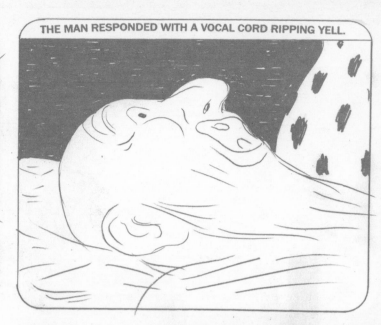

THIS IMMEDIATELY MADE THE CATS CEASE THEIR ACTIVITIES. THEY NOW LOOKED PLEASED, AS IF THE YELL HAD BEEN AN ORGASMIC EXPRESSION OF GRATITUDE FOR THEIR EFFORTS.

NOW THE CATS SETTLED DOWN BESIDE THE MAN. SOME STARTED GROOMING THEMSELVES, OTHERS YAWNED.

MEANWHILE GRANDPA HAD ROLLED HIMSELF INTO A BALL, AS IF POSING LIKE A SPINE-LESS HEDGEHOG COULD SAVE HIM.

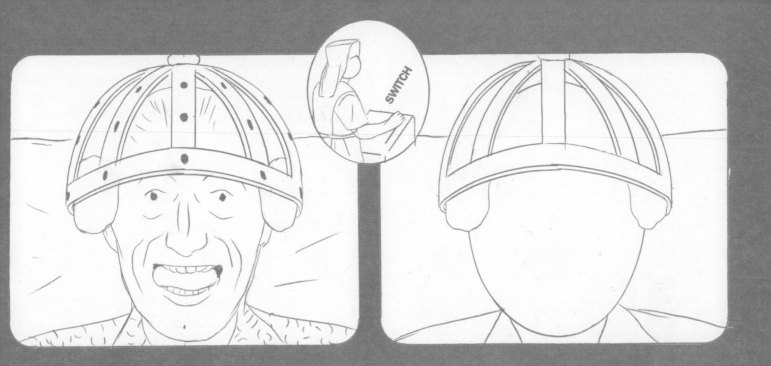

SUDDENLY ARSÈNE HEARD A DEAFENING BANG VERY CLOSE BY.

BANG

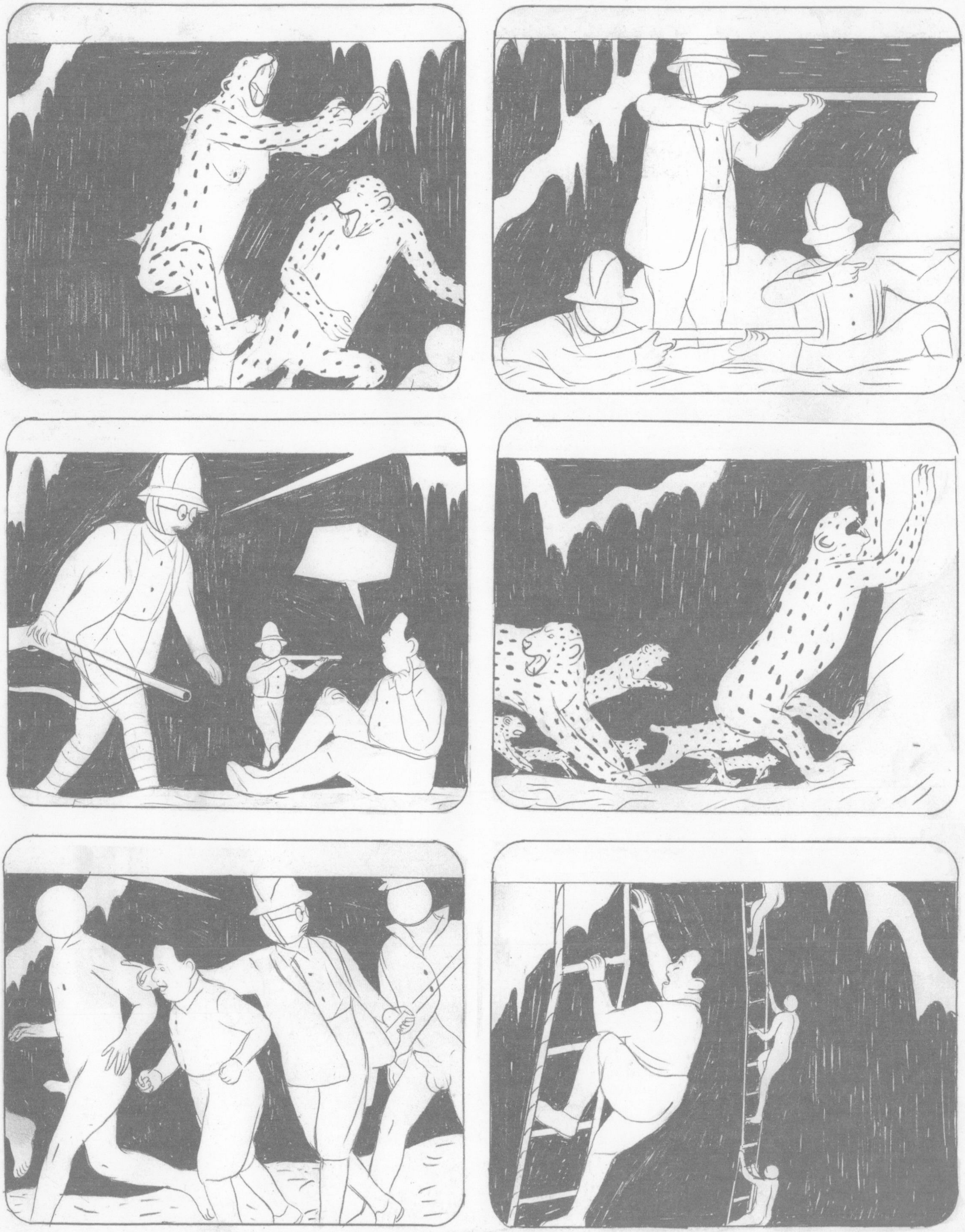

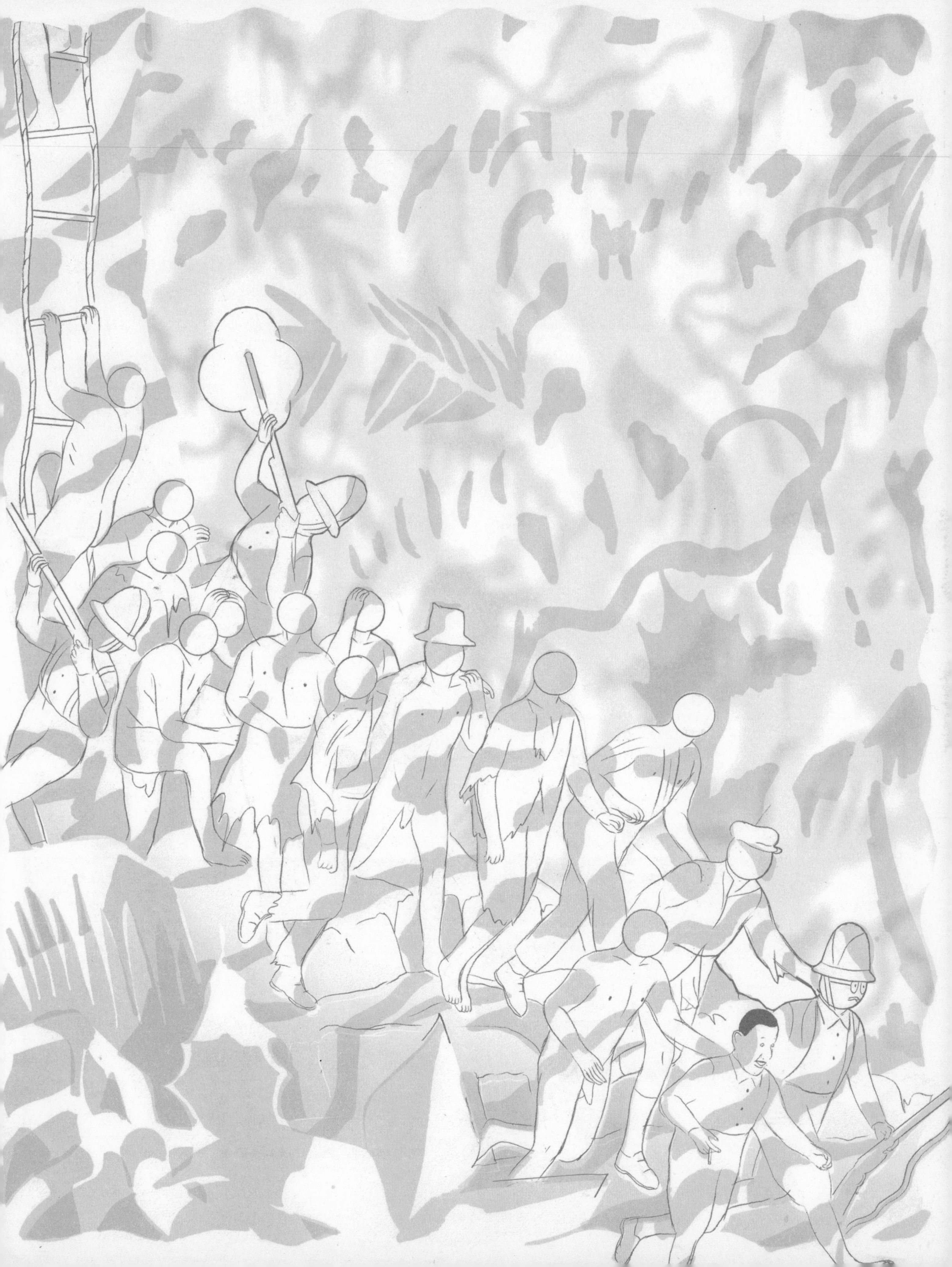

WHEN ARSÈNE REGAINED HIS HEARING, LOUIS WAS APOLOGIZING TO HIM AND MARIEKE FOR HIS UNSOLICITATED INTERVENTION.

HE'D FELT OBLIGATED TO FOLLOW THE EXPEDITION CLANDESTINELY AS HE'D INVESTED TOO MUCH OF HIMSELF IN PROJECT: FREEDOM TOWN TO SEE IT IN PERIL.

MARIEKE IMPRESSED UPON HIM, HER GRATITUDE ON BEHALF OF THE WHOLE CREW.

SHE WAS CERTAIN THAT HER FATHER WOULD NOT ONLY WITHDRAW LOUIS'S RESIGNATION, BUT WOULD ALSO GRANT HIM GENEROUS COMPENSATION FOR HIS COURAGEOUS INITIATIVE

SOON MARIEKE AND LOUIS WERE DISCUSSING THE ROUTE AND DECIDING ON A TRAJECTORY THAT WOULD LEAD THEM OUT OF THE JUNGLE AS EASILY AS POSSIBLE THE FOLLOWING DAY.

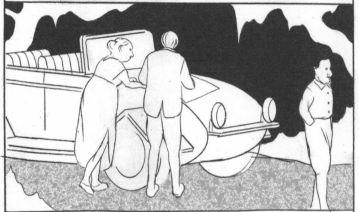

ARSENE WHO HADN'T MUCH TO ADD TO THE CONVERSATION, WANDERED OFF.

THE MEN WERE TRYING TO OBLITERATE THEIR MOST RECENT MEMORIES WITH A MASSIVE INTAKE OF TRAPPIST.

HE FELT COMPELLED TO PUT A HAND ON THE SHOULDER OF THE NOW RATHER PATHETIC LOOKING FOUL-MOUTHED MAN.

HE FLINCHED LIKE BEATEN DOG

ARSÈNE DECIDED TO SPEND THE NIGHT IN THE CAR.

WHILE PEERING INTO THE DARKNESS, HE TRIED TO MAKE SENSE OF ALL THAT HAD HAPPENED.

HOW, FOR INSTANCE, WOULD ONE RECOUNT THE LEOPARD-INCIDENT TO SOMEONE WHO HADN'T WITNESSED IT?

HOW DOES ONE TALK ABOUT SEX-CRAZED CAT-HUMANS WITHOUT SOUNDING LIKE A FOUL-MOUTHED BULLSHIT ARTIST?

EVERYTHING ABOUT THIS JUNGLE SEEMED INCONGRUOUS.

THINGS JUST DIDN'T ADD UP

YET WHAT OUGHT NOT GO TOGETHER WAS SOMEHOW JOINED IN AN UNHOLY BUT FERTILE MARRIAGE.

THIS, FOR SOME REASON, MADE HIM RECALL THE NIGHT HE'D SPENT WITH MARIEKE.

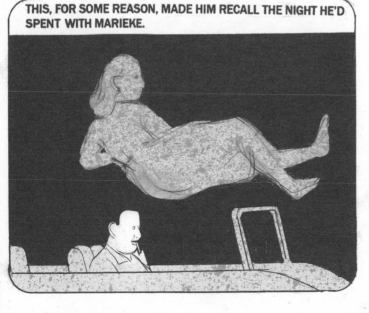

HOW THEY'D BECOME ONE...

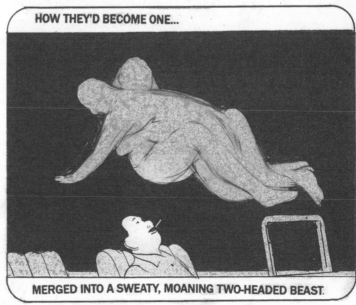

MERGED INTO A SWEATY, MOANING TWO-HEADED BEAST.

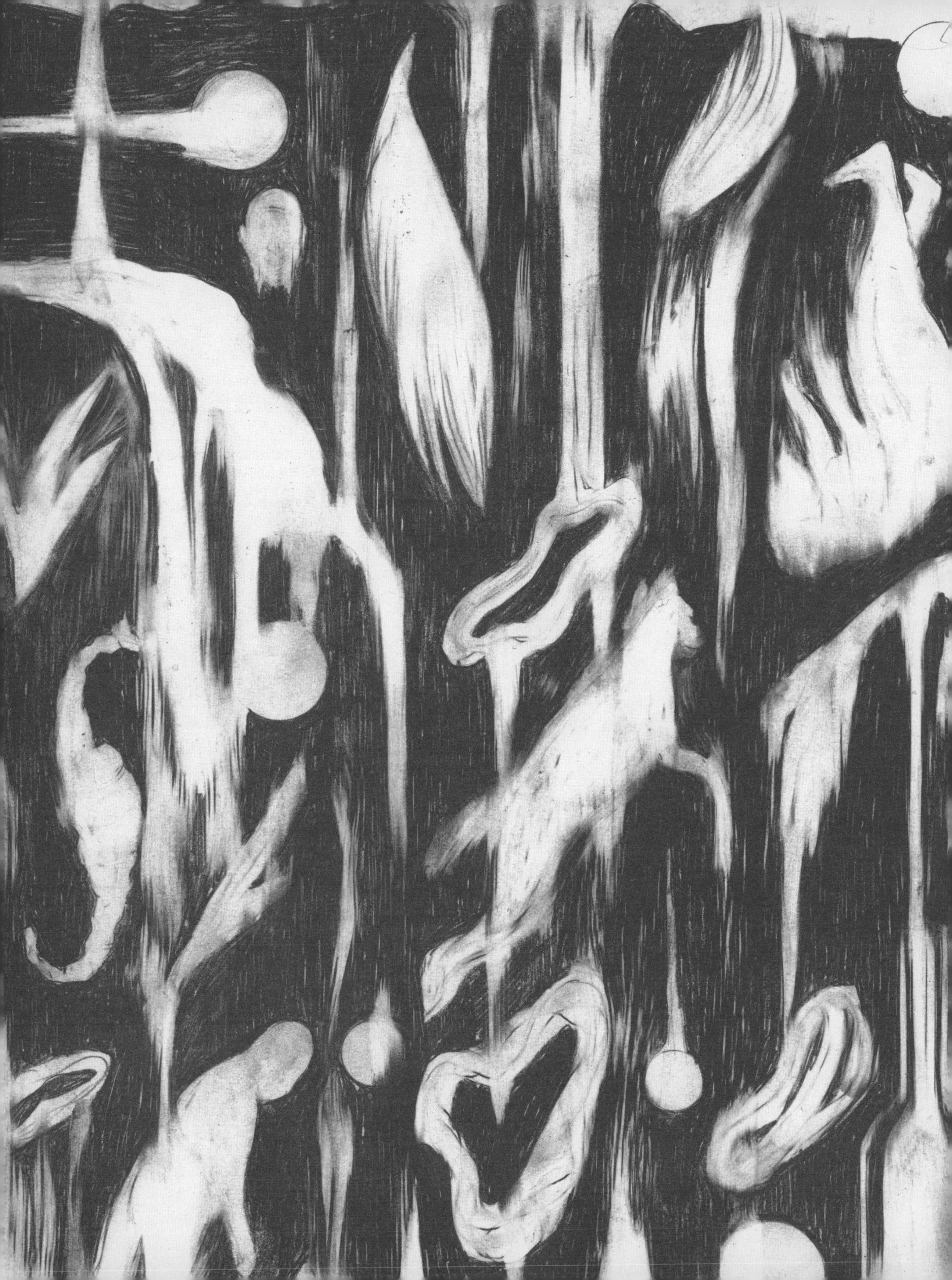

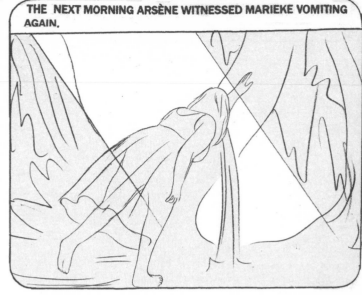

The next morning arsène witnessed marieke vomiting again.

Don't worry she'll be fine. It's quite normal for a woman who is ...

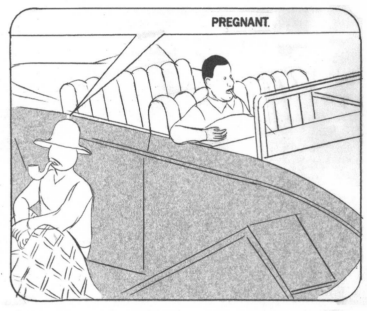

Pregnant.

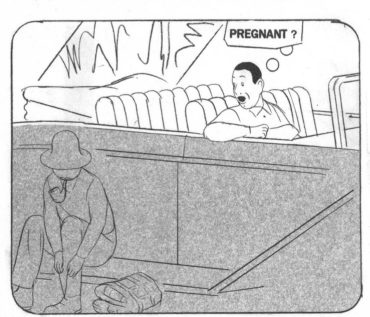

Pregnant ?

SOON THE CARAVAN WAS ON ITS WAY, THIS TIME UNDER THE COMPETENT GUIDANCE OF LOUIS.

ARSÈNE WAS GOING THROUGH THE MOTIONS. IN HIS MIND THERE WAS ROOM FOR ONLY ONE WORD AND IT SOUNDED INCREASINGLY LOUD:

PREGNANT

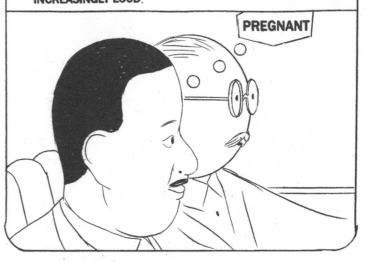

HE SAT IN THE FRONT OF THE CAR NEXT TO LOUIS, AND WAS HAPPY HE COULDN'T SEE MARIEKE.

LOUIS FOUND HIS WAY WITH CONFIDENT EASE. ARSÈNE DIDN'T REALLY NOTICE, ALL HE COULD THINK OF WAS...

PREGNANT

AFTER ABOUT 45 MINUTES, THEY REACHED THE EDGE OF THE WOOD. THEY NOW STOOD AT THE BANKS OF A RATHER BROAD, ROUGH RIVER.

PREGNANT

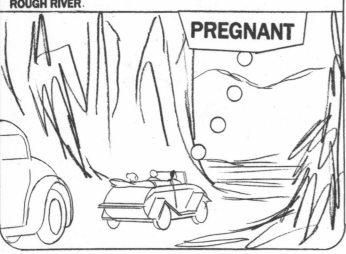

LOUIS AIMED HIS PENETRATING GAZE AT ARSENE AND ASKED:

SO HOW DO YOU FEEL, ARSENE?

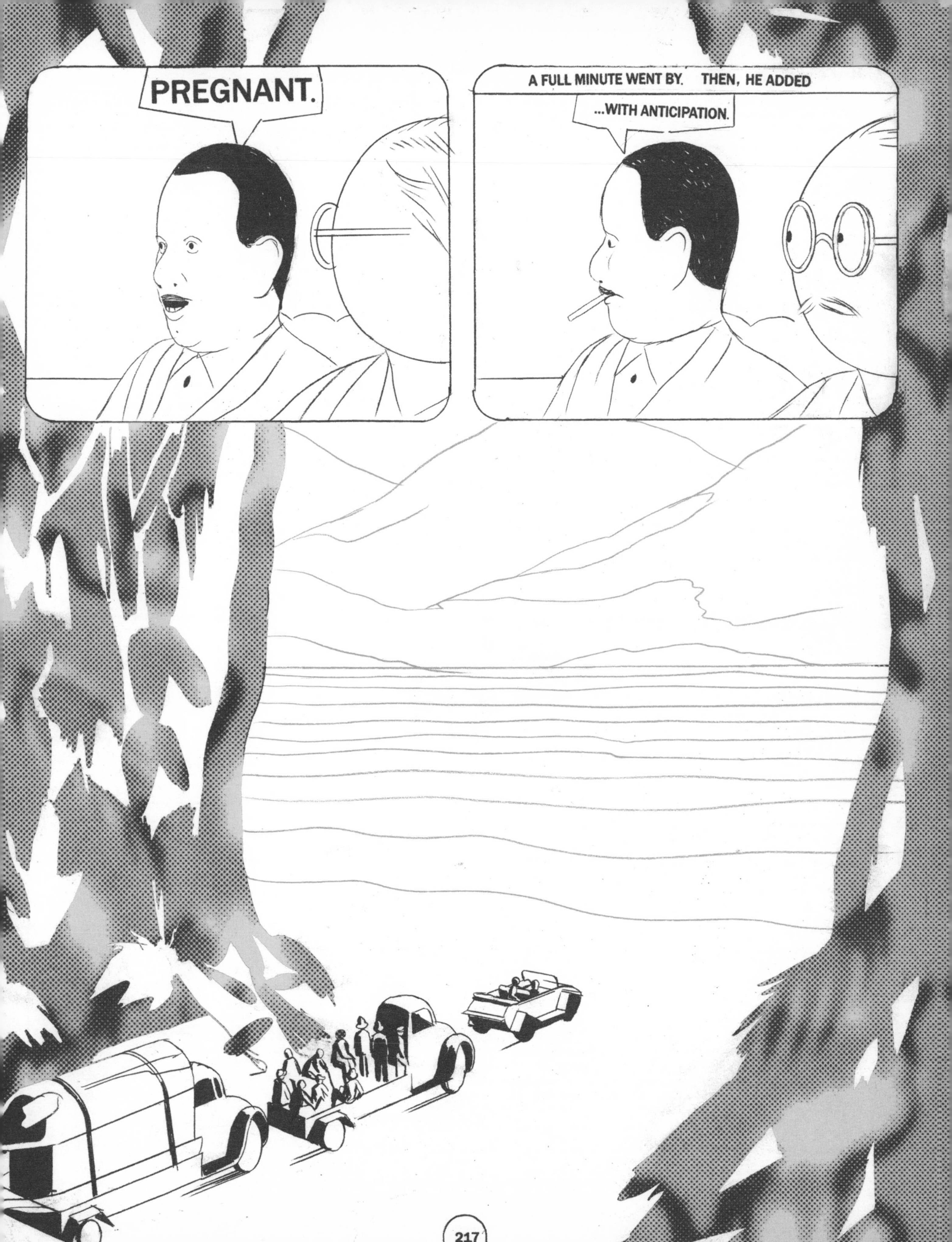
PREGNANT.
A FULL MINUTE WENT BY. THEN, HE ADDED
...WITH ANTICIPATION.

NOW THE CARGO ON THE BIG TRUCK HAD TO BE UNLOADED.

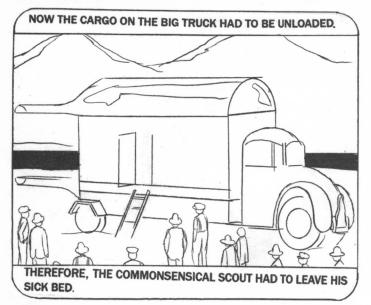

THEREFORE, THE COMMONSENSICAL SCOUT HAD TO LEAVE HIS SICK BED.

THIS WAS NOT A PROBLEM SINCE HE'D BEEN FEELING BETTER.

SEE, A GOOD NIGHT SLEEP CAN DO WONDERS!

NEXT, FURTHER PROOF OF ROGER DESMET'S INGENUITY WAS ON DISPLAY.

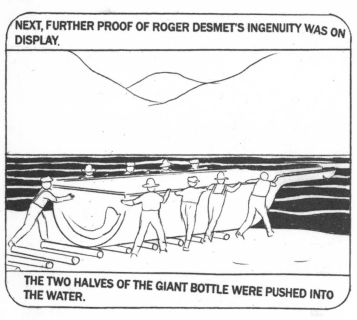

THE TWO HALVES OF THE GIANT BOTTLE WERE PUSHED INTO THE WATER.

THEY'D BE USED AS SLOOPS THAT WOULD CARRY BOTH THE CARGO, THE MEN, AND EVEN ONE OF THE TRUCKS.

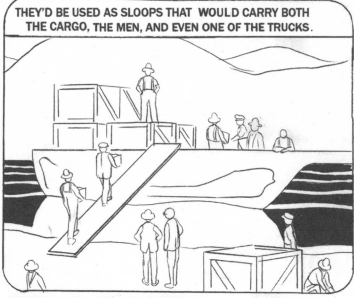

THEY WERE ATTACHED TO THE AMPHIBIOUS CAR, WHICH WOULD FUNCTION AS A TUGBOAT..

IT WAS TREMENDOUSLY CLEVER.

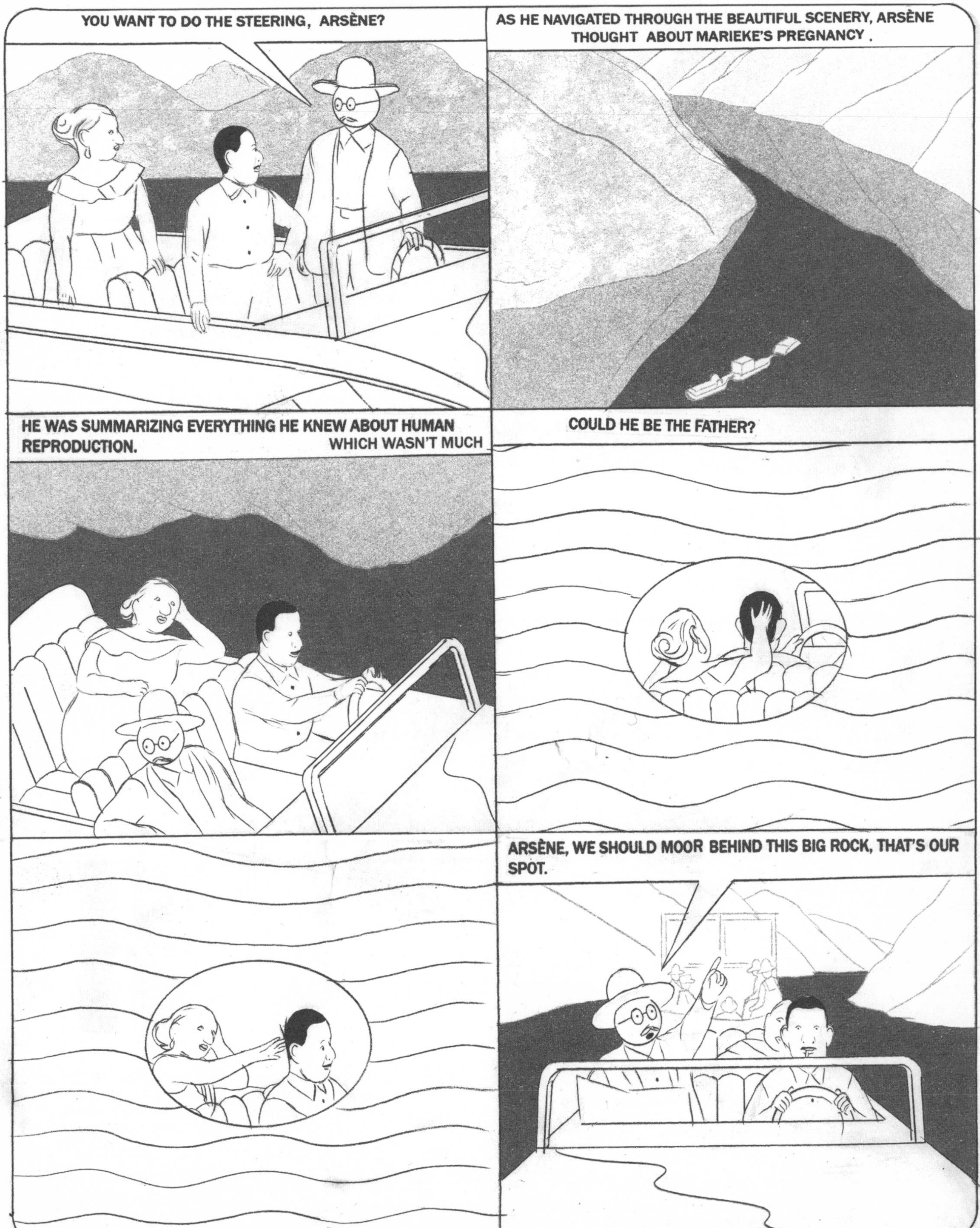
YOU WANT TO DO THE STEERING, ARSÈNE?
AS HE NAVIGATED THROUGH THE BEAUTIFUL SCENERY, ARSÈNE THOUGHT ABOUT MARIEKE'S PREGNANCY.
HE WAS SUMMARIZING EVERYTHING HE KNEW ABOUT HUMAN REPRODUCTION.
WHICH WASN'T MUCH
COULD HE BE THE FATHER?
ARSÈNE, WE SHOULD MOOR BEHIND THIS BIG ROCK, THAT'S OUR SPOT.

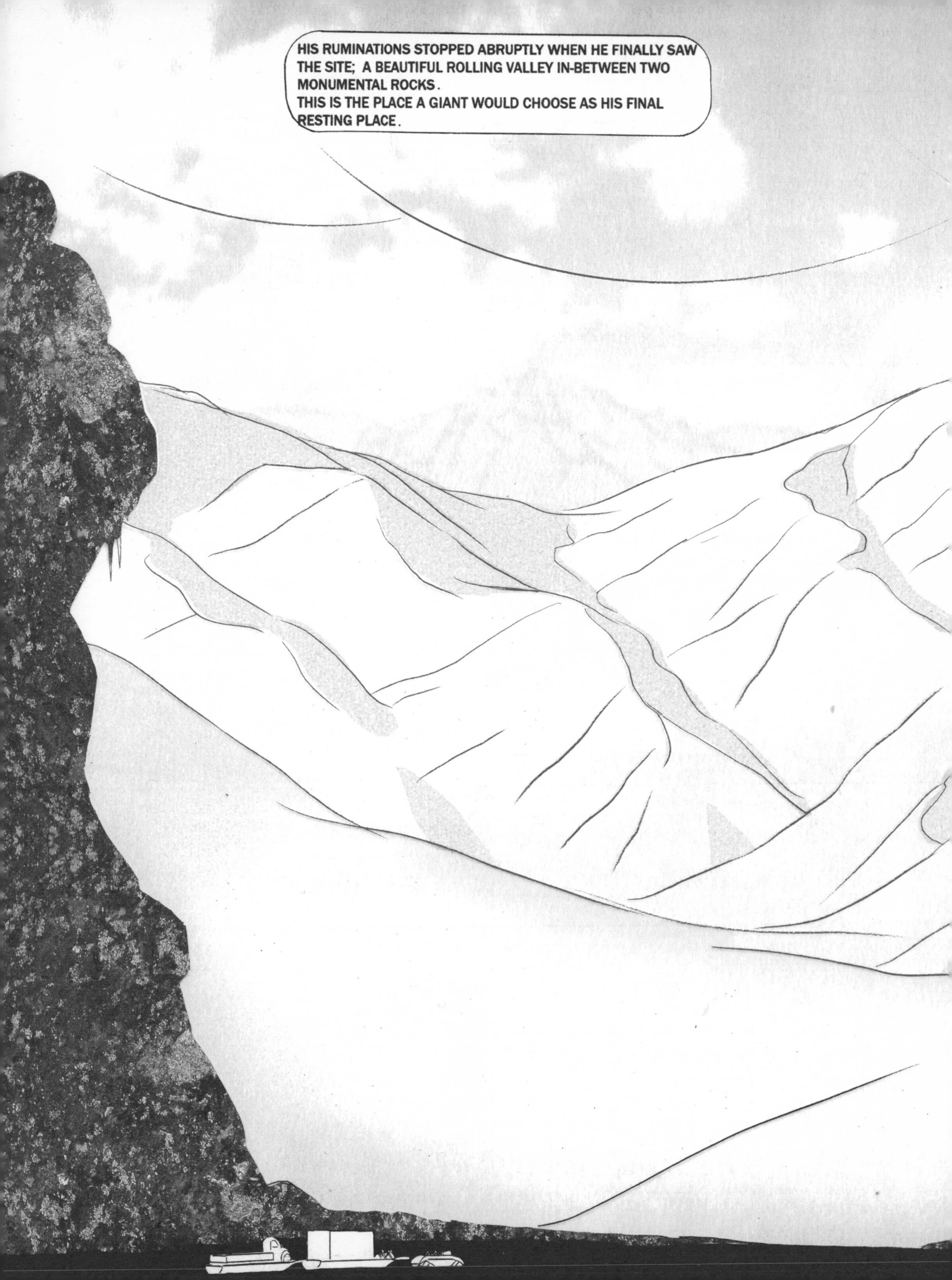
HIS RUMINATIONS STOPPED ABRUPTLY WHEN HE FINALLY SAW THE SITE; A BEAUTIFUL ROLLING VALLEY IN-BETWEEN TWO MONUMENTAL ROCKS.
THIS IS THE PLACE A GIANT WOULD CHOOSE AS HIS FINAL RESTING PLACE.

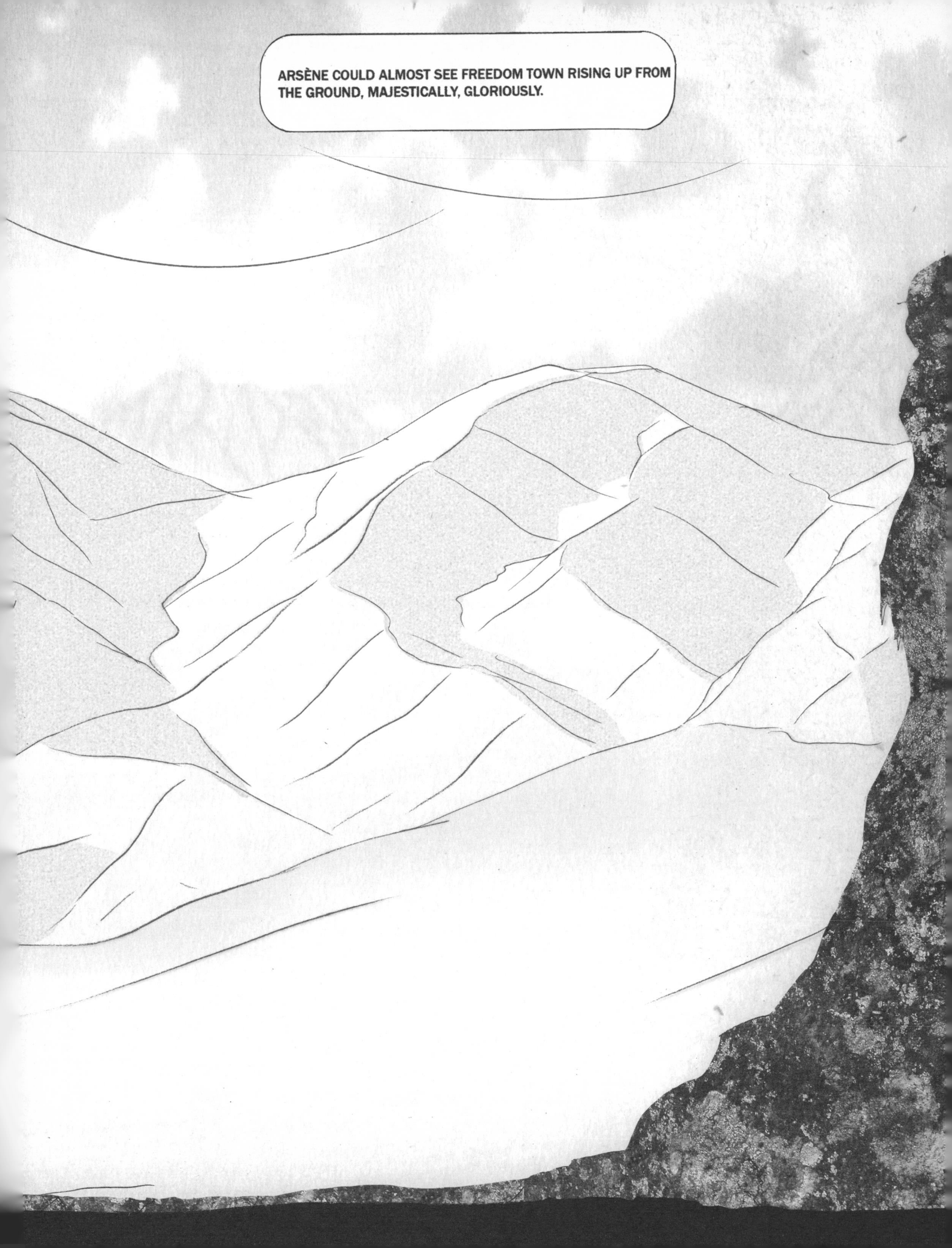
ARSÈNE COULD ALMOST SEE FREEDOM TOWN RISING UP FROM THE GROUND, MAJESTICALLY, GLORIOUSLY.

7. Freedo

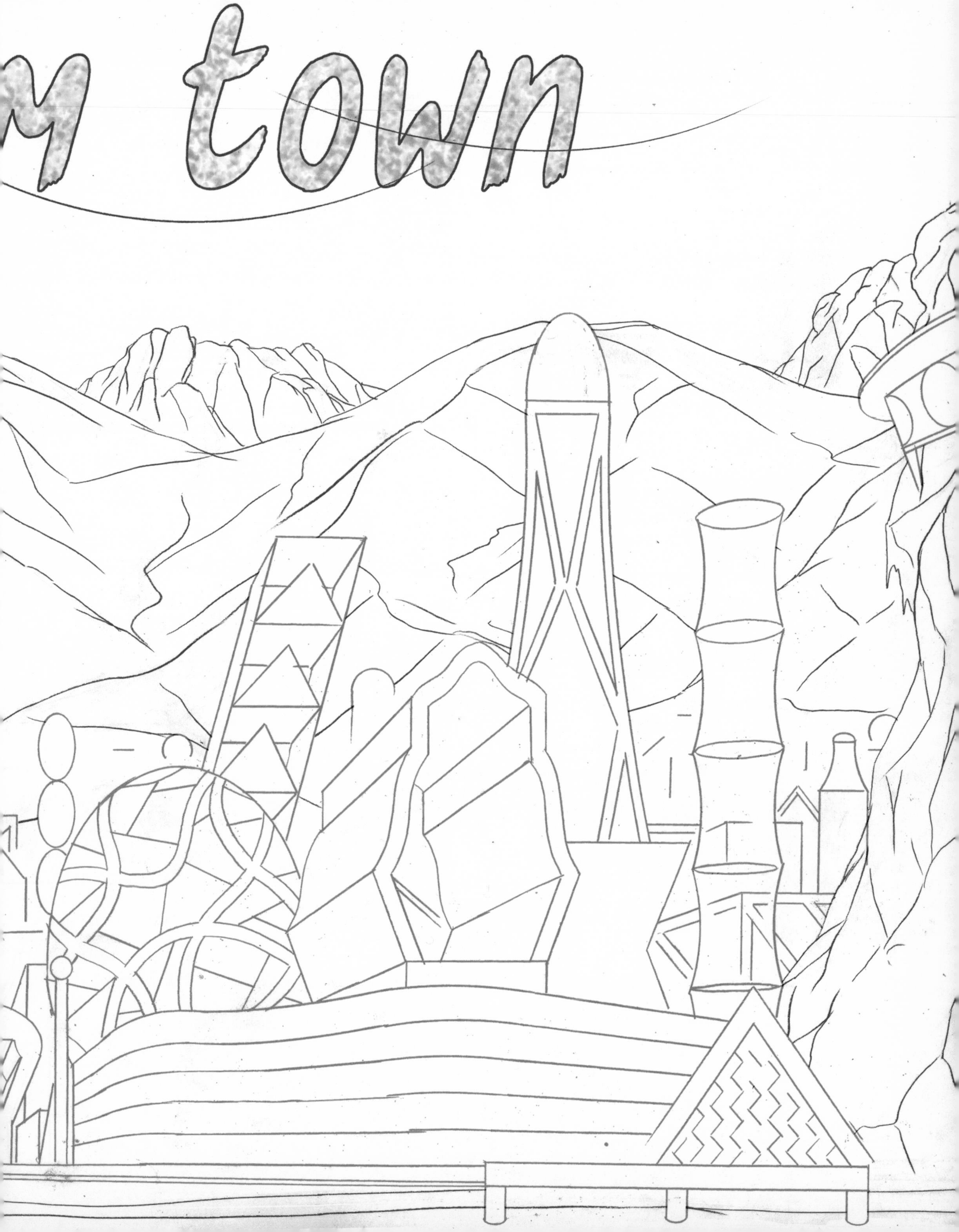
m town

ARSÈNE WAS THE FIRST TO SET FOOT ON LAND.

AS HE RAN THROUGH THE SWAYING, KNEE-HIGH GRASS, AND FELT A COOL BREEZE ON HIS SKIN, HE FORGOT ALL ABOUT THE ADULTEROUS PREGNANCY HE POSSIBLY HAD CAUSED.

THIS AWESOME LANDSCAPE WAS BRIMMING WITH POTENTIAL, FULL OF PROMISE.

SUDDENLY HE FELT COMPLETELY ATTUNED TO ROGER'S VISION. FURTHERMORE, HE WANTED TO SEE IT REALIZED AS SOON AS POSSIBLE.   IT ENCOURAGED HIM TO SHOUT:

LET'S GET TO WORK!

HIS CRY WAS MET WITH DUMBFOUNDED LOOKS FROM THE MEN, BUT AS THEY SAW HIM OSTENTATIOUSLY ROLLING UP HIS SLEEVES, THEY STARTED UNLOADING THE CARGO.

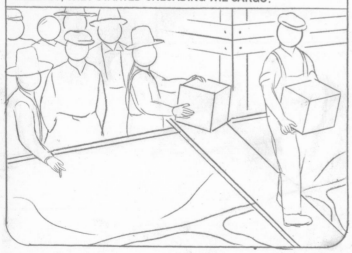

THEY UNLOADED EVERYTHING ONTO THE SHORE AND THEN BEGAN TO OPEN THE BOXES.

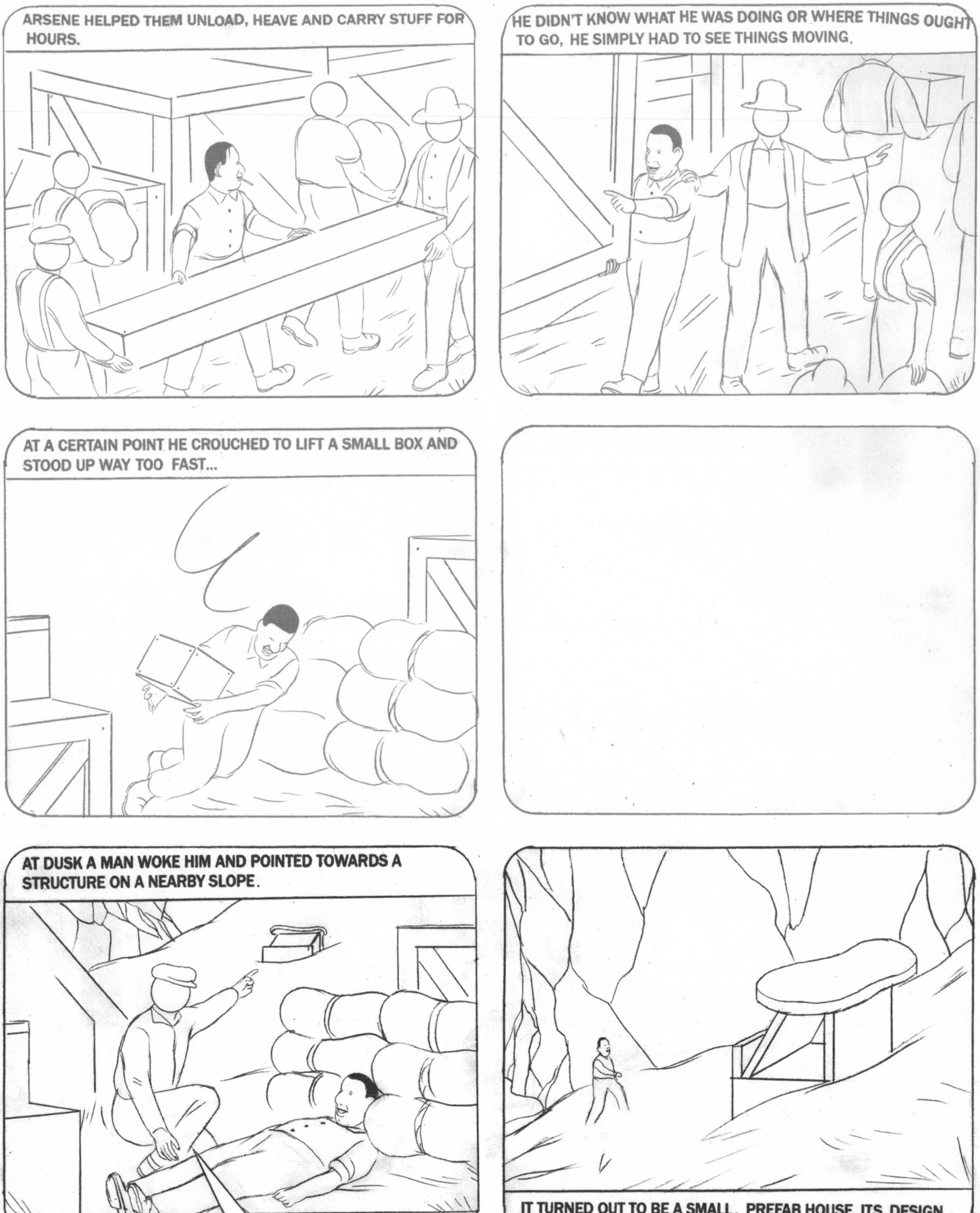
ARSENE HELPED THEM UNLOAD, HEAVE AND CARRY STUFF FOR HOURS.
HE DIDN'T KNOW WHAT HE WAS DOING OR WHERE THINGS OUGHT TO GO, HE SIMPLY HAD TO SEE THINGS MOVING.
AT A CERTAIN POINT HE CROUCHED TO LIFT A SMALL BOX AND STOOD UP WAY TOO FAST...
AT DUSK A MAN WOKE HIM AND POINTED TOWARDS A STRUCTURE ON A NEARBY SLOPE.
WE'VE PREPARED YOUR ACCOMMODATION SIR.
IT TURNED OUT TO BE A SMALL, PREFAB HOUSE. ITS DESIGN LOOKED VAGUELY FAMILIAR.

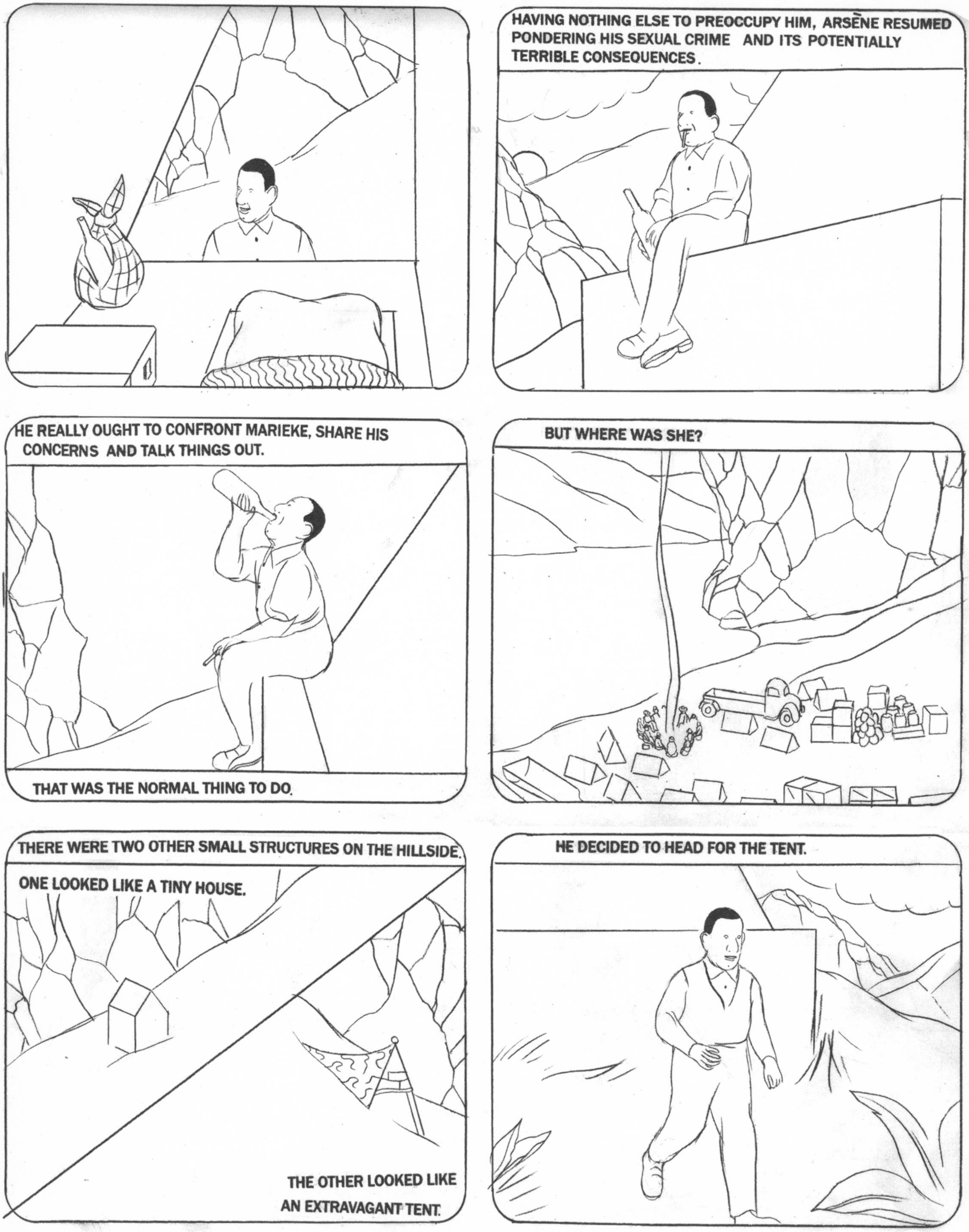
HAVING NOTHING ELSE TO PREOCCUPY HIM, ARSÈNE RESUMED PONDERING HIS SEXUAL CRIME AND ITS POTENTIALLY TERRIBLE CONSEQUENCES.
HE REALLY OUGHT TO CONFRONT MARIEKE, SHARE HIS CONCERNS AND TALK THINGS OUT.
THAT WAS THE NORMAL THING TO DO.
BUT WHERE WAS SHE?
THERE WERE TWO OTHER SMALL STRUCTURES ON THE HILLSIDE.
ONE LOOKED LIKE A TINY HOUSE.
THE OTHER LOOKED LIKE AN EXTRAVAGANT TENT.
HE DECIDED TO HEAD FOR THE TENT.

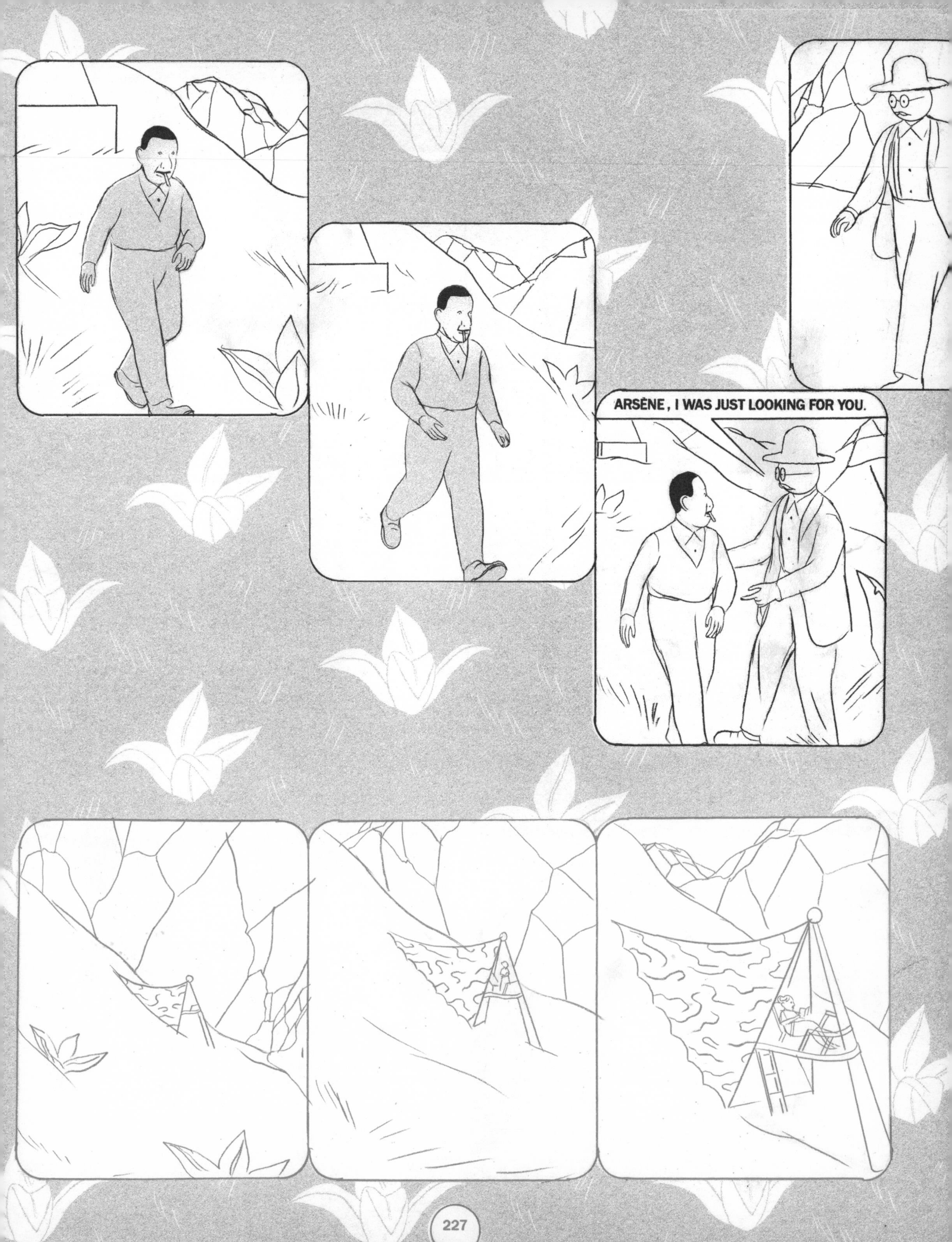
ARSÈNE, I WAS JUST LOOKING FOR YOU.

IN ABOUT A WEEK'S TIME A DELEGATION OF DIGNITARIES, FINANCIERS, AND JOURNALISTS WILL ARRIVE HERE TO ATTEND THE OPENING CEREMONY OF THE MONUMENT.

SINCE YOU ARE LARGELY RESPONSIBLE FOR BRINGING THIS PROJECT TO A GOOD END, IT WOULD BE GREATLY APPRECIATED IF YOU COULD WRITE A SHORT SPEECH FOR THE OCCASION.

WOULD YOU BE ABLE TO DO THAT?

LOUIS WAS LOOKING AT ARSÈNE AS IF HE WAS TRYING TO ASSESS HIS RETHORICAL SKILLS BY STARING AT HIS BRAIN THROUGH HIS SKULL.

ARSÈNE REPLIED, "SURE!", HE THEN TURNED AROUND AND STARTED BACK TO HIS LODGINGS, NON-VERBALLY COMMUNICATING A SENSE OF, "I'LL GET RIGHT TO IT!"

AND INDEED, BACK IN HIS HUT HE STARTED FORMULATING THE SPEECH RIGHT AWAY.

HE DESCRIBED HOW THEY ~~PENETRATED~~ ENTERED ~~THE TERRIFYING,~~ DARK JUNGLE. HOW THEY HAD TO DEAL WITH ~~THE ONSLAUGHT OF ELEPHANTWORMS~~ VILE PARASITES.

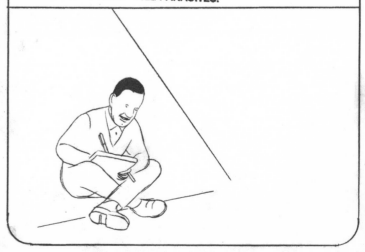

HOW THEY'D BEEN ~~SODOMIZED~~, ~~MOLESTED~~, ASSAULTED BY A GROUP OF LEOPARDMENS. HOW THEY ~~TRIED NOT TO CRACK UP~~ MANAGED TO REMAIN LEVELHEADED IN A REALM OF MADNESS.

AS GRANDPA KEPT CHANGING WORDS THAT HAD DUBIOUS OR UNWANTED CONNOTATIONS, THE TEXT SEEMED TO BECOME INCREASINGLY MEANINGLESS.

SO EVENTUALLY HE STOPPED WRITING AND DECIDED TO GO TO SLEEP ON THE PECULIAR FUTON LAID OUT FOR HIM.

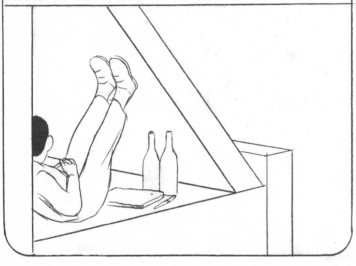

THAT NIGHT HE HAD A DISTURBING DREAM.

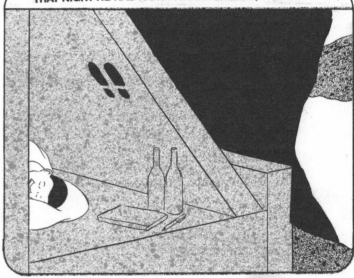

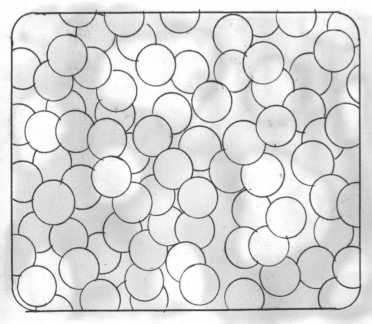

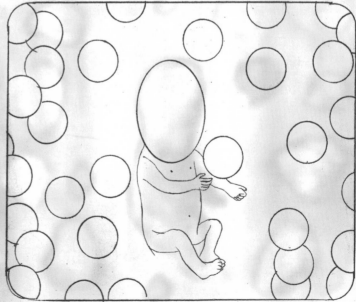

229

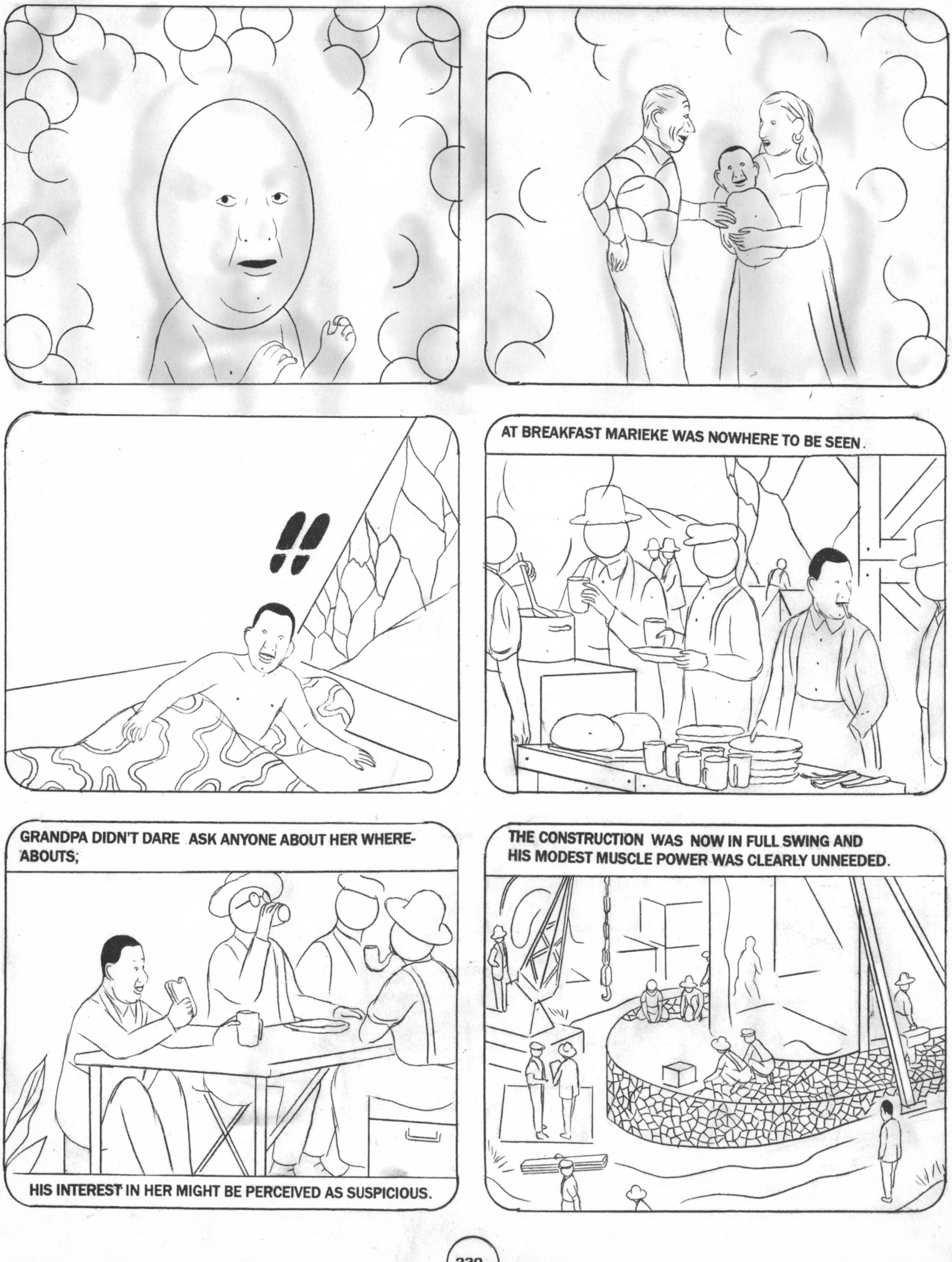
!!
AT BREAKFAST MARIEKE WAS NOWHERE TO BE SEEN.
GRANDPA DIDN'T DARE ASK ANYONE ABOUT HER WHEREABOUTS;
HIS INTEREST IN HER MIGHT BE PERCEIVED AS SUSPICIOUS.
THE CONSTRUCTION WAS NOW IN FULL SWING AND HIS MODEST MUSCLE POWER WAS CLEARLY UNNEEDED.

SO HE RETURNED TO HIS WRITING DUTIES.

ABOUT AN HOUR LATER HE SAW A TINY MARIEKE HEADING FOR THE MOUNTAINS.

HE TRIED TO CATCH UP ...

...BUT QUICKLY LOST TRACK OF HER.

HE COULD'VE CALLED OUT FOR HER...

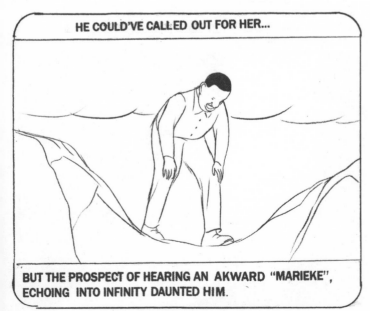

BUT THE PROSPECT OF HEARING AN AKWARD "MARIEKE", ECHOING INTO INFINITY DAUNTED HIM.

ARSÈNE KEPT REHASHING HIS TEXT UNTIL IT SEEMED AS IF THERE WAS NO RELATION AMONGST THE WORDS OTHER THEN THE FACT THAT THEY WERE ALL WRITTEN ON THE SAME PIECE OF PAPER.

EVENTUALLY HE PUT IT ASIDE AND FORMULATED A SHORT, MELANCHOLY POEM.

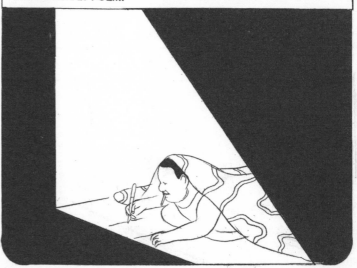

THE SENTENCES CAME ROLLING OUT FLUENTLY AND ORGANICALLY. ONLY AT THE VERY END DID HE HESITATE FOR A SECOND, THINKING THAT THE POEM NEEDED A FINISHING TOUCH.

HE LOOKED AROUND HIS ROOM AS IF HE'D FIND IT THERE.

A FEW DAYS LATER ARSÈNE SAW MARIEKE HANGING HER WASH.

PASSING BY ALL THE DRESSES HE HAS ADMIRED HER IN, ONE BY ONE, FELT LIKE A DOCUMENTARY OF HIS INFATUATION.

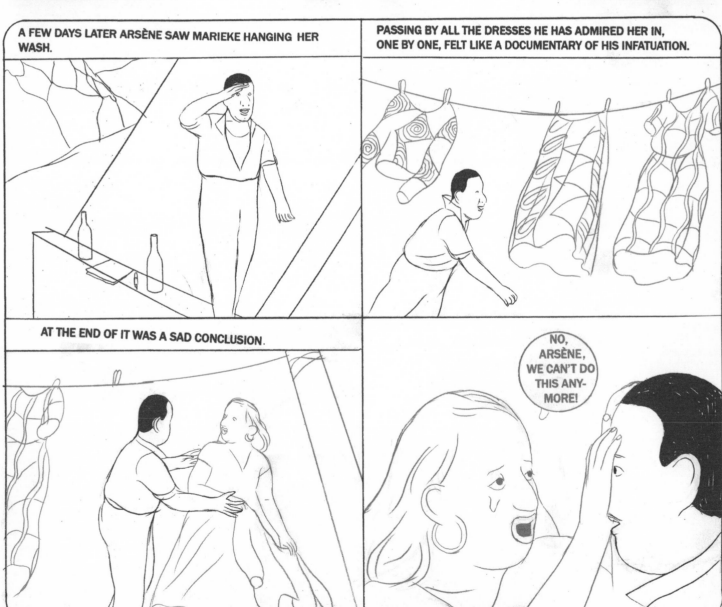

AT THE END OF IT WAS A SAD CONCLUSION.

NO, ARSÈNE, WE CAN'T DO THIS ANY-MORE!

BZZZZZZZZZZZZZZZZZZZZZZ
ARSÈNE WAS ANGRILY CONTEMPLATING THE FEMALE PSYCHE WHEN HE BECAME AWARE OF A GROWING BUZZING SOUND.
A SMALL MOVING DOT APPEARED ON THE HORIZON.
IT QUICKLY DEVELOPED INTO A BURLY, DRONING SEAPLANE.
EVERYBODY MOVED ONTO THE (NEWLY CONSTRUCTED) PIER TO WELCOME THE VISITORS.
ARSÈNE CAME RUNNING DOWN THE HILL WHILST SIMULTANEOUSLY PUTTING ON HIS SHOES.
AS SOON AS THE FOOTBRIDGE WAS PUT IN PLACE, A GROUP OF PEOPLE POURED OUT OF THE GATE.

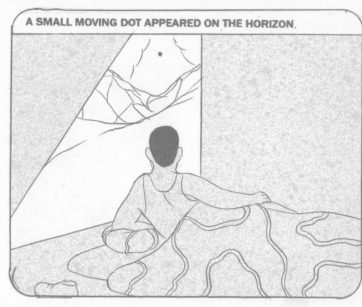

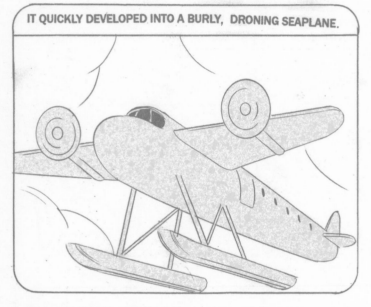

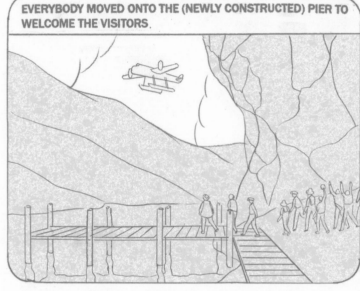

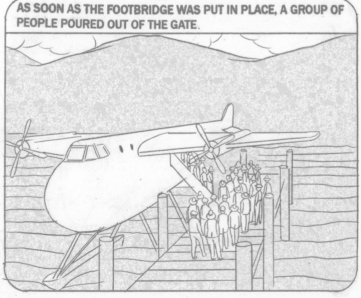

AT THE HEAD WAS A RATHER GAUNT LOOKING DESMET AND, RIGHT BY HIS SIDE, ARSÈNE RECOGNIZED THE OLD BULLSHIT ARTIST HE'D MET ON THE BOAT.

FATHER!

"MARIE-CHRISTINE, YOU LOOK WELL."

AS SHE BROUGHT HER LIPS UP TO HIS CHEEK, THE FAMILY RESEMBLANCE SUDDENLY BECAME BLATANTLY OBVIOUS.

GRANDPA WAS EXPRESSING HIS ASTONISHMENT IN A UNIVERSAL MANNER WHEN HE WAS APPROACHED BY THE OLD MAN.

"HOW ABOUT THAT, HUH? WHO WOULD THINK SUCH AN ENORMOUS BEAST COULD ACTUALLY FLY? HAHA!"

"YOU MIGHT WANT TO PREVENT ANYTHING ELSE FROM TAKING OFF."

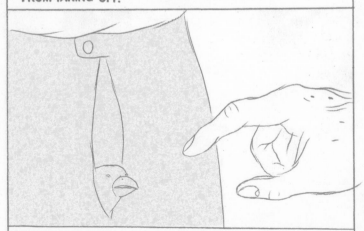

LIPPENS POINTED AN ARTHRITIS-RIDDEN FINGER AT ARSÈNE'S UNDONE ZIPPER.

MARIEKE AND ROGER WERE STANDING NEXT TO EACH OTHER, SOMEWHAT AWKWARDLY, WHEN ROGER NOTICED GRANDPA.

ARSÈNE!

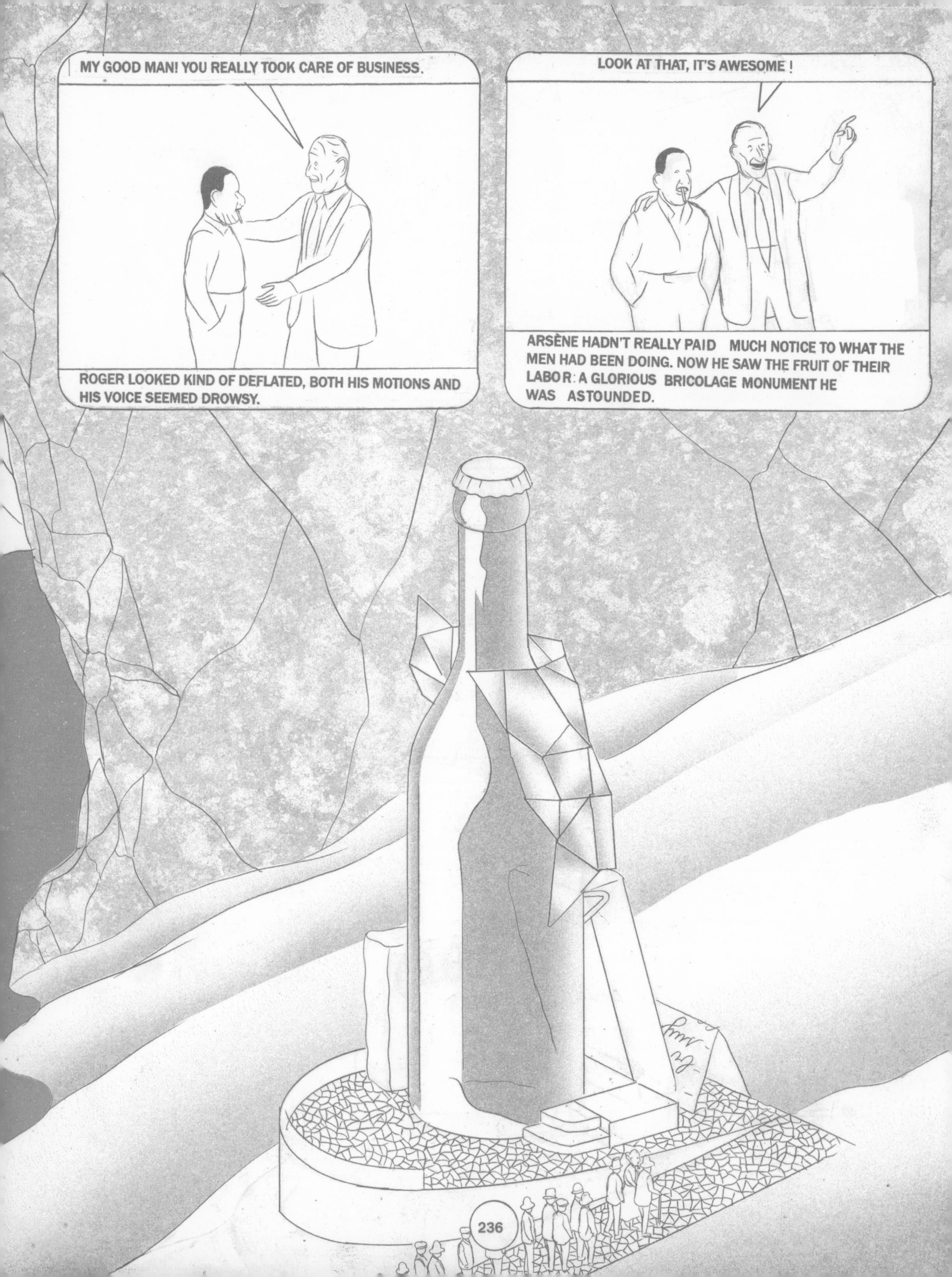
MY GOOD MAN! YOU REALLY TOOK CARE OF BUSINESS.
ROGER LOOKED KIND OF DEFLATED, BOTH HIS MOTIONS AND HIS VOICE SEEMED DROWSY.
LOOK AT THAT, IT'S AWESOME !
ARSÈNE HADN'T REALLY PAID MUCH NOTICE TO WHAT THE MEN HAD BEEN DOING. NOW HE SAW THE FRUIT OF THEIR LABOR: A GLORIOUS BRICOLAGE MONUMENT HE WAS ASTOUNDED.

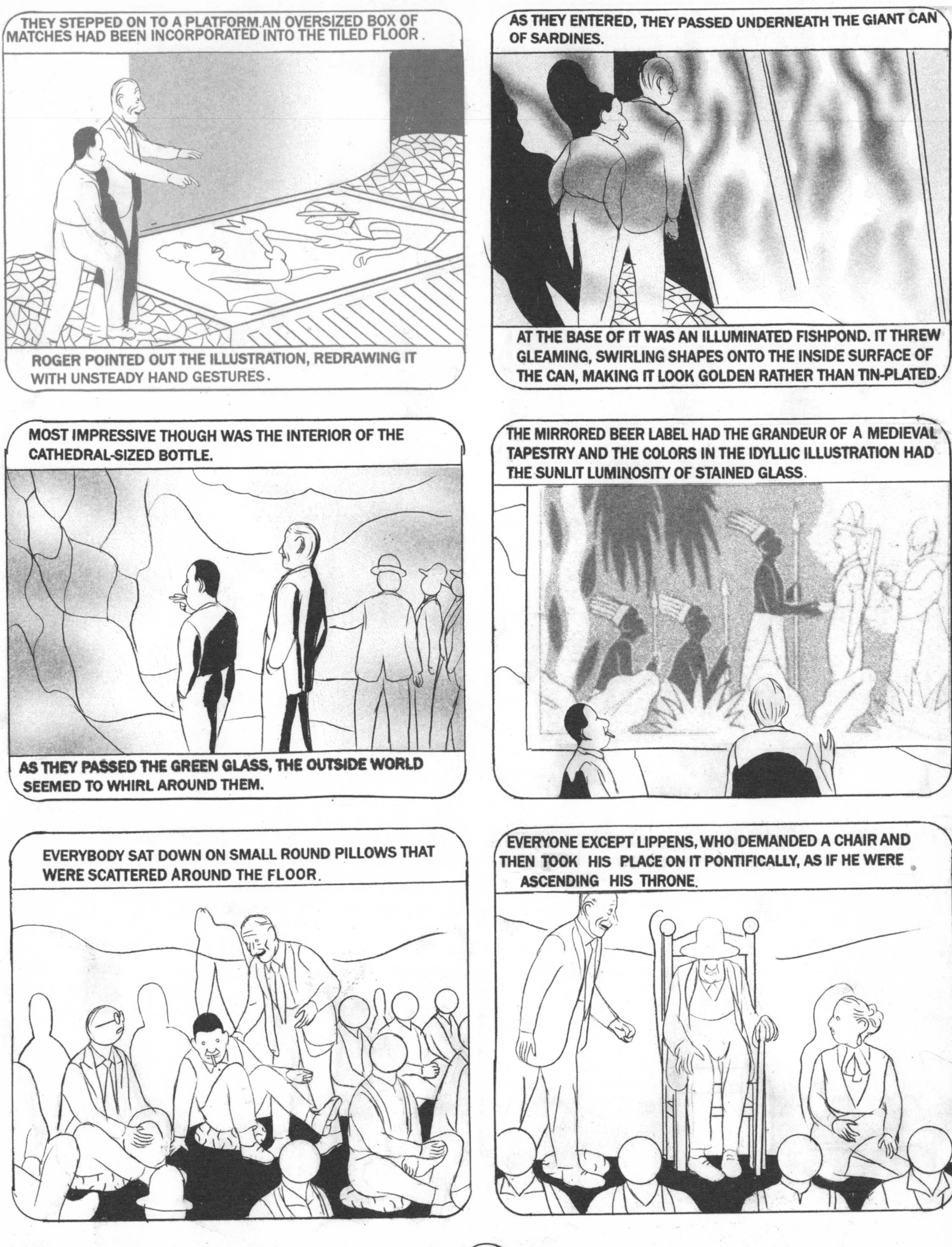
THEY STEPPED ON TO A PLATFORM.AN OVERSIZED BOX OF MATCHES HAD BEEN INCORPORATED INTO THE TILED FLOOR.
ROGER POINTED OUT THE ILLUSTRATION, REDRAWING IT WITH UNSTEADY HAND GESTURES.
AS THEY ENTERED, THEY PASSED UNDERNEATH THE GIANT CAN OF SARDINES.
AT THE BASE OF IT WAS AN ILLUMINATED FISHPOND. IT THREW GLEAMING, SWIRLING SHAPES ONTO THE INSIDE SURFACE OF THE CAN, MAKING IT LOOK GOLDEN RATHER THAN TIN-PLATED.
MOST IMPRESSIVE THOUGH WAS THE INTERIOR OF THE CATHEDRAL-SIZED BOTTLE.
AS THEY PASSED THE GREEN GLASS, THE OUTSIDE WORLD SEEMED TO WHIRL AROUND THEM.
THE MIRRORED BEER LABEL HAD THE GRANDEUR OF A MEDIEVAL TAPESTRY AND THE COLORS IN THE IDYLLIC ILLUSTRATION HAD THE SUNLIT LUMINOSITY OF STAINED GLASS.
EVERYBODY SAT DOWN ON SMALL ROUND PILLOWS THAT WERE SCATTERED AROUND THE FLOOR.
EVERYONE EXCEPT LIPPENS, WHO DEMANDED A CHAIR AND THEN TOOK HIS PLACE ON IT PONTIFICALLY, AS IF HE WERE ASCENDING HIS THRONE.

THEN TWO MEN DRESSED IN A PECULIAR GET-UP APPEARED. THEY WALKED ONTO A GIANT COIN IN THE MIDDLE OF THE SPACE. PLACED ON IT WERE AN ORGAN AND A BONGO DRUM.

THE PERCUSSIONIST STARTED PLAYING A HEARTBEAT-LIKE RHYTHM.

THEN THE ORGAN FELL IN, COMPLEMENTING THE PULSE WITH A SIMPLE, MOURNFUL MELODY.

THE PIECE WAS SURPRISINGLY BEAUTIFUL, A PERFECT MATCH TO ARSÈNE'S ALREADY MELANCHOLIC MOOD.

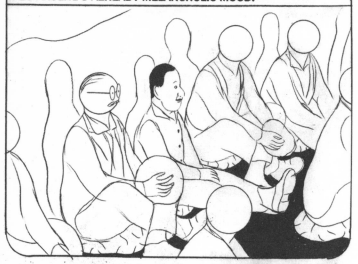

AT A CERTAIN POINT THE CROWN ON TOP OFF THE GLASS TOWER OPENED.
ONE COULD HEAR THE WIND BLOWING ACROSS THE OPENING.
THE AIR CAME BUZZING DOWN THE MOUTH AND NECK INTO THE BODY.

IT SOUNDED LIKE A VERY DEEP WIND CHIME, ADDING A DRONING BASS TO THE ORGAN TONES.

THE FREQUENCIES MADE THE WHOLE BOTTLE VIBRATE. IT MADE ARSÈNE'S BODY TINGLE FROM HIS PROSTATE TO HIS NOSE.

PEOPLE EXCHANGED GLANCES, SILENTLY ACKNOWLEDGING THE AWESOMENESS OF THE AMBIANCE.

THE ONLY THING DISTURBING THIS HARMONIOUS EXPERIENCE WAS THE SOUND OF LIPPENS TALKING LOUDLY THROUGH THE WHOLE PIECE.

AT LEAST YOU COULD'VE   ARRANGED A RIBBON-CUTTING CEREMON

SHUSH

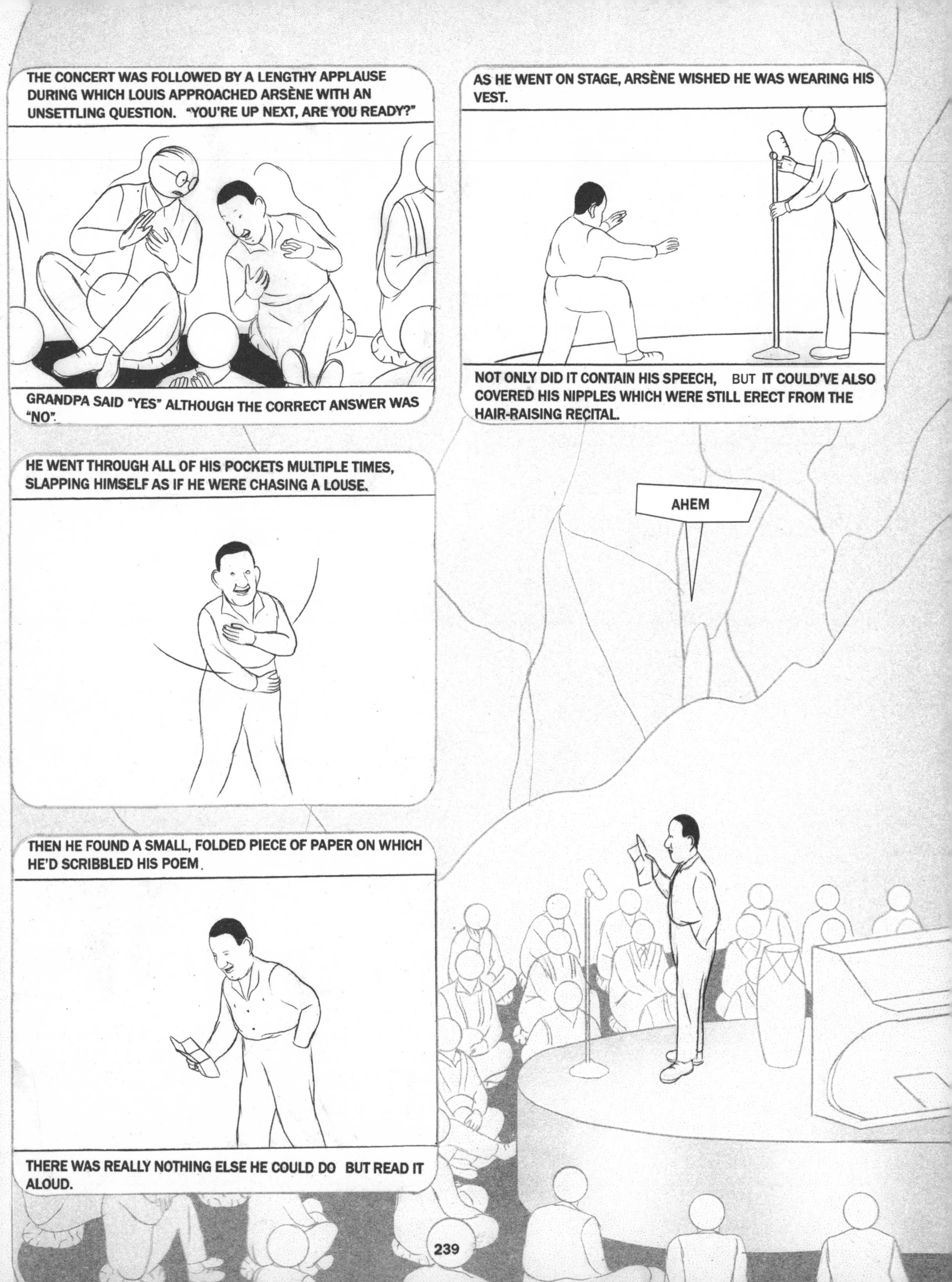
THE CONCERT WAS FOLLOWED BY A LENGTHY APPLAUSE DURING WHICH LOUIS APPROACHED ARSÈNE WITH AN UNSETTLING QUESTION. "YOU'RE UP NEXT, ARE YOU READY?"
GRANDPA SAID "YES" ALTHOUGH THE CORRECT ANSWER WAS "NO".
AS HE WENT ON STAGE, ARSÈNE WISHED HE WAS WEARING HIS VEST.
NOT ONLY DID IT CONTAIN HIS SPEECH, BUT IT COULD'VE ALSO COVERED HIS NIPPLES WHICH WERE STILL ERECT FROM THE HAIR-RAISING RECITAL.
HE WENT THROUGH ALL OF HIS POCKETS MULTIPLE TIMES, SLAPPING HIMSELF AS IF HE WERE CHASING A LOUSE.
THEN HE FOUND A SMALL, FOLDED PIECE OF PAPER ON WHICH HE'D SCRIBBLED HIS POEM.
THERE WAS REALLY NOTHING ELSE HE COULD DO BUT READ IT ALOUD.
AHEM

THE TITLE OF THE POEM WAS

Expectant

*I am a man
and I am expectant.*

ARSÈNE HELD THE PAPER IN FRONT OF HIS FACE SO HE WOULDN'T HAVE TO SEE THE BLANK STARES OF THE MEN NOR MARIEKE'S SAD EYES.

HIS "STAGE ACT" WAS MINIMAL; IT CONSISTED MAINLY OF SHIFTING HIS WEIGHT FROM ONE LEG TO THE OTHER, AND THEN BACK.

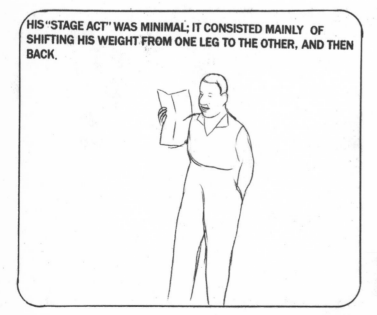

*I've got a belly
filled with hope.*

THE MECHANISM THAT MOVED THE LID ON TOP OF THE BOTTLE WASN'T WORKING PROPERLY. IT WAS CLOSING UP TOO SLOWLY.

SO, DURING ARSÈNE'S RECITATION ONE COULD HEAR THE LOW HUM GRADUALLY TUNING UP TO A HIGH-PITCHED SQUEAL. IT ADDED AN ODD SUSPENSE TO THE WHOLE AFFAIR.

IT DIDN'T BOTHER LIPPENS, WHO WAS EITHER CHECKING HIS TIE OR NODDING OFF.

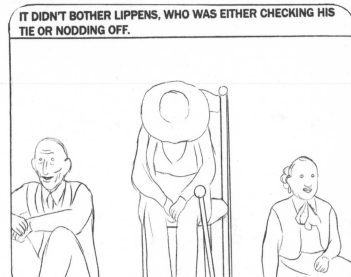

THE LAST WORD OF THE POEM WAS FOLLOWED BY A DOUBLE EXCLAMATION MARK, WHICH OBLIGED ARSÈNE TO ARTICULATE IT LOUDLY.

explode !!

THIS FORCEFUL ENDING MADE LIPPENS VEER UP AND BREAK INTO APPLAUSE.

HE WALTZED TOWARDS THE PODIUM AND SHOOK ARSÈNE'S HAND.

WHERE HAVE YOU BEEN KEEPING THIS DASHING YOUNG MAN?

THEN DRINKS WERE SERVED. GRANDPA WAS ASKED TO POSE FOR PHOTOS AND A GRINNING JOURNALIST ASKED IF HE COULD FEATURE HIS POEM PROMINENTLY IN THE NEWSPAPER.

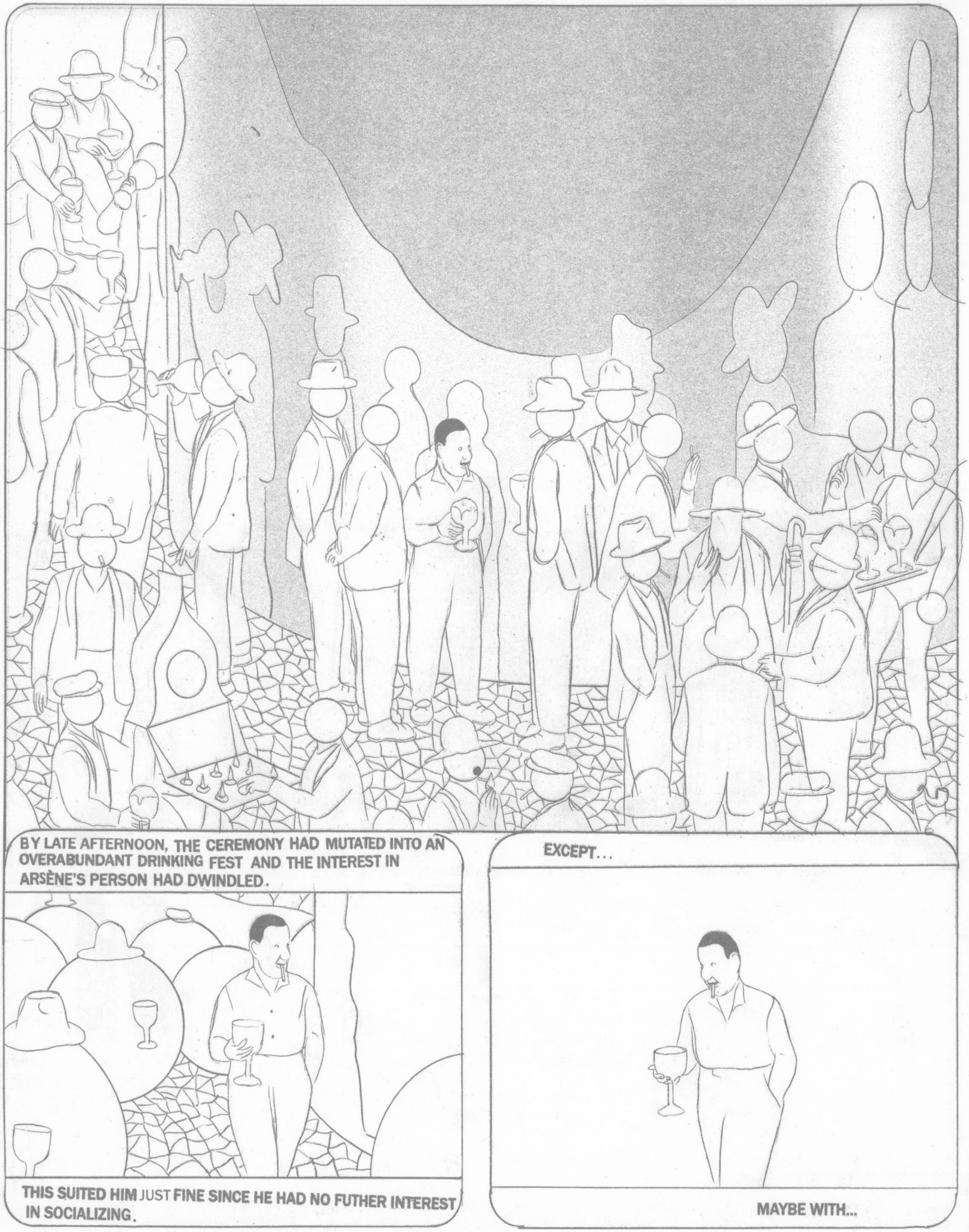
BY LATE AFTERNOON, THE CEREMONY HAD MUTATED INTO AN OVERABUNDANT DRINKING FEST AND THE INTEREST IN ARSÈNE'S PERSON HAD DWINDLED.
EXCEPT...
THIS SUITED HIM JUST FINE SINCE HE HAD NO FUTHER INTEREST IN SOCIALIZING.
MAYBE WITH...

ARSÈNE SPOTTED ROGER AND MARIEKE STANDING SOMEWHAT HIDDEN BEHIND A MEGA CIGARETTE PACK.

THEY WERE ENGAGED IN WHAT APPEARED TO BE AN INTIMATE CONVERSATION.

SUDDENLY ROGER PULLED HIS EMACIATED FACE INTO A PAINED GRIMACE.

HIS EXPRESSION SLOWLY FADED INTO A TIRED SMILE AND THEN, VERY TENDERLY, HE PUT HIS HAND ON MARIEKE'S BELLY.

A LITTLE FURTHER AWAY, COVERED BY THE SHADOW OF THE BOTTLE STOOD LOUIS, ALSO OBSERVING THE COUPLE.

ARSÈNE DECIDED TO GET AN EARLY NIGHT.

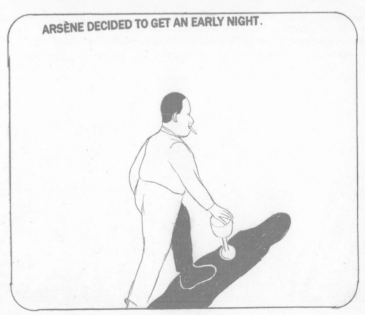

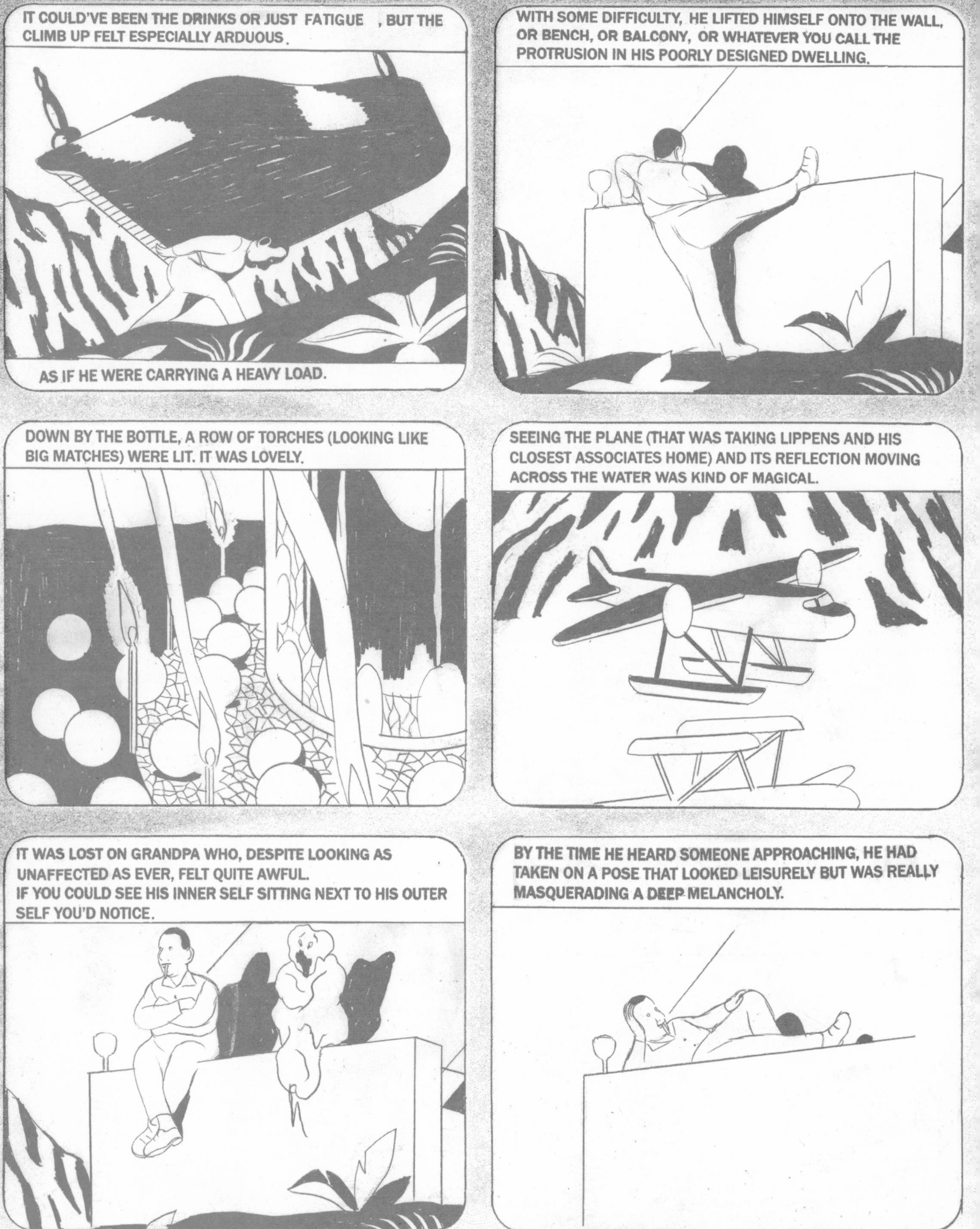
IT COULD'VE BEEN THE DRINKS OR JUST FATIGUE , BUT THE CLIMB UP FELT ESPECIALLY ARDUOUS.
AS IF HE WERE CARRYING A HEAVY LOAD.
WITH SOME DIFFICULTY, HE LIFTED HIMSELF ONTO THE WALL, OR BENCH, OR BALCONY, OR WHATEVER YOU CALL THE PROTRUSION IN HIS POORLY DESIGNED DWELLING.
DOWN BY THE BOTTLE, A ROW OF TORCHES (LOOKING LIKE BIG MATCHES) WERE LIT. IT WAS LOVELY.
SEEING THE PLANE (THAT WAS TAKING LIPPENS AND HIS CLOSEST ASSOCIATES HOME) AND ITS REFLECTION MOVING ACROSS THE WATER WAS KIND OF MAGICAL.
IT WAS LOST ON GRANDPA WHO, DESPITE LOOKING AS UNAFFECTED AS EVER, FELT QUITE AWFUL.
IF YOU COULD SEE HIS INNER SELF SITTING NEXT TO HIS OUTER SELF YOU'D NOTICE.
BY THE TIME HE HEARD SOMEONE APPROACHING, HE HAD TAKEN ON A POSE THAT LOOKED LEISURELY BUT WAS REALLY MASQUERADING A DEEP MELANCHOLY.

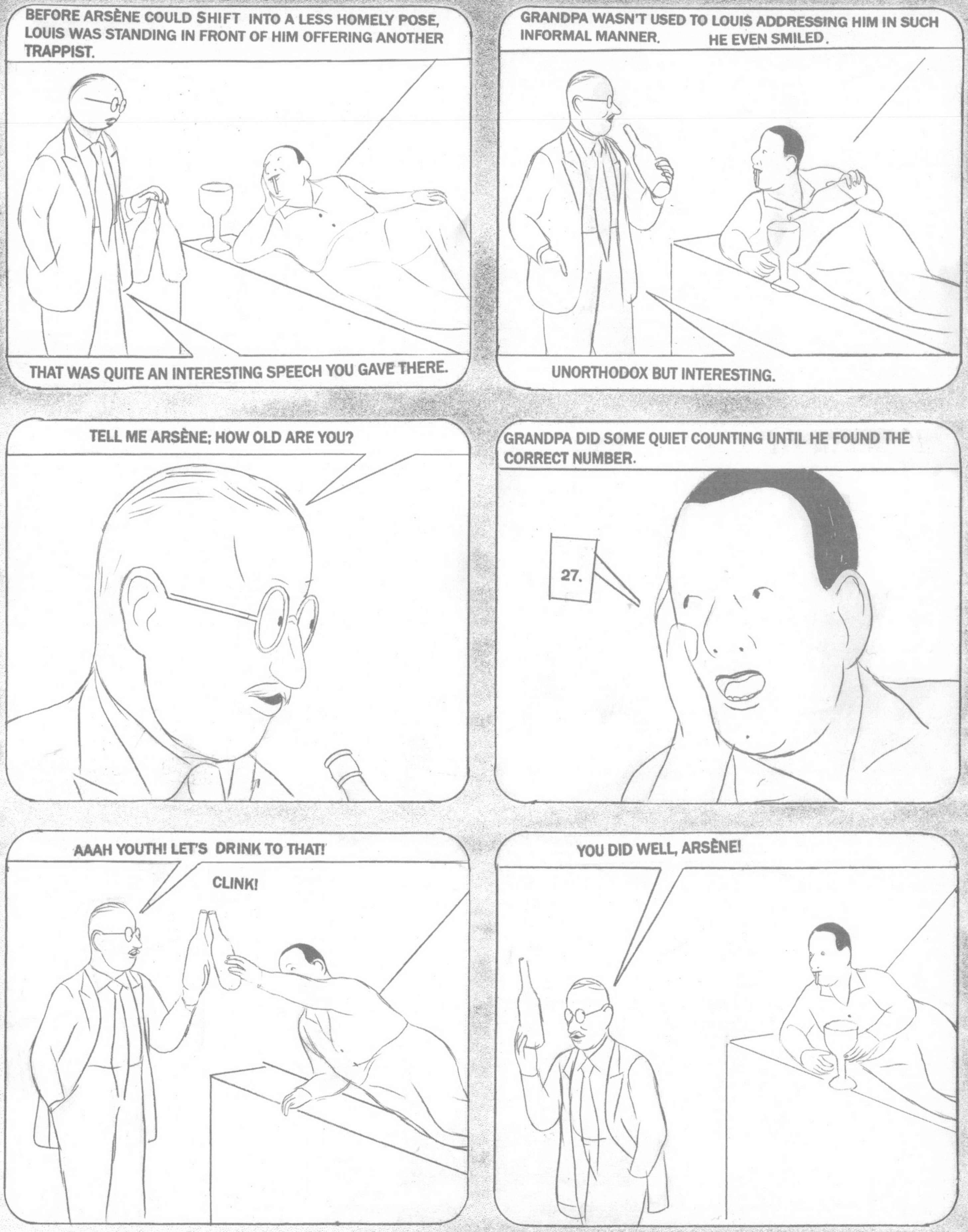
BEFORE ARSÈNE COULD SHIFT INTO A LESS HOMELY POSE, LOUIS WAS STANDING IN FRONT OF HIM OFFERING ANOTHER TRAPPIST.
THAT WAS QUITE AN INTERESTING SPEECH YOU GAVE THERE.
GRANDPA WASN'T USED TO LOUIS ADDRESSING HIM IN SUCH INFORMAL MANNER.
HE EVEN SMILED.
UNORTHODOX BUT INTERESTING.
TELL ME ARSÈNE; HOW OLD ARE YOU?
GRANDPA DID SOME QUIET COUNTING UNTIL HE FOUND THE CORRECT NUMBER.
27.
AAAH YOUTH! LET'S DRINK TO THAT!
CLINK!
YOU DID WELL, ARSÈNE!

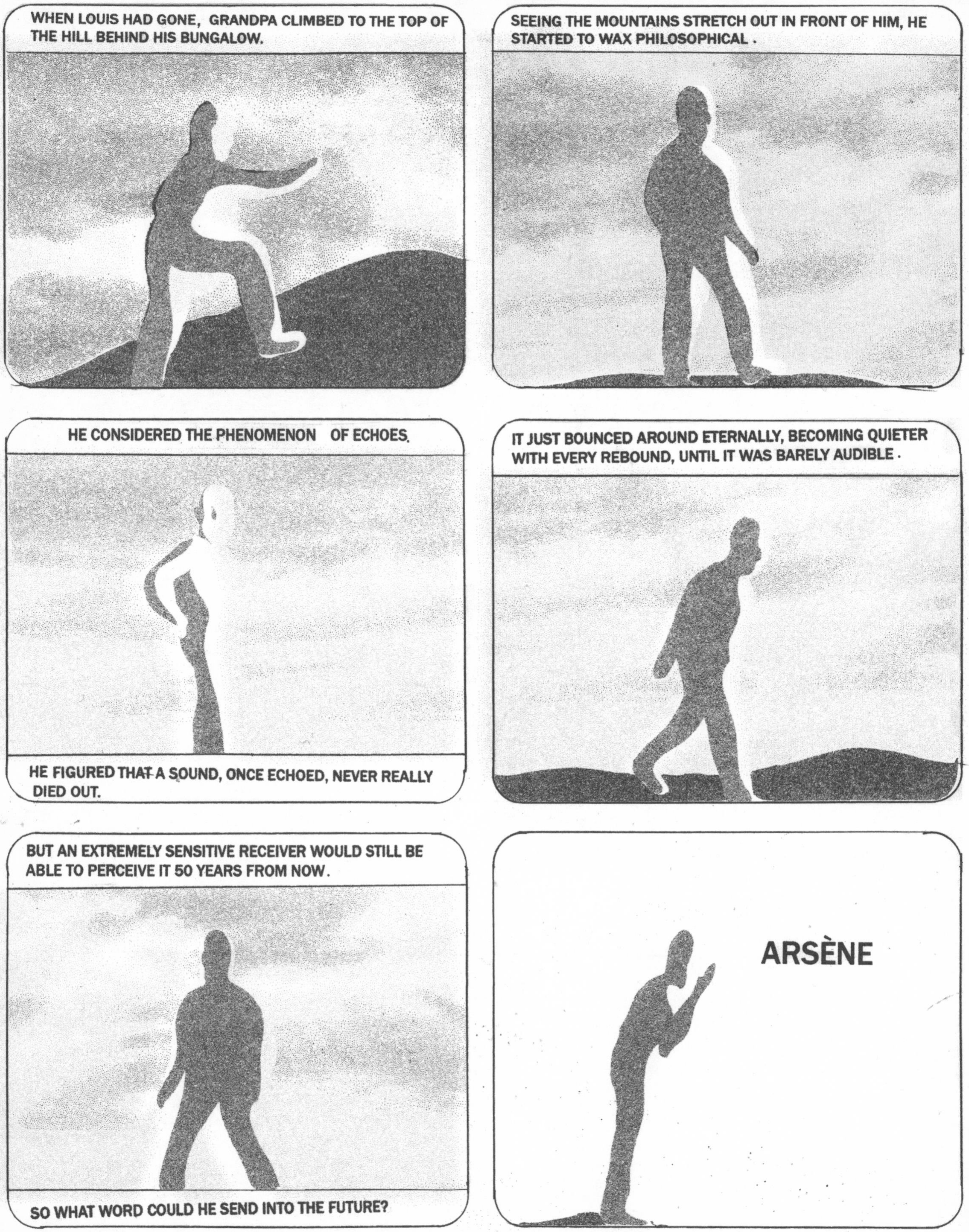
WHEN LOUIS HAD GONE, GRANDPA CLIMBED TO THE TOP OF THE HILL BEHIND HIS BUNGALOW.
SEEING THE MOUNTAINS STRETCH OUT IN FRONT OF HIM, HE STARTED TO WAX PHILOSOPHICAL.
HE CONSIDERED THE PHENOMENON OF ECHOES.
HE FIGURED THAT A SOUND, ONCE ECHOED, NEVER REALLY DIED OUT.
IT JUST BOUNCED AROUND ETERNALLY, BECOMING QUIETER WITH EVERY REBOUND, UNTIL IT WAS BARELY AUDIBLE.
BUT AN EXTREMELY SENSITIVE RECEIVER WOULD STILL BE ABLE TO PERCEIVE IT 50 YEARS FROM NOW.
SO WHAT WORD COULD HE SEND INTO THE FUTURE?
ARSÈNE

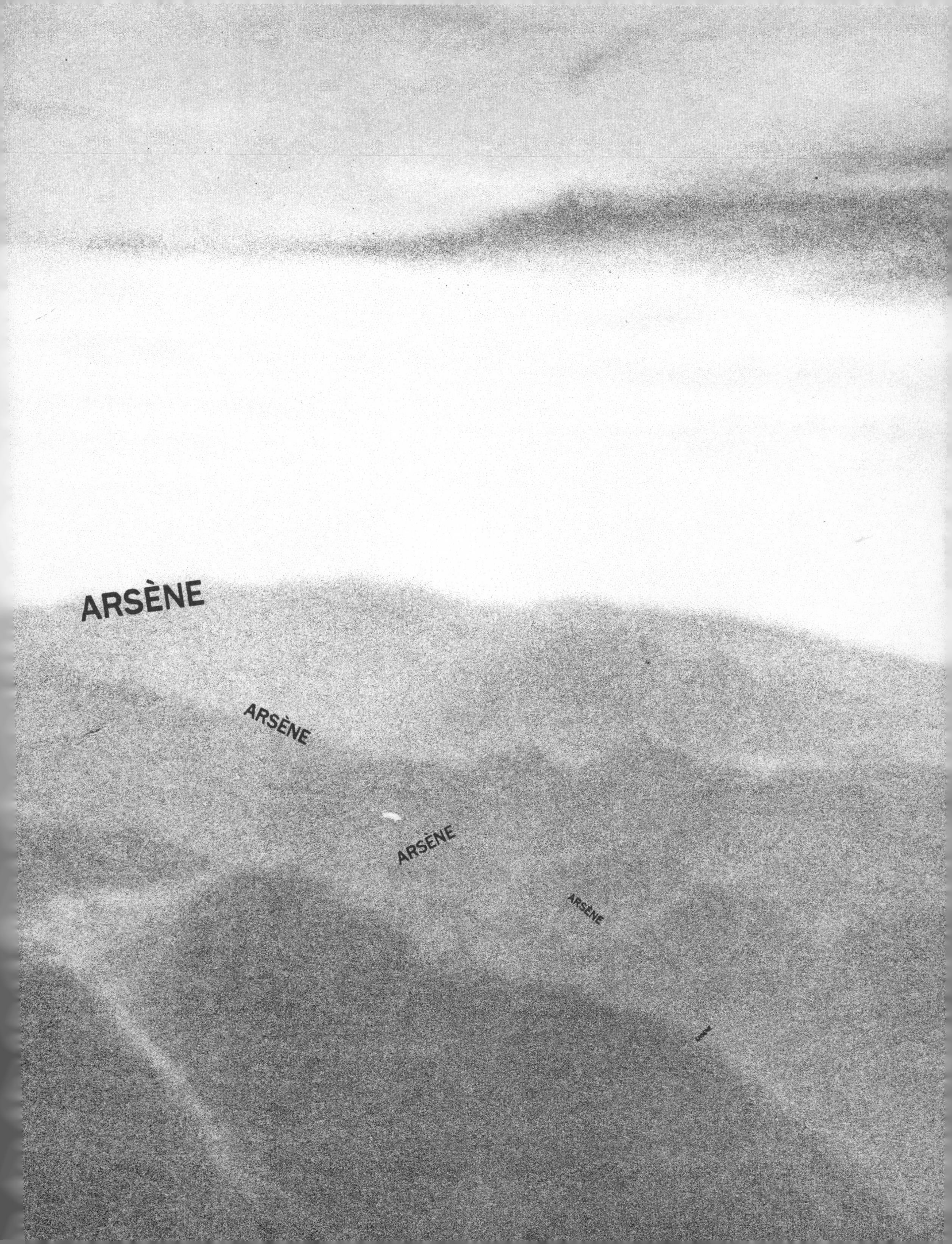
ARSÈNE
ARSÈNE
ARSÈNE
ARSÈNE

8. Arsène

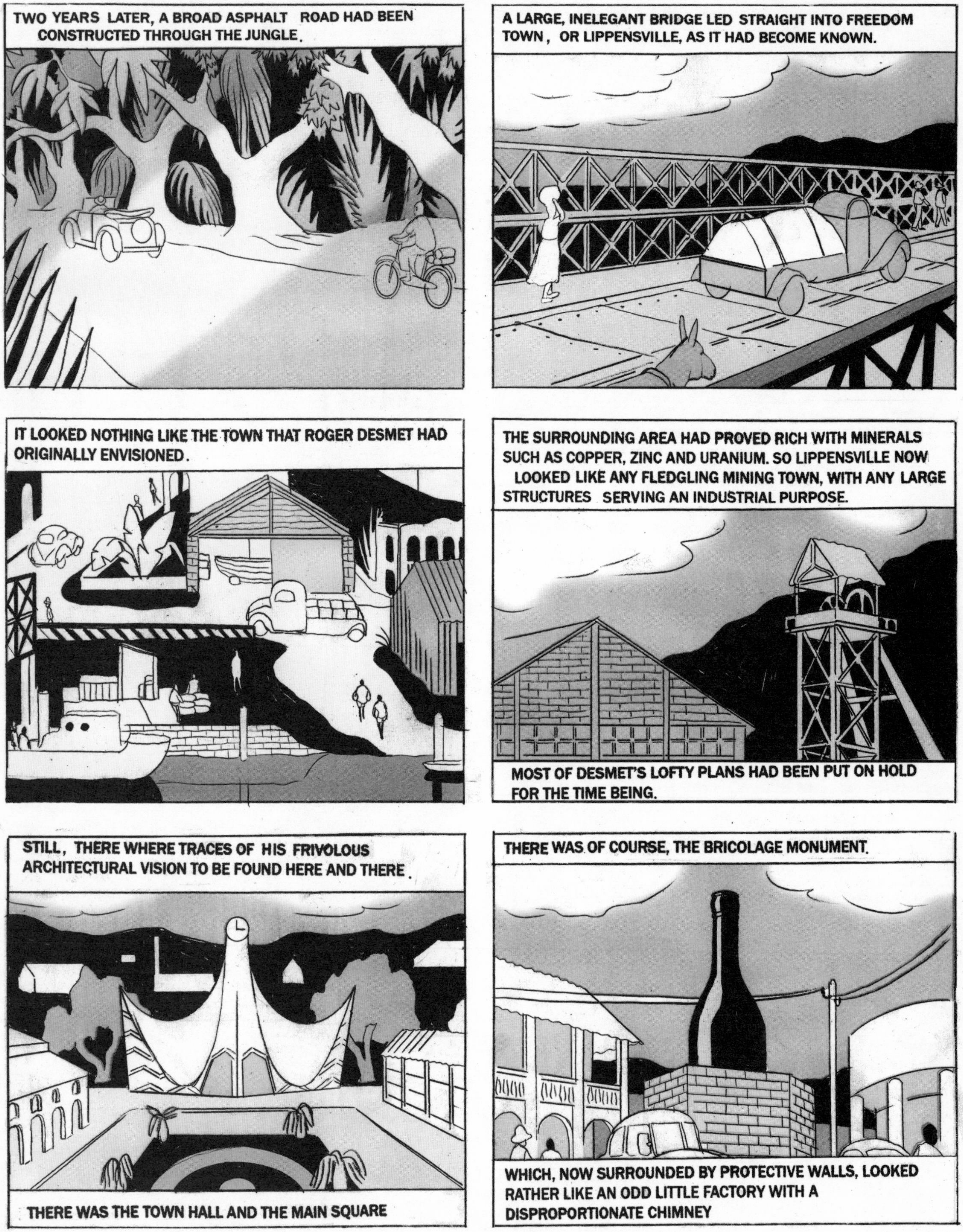
TWO YEARS LATER, A BROAD ASPHALT ROAD HAD BEEN CONSTRUCTED THROUGH THE JUNGLE.
A LARGE, INELEGANT BRIDGE LED STRAIGHT INTO FREEDOM TOWN, OR LIPPENSVILLE, AS IT HAD BECOME KNOWN.
IT LOOKED NOTHING LIKE THE TOWN THAT ROGER DESMET HAD ORIGINALLY ENVISIONED.
THE SURROUNDING AREA HAD PROVED RICH WITH MINERALS SUCH AS COPPER, ZINC AND URANIUM. SO LIPPENSVILLE NOW LOOKED LIKE ANY FLEDGLING MINING TOWN, WITH ANY LARGE STRUCTURES SERVING AN INDUSTRIAL PURPOSE.
MOST OF DESMET'S LOFTY PLANS HAD BEEN PUT ON HOLD FOR THE TIME BEING.
STILL, THERE WHERE TRACES OF HIS FRIVOLOUS ARCHITECTURAL VISION TO BE FOUND HERE AND THERE.
THERE WAS THE TOWN HALL AND THE MAIN SQUARE
THERE WAS OF COURSE, THE BRICOLAGE MONUMENT.
WHICH, NOW SURROUNDED BY PROTECTIVE WALLS, LOOKED RATHER LIKE AN ODD LITTLE FACTORY WITH A DISPROPORTIONATE CHIMNEY

THE ONLY BUILDING THAT WAS TRULY EMBLEMATIC OF WHAT FREEDOM TOWN COULD'VE BEEN WAS DESMET'S OWN WEEKEND RETREAT, NESTLED INTO THE HILLSIDE.

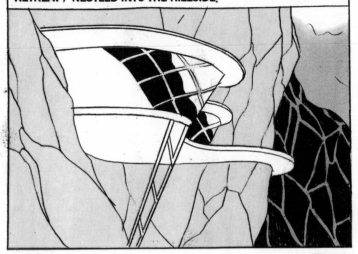

ARSÈNE WAS NOW LIVING IN A NICE LITTLE VILLA WITH A BEAUTIFULL GARDEN THAT LIPPENS HAD SET HIM UP WITH.

LIPPENS HAD ALSO GIVEN HIM A JOB HEADING AN URANIUM REFINERY, AFFORDED HIM A SYMPATHETIC SALARY.

THE JOB WAS EASY ENOUGH; HE COULD DELEGATE MOST OF HIS RESPONSIBILITIES TO LOUIS, WHO'D BECOME HIS RIGHT-HAND MAN.

ON SUNDAYS ARSENE COULD BE FOUND AT THE LOCAL MARKET WHERE HE MADE AN EXTRA BUCK BUYING ANIMAL HIDES AT BARGAIN PRICES.

Mr. Schrauwen?

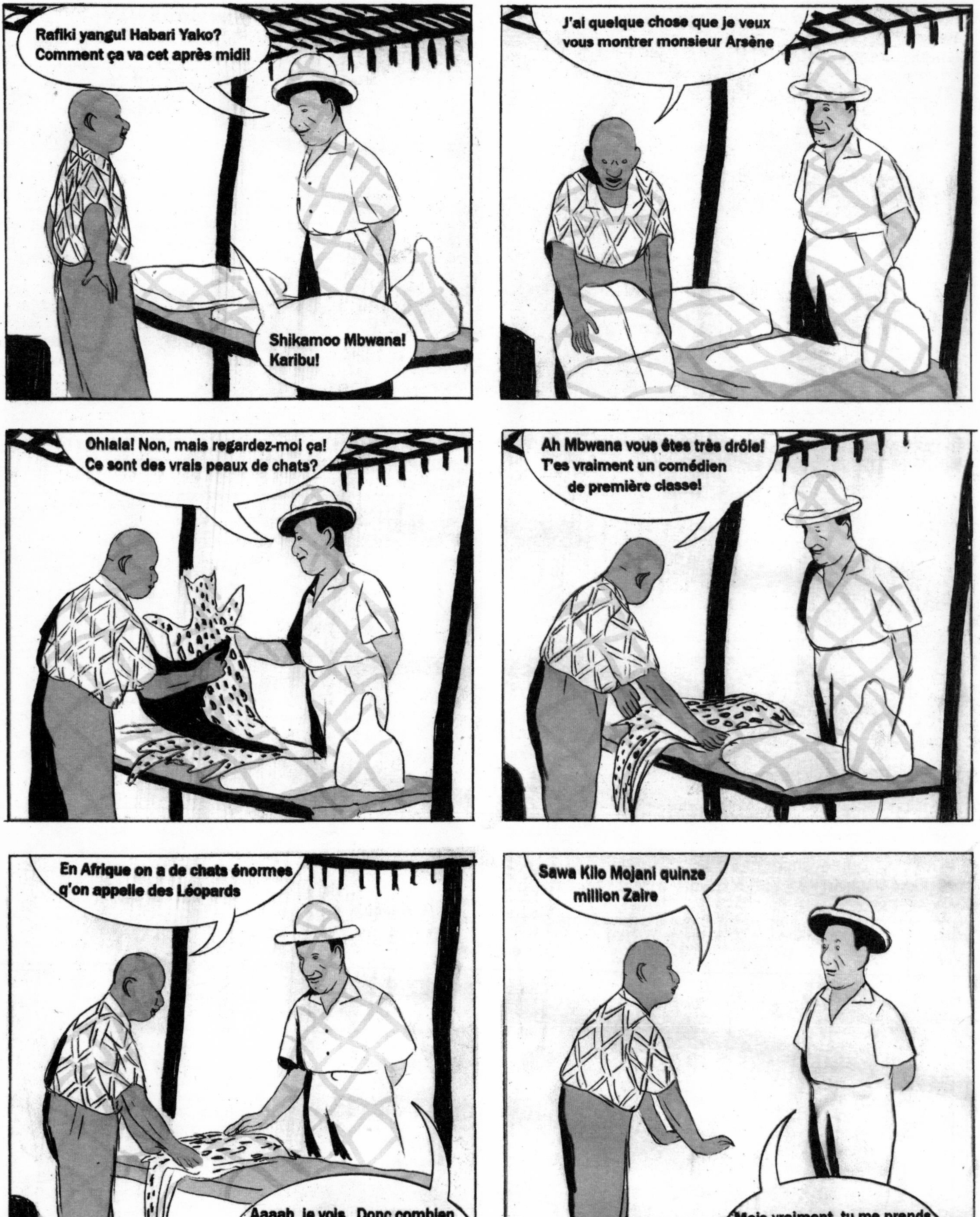
Rafiki yangu! Habari Yako?
Comment ça va cet après midi!
Shikamoo Mbwana!
Karibu!
J'ai quelque chose que je veux
vous montrer monsieur Arsène
Ohlala! Non, mais regardez-moi ça!
Ce sont des vrais peaux de chats?
Ah Mbwana vous êtes très drôle!
T'es vraiment un comédien
de première classe!
En Afrique on a de chats énormes
q'on appelle des Léopards
Aaaah je vois. Donc combien
pour toutes ces peaux de lapin
Sawa Kilo Mojani quinze
million Zaire
Mais vraiment, tu me prends
pour un clown idiote!

SOMETIMES HE WOULD RUN INTO ROGER AND MARIEKE, WHICH WAS ALWAYS A PLEASURE.

HIS ROMANTIC AFFILIATION WITH MARIEKE NOW SEEMED SOMETHING FROM A DISTANT, ALMOST UNREAL PAST.

THEIR RAPPORT WAS NOW COMFORTABLE AND FRIENDLY.

ROGER WAS COLLECTING HIS PENSION AND SEEMED QUITE HAPPY.

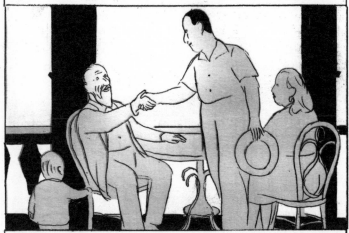

HE SPENT MOST OF HIS TIME TUTORING HIS SON, WHO LOOKED JUST LIKE HIM.

THEY REALLY WERE DEAD RINGERS. ROGER WOULD OFTEN DISPUTE THIS IN HUMOROUS FASHION.

He looks just like you Arséne, when you first arrived in the Congo.

MOSTLY, SEEING THEM REMINDED HIM THAT NOW, AS HE WAS VERGING ON HIS THIRTIES, IT WAS ABOUT TIME TO GO HOME AND START A FAMILY OF HIS OWN.

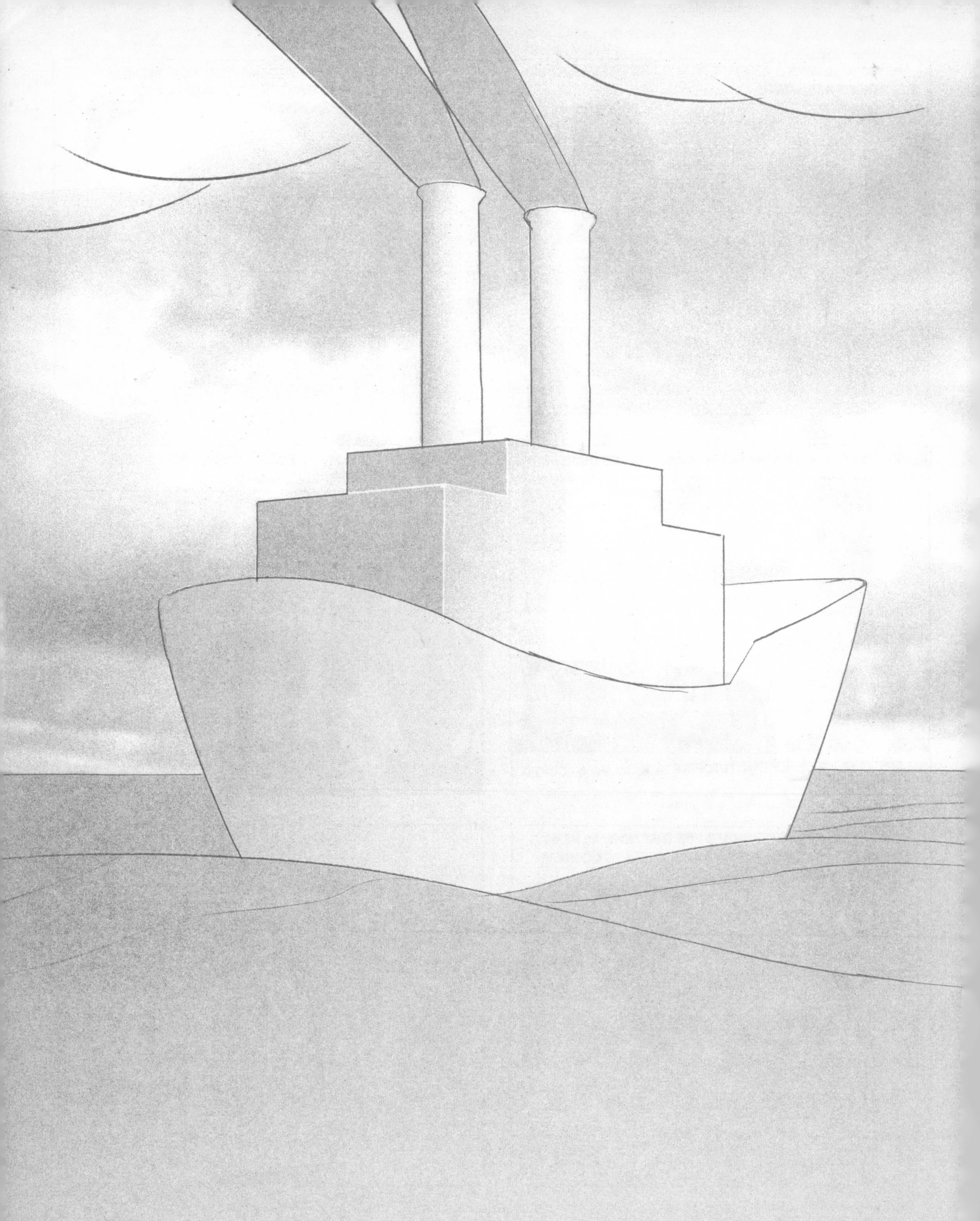

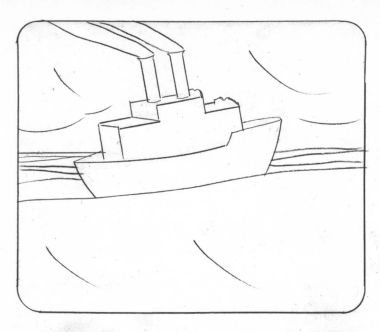

WHEN GRANDPA WALKED OFF THE BOAT HE WORE A LIGHT, COTTON SUMMER SUIT.

ON THE 20TH OF NOVEMBER 1949, THERE WAS NO SUN TO BE SEEN IN ANTWERP, IN FACT IT WAS FREEZING COLD.

HE COULD SURELY AFFORD A CAB (HIS VALISE WAS FILLED TO THE BRIM WITH CASH MONEY), BUT HE DECIDED TO TAKE HIS BIKE.
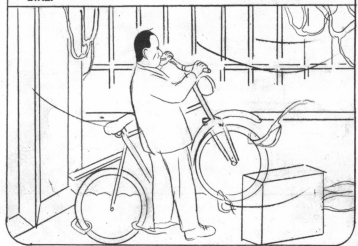

IT WAS IN FINE SHAPE, CONSIDERING THAT IT BEEN EXPOSED TO THE BELGIAN ELEMENTS FOR TWO YEARS.

SO HE JUST HOPPED ON IT AND RODE OFF.

BYE, GRANDPA!

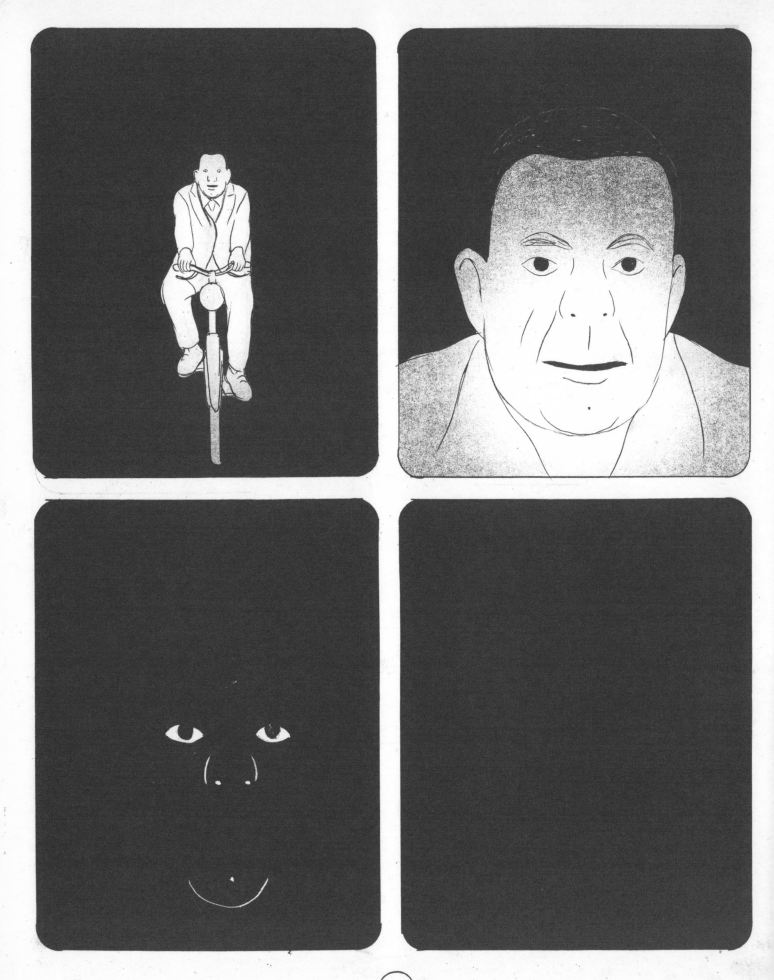

Editor and
Associate Publisher:
Eric Reynolds
Book Design: Olivier Schrauwen
Production: Paul Baresh
Publisher: Gary Groth
FANTAGRAPHICS BOOKS, INC.
Seattle, Washington, USA

ISBN 978-1-60699-730-7
Second printing: July 2015
Printed in
Singapore

Fantagraphics Books would like to thank:
Randall Bethune, Big Planet Comics, Black
Hook Press of Japan, Nick Capetillo,
Kevin Czapiewski, John DiBello, Juan Manuel
Dominguez, Mathieu Doublet, Dan Evans III,
Thomas Eykemans, Scott Fritsch-Hammes,
Coco and Eddie Gorodetsky, Karen Green,
Ted Haycraft, Eduardo Takeo "Lizarkeo" Igarashi,
NevdonJamgochian, Andy Koopmans, Philip Nel,
Vanessa Palacios, Kurt Sayenga, Anne Lise
Rostgaard Schmidt, Christian Schremser,
Secret Headquarters, Paul van Dijken,
Mungo van Krimpen-Hall, Jason Aaron Wong,
and Thomas Zimmermann

The author would like to thank: Ada, Arm,
Lin, Anton, Michael, Helge Florent, Gabe,
Jason, Aïsha, Eric, Cesar, Ria, Bart
and Arsene

Flemish
Literature
Fund

The translation and production of this
book are funded by the Flemish Literature
Fund (Vlaams Fonds boor de Letteren –
www.flemishliterature.be)

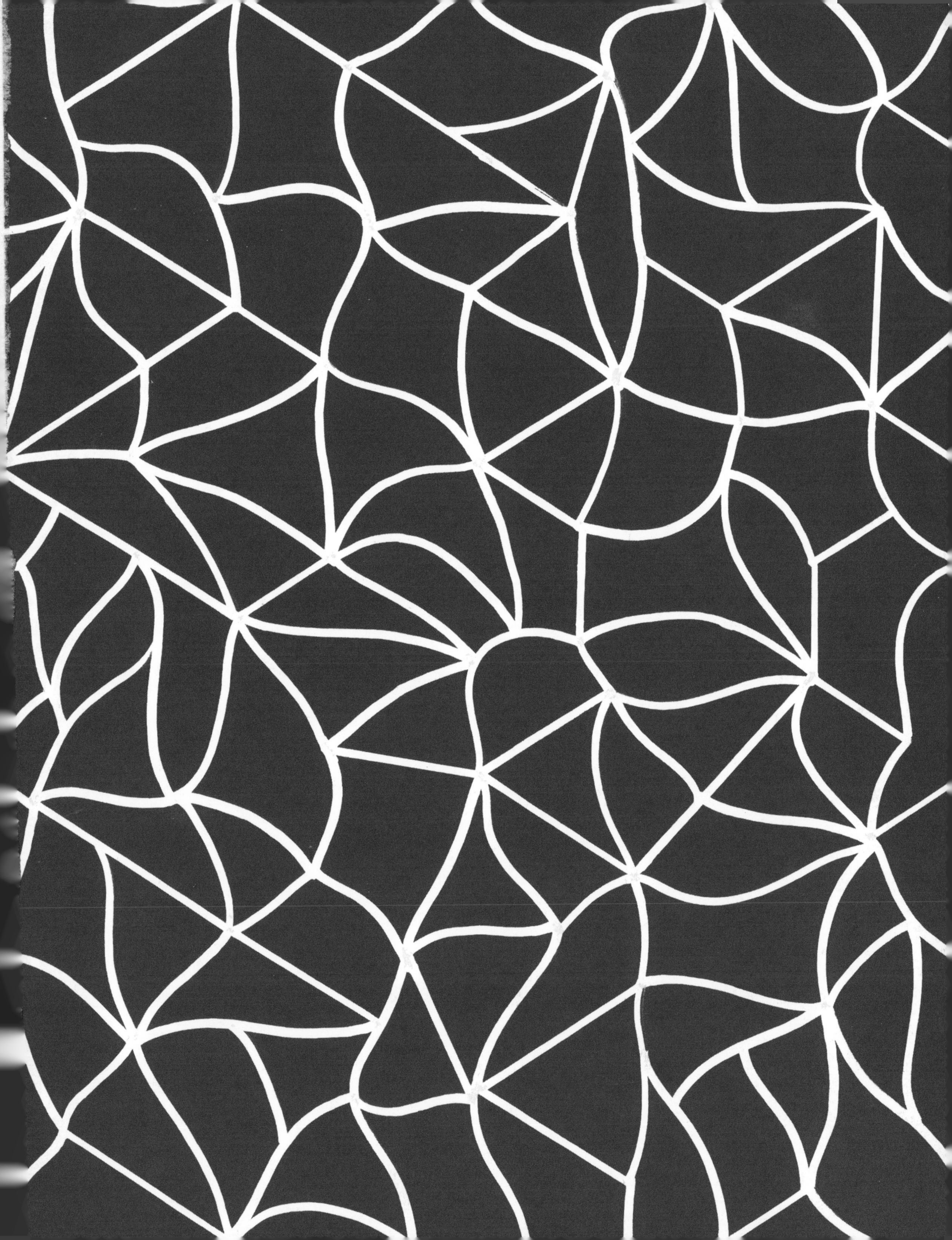

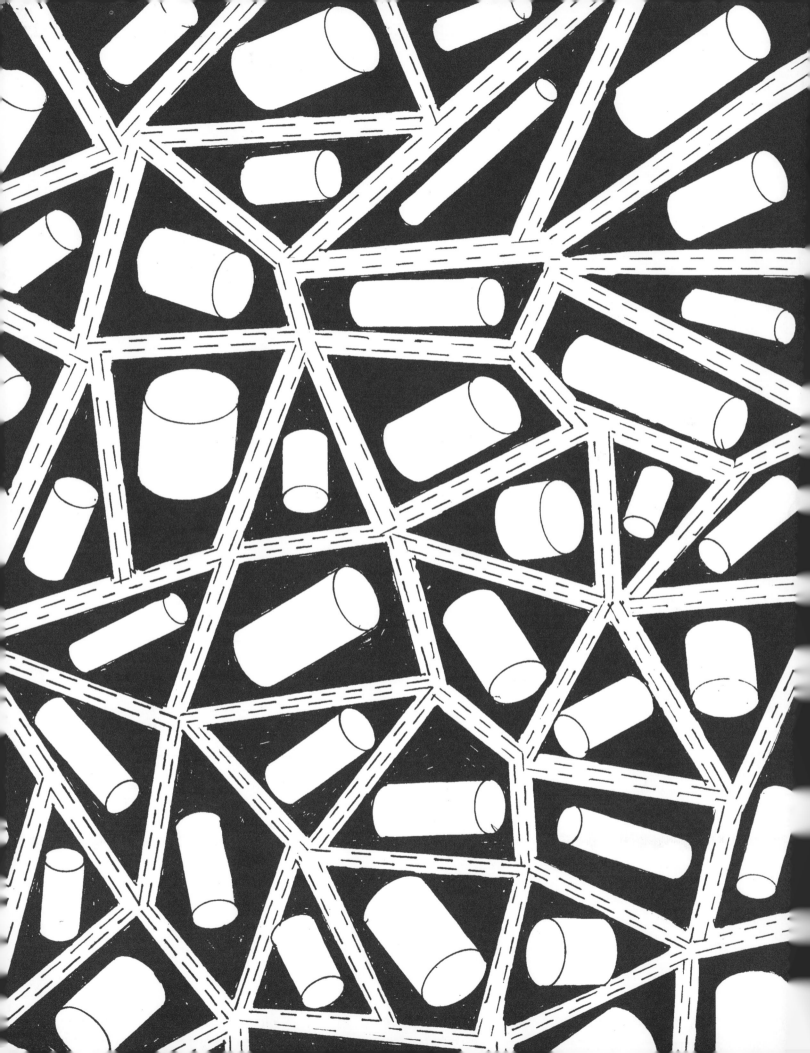